W9-BWD-997

THE GOLF BOOK

The Royal and Ancient Golf Club at St. Andrews, Scotland is the prototype of all golf clubs. The club itself has a very private membership, which includes golf's elite from around the world, but the courses (there are four: The Old Course, The New, The Eden and The Jubilee) are all open to the public. Playing the Old Course is one of the experiences every true golfer must enjoy.

THE GOLF BOOK

EDITED BY
MICHAEL BARTLETT

Illustrated with photographs by
TONY ROBERTS

ARBOR HOUSE
New York

for Charlie Bartlett
who always loved a good story

OTHER BOOKS BY MICHAEL BARTLETT

The New 1969 Golfer's Almanac

Bartlett's World Golf Encyclopedia

Books with photographs by Tony Roberts

Tom Ramsey's World of Golf

Great Golf Courses of the World
The Crosby: Greatest Show in Golf
The World Atlas of Golf

Copyright © 1980 by Michael Bartlett and Tony Roberts

All rights reserved, including the right of reproduction in whole or in part in any form. Published in the United States of America by Arbor House Publishing Company and in Canada by Fitzhenry & Whiteside, Ltd.

The following two pages constitute an extension of this copyright page.

Library of Congress Catalog Card Number: 80–67625
ISBN: 0–87795–297–3
MANUFACTURED IN THE UNITED STATES OF AMERICA

Designed by Antler and Baldwin, Inc.

Acknowledgments

- "The Golf Imperative," from *Golf: The Passion and The Challenge* by Art Spander and Mark Mulvoy. Copyright © 1977 by Art Spander and Mark Mulvoy. Reprinted by permission of the publisher, Rutledge Books, Inc.
- "Keep The Rules and They'll Keep You," from *The Pleasures of The Game* by Colman McCarthy. Copyright © 1977 by Colman McCarthy. Reprinted by permission of The Dial Press.
- "A Far, Far Better Thing," by Pat Ward-Thomas, from *The USGA Golf Journal,* June, 1976. Reprinted by permission of the author and the United States Golf Association.
- "The Game's Hidden but Accessible Meaning," from *Golf In The Kingdom* by Michael Murphy. Copyright © 1972 by Michael Murphy. Reprinted by permission of Viking Penguin Inc and Latimer New Dimensions.
- "The Principles of Golf," from *The Principles Behind The Rules of Golf* by Richard S. Tufts. Copyright © 1960 by Richard S. Tufts. Reprinted by permission of the author.
- "Pinehurst 30 Years Ago," by Charles Price, from *Golf Magazine,* January, 1977. Reprinted by permission of the author and *Golf Magazine.*
- "It's Your Honor, Comrade," by Nick Seitz from *Golf Digest.* Reprinted by permission from the November, 1971 issue of *Golf Digest* Magazine. Copyright © Golf Digest/Tennis, Inc.
- "How Golf Invented The Scots," from *The Glorious World of Golf* by Peter Dobereiner. Copyright © 1973 by Peter Dobereiner. Prepared and produced by the Ridge Press, Inc. All rights reserved. Reprinted by permission of the publisher.
- "13 Ways of Looking at the Masters," by John Updike, from *Golf Magazine*, April, 1980. Copyright © John Updike. Reprinted by permission of the author and *Golf Magazine.*
- "Following The Sun," by Al Barkow condensed from *Golf's Golden Grind, The History of the Tour*. Harcourt, Brace, Jovanovich, Inc. Copyright © 1974 by Al Barkow. Reprinted by permission of the author.
- "The Triumvirate," from *Out of the Rough* by Bernard Darwin. Copyright © 1932 by Bernard Darwin. Reprinted by permission of the publisher, Chapman & Hall, Ltd.
- "Pine Valley: Golf's American Shrine," by Joe Schwendemann, from *The Philadelphia Bulletin,* 1966. Used by permission of *The Philadelphia Bulletin.*
- "Monterey: or How I was Seduced by a Peninsula," by Cal Brown. Reprinted by permission from the January, 1971 issue of *Golf Digest.* Copyright © Golf Digest/Tennis, Inc.
- "Sam Snead With Hair," from *The Dogged Victims of Inexorable Fate* by Dan Jenkins. Copyright © 1970 by Dan Jenkins. All rights reserved. Reprinted by permission of the publisher, Little, Brown and Company and the Sterling Lord Agency. Expanded and revised from an article that originally appeared in *Sports Illustrated.*
- "Ben Hogan, Carnoustie, 1953," from *Great Moments In Sport: Golf* by Michael McDonnell. Copyright © 1974 by Michael McDonnell. Reprinted by permission of the publisher, Pelham Books.
- "The Maddening First Hole," from *Go For Broke* by Arnold Palmer with William Barry Furlong. Copyright © 1973 by Arnold Palmer with William Barry Furlong. Reprinted by permission of Simon & Schuster, a Division of Gulf & Western Corporation.
- "The 1964 United States Open: The Third Man, Ken Venturi," by Herbert Warren Wind, from "The Sporting Scene" in *The New Yorker,* July 11, 1964. Reprinted by permission of the author and publisher.
- "The Professional, Walter Hagen," from *Unplayable Lies* by Fred Corcoran and Bud Harvey. Hawthorn Books. Copyright © 1965 by Fred Corcoran and Bud Harvey. Reprinted by permission of the authors.
- "Elements of Greatness—A Classic Course," by Pat Ward-Thomas, from *The World Atlas of Golf* by Pat Ward-Thomas, Herbert Warren Wind, Charles Price and Peter Thomson. Copyright © 1976 by Mitchell Beazley. Reprinted by permission of the publishers, Random House, Inc., Alfred A. Knopf, Inc. and Pantheon Books, and Mitchell Beazley Marketing Ltd.
- "The Grand Slam: 1930–1980," by Peter Ryde, from the *1980 Bay Hill Classic Annual,* sponsored by Viceroy Rich Lights, Orlando, Florida. Reprinted by permission of the publisher.
- "The Trial of Dick Mayer," (original title "The trials and travails of Dick Mayer, Inverness' last champion"), by Dave Anderson, from *Golf Digest.* Reprinted with permission from the June, 1979 issue of *Golf Digest* Magazine. Copyright © Golf Digest/Tennis, Inc.
- "Developing A Style, Finding The Orthodox, Taking The Breaks In Stride," excerpted from *Bobby Jones On Golf* by Robert Tyre Jones, Jr. Copyright © 1966 by Robert Tyre Jones, Jr. Reprinted by permission of Doubleday & Company, Inc.
- "When A Player Hits The Ball—What Exactly Happens?" from *The Search For The Perfect Swing* by Alastair Cochran and John Stobbs. J.B. Lippincott. Copyright © 1968 by the Golf Society of Great Britain. Reprinted by permission of Harper & Row, Publishers, Inc. and Wm. Heinemann Ltd.
- "On Learning and Teaching," from *On Learning Golf* by Percy Boomer. Copyright © 1942, 1946 by Percy Boomer. Reprinted by permission of the publisher, Alfred A. Knopf, Inc. and The Bodley Head Ltd.
- "What Can Your Best Golf Be?" from *How To Play Your Best Golf All The Time* by Tommy Armour. Copyright © 1953 by Thomas D. Armour. Reprinted by permission of Simon & Schuster, a Division of Gulf & Western Corporation.
- "Harry Vardon, The Master Mold," by Ken Bowden, from *The Methods of Golf's Masters* by Richard Aultman and Kenneth Bowden. Copyright © 1975 by Richard Aultman and Kenneth Bowden. Reprinted by permission of the publisher, Coward, McCann & Geoghegan, Inc.

- "Why Golf Is So Different—And So Difficult," from *The Missing Links: Golf and the Mind* by David Morley. Copyright © 1976 by David C. Morley. Reprinted by permission of Atheneum Publishers, Inc.
- "Golf's One Unarguable, Universal Fundamental," from *Golf My Way* by Jack Nicklaus and Ken Bowden. Copyright © 1974 by Jack Nicklaus. Reprinted by permission of Simon & Schuster, a Division of Gulf Western Corporation.
- "Inner Golf," by Tim Gallwey, from *Golf Magazine*, May, 1979. Reprinted by permission of the author, *Golf Magazine* and Random House, Inc. Copyright © 1979 by Tim Gallwey and Random House, Inc.
- "What It Is All About," from *Swing The Clubhead* by Ernest Jones and David Eisenberg. Copyright © 1952 by Ernest Jones and David Eisenberg. Reprinted by permission of the publisher, Dodd, Mead & Company, Inc.
- "First, Understand What You Are Trying To Do," from *Practical Golf* by John Jacobs with Ken Bowden. Copyright © 1972 by John Jacobs and Ken Bowden. Reprinted by permission of *Times Books*, a division of Quadrangle/The New York Times Book Company, Inc. and Stanley Paul Ltd.
- "Golfers and Other Strangers," by Alistair Cooke, from *Golf Magazine*, 1975. Reprinted by permission of the author and *Golf Magazine*.
- "Golf Through TV Eyes," by Frank Hannigan, from *The USGA Golf Journal*, 1964. Reprinted by permission of the author and the United States Golf Association.
- "The Golfomaniac," by Stephen Leacock. Reprinted by permission of Dodd, Mead & Company, Inc., from *Laugh With Leacock*. Copyright © 1930 by Dodd, Mead & Company, Inc. Copyright renewed 1958 by George Leacock.
- "The Whitwams Go To The Masters," by Jolee Edmondson, from *Golf Magazine*, 1976. Reprinted by permission of the author and *Golf Magazine*.
- "Mr. Frisbie," from *Round Up* by Ring Lardner. Copyright © 1928 by Ellis A. Lardner; renewal copyright © 1956 by Ellis A. Lardner. Reprinted by permission of Charles Scribner's Sons.
- "Golf In Los Angeles: Part Royal and Ancient, Part Disney," by Jim Murray, from *Golf Digest*. Reprinted with permission from the January, 1973 issue of *Golf Digest* Magazine. Copyright © Golf Digest/Tennis, Inc.
- "The Heart of A Goof," from *The Golf Omnibus* by P.G. Wodehouse. Reprinted by permission of the publisher, Barrie & Jenkins, Ltd, A.P. Watt, Ltd. and Scott Meredith Literary Agency.
- "All To Play For/The Cup and the Lip," from *Goldfinger* by Ian Fleming. Reprinted with permission of Macmillan Publishing Co. Inc. from *Goldfinger* by Ian Fleming. Copyright © Glidrose Publications Ltd., 1959, and by permission of Jonathan Cape.
- "An Amateur on Tour," from *The Bogey Man* by George Plimpton (chapters 1, 11 and 12). Copyright © 1967, 1968 by George Plimpton. Reprinted by permission of Harper & Row, Publishers, Inc.
- "Up The Tower," by Henry Longhurst, from *The Best of Henry Longhurst*, edited by Mark Wilson, published by *Golf Digest*. Copyright © 1978.
- "Scenes From A Marriage: A Golfer's Lament," by Peter Andrews from The New York *Times*. Copyright © 1977 by Peter Andrews. Reprinted by permission of the author.
- "How Bobby Jones and I Blew the British Open at St. Andrews," by Charles Price, from *Golf Magazine*, July, 1978. Reprinted by permission of the author and *Golf Magazine*.

Contents

Part III: THE SECRET OF THE GAME   135

Part IV: THE FUN OF THE GAME   185

Part V: THE RECORD OF THE GAME   265

The Written Record

by **ALISTAIR COOKE**

EVERY sport pretends to a literature, but people don't believe it of any sport but their own. Ask Herbert Warren Wind or Ben Crenshaw to guess who is writing about what in the following passage, and he might cite Horace Hutchinson writing in 1903 on the never-ending problem of the swing: "The art, though difficult, may be acquired by imitation of a good practitioner, and, once it is mastered, constitutes one of those delightful combinations of strength and delicacy in which is found the chief charm of the higher athletics." The real author, however, had probably never heard of the golf swing, though he is or was—I am told—the revered master of the grilse, the gilaroo, the finnock, the sewin and every other guise of salmon. He is Sir Herbert Maxwell talking about the art of "casting the fly." Indeed, as I was settling to write the piece, my doctor was dangling before me the improbable dream of a million-dollar market for an anthology of fishing literature. All I could think of was Izaak Walton, Hemingway, and Red Smith (for that matter, Red Smith can create a literature of any sport he cares to write about). But, the doc insists, there is an enormous literature of fishing. I take his word for it and leave him to it.

I *know* there is a cricket literature, beginning —as far as I'm concerned (which is not very far) —with "a deathless hush in the Close tonight" and ending with Neville Cardus. And for the sake of peace at any price, we had better assume that there is an impressive literature also of curling, gin rummy and table tennis. But, now, golf. Does anybody—except the entire world of nongolfers —deny that "the gowf" has produced the richest literature of any known sport? How could it be otherwise with a game which, in Stephen Potter's famous reminder, "is not, as the popular fallacy has it, a microcosm of life: life, on the contrary, is golf in miniature."

Granted that to get any pleasure from golf reporting (i.e., "fired a three-iron to the tenth . . . sank a fifteen-footer at the twelve . . . fashioned four birdies, two bogeys and two long par-saving putts for a third-round sixty-eight") it helps to know the difference between a three-iron and a branding iron; although it is debatable whether, since the invention of the transistorized edit terminal, any pleasure at all is to be had from news-agency reporting. But this daily drone bears about as much relationship to the literature of golf as the stock market index does to the romance of money, as revealed in say, a biography of J.P. Morgan or the novels of Balzac. Every Sunday for forty years, the late lamented Henry Longhurst kept a devoted following, at least thirty percent of whom had never lifted a golf club or were likely to. He saw golf as an ample outdoor stage on which a cast of Dickensian characters was compelled by the firm etiquette of the game to act out a script by Jane Austen. The unique, the furtive pleasure that golf offers to the inveterate spectator—whether on the ground or on the box—is something that is not required of the ecstatic goal scorer or the tennis player in a tantrum: the tension of restraint. Once in a while, Johnny Miller may groan at the skies, Trevino may bark at his ball as at an errant puppy. But in moments of crushing disappointment, not even Sam Snead and Tom Weiskopf browbeat a marshal: they explode in a sigh. One great opportunity of tournament reporting, variously seized by such as Dan Jenkins, Bernard Darwin and Michael Williams, is to sense the turmoil or the ruefulness going on inside the placid exterior of a possible winner two strokes back with five holes to play. In short, character, and the tracing of its foibles, is only one of the things that the game is about. It has been enough to make memorable the entire golfing output of P.G. Wodehouse, Stephen Leacock, and Jim Murray.

But the game is complex enough, and beautiful and leisurely enough, to open up all sorts of specialties for all sorts of writers. Unlike, shall we say, tennis or chess, golf has an incomparable range of landscape, which encourages Pat Ward-Thomas to delineate the different pains and pleasures of the chase in Scotland and France and the California desert; John Updike to peel off the social layers from the artichoke of Augusta, Georgia; and Charles Price to enlarge on his lifelong feud with practically any course that gets the better of him.

There is the fantasy, indulged by every hacker on his pillow, of playing with Nicklaus or Palmer—and, here, George Plimpton to explore the dream as fact.

There is even—as with no other game—a fascinating detective literature, a wry commentary on the human comedy, implicit in the book of rules. I must say that for a game whose aim is to get a little ball in a hole in as few strokes as possible, the book of rules would seem to offer, at first glance, less excitement than the propositions of Euclid. In fact, and precisely because golf is played on a board of 120 acres or more, the vagaries of weather and topography, not to mention the unpredictable whimsies and prejudices of the human animal at play, have produced shelves of legal commentaries on the rules which suggest to the imaginative reader as many subtle, and hilarious interpretations as the Constitution of the United States. Anyone who doubts this should run, not walk, to procure the entertaining gloss on the rules recently written by Frank Hannigan, with Tom Watson standing watchfully at his elbow.

I suppose that the least satisfactory prose in the whole body of the literature (it is also of the literature of any other game) is that devoted to describing the technique of how it is done or ought to be done. This is a nearly inevitable failing, since God decreed that the doers of this world are seldom, if ever, writers. Nobody has yet written a *Sudden Death in the Afternoon* to compare with Hemingway's bone-clear exposition of how a bull is fought. But pending this masterpiece, several famous players and their ghosts have made a brave stab at it. And the great one who never needed a ghost, Robert Tyre Jones, Jr., has left us a file of lucid and literate commentaries which might well turn out to be The Missing Aristotle Papers On Golf.

More than anything else, though, to anyone who would write about it, golf offers a four-hour drama in two acts, which becomes memorable even in the tape-recorded reminiscences of old champs, and which—in the hands of someone like Herb Wind—can become a piece of war correspondence as artfully controlled as Alan Morehead's account of Gallipoli.

Introduction

by **MICHAEL BARTLETT**

THIS book celebrates fine writing about the game of golf. The argument is often made that golf has the richest literature in sport. Suggested reasons are that it is a gentleman's game covered by a more cultivated corps of journalists. That's snobbish. Maybe the answer is the sport's individualism, which puts a premium on solitary courage and nerve. But then so do mountain climbing and Grand Prix racing. Possibly it's the setting, simultaneously genteel and ruggedly natural. That seems correct enough. Its maddening absurdity gave us black (read golf) humor long before the term came into vogue. Adding the fact that no one has yet mastered the secret of teaching the swing to millions of devoted and doomed duffers helps create an instruction industry worth listing on the New York Stock Exchange. Last, there is the psycho-mystical element that produces poetic essays and other flights of golf writing fancy.

If this collection illustrates how good golf writing can be, it is also meant as homage to the writers themselves. Ever since the 16th century when scribes reported the handicaps of various and royal political types who were popularizing the game, golf's chronicle has been building. Here you'll find entries from the 20th century where the writing has kept pace with the game's sophistication without losing its sense of tradition or humor. The working formula for selection has been to include classic and contemporary stories about great golfers in great moments by great writers. If names like Keeler, Rice, Laney, Martin, Travis, Hutchinson, Potter and Graffis are missing, it is for lack of pages, not appreciation.

I have had the pleasure of spending time with many of the contributors. My thanks to them for their sage advice and untold anecdotes and for adding their names to the contents. Their talents include the renaissance erudition of Bernard Darwin, Herbert Warren Wind and Alistair Cooke and the heady speculations of Arnold Haultain and Michael Murphy. For great statements about the game that should not be taken *too* seriously, Dan Jenkins, Frank Hannigan and Charles Price lead the way. Reporters, humorists, essayists and novelists give you more to choose from.

To the writing we add the photography of Tony Roberts, who has spent the last decade recording the game through his lenses. Golf is a colorful world, and Tony, a colorful personality in his own right, has made much of that fact.

Finally, to those working behind the typewriter—Betsy Storm, Karen Walden, Sosha Wagner, Janet Seagle and Susan Shipman—sincere thanks.

Now to *The Golf Book.* Find a comfortable chair near your favorite hole, take an overlapping grip on the first few pages and keep your eye on the game . . . .   *New York City, 1980*

PART I

The Spirit of the Game

". . . And how beautiful the vacated links at dawn, when the dew gleams
untrodden beneath the pendant flags and the long shadows lie quiet on the
green; when no caddie intrudes upon the still and silent lawns, and you stroll
from hole to hole and drink in the beauties of a land to which you know you
will be all too blind when the sun mounts high and you toss for the honor!"

—from *The Mystery of Golf*
by Arnold Haultain

The Golf Imperative

by ART SPANDER and MARK MULVOY

Art Spander of the San Francisco Examiner *has covered golf for nearly two decades and garnered numerous awards for his work. Some years ago he and Mark Mulvoy, senior editor at* Sports Illustrated, *collaborated on* Golf: The Passion and the Challenge. *In the opening chapter Spander attempted to state in universal terms what drives people to play the game.*

YOU are alone. You are in full control of your destiny. You can create a masterpiece or a muddle and there will be no one else to credit or blame but yourself.

No perfect pitches get belted out of the park. No short lobs get belted into the net. No perfect passes get dropped; no missed jump shots get tapped in. There are no opponents and no teammates who ruin or reprieve you. Just you.

You have all the time you need to do what you want and an impartial standard against which to measure yourself.

Are you ready? Anyone with money and courage can play. Money for the clubs, the clothes, the balls, the greens fees, the club dues. Courage for the confrontation with yourself. For golf is a game of individual achievements and failures. You face the challenge of the course alone; your teammate is the self-indulgent belief that you can beat it. Your opponent, in the last analysis, is yourself—your inadequacies, your poor judgment, your helplessness. Par is an immediate and unrelenting yardstick. You either play well or you don't, and your score leaves no room for doubt.

And what does it all prove—this genteel, slightly absurd ritual of, as a 19th century logic tutor at Oxford put it, "putting little balls into little holes with instruments very ill-adapted to the purpose"? Just this: your worth. For golf is a game not just of manners but of morals. "Play it as it lies" is the first commandment: accept your fate and overcome it, if you can. Don't talk of the game's absurdity. That's not the point. A golfer finds out a great deal about himself during an eighteen-hole round, and besides, life itself could be regarded as an equally unwieldy venture. The fact is we must cope or cop out, and there is no finer place to learn that lesson than on the golf course. Whether your idea of coping is smelling the flowers as you go along or staring down the challenge of a three-foot character builder, golf allows you a chance to triumph over yourself. It's a game of the ego.

This challenge can be intimidating, and the game's trappings are often attempts to mitigate it. Consider, for example, the gentleman from Portland, Oregon, who shows up for his weekly round of golf wearing a shirt emblazoned with the logotype of the famous Doral Country Club in Miami. He hasn't played there, just visited to buy some conspicuous souvenirs. Pretentious? Perhaps. Or, put another way, it's a boost for the ever-faltering ego. If you can't conquer Doral, you can still dress as if you could. In golf the garb of the pros is not only accepted but expected from rank amateurs, not only copied but exaggerated. A bank president who barely permits himself a striped tie at work will appear on the course in blue and white polka-dot pants, an aquamarine shirt, and two-tone shoes. It's more than a little showing off. Those flashy clothes project an image of outrageous self-assurance for someone who needs all the self-assurance he can muster. Is it too much to suggest that such confidence may in fact be lacking and that the wild clothes are a means of bolstering it? Then what might have been a crash landing for the ego becomes only a bumpy one, the golfer having assured himself with his sporty clothes that he is sport enough to accept the verdict of the golf course, however harsh.

Clothes are not the only palliative for the cruelty of golf. Next to a full backswing and a smooth putting stroke, the excuse may be the most cultivated part of the game. Even the most proficient golfers, the touring pros, have a stockpile of excuses: the sun was in their eyes; the wind came up unexpectedly; they misread the yardage; the caddie gave them the wrong club; their spikes slipped; breakfast didn't agree with them; the sand in the bunkers was too soft, or too coarse; even—indeed—the grass grew too quickly. (The last excuse, a little contrived if not entirely untrue, is to be used only as a last resort, in major tournaments. It exploits the fact that the grass, after it is trimmed by the greenskeeper early in the morning, will grow a fraction of an inch on a sunny day. Thus, putting speed on the greens decreases. Moreover, the grass on the fairway may poke between clubface and ball and create a flying lie—the absence of backspin that is usually imparted by the grooves of the club.)

P.G. Wodehouse went so far as to create a character, ostensibly fictional, who whined about missing short putts because of the uproar butterflies made in an adjoining meadow.

When excuses pale, the golfer in search of success may be reduced to a temper tantrum. In other sports you can purge your frustrations by crashing into an opponent. Golf has no place for such catharsis; it is supposed to be a sport of decorum, of well-dressed men and women in a genteel atmosphere. And yet to the intemperate amateur this veneer of civility is hardly a deterrent. A favorite poster in many pro shops depicts an Oriental tourist musing. "I just come from America, where I learn about game called Ah Shit."

"Terrible Tempered" Tommy Bolt was the patron saint of such duffers. One day Bolt had a 350-yard shot to a green and asked for his three-wood. The caddie handed him a three-iron. Cursing darkly, Bolt demanded the wood again, insisting that no one would use an iron from that distance. The caddie shrugged helplessly. It was the only club he had left, he explained, except for a putter, and Bolt had broken the handle off that earlier in the round. In his later years Bolt claimed that many of the stories about him were contrived. But the evidence against him was compelling when *Sports Illustrated* ran a two-picture sequence from the 1960 U.S. Open at Cherry Hills in Denver, showing Bolt hitting a tee shot into a lake and then immediately hurling the club into the water. (A young boy dived in, retrieved the club, and handed it to a rather contrite Bolt, who mumbled his thanks.)

In the 1960s, apparently in an attempt to improve its image, the Professional Golfers Association (PGA) instituted an automatic fine for club throwing and club breaking. Then, modifying its edict as if to admit that a small show of temper was only natural, it ruled that no fine would be levied if the golfer kept hold of both sections of the club on breaking it.

Lefty Stackhouse, who played the pro tour in the 1930s and early 1940s, would treat various parts of his body as if they were independent beings and apportion them responsibility for his errors. One day Lefty hit a bad hook and immediately concluded that the trouble had been caused by his right hand turning over on the shot. "Take that!" he shouted, as he slapped the hand violently against a tree trunk. Stackhouse is the man who once attempted to strangle his putter and once after missing a short putt battered the club against the radiator of his car. Ky Laffoon was known to have plunged his putter into a lake and screamed, "Drown you son of a bitch, drown!"

Writer H. L. Mencken fumed, "If I had my way a man guilty of golf would be ineligible for any public office in the United States, and the families of the breed would be shipped off to the white slave corrals of the Argentine." But as Bolt and his fellow sufferers demonstrate, golf might be more accurately described as the punishment rather than the crime. The Scots, who invented the pastime, even theorized that the Almighty had provided golf to make man suffer and then bestowed Scotch whiskey on him to ease the pain.

Such quips bring to mind that other great salve of the golfer—humor, particularly black humor. A few years ago, so the story goes, a lawyer and his friend were playing at a course in West Los Angeles, and the friend sliced his tee shot into a road next to the third hole. The ball crashed through the windshield of an oncoming car and struck the driver, knocking him unconscious and causing the vehicle to run into a fence. Understandably upset, the man who had hit the ball turned to his lawyer/playing partner and asked, "What do you think I should do?" Whereupon the counselor advised, "Well, I'd turn the right hand under a little more and . . ."

A few years ago a golf magazine included a drawing of a skeleton lying in a clump of bushes next to a fairway, the bones of one hand wrapped around a golf club. A golfer standing nearby was thoughtfully regarding the macabre sight and telling his caddie, "You can't get out of this stuff with an eight-iron, apparently. Give me a wedge."

Sporty clothes, elaborate excuses, temper tantrums, black humor—all attempts to compensate for the cruelty of the game. Indeed the entire scenic and social setting of golf seems to fulfill a similar function. For the most part golf is a sport played in a very controlled, pretty setting. Nature has been tamed into a garden, the players into strolling garden partygoers. Studied casualness surrounds, almost obscures, the very intense contest. (To nongolfers this nonchalance often seems to *be* the game—golf as a social event rather than a sport.)

Logically enough, the golfer wants a soothing environment for his struggle. If you're going to undertake an ordeal of self-examination and testing, it may as well be amid pretty meadows and glades, and among companions who, presumably, are your friends. Ascetics may argue that it is more efficient to face up to the stark reality of yourself in a stark setting. But most of us prefer more gentle confrontations.

And so the intimidation of golf, the stark challenge to the individual that lies at the root of the game, is cloaked in reassuring blandishments with a quite different lure. Here is a sport that almost anyone is physically capable of playing—men, women and children, big and small, fit and fat. It offers physical exercise that, if no more strenuous than mowing the lawn or cleaning the attic, is at least more pleasant. How intimidating could such a do-able sport be?

The addicted golfer knows, since he has faced the formidable challenge of this game beneath its gentle accessibility. He experiences the game not just as a pastime but as an imperative. It is to him that the passion of golf reveals itself, and in him (and his eccentricities) that one finds the basic and most powerful lure of the game.

Journalist and television commentator Alistair Cooke came upon the game at middle age, shot 168 in his first round, and immediately became addicted. He calls golf, "an open exhibition of overweening ambition, courage deflated by stupidity, skill soured by a whiff of arrogance. . . . These humiliations are the essence of the game."

If golfers do not enjoy such pain and thus are not simply masochists, it does seem that they thirst for the discipline that inevitably produces pain. Golf is a kind of purgatory. It makes compelling demands on the golfer to confront himself, and as he acts on these demands, he experiences both pain and redemption. The game stimulates the player. But it is only a stimulus; it can itself be conquered no more than can life, that other purgatory.

The backbone of golf is the public course player, a pedestrian who pulls his cart through thousands of rounds.

Start with the swing, probably the single most important motion in sports. If it is right, the journey from tee to green becomes as easy as calculating distances and compensating for wind (tricky, but rarely as complicated as repairing an imperfect swing). And so the swing is endlessly scrutinized and analyzed. Every day sports pages across the country carry sidebar instructions from the ghostwriters of Arnold Palmer, Jack Nicklaus, Lee Trevino and Billy Casper. Aim the thumbs to the left, to the right; pull the left foot back from the line of flight; pull the right foot back; cock the wrists at the top of the swing; don't cock the wrists. Golfers absorb this advice reverently and diligently practice swinging everywhere—in elevators, meeting rooms, cocktail lounges, airports, even on television—as if serenity itself is to be found in constantly repeating the swing, like some chant. It soon transcends a mechanical motion and becomes a state of mind—ideally no longer a matter of straightened elbows or bent knees but of a tranquil, creative spirit, from which it will spring untroubled automatically.

Michael Murphy, author, cofounder of the Esalen Institute for behavioral science research, and student of the one-piece swing, calls golf the ultimate form of meditation. On the other hand, George Plimpton, whimsical writer and pedestrian duffer, hypothesized that while he is swinging, miniature beings are screaming instructions through megaphones from his brain to the muscles of the arms and legs. That turbulent condition, he recognized, produces equally turbulent swings.

But whether you meditate to transcendent calm or you fantasize to writhing neurosis, the game of golf remains unmoved by the game it moves you to play within yourself. Par is still par, the sand traps don't move, the fairways don't expand or contract. An unexpectedly bad lie here or a good one there is bestowed with, all in all, fairly random chance. Whether you're playing well or poorly, the game treats you impartially.

Not so other sports. In football, if your team is playing well and the opposition poorly, an eighty-yard touchdown drive can be a carefree romp. If you're playing poorly and the opposi-

tion well, a one-yard plunge can be a forced march. Other games are only what the interaction of opponents makes them. Golf is that and more—independent, indomitable.

It is indomitable too because it is so varied. Each course teaches the game differently. Other sports strive for similar if not always uniform playing fields, in size, composition, and condition. Golf celebrates variety, from booming par fives to petite par threes, from alligator-infested water hazards to sagebrush rough. It is almost as if the course is the game, and therefore each different course a different game. Golfers speak of "playing" Pebble Beach, or Oakmont, or Merion as if to say simply "playing golf" is meaningless. (Indeed in the case of courses such as Pebble Beach, where conditions fluctuate wildly, it is not enough to identify the course. You pretty well have to append a weather report if you want to convey what sort of game you were playing.) To conquer golf one would have to conquer all the different courses.

One Nathan Tufts considered the conquest of a course no more than surviving its eighteen holes, and in 1970 he announced his intention to play 300 rounds of golf that year, one each on 300 different American courses. A kindred spirit, Alfred Vlautin, of San Francisco, set himself the goal in life of playing every course in northern California. He tacked a map to a wall in his home and marked with pins the location of 160 courses. In time each pin was replaced with a black dot—mission accomplished. "I had to work to get on some of the private courses," Vlautin recalled with more than a hint of pride in his voice, "but I've played them all."

Some time later, Vlautin read of a hole-in-one at a local course he had never heard of. Badly shaken, he called to find out about it. He learned, to his relief, that he did know the course after all (and he had played it)—it had existed for years but had recently changed its name. Grateful but still disconcerted, he managed a few words of thanks.

Asked why he wanted to play all those courses, Vlautin responded with a mountain climber's sense of conquest, "Because they're there."

Bizarre? Not compared to the two intrepid souls who took it upon themselves to play courses that weren't there. In the summer of 1974, teenagers Bob Aube and Phil Marrone played the 400 miles from San Francisco (starting at Harding Park) to Los Angeles (ending at the Bel-Air Country Club) in a mere sixteen days and an estimated five hundred thousand shots.

Even allowing for the publicity gimmickry of these ventures, one can begin to appreciate a golf course's hold on a golfer. A round can be leisurely or intense, sociable or hostile, depending on the players, but to a great extent the course determines the atmosphere. You just don't feel the same playing Doral's Blue Monster as you do some cozy, familiar, gentle par 70 back home. And you haven't fully enjoyed the game until you have experienced its different settings. It takes only an appreciation of the game's possibilities, not some misguided notion of symbolic conquest or a craving for publicity, to want to embark on a golf odyssey.

The urge gripped Alan Shepard on February 6, 1971, when he plunked down a golf ball on the moon, shortly after arriving there himself, and proceeded to go to work with his six-iron. Restricted by his space suit, he missed with his first swing. "I said a few unprintable words under my breath," he confessed, "and called it a Mulligan." His next effort sent the little ball soaring through the nonresistant lunar atmosphere some 200 yards straight down the fairway, the highlands of Fra Mauro. (As a reward for that caper, Shepard was invited to the 1972 Bing Crosby Pro-Am Tournament.)

Whether or not you are charmed by teenagers bashing a golf ball down Highway 101 or by an astronaut wafting them over the lunar surface, it's hard to ignore the golfer's impossible yet irrepressible dream to concoct and conquer the ultimate golf challenge. It is as if there is something reassuring to many golfers about this indomitability of their game. They seem pleased to rediscover it continually, to be continually reminded of their inadequacy. "There is a certain romance in futility pursued," actor Efrem Zimbalist, Jr., an avid golfer, observed about golf. It is the romance of bringing some green monster

to its knees or of virtually falling to one's knees in reverence before it. Either way, the game is implacable, offering its lessons like some inexhaustible discipline of nature—the mountains or the seas. "A golfer always loses on the golf course," concluded Zimbalist, with no indication that it should ever be otherwise. Purgatory is demanding but cleansing.

One can even become honest at golf. In other sports, honesty is the referee's problem. Players do not readily admit to fouls or penalties when called for them and would not think of volunteering incriminating evidence that the ref has missed. Innocent until caught red-handed. In golf, for the most part there is no Big Brother watching, which gives you a chance to be the ref yourself. Power corrupts, it is said, but it has also been known to ennoble. Vested with the responsibility of calling the shots, even if they are his own, a golfer can become scrupulous. In the 1925 U.S. Open, to cite the most famous example, Bobby Jones nudged his ball while addressing it on the eleventh hole and called the penalty stroke on himself, though no one would have noticed had he failed to. That honorable act cost him the tournament (he fell into a tie with Willie Macfarlane and lost the playoff), but Jones showed no regret. "There is nothing to talk about, and you are not to write about it," he admonished newsmen, who were eager to work a little saintliness into their stories. "There is only one way to play the game."

You don't have to be quite that high-minded and moralistic to appreciate the rewards of honorable golf, to understand that it can be more satisfying to play a ball in the rough than to kick it out. Somehow, simple decency isn't as compelling in other sports. In golf it's easier to break the rules, but it's more rewarding to follow them, which may be part of the reason why the honor system survives.

Then there are the aesthetic fringe benefits of this discipline called golf. It was mentioned above that nature functions on a golf course to soothe the beleaguered player. But then too, it can inspire the tranquil one. Many a golfer has awakened on a beautiful morning, longed to go golfing for no reason other than that the golf course is an ideal place to appreciate a fine morning, and discovered the happy coincidence that the smells and sights of nature working its wonders can infuse one's game with a wonder-working spirit.

It's a big difficult to pin down, of course. Who knows whether those pros who stop to look at the brilliantly blooming azaleas behind the thirteenth green at the Augusta National are moved to brilliance on account of it? But the proper functioning of the body is often a sensual process (athletes are continually talking about how they feel), and a golf course abounds in richly sensual stimuli: the exquisite delicacy of dew on the greens, the perfume of freshly cut grass, the chill of a late-afternoon breeze. It's hard to visualize a player sensually impressed by such things who isn't able to feel how his body is functioning. And once he is in touch with what he is doing, it's a lot easier to do it right.

Suddenly, the pressure of golf all but dissolves, as the game ceases to be an internal test of the will and the other synthetics of the mind. It becomes a physical harmony, the golfer at peace with himself if not precisely at one with his surroundings. He plays serenely, expending great mental and physical energy without strain. Golf is no longer purgatory, just pleasure.

This is that exalted state, common to most sports, when the unsuspecting player sees everything going right and thinks he has conquered the game, when in fact he has only untangled himself. Foolishly, he begins to imagine the ideal, lucky game, over which he really has no control—sixty-foot putts dropping, pin-high approach shots stopping dead on the green. He fantasizes about the results of shots instead of continuing to concentrate on making the shots. Then a well-stroked putt unaccountably stays out or a solid drive finds a bad lie and he wonders whether the magic is gone. Soon his self-doubts are alive and well again, and he's back in purgatory, trying to confront and conquer them anew.

Playing golf well is not an elusive, ephemeral state of grace. But being lucky may very well be. You're well on your way toward coping with golf when you can tell the difference. Then you enjoy the exhilaration of good luck without getting intoxicated (losing touch with your game) and saddling yourself with a hangover when your luck turns sour. Being in a slump is a mental problem of not truly knowing what you can do. And there's no quicker way to get there than to mistake good luck for skill, because then bad luck inevitably seems to you to be a lack of skill.

If it's any consolation, many a pro has fallen out of touch with his game. After joining the tour in 1964, George Archer won an average of $77,000 a year for nine years. Then in the next three years he won less than $30,000 a year. "It's mass confusion," he moaned after one difficult day. "I'm guessing on every shot. About the only thing left for me is acupuncture in the brain."

At least Archer recognized where the problem lay. Many players, slumping and otherwise, will do anything to escape the conclusion that they are the cause (and the cure) of their problems. They swap up miracle remedies almost indiscriminately, so firm is their faith in self-helplessness.

We've come full circle—from the intimidating loneliness and purgative challenge, to the achievements of self-awareness, to the false paradise of good luck, to the self-doubts bred of failure. Then back to loneliness and challenge. Somehow golfers seem to be able to pick themselves up and start again.

We'll resist the urge to make of this pattern any more than a golf life cycle, and close simply by noting its consonance with the remarkable regenerative power of all species. Anyone wishing to pursue the investigation further is invited to make a field trip before dawn to any municipal course in or around a metropolitan center. There, in the darkness, he will come upon golfers stirring quietly, not yet quite awake, waiting to rise again.

Keep the Rules and They Keep You

by **COLMAN MCCARTHY**

One of a long line of golf essayists, Colman McCarthy, who makes his livelihood as a columnist for The Washington Post, *offers some reasons why learning and keeping the rules makes for more enjoyable golf.*

FORTY-ONE rules aren't so many—St. Benedict had seventy-three to keep the brethren on the straight and narrow. Yet, many golfers who have mastered the runics of the swing have not bothered much to master the simplicities of the rules, kept current by the vigilant fathers of the United States Golf Association and the Royal and Ancient Golf Club of St. Andrews, Scotland.

Most golfers are quite content with a mere acquaintance of the few basics that keep the game civilized—no kicking your opponent's ball into the rough when he's not looking, no stealing the honor on the tee—but after that, it often seems that anything goes. This attitude of abandon is more fitting for sports in which blood lust is an asset—like sparring with broken pool cues. Golf courses are havens for the nonhostile, where umpires and referees are not needed because the players themselves know the rules and obey them.

Is there a finer joy, short of clearing a pond by inches, than assessing an opponent two strokes who (as though playing croquet) strikes your ball on the putting green (breaching rule 35), cleans a muddy ball on the fairway (violating rule 23) or marks a line of flight on a blind shot over a hill (breaking rule 9)?

When calling attention to these rules and their unpleasant penalties, be prepared for pouting or fuming. You will be accused of unmentionable practices. But think of yourself, at such times, as Abraham Lincoln walking back those ten miles (a distance somewhat exceeding twenty-seven holes of golf) to return the penny. Your mission is honesty.

When someone tells you that you lead a dull life, deep in the sopor of rules and laws, tell them Arnold Palmer probably won the 1958 Masters because he knew the rules. On the par-three twelfth hole of the final round, on a soggy day in Augusta, Palmer flew the green and the ball imbedded in the back apron. A dispute arose when Palmer claimed he was entitled to a free drop; the official in the green jacket said no. Each was satisfied when Palmer played both a provisional ball, on which he scored three, and his first ball, on which he took a five. The tournament rules men then huddled and determined that Palmer was entitled to a free drop and the three stood.

If the alertness of a Palmer is not sufficiently

9

instructive, consider the wisdom of P.G. Wodehouse, who seldom broke 110. In one of his golf fables, Joseph Poskitt was playing Wadsworth Hemmingway for the President's Cup. On the ninth hole, over water, Poskitt hit one of his "colossal drives." He started to leave the tee but Hemmingway said, "One moment," and asked, "Are you not going to drive?"

" 'Don't you call that a drive?' Poskitt replied.

" 'I do not. A nice practice shot, but not a drive. You took the honor when it was not yours. I, if you recollect, won the last hole. I am afraid I must ask you to play again.'

" 'What?'

" 'The rules are quite definite on this point,' said Hemmingway, producing a well-thumbed volume . . .

"Poskitt returned to the tee and put down another ball. There was a splash. 'Playing three,' said Hemmingway. Poskitt drove again. 'Playing five,' said Hemmingway.

" 'Must you recite?' said Poskitt.

" 'There is no rule against calling the score.'

" 'I concede the hole,' said Poskitt."

I had a similar experience once, playing with Bobby Riggs, who knew the rules were there as much for his advantage as for orderly play. We were playing a course on Long Island, when on the first hole I happened to tee my ball ahead of the markers—by a matter of inches. The moment before my backswing, Riggs called out, "Wait!" Startled, I paused mid-swing. He sprung to the left marker, pulled it from the ground and moved it ahead by about a foot. "There," he said. "Swing away. You're behind the markers now." It was a subtle move and totally unnerving. My feelings were so vacillating between wonder at his nerve and rage that I sent my drive out of bounds. Riggs won the hole.

The St. Andrews' Scots who wrote the early rules were Calvinists who believed that although a golf course may look like paradise its users are potential wrongdoers. Shadows of sneakiness loom in us all, however sunny an aspect we present on the first tee. What is to prevent, say, a threesome of professionals from rigging their scores by signing cards two or three strokes lower than their actual tallies? Strikingly, it has always been one of the game's distinctions that the golf tour has never had a major cheating scandal. In 1972 Jane Blalock was accused of moving her ball in the rough by some other women on the tour, but the charges were never proven. In fact, she sued, in turn, the Ladies Professional Golfers Association and won a judgment that the LPGA was in violation of the Sherman Antitrust Act for not allowing her to compete in tournaments while her case was pending. In amateur golf, only the Deepdale scandal of the mid-1950s (in which phony handicaps were used by some of the contestants) is a splotch on the sport's purity. I have played with board members of corporations who lied, stole and cheated their way to the top, but who on the fairways were watchful of golf's rules and its etiquette.

Watchfulness goes to the heart of the matter, or at least to the aorta. It is not a great strain, for example, to avoid walking in the line of another's putt. Small effort is needed to keep from moving behind a player as he addresses the ball. And only moderate self-control is required to refrain from hitting into the foursome ahead. All that these standards of basic etiquette ask is that we simply be watchful of the other player, so that what we do on the golf course doesn't make it harder for our partners.

As a boy, I made a point of learning the rules. I would study them in the caddie yard while waiting to be assigned a loop. And, indeed, how often I came to use them. During the course of a round, I would watch closely whoever had matches against those I was caddieing for. When I saw a violation, I would call aside my employer and tell him what his opponent had just done. Usually, my man would be glad to get the facts and take action. Occasionally, though, my information was rejected. It would be too embarrassing, some thought. Others feared a stink. Some doubted that the rules made sense. But these were the exceptions. In time, I came to be sought out as a caddie, because my services went beyond merely carrying the clubs and attending the pin. They went directly to the heart of the game—the rules.

Founded in 1744, The Honourable Company of Edinburgh Golfers, known familiarly by its location, Muirfield, formulated the original golf rules, which now hang framed in the venerable clubhouse.

It is not by accident that the rules discuss "courtesy on the course" at the top of section 1. When golfers join private country clubs, and fork over high sums for initiation fees and monthly dues, invariably they talk with relief about no longer having to endure public course etiquette. They have something there: behavior on the nation's municipal and public fairways often makes a Route 66 truck stop seem like a well-mannered salon. In the past two decades, many of those taking up the game have been ruffians and rowdies. My suspicions are that golf began attracting the ruck when Arnold Palmer came along. Sitting on the barstools and looking blearily at the corner TV, the unrefined saw Palmer as their model. His thick neck, slashing swing and bullish play became the lightning rod down which the electrified masses slid on their way to the clubhouse. Many brought their rowdiness with them. If they take it anyplace else, it is when they walk behind

the ropes at a tournament in Arnie's Army. There, among shouting and shoving, crudeness and incivility rank high, as General Arnie is cheered on. Pros find it difficult to be paired with Palmer, for he attracts the rabble for whom etiquette, if they know the term at all, connotes questionable chromosomes. Palmer himself is often victimized by his own enthusiasts. I have seen him playing wretched golf only to walk the fairways thick with fans calling out, "Go get 'em, Arnie," when all he is capable of getting at that point is another struggle for par.

The point at which many golfers walk away from the rules is when they opt for preferred lies. The advantages of winter rules were intended to apply only when the earth is craggy, pocked by the harshness of the cold and other rudenesses of the winter weather. Such conditions rarely prevail mid-summer. Yet, the winter rules player counters that golf is hard enough without enduring the torment of uncivil real estate; if your Titleist lands in a vulgar piece of turf, move it to a more chaste spot. But rule 16 applies in all seasons: "The ball shall be played as it lies and shall not be purposely touched except that the player may, without penalty, touch his ball with his club in the act of addressing it and except as otherwise provided in the rules of local rules."

The challenge of accepting whatever lie we get is fundamental to the pleasures of golf. To accept the rub of the green, even when we must cross it against the grain, is to bring an objectivity to our play that refreshes the spirit. Once when I had the miffy luck of landing a tee shot in a divot hole, my companion called out, "Move the ball, it's OK. When I land in a divot I'll move mine." How tempting it was—to nudge the ball an inch or two to a tuft of grass waiting since the fourth day of creation for a golf ball to land. But who needs to go easy on themselves while at play? By accepting the conditions of turf on the fairways, you gather respect for yourself. When someone tells you, "Move the ball, it's only a game," answer, "No thanks." It's because golf *is* a game that we can accept its full reality.

In the end, some will always take the preferred lie, as others will ignore the sanctions of other rules. Fidelity to the rules is an acquired skill, and only the few who work at it experience its pleasures. For those who wish to bend the rules, there are always those putt-putt courses next to the truck stops. There, they can shout and stomp until their larynxes loosen when they miss that ten-footer off the sideboard. Amid the traffic and fumes, what could be more appropriate.

A Far, Far, Better Thing

by PAT WARD-THOMAS

Besides being a great golfer, Bobby Jones was an exceptional human being. Lifted to the heights at an early age, he accepted the prospect of a painful, slow death with equanimity. His friend, Pat Ward-Thomas, one of England's best golf writers, paid this tribute to Jones's final courage.

A lasting regret in the watching of golf is that I never saw Bobby Jones play, but I came to know him in the last ten years of his life and that was rich compensation for he was no ordinary man. Of all the great champions that ever lived he will be remembered as much for his qualities as a person as for his transcending skill at golf, and this in its time was beyond compare.

There is no call now to dwell upon his golfing achievements. They are indelibly etched on the tablets of history and cherished in the memories of numerous golfers, but the time for wondering at the essence of an exceptional human being is never done. As all the world knows he suffered, for twenty years and more, from syringomyelia, a rare disease of the spine. Probably from the outset he knew that there was no hope of recovery, that progressive physical decline was inevitable and that for the rest of his life he would have increasing discomfort, pain and immobility.

It is one thing to endure a grievous affliction with fortitude as many have done; it is another to do so without self-pity but often with ironic humor. Never did I hear him complain; rather would he make gentle mock of his incapacity so that one never felt the embarrassment and shyness that can happen when with the sorely stricken. Always he made his visitors at ease because, marvelously, the shrinking of the body had no effect on the crystal of his mind.

When thinking of Jones a sense of melancholy, even bitterness, is inescapable. It seemed unjust that the gods should exact so cruel a toll for the blessings they had bestowed upon him. Of these greatness at golf was only part. Recently, Eugene Branch, one of his partners in the Atlanta firm, told me what a capable lawyer he was. He had a degree in English at Harvard, one in engineering at Georgia Tech and withal the most cultured mind of all the great champions. I have sometimes thought that in a series of general knowledge examinations their collective efforts could not have matched his. And yet, in his spare time from intellectual pursuits, he could play golf better than all save two or three of them have ever done.

The legend of Jones was familiar to me as a boy, and in later years I envied those who had played with him and known him in his youth. Gene Sarazen competed with him as often as any

13

Courtesy United States Golf Association

Although Jack Nicklaus has surpassed the number of major championships won by Bobby Jones, 18 to 13, no golfer has ever duplicated Jones' Grand Slam. In 1930, at age 28, Jones won the Open and Amateur championships of both the United States and Great Britain. It remains a feat unparalleled in all of sport and the summit of golf achievement.

other golfer and before Jones died Gene said that "he was the only one of the great players of that era with whom I had a continuing friendship that was never marred. Jones and Francis Ouimet were the finest sportsmen the game has known." He went on to say that Jones was so unselfish on the course. "He would always consider you first in respect of the crowds." This has not always been conspicuous in the manners of some of the great modern players.

No greater privilege could befall a young British amateur than to partner Jones in an Open championship. Such was the good fortune at Hoylake in 1930, the celestial year, of Raymond Oppenheimer who was drawn with him for the first two rounds. Naturally he was nervous but recalls how charming and encouraging Jones was to him with the result that he played well and qualified comfortably for the final rounds. "Jones," he said, "was the most genuinely modest person I have ever met. When one had talked with him for a short time he gave you the feeling that the only difference between your golf and his was that he had been much more lucky."

Doubtless his chivalrous manners had a profound effect on golfers in Britain, as well as in America. Although such examples can be forgotten I think their influence was not lost on Jack Nicklaus whose first, and possibly only, hero in golf was Jones. Conceivably, this is why Nicklaus, greatest of today's champions, remains one of the game's most gracious losers.

My first meeting with Jones was in the shelter near the fifth green on the Old Course at St. Andrews one gray, bitter morning while the American team, of which he was captain, was practicing for the Eisenhower Trophy team championship. We talked of the course, then more like a meadowland than the swift running, burnished links that he recalled from his championship years, and the sight saddened him. I sometimes wonder what he would think of Augusta as it often plays nowadays with the experts firing shots at the flags like darts into a board.

When it was time for him to leave the course that day his electric cart faltered but with some pushing we managed to get him to the sanctuary of the hotel. He invited me to lunch, a memorable moment for a writer who had worshipped so long from afar. He was able then to walk very slowly with the aid of sticks, but writing was a considerable strain as I realized after asking him to sign one of his books. He did so and, as I cursed myself for imposing the task upon him, inscribed a message as well. This was my first experience of his innate kindness and courtesy.

Three years later, never having seen Augusta, I wrote and asked if he could arrange for me to do so. My wife and I were driving north through the eastern states, and it was arranged that Jones would collect us from our hotel in Atlanta and take us to East Lake, the old course where his genius first had bloomed.

One September morning he gave us lunch at the club. Previously that month I had seen Nicklaus win the Amateur championship at Pebble Beach and Jones spoke of how Nicklaus would become a great player and win many championships. In all his talk of young golfers there was no hint of the criticism that sometimes colors the opinions of distinguished elders when they discuss the coming generation. Later I learned that he was hardly recovered from a virus infection and that it was his first day abroad but, typically, he had made the effort rather than disappoint us.

At Augusta Jones had arranged that Jerome Franklin and Julian Roberts, two senior members of the club, would be our kindly hosts and reveal the beauties of the place to us. The course was being prepared for its winter season but I remember how easy it was to visualize the great deeds that had made the Masters a historic occasion. We saw too the cabin, amid its sheltering pines near the tenth tee, where in time one would call on Jones and receive the blessing of his perceptive observations of golf and golfers; but some years passed before I watched the Masters.

By then the change in Jones was heartrending to see. He could no longer walk; his hands were too frail to lift a glass and a supply of cigarettes had to be arrayed in holders within easy reach. It seemed as if his body had become too fragile to support the splendid head, which never lost its noble outlines, but the mind remained wonderfully sharp, the humor lively and the manner unfailingly gentle.

Always I shall remember his kindness. Not least one year when he learned indirectly, through Alistair Cooke as it happened, that *The Guardian* was having something of a crisis that winter and it was most unlikely I would be at the next Masters. Unknown to me Jones arranged through a friend of his that I could write articles for some American papers. This alone made possible my visit to Augusta where, incidentally, I saw the last great stretch of golf that Hogan ever played there when in the third round he came home in thirty.

At about this time I was involved in a possible book with the late Alfred Wright and we decided that Jones was the only eminent golfer we wanted to write a foreword. As everyone who has read his books must appreciate, he was a gifted writer and had no need of ghosts.

With some diffidence I wrote to him. He replied, "Believe me, there is nothing I dislike more than failing to accept enthusiastically any assignment you might give me; now, however, I simply must make some reservations.

"My health has been especially troublesome lately and I have been sorely pressed with personal matters. I am not one of those fortunate persons who can sit down before a typewriter and spill out words that make sense. The act of creation on a blank page costs me no end of pain." He went on to say that he could not then do the piece and concluded, "I hope you understand and will on your part act quite freely. If the uncertainty thus imposed is too great, I shall not be sensitive. On the other hand, I hope to be feeling better later on and perhaps may gain some grain of inspiration from the reading of your proof." Could anyone have declined what must have seemed a tiresome request more gracefully?

In 1968 Jones went to the Masters for the last time; thereafter the journey from Atlanta was too great a burden. By then it was a miracle that he still lived, so fragile had he become, weighing little more than eighty pounds. The agonies he must have borne can be imagined but the spirit was inextinguishable and still he welcomed "shooting the breeze," as he would say, in his bedroom.

It was deadly ironic that his final visit should coincide with the most disturbing hours the Masters has known—the affair of Roberto de Vicenzo's card—which caused all manner of anxiety to the Committee. I recall Mary, Bob's wife, telling us how, that Sunday evening, she suddenly saw a host of green jackets hastening across the lawn towards their cabin and wondered what on earth was amiss. They were coming to seek advice from Jones in the event that the consequences of de Vicenzo's aberration could be avoided. Bob, of course, said that nothing could be done and that, at all costs, the rules of the USGA and the R&A must be observed.

The following morning I called to say good-by and remember his distress at not having been strong enough to attend the presentation, although it was but 100 yards or so from his cabin. He knew that if ever the ceremony had needed his words it was on that haunted evening. Farewells were taken and he was carried to his car. I never saw him again but the memory of his courage and gentleness, the splendor of his mind and the pride of having known a great man will never perish.

The Game's Hidden but Accessible Meaning

by MICHAEL MURPHY

Not all who contribute to golf's literature are regular members of its writing corps. Michael Murphy, founder of the famed Esalen Institute, is also a low-handicap player who calls Pebble Beach his home course. In his remarkable book, Golf in the Kingdom, *Murphy wedded his love of the game with his explorations of human potential. At the Burningbush Golf Club he sat at the feet of the mystical pro Shivas Irons, whose vision of golf lifted Murphy to a new awareness.*

CERTAIN events may reflect the significant dimensions of all your life, mirroring your entire history in a passing moment. Have you ever had an experience like that? Have you been caught by an event that suddenly pulled the curtains back? Shivas Irons maintained that a round of golf sometimes took on that special power.

The archetypes of golf are amazingly varied, he said. That is the reason so many people gravitate to the game.

Golf as a Journey

"A round of golf," he said in his journal notes, "partakes of the journey, and the journey is one of the central myths and signs of Western man. It is built into his thoughts and dreams, into his genetic code. The Exodus, the Ascension, the Odyssey, the Crusades, the pilgrimages of Europe and the voyage of Columbus, Magellan's circumnavigation of the globe, the discovery of evolution and the March of Time, getting ahead and the ladder of perfection, the exploration of space and the Inner Trip: from the beginning our Western world has been on the move. We tend to see everything as part of the journey. But other men have not been so concerned to get somewhere else—take the Hindus with their endless cycles of time or the Chinese Tao. Getting somewhere else is not necessarily central to the human condition."

Perhaps we are so restless because like Moses we can never make it to the promised land. We tell ourselves that It is just over the next hill: just a little more time or a little more money or a little more struggle will get us there; ". . . even our theology depends upon that Final Day, that Eschaton when the journey will finally arrive, to compel our belief in God."

The symbol of the journey reflects our state, for man is surely on the move toward something. Many of us sense that our human race is on a tightrope, that we must keep moving or fall into the abyss. "This world is for dyin'," he said that night. We must die to the old or pay more and more for remaining where we are.

17

Yes, there is no escaping the long march of our lives: that is part of the reason people reenact it again and again on the golf course, my golfing teacher said. They are working out something built into their genes.

But there are other myths to govern our lives, other impulses lurking in our soul, "myths of arrival with our myths of the journey, something to tell us we are the target as well as the arrow."

So Shivas Irons would have us learn to enjoy what *is* while seeking our treasure of tomorrow. And—you might have guessed it—a round of golf is good for that, ". . . because if it is a journey, it is also a *round:* it always leads back to the place you started from . . . golf is always a trip back to the first tee, the more you play the more you realize you are staying where you are." By playing golf, he said, "you reenact that secret of the journey. You may even get to enjoy it."

The Whiteness of the Ball

What the golf ball was to Shivas has been hinted; what it has come to mean for me remains unsaid. And for a reason. Its power as a symbol is so complex and labyrinthine, so capable of lending itself to the psyche of each and every player, that once an attempt like this has begun to comprehend its "inner meaning," all bearings may be lost. For the golf ball is "an icon of Man the Multiple Amphibian, a smaller waffled version of the crystal ball, a mirror for the inner body; it is a lodestone, an old stone to polarize your psyche with." The more I ponder its ramifications the more I see that each and every bit of this world reflects the whole.

A friend of mine sees it as a satellite revolving around our higher self, thus forming a tiny universe for us to govern—a marvelous image really when you think about it, one I am sure Shivas Irons and Seamus MacDuff would have approved of. Our relation to the ball is like the Highest Self's relation to all its instruments and powers; the paths of its orbits reflect those of the planets and suns! The ball is then a symbol of all our revolving parts, be they mental or physical; for a while we reenact the primal act of all creation: the One casting worlds in all directions for

its extension and delight. Shivas anticipated the image in his notes: "For a while on the links we can lord it over our tiny solar system and pretend we are God: no wonder then that we suffer so deeply when our planet goes astray."

The ball is also a reflection, as Adam Greene said, of projectiles past and future, a reminder of our hunting history and our future powers of astral flight. We can then ponder the relation between projectile and planet, our being as hunter and our being as God; the hunter, the golfer, the astronaut, the yogi, and God all lined up in the symbol of the ball.

"The ball is ubiquitous. It is in flight at this very moment above every continent. Moreover, it is in flight every moment of the day and night. It may take flight one day on the moon, especially when you consider the potential prodigies of mile-long drives and the wonder they would bring to millions. Consider the symbolism inherent in that indubitable fact: a golf ball suspended in air at every moment!" There are so many golfers around the globe.

At rest, it is "like an egg, laid by man," for who can tell what prodigies the next shot will bring? In flight it brings that peculiar suspended pleasure which lies at the heart of the game; it is "a signal that we can fly—and the farther the better!"—it is a symbol of our spirit's flight to the goal. It is perfectly round, for centuries of human ingenuity and labor have made it so, and "the meanings of roundness are easy to see." (Parmenides and other Greek philosophers said that Being itself was a globe, that we must therefore "circulate" our words in order to tell a "round truth.")

So the symbols and meanings are endless. But when all these are said and done, there is a fact about the ball that overpowers all the rest. It is the whiteness of the ball that disturbs me more than anything else. "Though in many natural objects whiteness enhances beauty, as if imparting some special virtue of its own," said Herman Melville in a well-known passage, "and though certain nations have in some way recognized a certain preeminence to it, there yet lurks an elusive something in the color which strikes panic to the soul."

Only black so reminds us of the great unknown. Black and white, we throw them together in the old cliché, but somewhere deep in both there lies a hint of powers unforeseen. Do they remind us of the void, since they represent the absence of all ordinary hue? Is it annihilation we fear when we encounter them? "All colors taken together congeal to whiteness, the greatest part of space is black," say the journal notes. "What would happen if someone introduced a golf ball painted black?"

The Mystery of the Hole

In no other game is the ratio of playing field to goal so large. (Think of soccer, American football, lacrosse, basketball, billiards, bowling.) We are spread wide as we play, then brought to a tiny place.

The target then leads into the ground, leads underground. I realized this once reaching into one of the exceptionally deep holes our Salinas greenskeeper was cutting in 1949 (he had procured a new hole-cutter). What a strange sensation reaching so far into the ground. What was down there, underneath the ball?

There was a section in his notes entitled "The Psychology of Passageways," which has a bearing on the hole's mystery. In it there was a list of "holes and doorways in our ordinary life," which included a long paragraph about the significance of looking through windows (something to the effect that windows have a function other than letting us look outside, that we build them to simulate our essentially imprisoned state), another on the subject of toilets and the draining away of our refuse (including some sentences about the need to examine our stool whenever we feel disjointed), an essay on picture frames and other boundaries on art objects, and a list of all the "significant openings" in his own apartment (apparently, he had taken a careful inventory of these). There was also a list of "Extraordinary Openings." This included a constellation in the new zodiac he had made, various kinds of mystical experience—an entire catalog in fact of transports and ecstasies; a list of historic figures (including Joan of Arc, Pythagoras, Sri Ramakrishna, Seamus MacDuff, the Egyptian Pharaoh Ikhnaton, and a Dundee cobbler named

Typhus Magee); a list of historic events (including the outbreak of philosophy all over the world during the 6th century B.C., the first flights at Kitty Hawk, and a drive he had hit sometime during the summer of 1948); certain places in Burningbush and its environs (I think he compared these to the points on the body which are probed during treatments with acupuncture), a golf course in Peru (perhaps the Tuctu golf course, which he had mentioned during our conversation at the McNaughtons); certain phrases, philosophical terms, and lines of poetry (including the word *Atman,* the *Isha Upanishad,* and a limerick by one of his pupils); a list of coincidences in his life; and the unpublished manuscript of his teacher.

Our first passageways, he said, are the avenues of sense—our eyes, ears, nostrils and mouth. We build our houses and churches to simulate these, we relate to the earth itself as if it were our body, for "we start as someone looking out, and as soon as we look we think of escape."

"Life is a long obsession with passageways," the notes go on. "We are ever breaking through to the other side—of ignorance, isolation, imprisonment. Memory, catharsis, travel, discovery, ecstasy are all ways of getting outside our original skin."

He thought it significant that an entire fairway, with its green, rough, hazards, and traps was called a "hole," that the tiny target was used to characterize all the rest of the playing field. " 'How many holes have you played?' is the way the question is asked, not 'how many fairways?' or 'how many tees?' " He thought it had something to do with the fact that after all our adventures, all our trials and triumphs on the journey-round we are left with that final passage through.

As it turns out some of the most original thinking on the subject has been done by Jean-Paul Sartre, who ends Part Four of *Being and Nothingness* with a short essay on the hole and its implications. I don't recall Shivas quoting Sartre but their thinking on the subject has some extraordinary similarities. The French philosopher, admittedly, is not an accomplished golfer, but his apparent grasp of the hole's mystery suggests that he has had his problems and triumphs on the links. "Thus to plug up a hole," he says, "means originally to make a sacrifice of my body in order that the plenitude of being may exist." (How we golfers can sympathize with that.) "Here at its origin we grasp one of the most fundamental tendencies of human reality—the tendency to fill. . . . A good part of our life is passed in plugging up holes, in filling empty places, in realizing and symbolically establishing a plenitude." In establishing a plenitude! Perhaps this is the most fundamental clue. And the comprehension of that essential act of sacrifice involved in every disappearance of the ball into the hole (sacrifice and inevitable rebirth)! For— "In golf we throw ourselves away and find ourselves again and again. . . . A ball is in flight somewhere at every moment. . . ." What are all these but glimpses of plentitude!

Replacing the Divot

Our green-loving philosopher claimed there was no better way to deal with our existential guilt than replacing a divot or repairing a friendship. "We act on friendship every moment: with our fellows, our land, our tools, with the unseen spirits and the Lord whose world we are tending."

"Golf is a game of blows and weapons. In order that the game continue we must make amends for every single act of destruction. In a golf club everyone knows the player who does not replace his divot. One can guess how he leads the rest of his life."

Replacing the divot is "an exercise for the public good." It is also a reminder that "we are all one golfer." There would simply be no game if every golfer turned his back on the damage he did.

A Game for the Multiple Amphibian

Bobby Jones and other lovers of the game have attributed its widespread appeal to the fact that it reflects so much of the human situation: comedy, tragedy, hard work, and miracle; the agony and the ecstasy. There is something in it for almost everyone. Shivas liked to quote the

Religio Medici, especially the passage that described man as ". . . that great and true Amphibian whose nature is disposed to live, not only like other creatures in divers elements, but in divided and distinguished worlds." He believed that golf was uniquely suited to multiply our amphibious nature. It gives us a chance to exercise so many physical skills and so many aspects of our mind and character.

I need not catalog the game's complexity to make my point: you know about all the long and the short shots; all the nuance of weather, air, and grass; all the emotion and vast resolution; all the schemes for success and delusions of grandeur, and the tall tales unnumbered; the trials of patience and fiendish frustrations; all the suicidal thoughts and glimpses of the millennium. We all have a golfing friend we have had to nurse past a possible breakdown or listen to patiently while he expounded his latest theory of the game. How often have we seen a round go from an episode out of the Three Stooges to the agonies of King Lear—perhaps in the space of one hole! I will never forget a friend who declared after his tee shot that he wanted to kill himself but when the hole was finished said with total sincerity that he had never been so happy in his entire life. No other game is more capable of evoking a person's total commitment.

This immense complexity delighted Shivas. In fact, he would add more complexity to the game, perhaps to satisfy his endlessly adventurous spirit. Running, for example, has been left out, as well as jumping and shouting; so he advocated your exercising these basic functions sometime during the golfing day if you wanted to balance your mind and nerves. We must give these large needs adequate expression, he said, otherwise golf would "imprint too much of its necessarily limited nature on us." For ". . . every game must have its limits, simply to exist, just as every form and every culture does, but our bodies and our spirits suffer." So somewhere and somehow we should run and jump and sing and shout. (I don't want to give you any advice about this, especially when I think about some of the trouble I have had on golf courses when I have tried to follow his advice. Perhaps you should confine these more strenuous activities to your local schoolyard or gym. But you might find it interesting to see how your game fares when you exercise those muscles and functions that golf neglects.)

This is true for much more than running, jumping, and shouting though. For our golfing teacher maintained in his inexorable way that our "emotional and mental body" needed as much exercise as our physical body did. So "poetry, music, drama, prayer, and love" were essential to the game too. "There is no end to it," he said, "once you begin to take golf seriously."

Of a Golf Shot on the Moon

It can now be argued that golf was the first human game played on another planetary body. Those two shots Alan Shepard hit with a six-iron at the "Fra Mauro Country Club" have brought a certain stature and gleam of the eye to golfers the world over. Coming as they did while I was writing this book, they appeared to me as synchronicity: the game has a mighty destiny, the event said; Shivas Irons was right. In the shock I felt when the news appeared (I had not seen the television show) I thought that in some inexplicable way those shots had been engineered by Shivas (from his worldly hiding place) or by Seamus MacDuff (from his hiding place on the other side). But the subsequent news that Shepard and his golf pro, Jack Harden, had planned the thing ruled out Shivas and restored some perspective to my hopeful speculations. Still, the meaning of it continued to loom before me. Golf on the moon! And the command module named Kitty Hawk! (Shivas had called Kitty Hawk an "extraordinary opening" in this unfolding world and had worked with Seamus all those years on the possibilities of flight with "the luminous body.") The event was a tangle of synchronicities.

I wonder how many other golfers have felt the same way. So many of us are alive to the other edge of possibility (perhaps because the game has tried us so sorely) and ever alert for the cosmic meaning. This event confirms our sense of mighty things ahead.

There are other implications, however, some less promising. A trusted friend of mine, someone with a quick keen eye for injustice and intrigue, saw an ugly side to the whole affair. It was, he said, an imperial Wasp statement, however unconscious, that this here moon is our little old country club for whites, thank you, and here goes a golf shot to prove it. I hated to hear that, for I wanted to dwell on the hopeful meanings. And I hated to think what Seamus would do, being half-black, if he were fiddling around with it all from his powerful vantage point. The Kitty Hawk might not make it back to earth! But the heroes are back and so far so good. Still, I am left wondering what latent imperialism lay behind that six-iron shot.

And I am left with other thoughts about the character of Alan Shepard. What could have led the man to design that faulty club, smuggle it on board with those "heat-resistant" balls and risk some billion-dollar disaster from flying divots or tears in his space suit? What could have led him to such monumental triviality amid the terrors and marvels of the moon? The madness of the game had surfaced again, I thought, as I pondered his motives.

Had NASA put him up to it for public relations reasons? Maybe they wanted some humor in the enterprise or the backing of certain rich and powerful golfing senators. Perhaps he would collect on some stupendous bet (after all, he was interested in money and had made a pile in his astronaut years). Or could it simply be that all his golfer's passion to hit the ball a mile now had a chance to express itself, indeed the chance of a lifetime, the chance of history! Perhaps the collective unconscious of all the golfing world was delivering itself at last, seizing him as instrument for the release of a million foiled hopes for the shot that would never come down. And indeed the cry came down from space, ". . . it's sailing for miles and miles and miles," Alan Shepard was giving the mad cry of golfers the world over who want to put a ball in orbit and reassume their godlike power.

Yes, Shivas was right indeed: the game keeps giving us glimpses.

The Mystery of Golf

by ARNOLD HAULTAIN

One of the most unusual statements ever made about the game is The Mystery of Golf *by Arnold Haultain, a Canadian writer who tried very hard to look behind the meaning of the sport. If the following excerpts don't bring total illumination, they'll keep you thinking for a while.*

THREE things there are as unfathomable as they are fascinating to the masculine mind: metaphysics, golf, and the feminine heart. The Germans, I believe, pretend to have solved some of the riddles of the first, and the French to have unraveled some of the intricacies of the last; will someone tell us wherein lies the extraordinary fascination of golf?

I have just come home from my club. We played till we could not see the flag; the caddies were sent ahead to find the balls by the thud of their fall; and a low large moon threw whispering shadows on the dew-wet grass ere we trod the home green. At dinner the talk was of golf; and for three mortal hours after dinner the talk was —of golf. Yet the talkers were neither idiots, fools, nor monomaniacs. On the contrary, many of them were grave men of the world. At all events the most monomaniacal of the lot was a prosperous man of affairs, worth I do not know how many thousands, which thousands he had made by the same mental faculties by which this evening he was trying to probe or to elucidate the profundities and complexities of this so-called "game." Will someone tell us wherein lies its mystery?

. . . . .

I am a recent convert to golf. But it is the recent convert who most closely scrutinizes his creed— as certainly it is the recent convert who most zealously avows it. The old hand is more concerned about how he plays than about why he plays; the duffer is puzzled at the extraordinary fascination which his new found pastime exercises over him. He came to scoff; he remains to play; he inwardly wonders how it was that he was so long a heretic; and, if he is a proselyte given to Higher Criticism, he seeks reasons for the hope that is in him.

Well, I know a man, whether in the flesh or out of the flesh I cannot tell, I know such a one who some years ago joined a golf club, but did not play. The reasons for so extraordinary a proceeding were simple. The members (of course) were jolly good fellows; the comfort was assured; the links—the landscape, he called it—were beautiful. But he did not play. What fun was to be derived from knocking an insignificant-looking little white ball about the open country he did not see. Much less did he see why several

22

hundred pounds a year should be expended in rolling and cutting and watering certain patches of this country, while in others artfully contrived obstacles should be equally expensively constructed and maintained. Least of all could he understand (he was young then, and given to more violent games) how grown-up men could go to the trouble of traveling far, and of putting on flannels, hobnailed boots, and red coats, for the simple and apparently effortless purpose of hitting a ball as seldom as possible with no one in the world to oppose his strength or his skill to their hitting; and it seemed to him not a little childish to erect an elaborate clubhouse, with dressing rooms, dining rooms, smoking rooms, shower baths, lockers, verandas, and what not, for so simple a recreation, and one requiring so little exertion. Surely marbles would be infinitely more diverting than that. If it were football, now, or even tennis—and he once had the temerity to venture to suggest that a small portion of the links might be set apart for a court—the turf about the home hole was very tempting. The dead silence with which this innocent proposition was received gave him pause. (He sees now that an onlooker might as well have requested from a whist party the loan of a few cards out of the pack to play card tricks withal.)

Yet it is neither incomprehensible nor irrational, this misconception on the part of the layman of the royal and ancient game of golf. To the uninitiated, what is there in golf to be seen? A ball driven of a club; that is all. There is no exhibition of skill opposed to skill or of strength contending with strength; there is apparently no prowess, no strategy, no tactics—no pitting of muscle and brain against muscle and brain. At least, so it seems to the layman. When the layman has caught the infection, he thinks—and knows—better.

. . . . .

This modern rampancy of sport does not explain the fascination of golf. No; but it may help to explain its existence. Golf is some hundreds of years old; but only in the last two or three decades has it obtained its extraordinary footing. The interesting question is, Why is it that, amongst the thousand-and-one games today

played by men, women, and children in Europe and America, why is it that golf commands so large a share of attention, of serious and thoughtful attention? The literature of golf is now immense, and, much of it, good. Eminent men have devoted to it serious study; mathematicians try to solve its problems; prime ministers play it; multimillionaires resort to it; and grown men the world over jeopardize for it name and fame and fortune. Not even bridge quite so absorbs its votaries. Cricketers, footballers, tennis players do not so utterly abandon homes and offices for the crease, the field or the lawn. Only the golfer risks everything so he may excel in putting little balls into little holes—what is the clue to the mystery?

The clue is a compound one. To begin with, it is threefold: physiological, psychological, social. In the first place, no other game has so simple an object or one requiring, apparently, so simple an exertion of muscular effort. To knock a ball into a hole—that seems the acme of ease. It is a purely physiological matter of moving your muscles *so,* thus the tyro argues; and in order to move his muscles *so,* he expends more time and money and thought and temper than he cares, at the year's end, to compute. Without doubt the ball must be impelled by muscular movement: how to coordinate that muscular movement— that is the physiological factor in the fascination of golf.

In the second place, when the novice begins to give some serious consideration to the game, he discovers that there is such a thing as style in golf, and that a good style results in good golf. He begins to think there must be some recondite knack in the game, a knack that has to be learned by the head and taught by the head to the muscles. Accordingly he takes lessons, learns rules, reads books, laboriously thinks out every stroke, and by degrees comes to the conclusion that mind or brain has as much to do with the game as have hand and eye. It is here that the psychological factor comes in.

In the third place, having progressed a bit, having learned with a certain degree of skill to manipulate his several clubs; having learned also, and being able with more or less precision to put into practice, certain carefully conned rules as to how he shall stand and how he shall swing, the beginner—for he is still a beginner—discovers that he has not yet learned everything. He discovers that the character of his opponent and the quality of his opponent's play exercise a most extraordinary influence over him. Does he go out with a greater duffer than himself, unconsciously he finds himself growing overconfident or careless. Does he go out with a redoubtable player, one whose name on the club handicap stands at scratch, he cannot allay a certain exaltation or trepidation highly noxious to his game. And it is in vain that he attempts to reason these away. Not only so, but even after months of practice, when the exaltation or trepidation is under control, often it will happen that an opponent's idiosyncrasies will so thoroughly upset him that he will vow never to play with that idiosyncratic again. This we may call the social or moral element. It affects the feelings or the emotions; it affects the mind through these feelings or emotions; and, through the mind, it affects the muscles.

Now, I take it that there is no other game in which these three fundamental factors—the physiological, the psychological, and the social or moral—are so extraordinarily combined or so constantly called into play. Some sports, such as football, polo, rowing, call chiefly for muscular activity, judgment, and nerve; others, such as chess, draughts, backgammon, call upon the intellect only. In no other game that I know of is, first, the whole anatomical frame brought into such strenuous yet delicate action at every stroke; or, second, does the mind play so important a part in governing the actions of the muscles; or, third, do the character and temperament of your opponent so powerfully affect you as they do in golf. To play well, these three factors in the game must be most accurately adjusted, and their accurate adjustment is as difficult as it is fascinating.

· · · · ·

All true games, I have said, are contests. But in golf the contest is not with your fellowman. The foe in golf is not your opponent, but great Nature herself, and the game is to see who will overreach her better, you or your opponent. In almost all other games you pit yourself against a mortal foe; in golf it is yourself against the world: no human being stays your progress as you drive your ball over the face of the globe. It is very like life in this, is golf. Life is not an internecine strife. We are all here fighting, not against each other for our lives, but against Nature for our livelihoods. In golf we can see a symbol of the history and fate of humankind: careering over the face of this open earth, governed by rigid rule, surrounded with hazards, bound to subdue Nature ere we can survive, punished for the minutest divergence from the narrow course, and the end of it all. . . . And the end of it all? . . . To reach an exiguous grave with as few mistakes as may be—some with high and brilliant flight, others with slow and lowly crawl. . . .

But the ultimate analysis of the mystery of golf is hopeless—as hopeless as the ultimate analysis of that of metaphysics or of that of the feminine heart. Fortunately the hopelessness as little troubles the golfer as it does the philosopher or the lover. The *summum bonum* of the philosopher, I suppose, is to evolve a nice little system of metaphysics of his own. The *summum bonum* of the lover is of course to get him a nice little feminine heart of his own. Well, the *summum bonum* of the golfer is to have a nice little private links of his own (and, nowadays, perhaps, a private manufactory of rubber-cored balls into the bargain), and to be able to go round his private links daily, accompanied by a professional and a caddie. It would be an interesting experiment to add to these a psychologist, a leech, a chirurgeon, a psychiater, an apothecary, and a parson.

To sum up, then, in what does the secret of golf lie? Not in one thing; but in many. And in many so mysteriously conjoined, so incomprehensibly interwoven, as to baffle analysis. The mind plays as large a part as the muscles; and perhaps the moral nature as large a part as the mind—though this would carry us into regions deeper even than these depths of psychology. Suffice it to say that all golfers know that golf must be played seriously, earnestly; as seriously, as earnestly, as life.

· · · · ·

But may not also the simple delights of the game and its surroundings, with their effect upon the mind and the emotions, be included under the allurements and the mystery of golf? My knowledge of links up to the present is limited, but on mine there are delights which, to me a duffer, are like Pisgah sights: hills, valleys, trees, a gleaming lake in the distance, a grand and beloved piece of bunting lending gorgeous color to the scene; a hospitable club house with spacious verandas and arm chairs; shower baths; tea and toast; whiskey and soda; genial companionship; and the ever-delectable pipe. Has anyone yet sung these delights of the game: the comradeship in sport, the friendliness, the community of sentiment, the frankness of speech, the goodwill, the "generosity in trifles"? Or of the links themselves: the great breeze that greets you on the hill, the whiffs of air—pungent, penetrating—that come through green things growing, the hot smell of pines at noon, the wet smell of fallen leaves in autumn, the damp and heavy air of the valleys at eve, the lungs full of oxygen, the sense of freedom on a great expanse, the exhilaration, the vastness, the buoyancy, the exaltation? . . . And how beautiful the vacated links at dawn, when the dew gleams untrodden beneath the pendant flags and the long shadows lie quiet on the green; when no caddie intrudes upon the still and silent lawns, and you stroll from hole to hole and drink in the beauties of a land to which you know you will be all too blind when the sun mounts high and you toss for the honor!

The Principles of Golf

by RICHARD S. TUFTS

Pinehurst sprang from the sandhills of North Carolina and the vision of the Tufts family. Richard S. Tufts, a former member of the USGA Rules Committee, believed deeply enough in The Principles Behind the Rules of Golf *to publish it himself. Here are the core chapters which reduce all of the code to two simple laws.*

HOW, then, is it possible to give an understanding of the rules to those unable or unwilling to devote long hours to their study? How can we humanize a subject which is admittedly complex and pedantic? How can the cold rules be made to seem part and parcel of a warm game like golf?

Fortunately there is a way. Running through the rules are underlying principles, that, like the steel rods which lie below the surface of reinforced concrete, serve to bind together the brittle material and to give it strength. Whereas these principles are seldom specifically referred to in the rules, they are well recognized by all who work with the rules and can serve excellently as a guide, not only in working with the rules but also in becoming acquainted with them.

These basic principles fortunately are simple, logical, practical and expressive. By their recognition and by their application to specific rules, it is possible to bring warmth and an understanding to the austerity and complexity of the rules.

The one serious warning that must be made is that these principles can never become an adequate substitute for the rules themselves. The more exact descriptive wording of the rules is essential to provide adequate answers to the many complicated questions which arise in the play of the game.

Since the purpose of this work is limited to the development and study of these principles, it cannot be used as a substitute for the rule book, nor should it be used as a reference work. The sole purpose in its preparation has been to provide an introduction to and a broad, overall understanding of the rules of golf. This can best be accomplished by following the thread of each principle separately as it weaves through the rule book.

. . . . .

If there is one principle more basic than any of the rest, it must be that *you play the course* [def. 11] *as you find it.* This simply means that the player must accept the conditions he encounters during play and may not alter them to suit his convenience.

This principle is first established under rule 16 [rule 16], but it is the rule that follows which

The Rules of Golf state the ball must be played as it lies. Very often the "rub of the green," or bad breaks, leaves the golfer an impossible situation, requiring a penalty stroke to keep the ball in play or some very creative shotmaking.

firmly nails down the fact that the ground and everything that grows or is fixed in it is a part of the player's lie and must not be moved [rule 17]. Unfortunately there is no rule in the book which is more frequently violated and if this work carries the reader no further than the careful reading of rule 17, it will have served a useful purpose.

The object of this rule is obvious. One of the great features of golf is that it tests the player's ability to execute a great assortment of strokes under a perplexing variety of conditions. Golf would cease to be a game of skill if the player were permitted to get the best of the conditions which confront him through their elimination rather than to overcome them by the expert execution of his stroke.

Golf, like life, is full of breaks. It is a game of chance, one of its fascinations being in "the way the ball bounces." To be able to accept the breaks and still go on playing your game has always been one of the tests of the true champion, a test which it is more important to meet successfully in golf than in any other sport. The acceptance of the conditions which the player finds on the course is therefore a vital part of the game.

Rule 17 is to be taken literally. When subparagraph 1 [rule 17–1] prohibits improving the surface it means just that. It is just as much a violation of the rule to sole your club in a sandy lie in the fairway as it is in a bunker, if by so doing the lie of your ball is improved. As a matter of fact that part of the hazard rule which prohibits touching the ground could just as well be covered by rule 17–1. Both rules are in the book for the same purpose, namely to assure that the player plays the course as he finds it.

Subparagraphs 2 and 3 of rule 17 [rule 17–2 and rule 17–3] are equally rigid. Grass may not be bent to one side either in finding the ball or in the act of address. In subparagraph 3, the principle of playing the course as you find it is extended to cover more than just the lie of the ball. The prohibition covers everything on the line over which the ball may conceivably travel. Subparagraph 4 [rule 17–4] even makes it clear that the player has to take his stance on the course as he finds it.

Further support of this principle is found in the special rules covering hazards [rule 33, first paragraph] and the putting green [rule 35–1a and rule 35–1f]. In rule 35–1a the principle of not adjusting anything (except ball marks on the putting green) in the line over which the ball may travel is again specifically covered.

The reader will have noted that subparagraph 3 of rule 17 provides for two exceptions to the principle which the rule establishes. The player may move things in order to take his stance, but the use of the word "fairly" restricts such bending or breaking to those things which interfere with the act of placing himself in the normal position to play his stroke, and any unreasonable action made for the purpose of removing anything which could interfere with his stroke is, of course, completely prohibited. Also, the player is not penalized if things be moved or broken in the execution of the swing with which he makes his stroke [def. 30], but this exception does not cover actions caused by the preliminary waggle, practice swings or the indiscriminate waving about of the club before making the stroke.

The character of the exceptions therefore serves only to strengthen the principle. Obviously if he is to make any progress the player must be permitted to stand and hit his ball. It can therefore be said that fundamentally the rules do not permit any departure from this principle.

In connection with the above quite positive assertion, it is necessary to recognize that the rules do grant what at first may appear to be certain additional exceptions to the principle of playing the course as you find it. However, all these added circumstances are not actually exceptions to the principle; they are in the nature of granting relief from a part of the course not in proper condition or from objects which are not a part of the course or which, if attached to the course, are not a proper part of it. Included are casual water, ground under repair, ball marks on the putting green, objects not attached to the course and such immovable obstructions as rain shelters. Reference to these matters has been inserted here because of their close affiliation with the principle under consideration.

Of all the basic principles, the playing of the

course as you find it is certainly one of the most sacred and those who violate it can hardly have acquired an understanding or appreciation of the game.

· · · · ·

The second great principle of golf is that *you put your ball in play* at the start of the hole [def. 5 and def. 32], *play only your own ball and do not touch it* until you lift it from the hole. To indicate the importance of this principle, the rule that covers it has been assigned the first position in the rule book [rule 1].

It is the chief purpose of the rules, the definitions and such local rules as may be in force, to inform the player as to the way in which he shall comply with this principle, in the process of moving his ball from the tee into the hole. For example, he may not purposely touch the ball [rule 16 and rule 23–3] and he must strike it [rule 19–1] using a limited number of clubs [rule 3] of approved design [rule 2].

Confirmation of the principle is liberally provided in the rule by the many situations wherein penalties are invoked for violations of the principle. For example, a player must hole out with the ball played from the tee [rule 21–1] and there is a penalty if you play any ball other than your own [rule 21–2, rule 21–3, rule 40–3f and rule 41–6]. As protection against such disaster, the player is advised to place a mark on his ball [note under the heading to rule 21] and he is permitted to touch his ball in order to lift it for purpose of identification [rule 23–1], except when his ball is in a hazard, which exception is due to the fact that there is no penalty for playing a wrong ball while it is in a hazard [rule 21–2, rule 21–3, rule 40–3f and rule 41–6].

Another rule which restricts the player to the play of the ball driven from the tee relates to practice. The player may not prepare for the strokes to be played by practicing during the play of the hole [rule 8–1] and may not practice from a hazard between the play of holes or on or to the putting green of the holes yet to be played [rule 8–2] or if he otherwise causes any undue delay [rule 37–7]. Practice between the play of holes covers practice putting made after holing out and delay of play includes either any delay which

such practice may cause in the start of the next hole or in holding up the match following, which may be playing to the green.

However, it is obvious that there will be circumstances in golf when the player will be unable fairly to complete the play of the hole unless he is granted some exceptions to the principle of advancing the ball without touching it. The exceptions are rather numerous—unfortunately they have to be—and as a consequence a rather casual handling of the ball is encouraged and one of golf's really basic principles is thereby weakened. Unhappily few golfers seem to appreciate that the safeguards with which the rules surround the exceptions actually serve to strengthen the principle that you do not touch your ball while it is in play. Every golfer would do well always to be sure of his rights before touching his ball during the play of a hole.

A few of the situations where exceptions to this principle are granted are as follows: when cleaning is permitted [rule 23–2 and rule 35–1d]; when the ball has been moved by another agency and must be put back [rule 27–1a]; when it becomes unplayable [rule 29–2]; when it is in ground under repair from which it may be dropped [rule 32–1]; when it is close to an immovable obstruction which interferes with the stroke [rule 31–2]; and many others.

It should be carefully noted that in all the situations in which the player is permitted to touch his ball, it must always be put in play again no nearer to the hole than the spot at which it came to rest [rule 22–2d]. Thus the principle is carefully maintained that the player may not advance the ball toward the hole by any other means than the striking of the ball with the club.

An impressive confirmation of this principle is found in the first notes under rules 29 and 33, which read: "A serious breach of this rule should be dealt with by the Committee under rule 1." What does this mean? Rules 29 and 33 concern the procedure for putting a ball in play when the original ball is lost, out of bounds, unplayable or lost or unplayable in a water hazard. The two rules provide a penalty of two strokes in stroke play for failure to proceed as called for but the note says in effect that if the violation be of sufficient extent to create a breach of the principle established by rule 1, then the Committee may increase the penalty to disqualification. Thus a ball dropped for a lost ball a few feet nearer to the hole than the spot from which the lost ball was played would represent a violation of rule 29, for which the penalty in stroke play is two strokes. However, if the ball be dropped where the ball was lost instead of at the spot from which it was played or if it be dropped so as to avoid some interference with the flight of the ball, such as a large tree, then obviously the player will not have played the full course. He will be in violation of one of the two basic principles of golf and should be disqualified in stroke play.

A combination of the two preceding great principles supplies a fine definition of the game of golf. You put your ball in play at the start of the hole, you play the course as you find it, you play only your own ball, and you do not touch it until you lift it from the hole.

Those who do not understand golf or who have never acquired the spirit of the game should memorize this simple definition and repeat it during the course of play. It beautifully simplifies the complexities of the game. With its acceptance the rules become merely regulations through which these two great principles of the game are maintained in the face of the overpowering variety of complicated situations produced by the conditions under which golf is played.

The principles to be developed hereafter serve to give an understanding of the application of the rules to golf as defined by the two great principles. To this extent they are the working principles of the game. They provide the answers to the specific questions on procedure which develop in the play as it proceeds from tee to green around the course. They serve an important and a useful purpose but they must always be subsidiary to these first two basic principles.

Pinehurst Thirty Years Later

by CHARLES PRICE

The more things change, the more they remain the same. In the case of Pinehurst in the thirties and forties, things have changed but they aren't the same. This nostalgic piece by Charles Price won first prize in the 1978 Golf Writers' Awards and shows the penetrating and comic style which makes Price one of the game's finest chroniclers.

IT has been thirty years since I first visited Pinehurst, North Carolina, and then, soon afterward, began working there. I became the star reporter for *The Pinehurst Outlook*, this because I was the only kid they could find who could spell Mississippi without dropping an "s," had a mail order sheepskin and knew the difference between a backswing and a bogey. Also, I was willing to work for fifty dollars a week.

Pinehurst then was an exciting beat for a young man who intended to be a two-fisted, hard-drinking, Chicago-style newspaperman, constantly on the lookout for action. I covered flower shows, pony races, putting contests, lawn bowling, birdwatching, croquet tournaments, whist matches, church sermons, road pavings, barn burnings, haircuts and the big movies starring Leslie Howard or Abbott and Costello. Because I owned a suit, I also wrote the society

column; I was the local Cholly Knickerbocker, you might say. I particularly remember one item I wrote. It had set the whole town on its ear. "Mrs. Abigail Van Heusenduff, of Piney Thorn Drive," it said, "recently returned from a trip to her hometown of Baltimore, where she had her watch set."

If all this seems to imply that Pinehurst thirty years ago during the height of its sporting and social season was a sleepy little village, you should have seen it in the summers. At that time of year, it went into a positive coma. *Everything* closed down. The movie theater, which is now an antique shop. The barber shop and the beauty shop, although I'm not too sure if the town even had one. The drug store. Two of the country club's three golf courses, although it was a mystery why not all three. The Carolina Hotel. Holly Inn. The Pinecrest. The Magnolia. And every other place of lodging. And both the restaurants, even Henri's.

Ah, Henri's! How well I remember my lonely dinners there, listening to Beniamino Gigli singing arias on ancient records while I supped on my *coq au vin* and Pouilly Fuisse, now and then to stop and listen to Henri and Madame Henriette tell me of the old days on the Left Bank. Gawd! You would have thought I was Lucius Beebe. All on fifty bucks a week. Don't feel sorry for me, though. In Pinehurst during the summers, you couldn't *spend* fifty bucks a week.

During the fall and spring, the two big seasons then, I supplemented my Dickensian income by moonlighting at the Dunes Club, a supper club with a floor show and a gambling casino that stood just off the road that runs from Pinehurst to Southern Pines. It was not altogether an honorable job, but it beat being a busboy.

To be blunt, I was a shill. I used to saunter into the club with my date for the evening on my arm, talk golf with tourists at the bar over our martinis, watch the dinner show with a couple of steaks Diane and then cavalierly sign the check—for which I never got a bill.

After dinner, I would saunter into the casino, where I would purchase fifty dollars' worth of chips, making sure that nobody but the cashier noticed that I wasn't paying for them. If there was an empty craps table, I would start there. Sooner or later, other customers would join in. Then I'd nonchalantly move over to the roulette wheel, play a combination that couldn't possibly come off, and then move over to any empty blackjack table when the roulette wheel got rolling. If by some miracle I won, I would cash in my chips and tell them to credit them to my account.

All the young broads then in and around Pinehurst thought I was some rich, young romantic who had somehow materialized out of the west, a downy-faced combination of Titanic

For many players the work of Donald Ross, a Scottish emigrant who created some of America's greatest courses, is too subtle. Pinehurst #2 (the 17th hole is shown here) is Ross's most famous effort, and only by walking the course and examining the varied contours of each fairway can his genius be appreciated.

Thompson and Errol Flynn. From September to May, when the Dunes Club was open, I had to beat them off with a brassie. From May to September though, when I was forced to dine at a sleazy luncheonette in Southern Pines, those same girls didn't even speak to me.

Well, with the passage of thirty years, all that has changed. The Dunes Club burned down years ago. A girl I used to take there is now a grandmother, and when last I saw her—during the World Open in September—she somehow recognized me. "Well, I declare!" she said. "If it isn't old Charley Pride!"

The Pinehurst Country Club is now open year round, and has added two courses to its original three, with a sixth under construction by George and Tom Fazio. Other country clubs have sprung up all over the area, such as Foxfire and the magnificent Country Club of North Carolina, which is called CCNC by initiates. Henri and Henriette have long since retired. Their restaurant has since been replaced by the Red Door, which is fine, but I still miss the scratchy records of Beniamino Gigli singing "Donna Mobile" over my *coq au vin.*

During the World Open, Ray Floyd and Jerry McGee shot the grass off Pinehurst Number Two with ten-under-par totals of 274, Floyd to win the playoff with a birdie three. Thirty years ago, those scores would have been *fourteen* under par, a total that would have been regarded as sacrilege among such Pinehurst puristic, but highly talented, players as Dick Chapman and George Dunlap, two former Pinehurst residents when the course had a par of seventy-two for tournaments and when anybody who had been around at all regarded the layout as easily one of the ten best in the world. It still is, but the PGA lowers the par a stroke for any of its tournaments, although most pros, notably Jack Nicklaus, who failed to make the cut for the first time in seven years, regard par as "just a figure on the scorecard." To Chapman and Dunlap, that 274 must have struck them the same way news would to an archbishop that somebody had torn to shreds the altar cloth at St. Patrick's Cathedral.

The galleries at the World Open reached a daily high of 20,000, almost twenty times the population of the town. Thirty years ago, the gallery for the whole week of the old North and South Open would not have surpassed 5,000. But then the week of the North and South Open only presented a bunch of bums—like Ben Hogan, Byron Nelson, Jimmy Demaret, Lloyd Mangrum, Horton Smith, Paul Runyan, Gene Sarazen, Henry Picard, and a guy named Sam Snead.

I'm not quite sure how these young men can shoot a truly great course like Number Two in such publinx figures. Some of them couldn't understand the scores themselves. Nicklaus won the same tournament the year before with a total of 280, four under, a score that would have won the old North and South Open easily. For sure, great individual rounds have been shot in the past. As far back as 1934 George Dunlap won the medal for the North and South Amateur with a sixty-seven, a score not to be matched for sixteen years, this by Harry Haverstick of Pennsylvania, and broken six years later by an amateur named Douglas Sanders—whoever he was. But for sustained golf, nothing matched this year's World Open. I was stopped in the lobby of the Pinehurst Hotel, the old Carolina, by Chi Chi Rodriguez, himself under par at the time, who asked me if I could account for the low scoring. "How should I know?" I said. "You're one of the guys doing it."

Looking back, I realize now that was a trite answer. The Number Two course, like every other course then in the area, has changed in nature without gaining an inch in length. The greens are Penncross bent, a strain of grass that would not have survived two weeks in June thirty years ago, much less July, August and September, what with the heat. Having played in the World Open's pro-am, with a practice round at CCNC, I can say I have never putted or played shots to finer greens anywhere, and I am not excluding Merion or Oakmont. They were perfection. You could stroke a putt of ninety feet, and the ball would not waver an inch. It must be allowed that thirty years ago the greens were perfection too, but the grass was Bermuda, not bent, and a putt of ninety feet or much, much less left you with a bunt, not a stroke. And the greens of thirty years ago were so much larger than they are now that a putt of ninety feet was commonplace, not, as it is now, a chip or a pitch. Ask any pro you know, he'd rather have a chip or a pitch from ninety feet than a putt of the same length. Putting from that distance is a little like trying to touch a girl sitting on the far side of a couch. You can reach her, but you're not likely to accomplish much.

To stick one more moment to the this year's World Open and its phenomenal scoring, Number Two's superb fairways now seem to lend themselves to more roll than they used to. Take the eighteenth hole. During the old North and South Open thirty years ago, big hitters such as Clayton Heafner and Chick Harbert used to play the hole with their best drive and a three- or four-iron. Today, kids I never heard of use eight-irons. In my day, their drives would have bounced back at you, not roll twenty yards farther, all uphill. It could be that the ball today is twenty yards longer. But, then, I'm thirty years older. So what's the diff?

If all of what I have said about Pinehurst and how it has changed in thirty years sounds as though I were saying only the dead know Brooklyn, let it go on the record that I still love the village, thirty years of a few wrinkles here and there on both of us notwithstanding. It still has the feel, the ambience, of total golf on every driveway, every footpath, every fairway. Pinehurst exudes golf, it doesn't just imitate it with phony street names, jerry-built courses, and sweater-and-shoe pros who couldn't give a lesson of any use to a cross-handed fat lady.

The Carolina Hotel is now called the Pinehurst Hotel—"for promotion purposes, to integrate the name," says a spokesman there. Black tie and evening gowns are no longer required for dinner; but the food, if anything, has improved under the direction of *maitre d' hotel* Otto Sesin.

The clubhouse at the Country Club has been extended to more than twice its original size, the new wings quite naturally being more modern than the original. But they are architecturally tasteful and undoubtedly will be standing resplendently long after the original has collapsed from old age. A nod of approval from the Old Guard of Pinehurst exists in the fact that the Tin Whistles, a kind of ultra-exclusive club within the country club, now accepts members under the age of eighty and has its headquarters in one of the new wings. It probably comes as news to long-time Pinehurst visitors, and some Tin Whistle members as well, that the name of the club-within-a-club comes from the antiquarian booze laws of North Carolina, which date back to George the Fifth and, since then, have cost the state roughly $20 billion in tax revenue from resort business. I mean, Stuckey's candy is dandy. Grits are great. But business is business, and the first thing a convention director is going to ask a convention manager—anywhere!—is what are your liquor laws. He is not about to bring 200 persons from ten different states and then find out that they have to go to a state-approved store to buy their cocktails and then take them back to the hotel in a brown bag.

To get around these laws half a century or more ago, and particularly during prohibition, liquor was delivered to a cottage within earshot of the clubhouse. The bootlegger would then blow a tin whistle to let the members know that they could walk (run?) over to the cottage and buy all they wanted. Hence, the name. So Pinehurst has not always been as blue-nosed as it has seemed.

As to some other change during the past thirty years: There used to be an old redneck named Happy, who drove an antiquated bus from the clubhouse to the hotel. Happy would walk into the lobby of the clubhouse every half hour or so and announce in stentorian tones, "Bus to the OWE-tell! Bus to the OWE-tell!" Then everybody would clamber on to the bus and hold their breath while it coughed and chugged its way back to the Carolina, half a mile away. I doubt anybody in the world could have driven that bus other than Happy. He was a genius with machinery but had a failing in that he could never remember anybody's name. So he had nicknames for all of us. I was "Mr. Types" because I used to typewrite letters he dictated to me in my office nearby. Sam Snead was "Mr. Hips" from the pantherlike way Sam had of walking. And Eberhard Faber, a frequent visitor then who had practically invented the lead pencil, was called "Mr. Pencils." What else?

Happy was part and parcel of Pinehurst thirty years ago. And much of its other charms still remain. Number Two may be the last of the great American courses on which golf cars are not allowed. You must use a caddie. Sam Snead's favorite course was always Number Two, and still is, and his favorite caddie, Jimmy Steed, is still there, making his daily swing. When I played in the World Open's pro-am, I had a man who must have been near seventy carrying double. His name was John. Knowing old Pinehurst caddies are nearly psychic in summing up a stranger's game, I let John "club" me for the first five holes.

On the sixth hole, the first par three, I wanted to use a two-iron. John insisted I use a three. The ball hit short of the green and stayed there. Not wanting to hurt his feelings, I did not mention to John that that shot was as long as I can hit a three-iron.

John walked in silence until after I had chipped and putted out. On the next tee, John turned to me as I pulled my driver out of the bag. "Mr. Types," he said. "You ain't as long as you used to be."

"Huh?" I said.

"You don't remember me, do you?" said John.

"No," I said. "I'm afraid I don't. But nobody has called me 'Mr. Types' in years. You must have known Happy."

"Sure, I did," said John. "I carried for you in the 1947 North-South. Happy was my cousin." And he smiled.

So thirty years have not altogether dimmed the memory of all of us about Pinehurst. Happy is gone, but "cousins" like John will linger on forever. The Carolina Hotel is now the Pinehurst. Henri and Henriette are on the Left Bank of somewhere nice, I am sure. Number Two still has its caddie-wizards, you still can walk it in all its golfing majesty, and it is being restored to its original conception of Donald Ross, America's master architect and a Pinehurst resident since near the turn of the century and who regarded it as his masterpiece.

I had the fortunate experience of talking long hours with Mr. Ross thirty years ago, and the unhappy experience of writing his obituary in 1948 for *The Pinehurst Outlook*. Donald Ross was a strict man, with himself and everybody else. But he thought, really thought, and all those thoughts were channelled through golf. If golf can be regarded as some kind of religion among some people then Donald Ross regarded Pinehurst as his Vatican City.

I think, in retrospect, that Donald Ross would still be pleased with Pinehurst as the advance of thirty years have gone by. Pinehurst Inc. —the company that included all the courses and hotels and 7,000 acres of the community—was sold to the Diamondhead Corporation a few years ago for $9,500,000. Diamondhead is owned largely by Malcolm McLean, whose trucks you see on every highway in America, and whose president is William Bru, a handsome, young, low-key executive who obviously knows how to balance profits with tradition. Frankly, had I been in Malcolm McLean's position, I would have put the torch to the Carolina rather than spend the $2,500,000 they used to modernize it. Nor would I have spent the same amount they did to build the first hall of fame this game truly deserves. It is now a public foundation, receiving donations tax-free ranging anywhere from $10 to $10,000, and it makes baseball's Cooperstown look like an outhouse.

Pinehurst has changed to some, notably to Richard Tufts, grandson of the man who founded Pinehurst before the turn of the century. He did not want to sell the old property, despite the fact he was president of the corporation. But he was overruled by his brothers, stockholders both, and so 7,000 acres of golfing paradise passed on to Diamondhead Inc.

Perhaps no one alive in golf has given so much to golf and taken away so little as Dick Tufts. He was president of the USGA for a while, and served faithfully before and after on every committee they had. For this, embarrassing to him, he was given every award there is to be given to a dedicated amateur golfer. When the $2,500,000 World Golf Hall of Fame was finished and the idea came to its president, Don

Collett, that a distinguished award should go out to amateurs who have given a part of themselves unselfishly to this too often selfish game, Dick Tufts was one of the first to be mentioned. Before Collett could even bring Dick Tufts's name to the nominating committee, Dick sent a polite note to them saying that he would like not to be considered for such an honor, this from a man who more than any other individual had turned 7,000 acres of sandhills into the premier golf resort of the world.

Dick Tufts is a man dedicated to golf, a kind-hearted person to whom golf is everything short of life itself, a man who with all his long strides in the game can take or leave it with a smile or chuckle or a laugh. I know it damned near crushed him when Pinehurst was sold to Diamondhead; he told me so from a sickbed not two weeks after the transaction took place. But, I am glad to say, Dick is today a happy, contented man robust and full of good humor about Pinehurst in the old days when Jimmy Steed caddied Sam, when Henri and Henriette ran the French restaurant, when Donald Ross consulted him about the conduct of Number Two.

Perhaps Dick Tufts heard the owl call his name. But knowing Pinehurst as I have for thirty years, I would rather think he heard that of Happy in the lobby of the Country Club. "Bus to the OWE-tell!" Happy would say. "Bus to the OWE-tell! Bus to the OWE—!" And then his voice would fade away.

It made no difference. We all knew where we were going. And the name of the place was "golf."

It's Your Honor, Comrade

by NICK SEITZ

"Goodwill Through Golf" is the motto of the World Cup, an international competition which draws teams from fifty countries, even from countries behind the Iron Curtain. In 1971 Nick Seitz, editor of Golf Digest, *went to Buenos Aires and met the Rumanian entry, Paul Tomita, who proved again why the World Cup is a great idea.*

WHEN I learned I would play in the World Cup pro-am in Buenos Aires with Rumania, the only communist country in the forty-three nation field, my imagination set feverishly to work. I spared no sordid detail envisioning the two Rumanians. They would be young and muscular. They would not speak English or smile. They would wear severe, square-shouldered uniforms, probably topped by cosmonaut helmets. They would stride onto the first tee with machine-like precision and swing the same way. Right?

Wrong. The junior member of the partnership, Dumitru Munteanu, turned out to be young, and did not speak English. But the other Rumanian was Pavel (Paul) Tomita, and he was a surprise in many ways. In a tournament that has given the world some great characters in its eighteen years, Tomita has become a memorable personality. He is sixty-ish, easily the oldest

player in World Cup competition. He speaks excellent English and French, good German, and is conversant in several other languages. He wears casual golf clothes that could have come right out of your friendly neighborhood pro shop. He smiles disarmingly from behind a pipe which, it developed, he smokes right through his elegantly fashioned shots. So much for my uneducated preconceptions.

Short and solid, his avuncular gray mustache dancing above his words, Tomita rose at last year's pre-tournament banquet and delivered a brief speech that captured the spirit of the gathering. "This is a wonderful idea, excellencies," he said emotionally with a slight Balkan accent. "The World Cup is not a place to make money, but a place to meet people from all over, thank God. Some of us are not the best of players, but we go home and speak well of bonds formed here."

As golfers, the Rumanians might have trouble making the second flight in a good California member-guest. They occupied last place in Buenos Aires after Paul shot 86–89–82–92 and his partner did even worse. Together they finished 151 strokes over par and 183 under winning Australia. Scores, however, are not the essence of the World Cup, and in Tomita's case they mean even less than usual.

37

Once, he was probably a world-class player —or would have been, had he been free to compete outside Rumania. For thirty-one years he played one course—Rumania's only one, where he is now in his fifth decade as "trainer of golf" —the Diplomatic Club in Bucharest. There was a time when he could shoot sixty-seven every day of the week and twice on Sunday, but no one knew except the foreign diplomats who, uniquely, comprise most of the club's membership.

The wonder today is that he's playing at all. During World War II, infantryman Tomita marched 1,900 miles in six months against the Russians. He says his legs never regained their full strength. But if he is bitter over missing the opportunity to broaden his golfing career, he gives no indication. He expresses gratitude to the foreign ambassadors whose effort induced the Rumanian government to let him play in his first World Cup in 1968, in Rome. He arrived during the second round of the tournament, with no partner. He walked into the press tent and stunned reporters there by announcing in flawless English that he was Paul Tomita from Rumania and was sorry he was late.

Fred Corcoran, the dandy little manager of the cup event, is not known as a promoter's promoter for nothing. He hastily arranged for a playing partner and full ceremonial send-off at the first tee, and Tomita played a symbolic nine holes, shooting thirty-nine. "I just wanted to see the Rumanian flag raised with all the others," he said.

In 1969, he brought his partner and played in Singapore, and last year they were back, in Argentina. When he entered Argentina, customs officials ransacked Tomita's luggage, breaking a lock. "I guess they thought I was a spy," he said, "but they found only dirty clothes." At the Jockey Club course, one frequently heard that his partner was actually a Rumanian secret agent keeping an eye on Tomita. I began to wonder if the rumor might be true after I—with my four-piece swing—tied his partner in the pro-am.

But Paul later visited me in the United States on his way home, and was traveling alone. His partner, he pointed out, is his shop assistant at the Diplomatic Club, more an amateur golfer than a pro, and certainly not a figure in international intrigue. Paul suffered these indignities with transcendent good humor, as he did his lack of success on the long Jockey Club course.

"It's hard for me to play my game," was his only lament. "I'm outdriven by fifty yards all the time. I know how to relax, but I don't. I've been too long teaching others."

His teaching background caught up with him in more ways than one in Buenos Aires, a cosmopolitan city. Dozens of diplomatic people who had taken lessons from Tomita in Bucharest were stationed there. They all wanted him to come to cocktail parties and fashionably late dinner parties, and Tomita sought to oblige them. By the third round, he was weary, and barely made his morning tee time. "Having too many friends is no good," he sighed, reloading his pipe, "but having no friends is worse. If you see smoke coming from a bunker, you will know I have fallen asleep."

On the final day, Tomita played early, with the team from Libya; the pairings change daily to mix the players as much as possible. Then he galleried the feature Argentina-Australia group. "I must be here for my friend Roberto de Vicenzo," he said, "because he is an old goat like me." Later, at the presentation program in front of the huge scoreboard, Paul was an attentive observer as the president of Argentina (since overthrown in a coup) handed out trophies and cash awards to the top finishers. As Tomita pointed out, the money isn't much—first prize is $1,000. Each player receives a $500 honorarium, $100 walking-around money, his hotel room and round-trip economy-class plane tickets. "But everyone hates to leave," Tomita says.

Dusk was falling as the players gathered their gear and boarded chartered buses for the airport, there to scatter to different parts of the globe. Paul, hugging and beaming his good-bys in the airport waiting room, was bound for New York first, to fulfill a forty-year ambition to visit the U.S.

While in America, Tomita met me to play golf at Winged Foot, the 1974 U.S. Open site. He was awestruck by this, the first American course he had seen—and particularly by the quality of its caretaking (in Bucharest, he is his own greenskeeper). "I would be happy to have this fairway for a front lawn," he said frequently.

Our caddies addressed him as "Mister Paul" and raved about the way he drove the ball precisely where they suggested. Relaxed, he shot a seventy-five. "I'd like to have seen him when he could knock it farther," said one of the caddies.

I was struggling to play bogey golf myself. At my insistence, Tomita periodically gave me tips on my swing. "You are too stiff," he pointed out once. "Grip the club lighter. Don't hurry your swing, and swing bigger to give yourself time to stay in balance." That helped. Another time he said, "Feel the clubhead with your hands." I began to gain distance with less effort. Then he gave me a word-picture to straighten out my drives. "Keep your swing down the middle," he said. Something clicked, and on the last hole our balls were resting together a respectable distance off the tee and in the best position in the fairway, and he said happily, "You see? You don't have to make it such a difficult game."

I complimented him on his teaching ability, and he said, "I am from the old school. I first came under the influence of a French professional, a friend of my older brother. I was a peasant boy in need of work, and began caddieing at the Diplomatic Club at fourteen. The Frenchman was succeeded at the club by Joe Baker, an Englishman, later the captain of the British PGA. Joe was my mentor. I studied in Great Britain before taking the job at the Diplomatic Club myself."

Over his favorite dinner of baked fish and white wine, Tomita talked more about his unusual club. "We have 600 members from forty-eight countries and almost all of them are diplomats. I go home and make more propaganda for the World Cup than anyone."

Paul continued, "I live at the club with my wife. My only regret in life is that we have no children. We waited ten years because of the war, then lost two. The war also made it difficult to keep golf in Rumania. I was always running to different big leaders. I had designed two other courses, on the Black Sea, but in twenty-four hours the Germans dug them up and planted crops. My club was eighteen holes and over 6,-000 yards, but now is nine tricky, hilly holes. When the state asked for playground space, I couldn't say no.

"Now I am helping a tourist company plan two courses near Bucharest. American tourists are just beginning to discover Rumania. They travel so much, they want something different, like our capital, which is a little Paris. And your dollars go far in Rumania. Our people like Americans. President Nixon has been to Bucharest twice, and was very popular."

Tomita is proud that golf has been included in the government-sponsored Sports Association of Rumania. "At last the game is going to grow with us," he said.

It was late evening when I saw Paul onto a train back to New York City. Plainly garbed and carrying his modest golf bag over his shoulder, he paused in the door of the Penn Central car and waved with his pipe, a simple man with marvelous style. "Don't forget," he called. "Keep your swing down the middle."

The Drama of the Game

"He hadn't hit bad shots, and he hadn't panicked; he just was screwed a half-turn too tight to get a par. The gallery of 40,000 felt for him, right to the pits of our golf-weary stomachs, when his last hope of winning it clean hung on the lip of the seventy-second hole. It so easily might have been otherwise. But then that's life, and that's golf, a game even masters don't master."

—from *Thirteen Ways of Looking at the Masters* by John Updike

How Golf Invented the Scots

by **PETER DOBEREINER**

One of the most beautiful golf books ever produced is The Glorious World of Golf, *full of wonderful pictures accompanied by the writing of Peter Dobereiner, golf correspondent for the* London Observer. *Dobereiner is at once droll and graceful and his eye enlivens his account of golf's first days.*

AT the beginning of the new century, a treaty of perpetual peace was signed between England and Scotland. The optimism of this document may not have been entirely justified by subsequent events, but by and large the heat was off. It was no longer necessary to keep armies in readiness for war and the way was open for golf to develop and spread.

Shall we shed a tear for the men who made bows and arrows and who now, in these peaceful times, found themselves in a falling market? Not at all. One reason for the spread of golf was that the game inherited a ready-made industry to service it. The bowyers and fletchers were craftsmen wise in the properties of native woods and skilled in the arts of turning and balancing shafts and forging iron. A man who could shape the arrow for a longbow or a crossbow's bolt had at hand the tools and skills to make golf clubs. Who better than a bowyer to know about the flex and torsion of a blackthorn bough, or the security to be found in a rawhide grip?

They turned naturally to clubmaking as a profitable sideline and golf's debt to archery has never been properly appreciated and acknowledged. If golf had relied on the rude agricultural implements used for *kolven* the game would surely never have achieved such popularity. By later standards, when clubmaking became a highly developed art, the early clubs may have seemed crude but at least they proved effective.

For something like 200 years after that first proclamation outlawing golf the game was an informal affair. There were no codified rules, although no doubt there were conventions on how the game should be played, probably varying from one community to another. (This is another reason for doubting whether the distinction of having invented golf can ever be ascribed to an individual. The game had been evolving for 300 years before it achieved anything like a standardized form.) There were no set "courses" as we know them today; you simply played over whatever suitable ground happened to be available, cutting holes where necessary with a pocket knife.

The game went through vicissitudes, at times being repressed by decrees forbidding it on Sundays, sometimes being encouraged by royal patronage. Most of the Scottish kings were golfers and poor Mary Queen of Scots was accused of callously playing golf immediately after the murder of her husband. For the keen student of the history of golf it is a fascinating period, with a wealth of documented evidence, but the next significant change did not occur until the early part of the 17th century with the introduction of the feather ball, or "featherie."

At its best, the featherie must have represented a considerable improvement on the earlier balls of turned boxwood. Its irregular surface pattern would have given it far better flight characteristics. Distance records are unreliable because one can never be quite sure what the conditions were like at the time but, taking a cautious average from contemporary accounts, it is clear that a good player could drive a featherie 200 yards. And in 1836, a French schoolmaster at St. Andrews, on a frosty Old Course and with a gentle following wind, hit a measured drive of 361 yards. In wet weather the featherie was not nearly so effective since it absorbed water and became heavy and soggy. And, of course, one injudicious blow with the sharp edge of an iron club was liable to split the cover and disembowel this expensive missile.

The featherie was made by the same process employed by the Romans. A cover of untanned bull's hide was stitched, leaving a small aperture so that it could then be turned inside out, with the raised seams inside, and stuffed with boiled feathers—traditionally, enough to fill a top hat. The aperture was then stitched shut and the ball pounded into shape. As the feathers dried they expanded to make a hard, resilient ball, ready for painting. It was a skilled operation to make a featherie and a craftsman was doing well if he turned out half a dozen a day.

Compared with the earlier boxwood balls, the featheries were prohibitively expensive, costing twelve times as much, and this inflationary move was reflected in a social change in the game. Golf became a luxury, and although the Scots managed to keep the classless tradition of the game alive, the situation was very different in the game's missionary fields. The golf which spread to England early in the 17th century, largely through the enthusiasm of her Scottish-born king, James the First, was most definitely a game for the nobility. The idea of golf as a pursuit of the well-born and wealthy proved to be

enduring and damaging to the development of the game. Even today, 300 years later, when the talk at the pit face among coal miners is just as likely to concern how they scored in the monthly medal competition, the notion persists in some quarters that golf is a game of the privileged minority. In England, local authorities of a socialist bias still refuse to consider the provision of municipal golf courses on the grounds that public money should not be spent on amenities for "toffs."

If the featherie must take initial responsibility for this state of affairs, it also advanced the game considerably. The improvements arose not only through the superior properties of the ball itself, but because of the new challenge it offered to the clubmaker. Whereas a club which had to withstand constant impact with unyielding wooden balls had of necessity to be of sturdy construction, the featherie presented opportunities for refinement. From this time the craft of clubmaking developed into an art.

The oldest surviving clubs date from the 17th century and provide some evidence of what golf was like in the early days. The set consists of six woods and two irons, which confirms the theory of the historical development of golf. Probably in the very beginning golf was played with a single wooden club. Then variations were introduced to deal with specific situations. One such would be the baffing spoon. The original play club (later called the driver) would have served its purpose well enough when the ball was teed up on a pinch of sand. But the straight-faced play club would have been ineffective from a tight fairway lie. Hence, the introduction of a club with an angled face and the technique of baffling, or bouncing the clubhead into the turf just behind the ball to make it rise. From that point we may surmise the introduction of further variations, such as the long spoon and the holing-out club, or putter. The 17th century set marks the transitional period when iron clubs were becoming popular and the proliferation of woods began to decline. It gives an impression of size and crudeness. Each is about six inches longer than the equivalent club of today. The heads are deeper and more heavily weighted. In every case

Right: early golf clubs and balls were made by craftsmen who often turned them into works of art, so that today wooden "play clubs" and "featherie" balls are valuable collector's items. The era of the featherie lasted from about 1600 to 1848, when the gutta percha ball, made from rubber, was developed. The play club was the forerunner of the driver.

Lower left: until the invention of the rubbercore ball and steel shafts in the 20th century, most golf implements were made at a workbench like that pictured above. Most golf professionals, until recently, were required to learn the art of making and repairing clubs. Their hope was to make players more adept and less inclined to ruin their equipment.

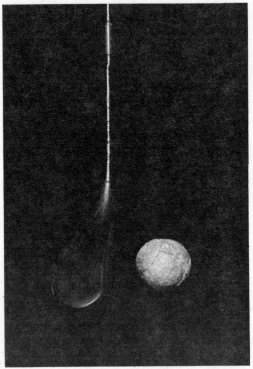

Below: the featherie, which could fly over 300 yards when struck properly, was very expensive because it required painstaking effort by a ballmaker who could manufacture only four or five a day. The amount of feathers used in each ball was measured by filling a top hat to the brim.

the face is slightly concave, presumably in an attempt to impart control. This hollowing of the face, combined with the name "spoon," may give us a clue to the method of using the clubs. The inference is that the ball was spooned, with a scooping action, which would tally with the club's general dimensions. Anything in the nature of a "hit" would be impossible with implements of this weight and size. Restoration golfers would most certainly have had to "wait for it" as those great, weighted heads built up a ponderous speed on the periphery of their wide arc. These clubs would need to be swung with a lazy, sweeping action, probably embellished by a dipping or scooping motion in the contact zone. As to the outcome of the shot, we can only apply our modern knowledge of aerodynamics and insist that the balls must have been roughened in some way to produce an approximately true flight path. In constant play any ball, whether of boxwood or bullhide with feather interior, would become scuffed, and we do know that the tradition arose of the need for golf balls to "mature."

We should not assume that, simply because the equipment was crude by modern standards, it was many times less effective. As soon as authenticated records appear we find surprisingly good results being recorded. The laws of dynamics have not changed over the ages and the distance a ball may be struck was governed in the 17th century by the same forces that govern it today: the size, density, and resilience of the ball combined with the mass and speed of the clubhead. The resilience of the ball would have been inferior, but if it were smaller and heavier than today's artificially regulated examples the overall difference might well have been small.

The other fundamental change, the use of the steel shaft, does not make the slightest difference in the speed of the clubhead. It is vastly more convenient, and it makes the task of swinging a club somewhat easier, but a modern set of irons could be fitted with wooden shafts without altering their performance in the slightest degree. So, if we assume that these early golfers mastered a technique of extracting the maximum theoretical performance from their clubs—and the continued popularity of the game suggests at the very least that golf for them was a highly satisfying pastime—we must suppose that they hit a proportion of shots which were good by any yardstick. Of necessity, it would be low-trajectory golf, since their equipment simply would not produce the high-soaring modern shot. But on hard, unwatered linksland a low shot which pitches and runs is often the most effective, especially in windy conditions.

We may, in summary, rest assured that this early golf was, at its highest levels, considerably more refined than the popular notion of bumbling the ball along the ground in hundred-yard stages. At the same time, looking at those hollowed faces with the knowledge that even the finest of contemporary professionals does not strike every shot exactly off the "meat," we must accept that the perfect shot was a somewhat rarer occurrence in the 17th century than it is today. They must have had plenty of foozles in every round. No wonder they drank such prodigious quantities of alcohol afterwards.

Incidentally, although the use of numbers to distinguish clubs may be appropriate to this computer age, golf surely has been impoverished by the loss of those wonderful Scottish names for clubs. Dull of soul is he who feels no difference between a five-iron and, as it once was called, a mashie. The driver retains its name, although of comparatively recent origin (being the successor to the play club). The wedge (much more recent) continues to resist attempts to submerge its individuality in the number ten. And the putter defies the passion for numerology, which is only proper since of all the clubs it is the most personal—indeed, in temperament the most human. There would be little satisfaction in breaking a number eleven across your knee, and the love-hate relationship most golfers enjoy with their putters could scarcely survive the substitution of an anonymous number. But the brassie and spoon are disappearing from the language of golf while cleek, baffie, mashie, and niblick have already vanished.

For tournament professionals golf has become a science rather than an art and for them numbered clubs may be appropriate. But club golfers who play the game for pleasure, and for whom aesthetic considerations are half the charm of the game, would surely get satisfaction from a revival of those wonderful names. Those soulless businessmen who mass-produce matched sets and are concerned with balance sheets rather than traditions, say that numbers are necessary because there are not enough names to go round. What they overlook, because it suits their pockets, is that the average golfer does not need fourteen clubs and is quite incapable of benefiting from such a range.

In the hands of a powerful pro a four-iron will hit the ball fifteen yards farther than a five-iron. For a handicap golfer this differential comes down to ten yards. However, the average amateur is not consistent enough to exploit that small difference. His well-hit five-iron goes farther than his indifferent four-iron shot. For him —and he represents well over ninety percent of the world's golfers—a set of irons graduated according to the modern scale, that is, a three, four-and-a-half, six, seven-and-a-half, and nine, would adequately cater to his needs. In other words, cleek, mashie, mid-iron, mashie-niblick, and niblick. Add a driver, brassie, and spoon with lofts equivalent to one-wood, two-and-a-half-wood, and four-wood, plus a sand iron, wedge, and putter, and he has a set of eleven clubs, which is two more than Harry Vardon needed to win his six Open Championships.

Quite apart from the considerable financial saving such a set would represent and the added pleasure the player would find in his named clubs, the game itself might well become more enjoyable by bringing back the need to "invent" half-shots, cut-ups, and the "feel" strokes. Golf's appeal lies in the combination of power and artistry. In this brutal golfing age anything which tends to emphasize the artistry is to be encouraged. However, we dupes allow ourselves to be persuaded that fourteen clubs constitute a "set," and that unless we are equipped like Jack Nicklaus we cannot hope to play like him. The premise is as absurd as the aspiration.

After the formation of proper clubs, a process that began around 1740, the next significant development in golf was the standardization of courses and rules. This was the period when golf ceased to be a happy-go-lucky activity and formality entered into the game. Nowadays golfers who travel around the countryside like to tell each other, "What a place this would be to build a golf course." In those early days that thought was enough. If you had clubs and balls to hand you played wherever you found a piece of suitable country. In Scotland the golfing grounds were of necessity the common lands, but when we read of royal personages playing golf in the royal park at Greenwich, it does not mean a golf course was there.

The earliest references to stroke play date from this era in the middle of the 18th century, as does the earliest surviving code of rules. It is interesting to note that our ancestors managed to get along on thirteen brief laws, compared with the present proliferation of forty-one, many of them divided into numerous subclauses, definitions, appendices, and instructions on etiquette.

Although the game was in a fairly advanced state of development, there still was no such thing as a formalized golf course as we know it today. At one of the earliest links, for instance, at Leith, near Edinburgh, the game was played over five holes measuring 414, 461, 426, 495 and 435 yards. If these distances are adjusted for the equipment of the day, they are the equivalent of about 600 yards for each hole, good three-shotters for the best players. Here again we have direct evidence to refute the modern view that putting is half of golf. Nowadays, on a par seventy-two course, the first-class golfer is allowed a "ration" of two putts a hole, thirty-six in all. The ratio of shots through the green to putts in the days when Leith was a five-hole course must have been nearer two to one. A round at Leith probably consisted of three circuits, so there could be no basis for comparison with the golfers of, say, Perth, whose course had six holes, or Montrose, which had twenty-five.

In any case, stroke-play golf with card and pencil had not yet become popular. Golf was mainly man-to-man encounters, blood-and-guts matches with all the interest of private wagers and the interplay of personality. Those of the generation reared on a diet of almost unrelieved match play tend to regard it as the "real" golf, and find stroke play insipid stuff by comparison.

In this respect at least we must concede that the traditionalists are right. One of the regrettable trends of modern times is the decline of match play, following the pervasive example of the professional tournaments with their necessary emphasis on scores.

Whether or not the first golf was played at St. Andrews, the city of Edinburgh must be given credit for forming the first club. In 1744 a group of "honorable gentlemen golfers" petitioned the city fathers to provide a silver club for open competition among the golfing community. The trophy was duly provided and the championship announced by proclamation and tuck of drum. Twenty years later the Honourable Company of Edinburgh Golfers was formally constituted as a club, although it had no clubhouse, nor indeed did it own the golfing grounds at Leith. Nevertheless, minute books were kept of the club's activities and from such records we can get an accurate picture of the golfing way of life of those days.

Let us take a typical Saturday in, say, 1780, when the club tradition was well established, and follow the movements of a prosperous merchant. The only paid official of the club was a boy whose job was to call on every member and inquire if he proposed to dine with the club on Saturday. Having given due notice of his intention to be present at dinner (cost: one shilling) the merchant would dress in his scarlet club uniform with crested buttons, and call for his carriage to take him to his appointment on the links. There he would meet his prearranged opponent, possibly a surgeon or an officer from the castle garrison, and their regular caddies. These caddies, probably reeking and fuddled from their ale-house excesses of the previous night, would take their owners' clubs in a bundle under their arms and play could begin. Undoubtedly it would be a match, and after pinching up a small pyramid of loose sand, the golfers would tee their balls and strike off with their play clubs.

The sight of these two splendid creatures in their finery would certainly attract a gallery of casual strollers, and the caddies would be kept busy clearing picnic parties and dog-walkers from the path of the match. By all accounts the caddies would not be too particular about the language they employed in their control of the public. For all their faults, the caddies were fiercely partisan and jealously protected the rights of their masters. The tradition among caddies of knowing how to milk a fat tip is as old as golf itself. On one occasion, when a spectator was crowding the hole so closely that he impeded the player's stroke, the caddie grabbed the onlooker by the back of the neck and thrust his nose into the hole with the words: "There now! You can see the ball's in the hole right enough."

After the game the serious business of the club would begin. The golfers would change into their dining uniforms, possibly blue or gray coats with black facings and gilt buttons, and repair to a private room in a local tavern for dinner, presided over by the captain (an office automatically assumed by the winner of the club championship). It was customary for members to provide food from their own estates, and these golfers did themselves well. Club minutes recall feasts of a round of beef stewed in hock, haunch of venison, saddle of mutton, reindeer's tongue, pigeon pie and sheep's-head pasty. The Royal Aberdeen club accounts show an average consumption in excess of three bottles of liquor per man at their dinners, and Tobias Smollett writes of the club golfer customarily retiring with a gallon of claret in his belly. The business of the club was transacted during the meal. A member who had been observed playing golf out of uniform might be fined half a dozen bottles of rum or Highland whiskey. And then the wagers would be recorded. This ritual was the normal method of organizing matches for the following week. One member might challenge another to a match for a gallon of whiskey and the details would duly be recorded in the book. At the same time, from reference to the previous week's entries, settlement would be demanded for that day's results. Since booze in some form was the common currency of golf wagers and payment was exacted at dinner, we can imagine that late in the evening some imprudent challenges were made. Never mind. It was an age of high conviviality and good fellowship; golf was not the solemn affair it later became. And the morrow was a day of rest.

Thirteen Ways of Looking at the Masters

by JOHN UPDIKE

The Monday after the 1979 Masters, novelist John Updike carded "a nifty ninety-four" at Augusta National Golf Club, site of the Masters Tournament, in what he feels was a memorable experience. A master of the English language, Updike also turned his skills to creating an impression of the Masters ritual in his major effort thus far as a golf writer.

1. As an Event in Augusta, Georgia

In the middle of downtown Broad Street a tall white monument—like an immensely heightened wedding cake save that in place of the bride and groom stands a dignified Confederate officer —proffers the thought that

> *"No nation rose so white and fair;*
> *None fell so pure of crime."*

Within a few steps of the monument, a movie theater, during Masters Week last year, was showing "Hair," full of cheerful miscegenation and anti-military song and dance. This is the Deep/Old/New South, with its sure-enough levees, railroad tracks, unpainted dwellings out of illustrations to Joel Chandler Harris, and stately homes ornamented by grillework and verandas. As far up the Savannah River as boats could go, Augusta was a trading post since 1717 and was named in 1735 by James Oglethorpe for the mother of George the Third. It changed hands several times during the Revolutionary War, thrived on tobacco and cotton, imported textile machinery from Philadelphia in 1828, and during the Civil War housed the South's largest powder works. Sherman passed through here, and didn't leave much in the way of historical sites.

The Augusta National Golf Club is away from the business end of town, in a region of big brick houses embowered in magnolia and dogwood. A lot of people retire to Augusta, and one of the reasons that Bobby Jones wanted to build a golf course here, instead of near his native Atlanta, was the distinctly milder climate. The course, built in 1931–1932 on the site of the Fruitlands Nursery property, after designs by Dr. Alister Mackenzie (architect of Cypress Point) and Jones himself, has the venerable Augusta Country Club at its back, and at its front, across Route 28, an extensive shopping-center outlay. At this point the New South becomes indistinguishable from New Jersey.

2. As an Event Not in Augusta, Georgia

How many Augusta citizens are members of the Augusta National Golf Club? The question, clearly in bad taste, brought raised eyebrows and a muttered, "Very few" or, more spaciously, "Thirty-eight or forty." The initial membership fee is rumored to be $50,000, there is a waiting list five years' long, and most of the members seem to be national Beautiful People, Golfing Subspecies, who jet in for an occasional round during the six months the course is open. When Ike, whose cottage was near the clubhouse, used to show up and play a twosome with Arnold Palmer, the course would be cleared by the Secret Service. Cliff Roberts, chairman of the tournament from its inception in 1934 until his death in 1977, was a Wall Street investment banker; his chosen successor, William H. Lane, was (until his recent death) a business executive from faraway Houston.

A lot of Augusta's citizens get out of town during Masters Week, renting their houses. The lady in the drugstore near the house my wife and I were staying in told me she had once gone walking on the course. *Once:* The experience seemed unrepeatable, like her first kiss. The course had looked deserted to her, but then a voice shouted "Fore" and a ball struck near her. The ghost of Lloyd Mangrum, perhaps. The only Augustans conspicuous during the tournament are the black caddies, who know the greens so well they can call a putt's break to the inch while standing on the fringe.

3. As a Study in Green

Green grass, green grandstands, green concession stalls, green paper cups, green folding chairs and visors for sale, green-and-white ropes, green-topped Georgia pines, a prevalence of green in the slacks and jerseys of the gallery, like the prevalence of red in the crowd in Moscow on May Day. The caddies' bright green caps and Sam Snead's bright green trousers. If justice were poetic, Hubert Green would win it every year.

4. As a Rite of Spring

"It's become a rite of spring," a man told me with a growl, "like the Derby." Like Fort Lauderdale. Like opening day at a dozen ballparks. Spring it was, especially for us Northerners who had left our gray skies, brown lawns, salt-strewn

highways and plucky little croci for this efflorescence of azaleas and barefoot *jeunes filles en fleurs.* Most of the gallery, like most of the golfers, had Southern accents. This Yankee felt a little as if he were coming in late on a round of equinoctial parties that had stretched from Virginia to Florida. A lot of young men were lying on the grass betranced by the memories of last night's libations, a lot of matronly voices continued discussing Aunt Earlene's unfortunate second marriage, while the golf balls floated overhead. For many in attendance, the Masters is a ritual observance; some of the oldtimers wore sun hats festooned with over twenty years' worth of admission badges.

Will success as a festival spoil the Masters as a sporting event? It hasn't yet, but the strain on the tournament's famous and exemplary organization can be felt. Ticket sales are limited, but the throng at the main scoreboard is hard to squeeze by. The acreage devoted to parking would make a golf course in itself. An army of over 2,000 policemen, marshals, walkway guards, salespersons, trash-gleaners and other attendants is needed to maintain order and facilitate the pursuit of happiness. To secure a place by any green it is necessary to arrive at least an hour before there is anything to watch.

When, on the last two days, the television equipment arrives, the crowd itself is watched. Dutifully, it takes its part as a mammoth unpaid extra in a national television spectacular. As part of it, patting out courteous applause at a good shot or groaning in chorus at a missed putt, one felt, slightly, *canned.*

5. As a Fashion Show

Female fashions, my wife pointed out, came in three strata. First, young women decked out as if going to a garden party—make-up, flowing dresses, sandals. Next, the trim, leathery generation of the mothers, dressed as if they themselves were playing golf—short skirts, sun visors, cleated two-tone shoes. Last, the generation of the grandmothers, in immaculately blued hair and amply filled pants suits in shades we might call electric pastel or Day-Glo azalea.

Among American golf shrines, Augusta National Golf Club, home of The Masters Tournament, is unique in its ambience. The course was designed by Bobby Jones and Alister Mackenzie and the tournament is really golf's rite of spring, whose elegant hub is the famous oak tree in front of the Georgian clubhouse.

6. As a Display Case for Sam Snead and Arnold Palmer

Though they no longer are likely to win, you wouldn't know it from their charismas. Snead, with his delicately swagged belly, rakishly tilted panama and slightly pushed-in face—a face that has known both battle and merriment—swaggers around the practice tee like the sheriff of Golf County, testing a locked door here, hanging a parking ticket there. On the course, he remains a golfer one has to call beautiful, from the cushioned roll of his shoulders as he strokes the ball to the padding, pantherlike tread with which he follows it down the center of the fairway, his chin tucked down while he thinks, apparently, rueful thoughts. He is one of the great inward golfers, those who wrap the dazzling difficulty of the game in an impassive, effortless flow of movement. When, on the green, he stands beside his ball, faces the hole, and performs the curious obeisance of his "sidewinder" putting stroke, no one laughs.

And Palmer, he of the unsound swing, a hurried slash that ends as though he is snatching something hot back from a fire, remains the monumental outward golfer, who invites us into the game to share with him its heady turmoil, its call for constant courage. Every inch an agonist, Palmer still hitches his pants as he mounts the green, still strides between the wings of his army like Hector on his way to yet more problematical heroism. Age has thickened him, made him look almost muscle-bound, and has grizzled his thin, untidy hair, but his deportment more than ever expresses vitality, a love of life and of the game that returns to him, from the multitudes, as fervent gratitude. Like us golfing commoners, he risks looking bad for the sake of some fun.

Of the younger players, only Lanny Wadkins communicates Palmer's reckless and debonair determination, and only Fuzzy Zoeller has the captivating blitheness of a Jimmy Demaret or a Lee Trevino. The Masters, with its clubby lifetime qualification for previous winners, serves as an annual exhibit of Old Masters, wherein one can see the difference between the reigning, college-bred pros, with their even teeth, on-camera poise and abstemious air, and the older crowd that came up from caddie sheds, drove themselves in cars along the dusty miles of the tour and hustled bets with the rich to make ends meet. Golf expresses the man, as every weekend foursome knows; amid the mannerly lads who dominate the money list, Palmer and Snead loom in three dimensions, as men.

7. As an Exercise in Spectatorship

In no other sport must the spectator move. The builders and improvers of Augusta National built mounds and bleachers for the crowds to gain vantage from, and a gracefully written pamphlet by the founder, Robert Jones, is handed out as instruction in the art of "letting the tournament come to us instead of chasing after it." Nevertheless, as the field narrows and the interest of the hordes focuses, the best way to see anything is to hang back in the woods and use binoculars. From within the galleries, the players become tiny walking dolls, glimpsable, like stars on a night of scudding clouds, in the gaps between heads.

Examples of Southern courtesy in the galleries: (1) When my wife stood to watch an approach to the green, the man behind her mildly observed, "Ma'am, it was awful nice when you were sittin' down." (2) A man standing next to me, not liking the smell of a cigar I was smoking, offered to buy it from me for a dollar.

Extraordinary event in the galleries: On the fourth hole a ball set in flight by Dow Finsterwald

struck a fuzzy-haired young man sitting beside the green solidly on the head. The sound of a golf ball on a skull is remarkably like that of two blocks of wood being knocked together.

Single instance of successful spectatorship by this reporter: I happened to be in the pines left of the seventh fairway on the first day of play, wondering whether to go for another of the refreshment committee's standardized but economical ham sandwiches when Art Wall, Jr., hooked a ball near where I was standing. Only a dozen or so gathered to watch his recovery: for a moment, then, we could breathe with a player and experience with him—as he waggled, peered at obtruding branches, switched clubs and peered at the branches again—that quintessential golfing sensation, the loneliness of the bad-ball hitter.

Sad truth, never before revealed: By sticking to a spot in the stands or by the green, one can view the field coming through, hitting variants of the same shots and putts, and by listening to the massed cheers and grunts from the other greens one can guess at dramas unseen: but the unified field, as Einstein discovered in a more general connection, is unapprehendable, and the best way to witness a golf tournament is at the receiving end of a television signal. Many a fine golf reporter, it was whispered to me, never leaves the set in the press tent.

The other sad truth about golf spectatorship is that for today's pros it all comes down to the putting, and that the difference between a putt that drops and one that rims the cup, though teleologically enormous, is intellectually negligible.

8. As a Study in Turf-Building

A suburban lawn-owner can hardly look up from admiring the weedless immensity of the Augusta National turf. One's impression, when first admitted to this natural Oz, is that a giant putting green has been dropped over acres of rolling terrain, with a few holes for ponds and trees to poke through. A philosophy of golf is hereby expressed in Jones's pamphlet: "The Augusta National has much more fairway and green area than the average course. There is little punishing rough and very few bunkers. The course is not intended so much to punish severely the wayward shot as to reward adequately the stroke played with skill—and judgment.''

It is an intentional paradox, then, that this great championship course is rather kind to duffers. The ball sits up on Augusta's emerald carpet looking big as a baseball. It was not always such; in 1972, an invasion of *Poa annua,* a white-spiked vagabond grass, rendered conditions notoriously bumpy: in remedy a fescue called Pennlawn and a rye called Pennfine were implanted on the fairways and greens respectively and have flourished. Experimentation continues; to make the greens even harder and slicker, they are thinking of rebuilding them on a sand base —and have already done so on the adjacent par-three course.

From May to October, when the course is closed to play, everything goes to seed and becomes a hayfield, and entire fairways are plowed up. The caddies, I was solemnly assured, never replace a divot; they just sprinkle grass seed from a pouch they carry. Well, this is a myth, for I repeatedly saw caddies replace divots in the course of the tournament. The only difference is at Augusta the divots tear loose on dotted lines.

9. As Demography

One doesn't have to want to give the country back to the Indians to feel a nostalgic pang while looking at old photos of the pre–World War II tournaments, with their hatted, necktied galleries strolling up the fairways in the wake of the baggy-trousered players, and lining the tees and greens only one man deep.

The scores have grown crowded, too. The best then would be among the best now—Lloyd Mangrum's single round sixty-four in 1940 has not been bettered, though for the last two years it has been equaled. But the population of the second-best has increased, producing virtually a new winner each week of the tour, and stifling the emergence of stable constellations of superstars like Nelson-Hogan-Snead and Palmer-Player-Nicklaus. In the 1936 and 1938 Masters, only seven players made the 36-hole score of 145 that cut the 1979 field to forty-five players. Not until 1939 did the winner break 280 and not again until 1948. The last total over 280 to win it came in 1973. In 1936, Craig Wood had a first-day round of eighty-eight and finished in the top twenty-four. In 1952, Sam Snead won the Masters in spite of a third-round seventy-seven. That margin for intermittent error has been squeezed from tournament golf. Johnny Miller chops down a few trees, develops the wrong muscles and plummets. Arnold Palmer, relatively young and still strong and keen, can no longer ram the putts in from twenty feet, and becomes a father figure. A cruel world, top-flight golf, that eats its young.

10. As Race Relations

A Martian skimming overhead in his saucer would have to conclude that white earthlings hit the ball and black earthlings fetch it, that white men swing the sticks and black men carry them. The black caddies of Augusta, in their white coveralls, are a tradition that needs a symbolic breaking, the converse of Lee Elder's playing in the tournament. Yet, to be fair, these caddies are specialists of a high order, who take a cheerful pride in their expertise and who are, especially during Masters Week, well paid for it. Gary Player's caddie for his spectacular come-from-nowhere victory of 1978 was tipped $10,000, a sum that, this caddie assured an impudent interrogator, was still safe in the bank. In the New South, blacks work side by side with whites in the concession stands and at the fairway ropes, though I didn't see any in a green marshal's coat. I was unofficially informed that, at the very time when civil rightists were agitating for a black player to be invited to play even if one did not earn qualification—as Elder did in 1975—blacks were not being admitted to the tournament *as spectators.* I wonder about this. On pages 26–27 of the green souvenir album with a text by Cliff Roberts, one can see a photograph of Henry Picard hitting out of a bunker; behind him in the scattering of spectators are a number of ebony gentlemen not dressed as caddies. At any rate, though golf remains a white man's game, it represents in the player and caddie an active white-black partnership in which the white man is taking the advice and doing the manual work. Caddies think of the partnership as "we," as in "We hit a drive down the center and a four-iron stiff to the pin, but then *he* missed the putt."

11. As Class Relations

Though the Augusta National aspires to be the American St. Andrews, there is a significant economic difference between a Scottish golf links thriftily pinked out on a wasteland—the seaside sandy hills that are "links"—and the American courses elaborately, expensively carved from farmland and woods. Though golf has plebeian Scottish roots, in this country its province is patrician. A course requires capital and flaunts that ancient aristocratic prerogative, land. In much of the world, this humbling game is an automatic symbol of capitalist-imperialist oppression; a progressive African novelist, to establish a character as a villain, has only to show him coming off a golf course. And in our own nation, for all the roadside driving ranges and four o'clock factory leagues, golf remains for millions something that happens at the end of a long driveway, beyond the MEMBERS ONLY sign.

Yet competitive golf in the United States came of age when, at the Country Club, in Brookline, Massachusetts, a twenty-year-old ex-caddie and workingman's son, Francis Ouimet, beat the British masters Vardon and Ray in a playoff for the U.S. Open. And ever since, the great competitors have tended to come from the blue-collar level of golf, the caddies and the offspring of club pros. Rare is the Bobby Jones who emerges from the gentry with the perfectionistic drive and killer instinct that make a champion in this game which permits no let-up or loss of concentration, yet which penalizes tightness also. Hagen acted like a swell and was called Sir Walter, but he came up from a caddie's roost in Rochester. The lords of golf have been by and large gentlemen made and not born, while the clubs and the management of the tour remain in the hands of the country club crowd. When genteel Ed Sneed and Tom Watson fell into a three-way playoff for the

1979 Masters title, you knew in your bones it was going to be the third player, a barbarian called Fuzzy with a loopy swing, who would stroll through the gates and carry off the loot.

12. As a Parade of Lovely Golfers, No Two Alike

Charles Coody, big-beaked and stooped like a gentle predatory bird. Billy Casper, once the king of touch, now sporting the bushy white sideburns of a turn-of-the-century railroad conductor, still able to pop them up from a sand trap and sink the putt. Trevino, so broad across he looks like a reflection in a funhouse mirror, a model of delicacy around the greens and a model of affable temperament everywhere. Player, varying his normal black outfit with white slacks, his bearing so full of fight and muscle he seems to be restraining himself from breaking into a run. Nicklaus, athlete of the decade, still golden but almost gaunt and faintly grim, as he feels a crown evaporating from his head. Gay Brewer, heavy in the face and above the belt, nevertheless uncorking a string-straight mid-iron to within nine inches of the long seventh hole in the par-three tournament. Miller Barber, Truman Capote's double, punching and putting his way to last year's best round, a storm-split sixty-four in two installments. Bob Clampett, looking too young and thin to be out there. Andy Bean, looking too big to be out there, and with his perennially puzzled expression seeming to be searching for a game more his size. Hubert Green, with a hunched flicky swing that would make a high school golf coach scream. Tom Weiskopf, the handsome embodiment of pained near-perfection. Hale Irwin, the picture-book golfer with the face of a Ph.D. candidate. Johnny Miller, looking heavier than we remember him, patiently knocking them out on the practice tee, wondering where the lightning went. Ben Crenshaw, the smiling Huck Finn, and Tom Watson, the more pensive Tom Sawyer, who, while the other boys were whitewashing fences, has become, politely but firmly, the best golfer in the world.

And many other redoubtable young men. Seeing them up close, in the dining room or on the clubhouse veranda, one is struck by how young and in many cases how slight they seem, with their pert and telegenic little wives—boys, really, anxious to be polite and to please even the bores and boors that collect in the interstices of all well-publicized events. Only when one sees them at a distance, as they walk alone or chatting in twos down the great green emptiness of the fairway, does one sense that each is the pinnacle of a great buried pyramid of effort and invest-ment, prior competition from preteen level up, of immense and, it must be at times, wearisome, accumulated hopes of parents, teachers, backers. And with none of the group hypnosis and exhila-ration of team play to relieve them. And with the difference between success and failure so feath-er-fine.

13. As a Religious Experience

The four days of last year's Masters fell on Maundy Thursday, Good Friday, Holy Saturday and Easter Sunday. On Good Friday, fittingly, the skies darkened, tornados were predicted, and thousands of sinners ran for cover. My good wife, who had gone to divine services, was pre-vented from returning to the course by the flood of departing cars, and the clear moral is one propounded from many a pulpit: golf and church-going do not mix. Easter Sunday also happened to be the anniversary of the assassination of Abraham Lincoln and the sinking of the Titanic, and it wasn't such a good day for Ed Sneed, either.

About ninety-nine percent of the gallery, my poll of local vibes indicated, was rooting for Sneed to hold off disaster and finish what he had begun. He had played splendidly for three days, and it didn't seem likely he'd come this close soon again. When he birdied the fifteenth and enlarged his once-huge cushion back to three strokes, it seemed he would do it. But then, through no flagrant fault of his own, he began "leaking." We all knew how it felt, the slippery struggle to nurse a good round back to the club-house, with the ball getting smaller and the ter-rain meaner. On the seventeenth green, where I was standing, his approach looked no worse than his playing partner's; it just hit a foot too long, skipped into the sloping back part of the green and slithered into the fringe. His putt back caught the cup but twirled away. And his putt to save par, which looked to me like a gimme, lipped out, just the way my two-footers do when I lift my head to watch them drop, my sigh of relief all prepared. Zoeller, ten minutes before, had gently rolled in a birdie from much farther away. Sneed's fate seemed sealed then: the eigh-teenth hole, a famous bogey-maker, waited for him as ineluctably as Romeo's missed appoint-ment with Juliet.

He hadn't hit bad shots, and he hadn't pa-nicked; he just was screwed a half-turn too tight to get a par. The gallery of 40,000 felt for him, right to the pits of our golf-weary stomachs, when his last hope of winning it clean hung on the lip of the seventy-second hole. It so easily might have been otherwise. But then that's life, and that's golf, a game even masters don't mas-ter.

Following the Sun

by AL BARKOW

Al Barkow's golf credentials include qualifying for the U.S. Amateur, as well as being a former editor of Golf *magazine and writer of the* Shell's Wonderful World of Golf *series. His major contribution to the game's library is* Golf's Golden Grind, *the best-ever history of the pro tour. "Following the Sun" details the rhythm and routine of one tournament, the 1973 Westchester Classic.*

THEY live by the sun and pay its dues. They are burnt red around chins and cheekbones, backs of necks are Oklahoma in drought—deep, dry crevices in baked hide; backs of hands are crumpled onionskin; permanent squint lines are deeply etched; lips are camphored. Few use oils. They are not on vacation. They are at work under King Hot, and oils can get on hands and make them slippery. Slippery is bad, dry is good . . . on the outside. On the inside, all the nerve ends, tendons, muscles, ligaments want to be, should be, as slick and free-flowing as a fire pole. But the stuff of such inner lubrication does not come so easily, is not as cheaply applied as a bit of lip balm. They are professional tournament golfers, swimmers in the goldfish bowl of golf, or what is known simply as the tour. This week the tour is in Harrison, New York, for the playing of the Westchester Classic.

When fishermen throw loose chunks of bait into the water to attract fish, it is called chumming. At the Westchester Classic the chum is very good indeed. The total purse is a quarter of a million dollars, and the water is a turmoil of all make and manner of catch. Some of the pros are in vivid clothes—tight-fitting slacks in checks or stripes and brightly printed shirts and red, white and blue shoes. There are others wearing dark baggy pants and dull tan shirts and plain brown shoes. They run the gamut of sizes, come from all corners of the nation, the world. There's a flat flounder from Illinois, an eel from Colorado, a chub from Florida, a piranha from South Africa. Somehow, though, the polyphony of accents has a veneer of American South—soft cushions on hard consonants, casual melding of one word into another. Patois.

"Hey pard, got meuh new driver. Looguh this dude. Juss what ah need for this track. Airmail it. Gonna get me a goood check'ear. You goinuh Hortford?"

"Ah may."

"Lotsuh guys pass it. Can getchuh goood check up'air."

"Whereyuh stayin' ear?"

"Ramada."

"Heard theresuh new Holiday in Mount Crisco."

55

"Kissgo."

"Yeah. Only twentyuh night."

"Price is right, for Nooo Yawk. Hey, had me some cute l'il things in my gallery in Montreal. Horda unnerstanem'o. Teenyboppers."

"Hey muff, you eat yet?"

"You won't catch me eatin' in this'ear clubhouse. Got a tab here'll makeyuh play."

"Noooo Yawwwwk!"

Little fish, big fish, all in the same pond.

Before the sun coming up out of Long Island Sound is high enough to dry the heavy dew covering the Wee Burn Country Club golf course, in Darien, Connecticut, 111 golfers begin an eighteen-hole round of golf that will make or break their week . . . at least. It is Monday morning of Westchester Classic Week, and these are the so-called rabbits of the pro tour, Monday's Children, the odd-lot pros who are not exempt and must qualify for a place in the field of the 1973 Westchester Classic. One hundred and eleven of them out for twenty-two places. Some are local club pros larking it. If they get in, fine; if not, back to their jobs. The others want to succeed strictly as players.

It is lonely, quiet, wet, and too early in the day to feel easy in the shoulders, thin in the hands, clear in the head. But play they must. A few have been winners on the tour—Cerrudo, Henry, Brown—but have fallen on the evil times of a lost touch, poor concentration, negative attitude, injury or illness. Most have never been there, or even thereabouts—young, pocket-frayed, worried, numb. Miss here and it's down the road to the next qualifying round for the next tournament, maybe just a ride on home to pack it all in. One of Monday's Children went thirteen straight without once getting into a tournament proper. The dew sweepers, dragging in the eerie, beaded sea a trail of footprints that by noon will have disappeared as quickly and unobtrusively as those who made them. Only some numbers on a sheet of paper thumbtacked and flapping in the twilight breeze is their mark. No one will see them but themselves.

Out of that same Monday's twilight a sleek two-engine jet plane glides into the approach pattern for its landing at New York City's La-Guardia Airport. It tips to the right above the Hudson River and puts the lowering sun behind it, passes over Yonkers, where, less, than a hundred years before a few gentlemen parked horse and buggy beside an untilled pasture and gave birth to American golf, skims close to the East River, and finally touches down. The executive jet has been chartered by Jack Nicklaus, "the greatest golfer in the world," to bring him up from Baltimore.

The plane's engines whine down and the solid, self-assured figure of Nicklaus emerges. A presence. Sun-bleached hair swept carefully across the top of his forehead and sprayed to stay. He is immediately recognized by other businessmen arriving and departing, and he acknowledges the stares and smiles with darty glances. A visceral reaction. No one, no matter how long a celebrity, can fail to notice recognition.

In 1972 Nicklaus earned over $300,000 in prize money playing in only twenty tournaments on the U.S. tour. That's over $64,000 a month, and change. Or, by the reckoning of the everyday clock puncher, $400 an hour, and change. For playing golf. It represents only a portion of his annual income. He has a golf course design firm, an automobile agency, does lucrative television commercials for Hathaway and Hart Shaffner and Marx, who provide him his clothes. He buys his own street shoes, by Gucci. He goes in style. The flight from Baltimore cost him $1.25 an air mile, plus pilot's salary, landing fees. He likes fine wines, good food, pays his caddie-valet around $20,000 a year. It will cost him about $1,500 to play in the Westchester Classic. He will not take a loss.

Those of Monday's Children who qualified at Darien are looking for an inexpensive motel, planning strategy for the Westchester Classic. The strategy is simple; sink a lot of putts, make the thirty-six-hole cut, which means qualifying for the rest of the tournament, which means that the following Monday they won't have to sweep dew. Those who failed at Darien have dropped their heavy golf bags into car trunks, checked to see if caddies swiped any of their golf balls, asked

Keith Fergus, one of the bright, blond hopes of the new tour, enjoys the fun of making a long birdie putt.

how to get onto Interstate Something going Somewhere, and figure on grabbing a bite to eat at Howard Johnson. The fries aren't bad.

Nicklaus takes rooms in the Hilton Inn, Rye, New York, which is only a few minutes from the Westchester Country Club, site of the Classic. He drives a Pontiac to and from the course. A Pontiac because he endorses the make and has the use of a new one in every town he visits, compliments of GM and a local dealer who perhaps picks up a sales point: "Jack Nicklaus, pal. Turned this steering wheel with hands that have

won more major championships than any other golfer alive or dead. May help your game, pal."

Charles Coody is also a professional golfer. In the middle range. Won the Masters one year, a few lesser events. Tall, rather round-shouldered, with a thin, straight-boned nose a touch too short for the whole face. Friendly, modest, unassuming. Waits for you to speak first. A good grinder.

On Monday, while Jack Nicklaus was playing an eighteen-hole exhibition in Maryland for $12,500, which he gave to charity, and while the dew sweepers were agonizing in Darien, Connecticut, Charles Coody was playing an exhibition at the Winged Foot Country Club, not far from Westchester Country Club. The day before, he concluded play in Montreal (the Canadian Open), where he won a little over a thousand dollars, then drove nine hours to the New York area. ("Not countin' six stops. Two for meals, one for popcorn, potato chips and gas, three for kidneys.") Coody would have liked to stay overnight in Montreal, but the exhibition data at Winged Foot was worth $1,200. Like all regular pros on the tour, Coody gets his playing equipment for nothing. He has a small contract with a clothing manufacturer, an association with a Florida real-estate/golf operation, and some other bits and pieces. He's been earning about $65,000 in prize money every year for the past few, spends about $30,000 to get it, and counts on the extras, the $1,200 exhibitions, for the cream. Half-and-half, all things being relative.

Unlike Nicklaus, who grew up with some money, played country club golf, and started making it soon after turning pro, Coody knew some hard times. Son of a roustabout in the oil fields of west Texas, in his first year on tour he was allotted only $250 a week for expenses. He and his wife, Lynette, drove around Orlando, Florida for two hours once trying to make a decision, a big one: should they spend thirty-two dollars for a motel with a cook-in dinette, or forty dollars for one closer to the course and on the beach? They went for thirty-two . . . a week. Still, it was better than pulling rod and tubing or tinking batteries for someone else around some oil hole.

Coody puts half of the 100,000 miles he travels each year on his own Cadillac, and then trades for a new one. He plays in thirty-two to thirty-six tournaments annually. It's a lot of golf, but there's nothing much else on his mind to do, for now. He had gone to college—Texas Christian—and took a degree in business administration, but, "I probably wouldn't have gone if not for the golf scholarship. Got to admit I just walked through. School was a conduit to the tour."

During the summer months, Coody closes up the family home in Abilene, Texas, and takes his wife and three children with him on the tour. He spends about $500 a week, although it is not much less without the family. "If you eat and sleep cheap, you play cheap." In 1965 Coody pulled a trailer on the golf tour. Coming to Westchester for the first time he had no idea where to put the rig. He was told of a good trailer park on Long Island. Coody hooked up and drove an hour-and-a-half each way to play the Westchester. He's learned since. Has been around. And this year he has a better deal. An old friend has a home in Ridgewood, New Jersey, forty-five minutes from the Westchester Country Club, and the Coodys stay there. They save rent for the week, and can beat the restaurant food for the time. ("About July the steak in St. Louis looks like the same one you had in L.A. Don't talk about the potatoes and peas.")

Many months prior to eight o'clock Thursday morning, August 2, 1973, when the first golf shots are struck that get the Westchester Classic officially under way, preparations were begun to make it all happen. Since it was in its seventh annual renewal, it was mostly a matter of dusting off the working parts.

With the calendar dates agreed upon, the contract between the sponsors and the Tournament Players Division (TPD) of the Professional Golfers Association of America (PGA) was signed. The sponsoring group puts up the prize money, the stands, the ropes; rents the golf course and courtesy cars, hires a security force, prints the tickets and sells them, buys insurance, gathers together a force of volunteers to run the show.

The TPD provides the players, of course, and runs the competition. It does a smooth and efficient job, as befits the supervisor, an ex-FBI agent named Jack Tuthill who seldom loses the bland cool of the cop. Tuthill and his assistants administer Rabbit Monday, set up the Classic course—cut the holes in the greens, position the tee markers, line out ground under repair, handle the pairings and starting times. Tuthill and his men also make all rules calls—all are excellent golfers in their own right—and continually drive around the course talking to each other over walkie-talkies to maintain the flow of play: "Wade, there's a big hole opened up between groups here at thirteen." "I know, Tut, player has lost his ball here on eleven." "You timing him?" "He's got thirty more seconds to look for it." "Over and out."

The sponsors of the Westchester Classic are Eastern Airlines and the volunteer TWIG Organizations of United Hospitals. All profits from the tournament go to six hospitals in Westchester County, New York ($1.8 million in six years). Eastern Airlines puts up a portion of the purse money the pros play for, the rest is raised by the hospital group from various sources. A thick, expensively produced program sells for a dollar, has 190 pages, 106 of which are paid advertisements. The revenue goes into the tournament pot. There is an advance ticket sale. A season ticket (a golf tournament's season is one week long) can be purchased for forty-four dollars, parking not included. The ticket gets the holder onto the grounds for the "season" and allows him into the Sports Hospitality Area, a roped-off section that amounts to a clubhouse porch. A $27.50 season ticket is good for grounds-only. The advance sale is important, the only insurance against rainouts; Lloyds of London is too expensive.

Grand patrons and patrons are solicited. The former, generally a corporation, sometimes only a wealthy, benevolent individual, donates $5,500, for which he gets a color ad in the program, a bunch of tickets, parking privileges, and four places in the professional-amateur event. A patron puts up $1,650 and gets one place in the pro-am, a black-and-white ad in the program, some tickets. All monies go into the tournament pot.

Fund-raising drawings are held, and the Westchester Classic takes a cut of the concessionaires' action. The people who sell the hamburgers (one dollar), hotdogs (seventy-five cents), soft drinks (fifty cents) figure each spectator spends, on average, three dollars a day with them. About 80,000 persons attended the 1973 Westchester Classic.

The pro-am event is unique to professional tournament golf. It is like a fan taking batting practice with Reggie Jackson or Ty Cobb—the first U.S. PGA championship, in 1916, had a pro-am. But it costs. Each amateur pays $1,500 to play an eighteen-hole round of golf with a pro entered in the Westchester Classic. There is a small purse for the pros, merchandise for the amateurs. Is it worth $1,500 to play eighteen holes with a pro?

If you get Chi Chi Rodriguez, yes. "Helluva nice guy." Sometimes, not so much fun. Many pros grumble about having to play golf with "hackers" and say hardly a word to them during the entire round. But the pros are beginning to get less bumptious about this. Pro-ams help build bigger purses for the tournament proper. In the 1973 Westchester Classic, ninety-six amateurs contributed $144,000 to the tournament pot. The pro-am is run off the day before the Classic begins. Westchester does not go in for "celebrity" pro-ams—a lot of show business personalities—but Joe DiMaggio is in town to make some television commercials for a local bank, and is playing.

"Oh, there's Arnie Palmer," says a teenager.

"Well, I want to see Joe D.," says her mother.

Almost every function of the tournament outside of the running of the competition itself is done by volunteers—the fund raising, the ticket sales, program sales, marshals, etc. Close to a thousand persons donate their time and energy to this work. Such free labor is a keystone in the structure of the tour. Without it, the purse money would surely not be as high as it is. Consider. Say the 1,000 volunteers at Westchester work seven days from Monday through Sunday of the tournament. Almost all work much more, but let that be. If they put in an average of ten hours a day and are paid a minimum wage of two dollars an hour, you have $140,000 worth of labor . . . for free.

Few of the volunteers are two-dollar-an-hour persons in "real" life. Arthur Nardin, for example, is a contractor and house builder, one-time owner of national champion trotting horses, a member of Westchester Country Club. He stands at a desk passing out entry blanks to arriving pros, takes entry fees, tells the pros where they might find a room for the week, where they can cash a check, relieve themselves. Why does he do it?

"I've been around golf for years. Love the game. And, it's for charity," says Nardin. "I enjoy it," he goes on. "Some of the pros can be, you know, a pain. Like Sam Snead giving us a hard time about paying his entry fee. Something about last year he had to withdraw because of an injury and someone else paid another fifty bucks to take his place, so he should be able to use his fifty from last year for this year."

"He was kidding?"

"Maybe. You know how Sam is. Then you get something like Larry Hinson and Ed Furgol coming in at the same time to sign their entry. Both have withered left arms. Two generations together. Isn't that something."

Among the volunteers are about 300 TWIGS. TWIG is not an acronym. It stands for a group of women who see themselves as branches on the big tree of charity. The Westchester Classic is but one of their good works. They dress in smart blue-and-yellow dresses, sell tickets, type letters, distribute programs, handle myriad details in the cause of United Hospitals . . . and the tour.

Two months before play is to begin, television technicians scout the course to set up camera positions, construct camera towers, lay cable. Fourteen cameras will cover the action on the last six holes. At the same time, television time salesmen begin calling on clients. Among those who "come in" are Eastern Airlines, of course, and Texaco, Mercedes-Benz, Liberty Mutual Insurance, IBM, American Express, Schweppes. The list is indicative of that strata of the American public that is into golf; solid middle-class. The TPD negotiates all television contracts (except for a few, such as the Masters and U.S. Open), and each sponsor on the tour gets a share of the total "package." Westchester's comes to about $60,000. Into the pot.

On Tuesday most of the pros arrive at Westchester Country Club. Trunks of big cars open, and from each is lifted a great sack of golf clubs wrapped in an airline travel bag. Each rounded mass of leather or Naugahyde looks, to a Chicagoan raised on gangland murder headlines, like a small-time loser. The pros sign in with Arthur Nardin, move into the locker room and there check the brown accordion file that follows the tour and carries their mail. Write a touring pro at home, that is, where he stores his insurance policies and old tax records, and you may not reach him for months.

In every pro's locker, manufacturers representatives have stacked three one-dozen boxes of new golf balls. Each player in the starting field of every tournament gets thirty-six new balls, no charge, from somebody. Pros with no manufacturer affiliation get them from a company that specializes in golf balls but does not sign pros to contracts. Pros contracted to companies that make only clubs shop around for a ballmaker representative of their choice. Pros contracted to full-line companies usually adhere to their agreement to play the company ball, not always happily. For example, a rep asks a staff pro how he likes the new cover on "our" ball. The pro shakes his head slowly from side to side.

"A lot of 'em are going to the right," says the pro.

"Well, you sometimes get to hitting a fade," says the rep.

"Man, I've been hooking the ball for forty years."

Embarrassed silence, eyes to the floor, and, "Good luck in the tournament." "Thanks a lot." The rep slips away.

Golf-glove reps ask pros how their supply is holding up.

"Ah need me some blue ones, some green ones, 'n white ones. And oh year, a couple uh red ones. Got me some new red slacks. Looky heah, canya matchem?"

"I think so."

"Super. Medium large, buddy."

A representative from the Southern Open, to be played in two months' time, is lining up entrants at Westchester.

"Y'all cominuh Southern, aint yuh?"

"Yeah, ah reckon, if ah can git it goin' good.

Sheeet! Yuh git it goin' good yuh can't hordly go on home."

"We got the purse up some, and we getchuh goood deal on a room."

"Lemme get back to yuh, buddy."

"Fahn. Have a good tournament, hear."

The caddies gather near the first tee, or at the entrance to the locker room, where the pros arrive. They are a variegated band: old men with gray-stubble chins, rheumy eyes, wearing sagging trousers torn at the inseams and Woolworth white dress shirts permanently stained across the shoulders from the straps of heavy golf bags; middle-aged men with a professional mien wearing white visors or baseball caps, thin tan windbreakers, golf shoes; young school kids working their way through the summer, wearing Joe Namath football shirts, gym shoes. The caddies who get a bag in the Classic will be given one-piece jump suits to wear, courtesy of the sponsor.

The caddies wait for an assignment. Some have "influenced" the caddiemaster to get a pro for the week; most wait on chance. It can be a profitable week for a caddie who works. Pack a sack for the winner and it can be worth as much as $1,000—five percent of the first prize. All for keeping the clubs clean, doing an early morning reconaissance to spot pin placements and so advise his man, help pick the right club for shots, help judge the roll of the greens, and shag practice balls, which is the next worst thing to being a standing target on a live mortar range.

The practice tee at the Westchester Country Club is a polo field except for this one week of the year when it takes a heavy gouging from those who, in the long ago, were thought to be horseless polo players. As the week progresses toward Saturday and Sunday, the practice field becomes a parking lot and the pros are allowed to dig trenches in the softer turf of the club's second course, much to their joy, if not the members'.

If the golf course is the pros' office, as many refer to it, the practice tee is their laboratory. Their rock pile, too, hard ground or soft, where they hammer away at ball and turf-building muscle memory, trying something a little different that may get their game going, or keep it coming. Some of the pros can be likened to Sisyphus and his gravity-prone boulder. On the practice tee they work out an altered swing plane or readjusted address position, and shot after shot is the rifle work of a super marksman. The boulder has been pushed to the top of the hill. But when they get on the golf course—the top of the hill—the stone may come tumbling down again. It usually does. Champions are indeed made on practice tees, but many pros leave their best stuff on that well-worn rehearsal ground.

The writers and editors of golf periodicals shuffle up and down behind the practicing pros, note pads in hand, looking at swings and picking brains for instruction articles they can produce for their how-to starved readers. ("You've got to get the pros Monday through Wednesday," says one writer. "When the bell rings they don't want to know about supination, lateral shifts and setting the angle early.")

The editors are trailed slavishly by photographers with chests crowded with Nikons. Two of them have $2,000 Hultcher cameras that roll at fifty frames per second and produce negatives from which sharp still photographs can be made of Lanny Wadkins's wrists beginning to break at the right knee, breaking more at the right hip, even more at the armpit, cocking completely above the shoulder line, remaining cocked until the moment of impact with the ball, then releasing an instant later.

"How Lanny Wadkins Achieves the Late Hit . . . and How You Can, Too," will read the headline on the magazine article.

The newspaper guys hang around in the locker room, mostly, eyes and ears out for items to fill a column or a pretournament feature before they must file the simpler play-by-play reports.

"Tommy, how do you account for this sudden burst of winning form?"

"When my father died I realized I had left him down by not working hard enough at my game and becoming the winner he wanted me to be. The Almighty gave me this talent and I wasn't using it. But I hope they keep those god-damn cameras off the course. Jeesus Christ, they're bugging the crap out of me."

"Photogs Menace Pro's Concentration" reads the headline on the column, or item.

The golf course has been massaged and manicured. The maintenance superintendent (greenskeeper, to oldtimers) has had his crew carefully raking the sand in the bunkers ("No pockmarks, fellas. Keep the ridges shallow."), and trimming the scraggly grass from their lips. The greens have been rolled and cross-cut to make them as smooth as a flatiron. The long grass just off the fairways has been allowed a good growth then cut to a height of two or three inches a week before play begins. It will be tough, but playable. The long grass well off the fairways is left to grow full. It will be trampled flat by the crowds, and if not, "A man hits it that far wide *deserves* hay." The rear portions of the teeing grounds, from where the pros play, have been screened with chicken wire to keep every-one off until tournament time. The deep scars of shots misbehit by members have been filled with seed. Sprinklers have been turned on every eve-ning, their metal fingers spinning prescribed arcs and sending out diaphanous sprays that, when seen from a distance in concert, are like a gentle, aqueous ballet. The course is ready.

Now come the spectators, the ultimate do-nors to charity and the wallets of the pros. The 80,000 at Westchester put nearly a half-million dollars in the till in the form of gate receipts. They park their cars for two dollars a day (into the pot, less parking attendants' salaries) and God help them if on a hot day they can't find a spot under a tree. Most don't. They walk about a mile from car park to main gate, pay three dollars to watch Monday and Tuesday practice rounds, six dollars to watch the pro-am on Wednesday, seven dollars on Thursday and Fri-day, eight dollars on Saturday and Sunday. To prove they have paid they wear tags looped around buttons. They look like they're on sale.

The gallery carries any essentials they may need during their nomadic four to eight hours in the great out of doors: umbrellas, suntan lotion, small canvas chairs, collapsible combination chair/walking sticks, a golf club (should the muse strike), binoculars, lightweight kitchen stools and elongated cardboard rectangles with an inset mirror that allows them to stand low and see high. Seeing is not easy at a golf tournament.

The spectators wear the same clothes Arnie and Jack and Lee and Johnny wear in the maga-zines and on the course—shirts with alligators, penguins, umbrellas, golden bears or sombreros sewn over the left teat, and double-knit, two-, three-, and four-tone slacks and all-white or white-and-red or blue-and-red golf shoes—but somehow they never look like the players. The drape is not quite the same, the combinations not as carefully selected. Something. Perhaps it's their carriage, born of the knowledge that they can't play like the pros and all the insignia on their bodies are not going to make up the differ-ence.

Many pieces have been thrown together. A cake has been baked. A number of interests are served—charitable, commercial, social—and a golf tournament is staged. When it is finished at Westchester, the ingredients are put together again in Cleveland; Sutton, Massachusetts, Bet-tendorf, Iowa. Each event has its variations; a little less prize money, a little more, a different charity, sometimes no charity. Each offers an en-tirely different golf course in topography and in the demands made on the pros' skills, which makes tournament golf quite different from other sports. Not all the same players will be in each tournament, although cynics or the jaded among those who travel the circuit will say they all look alike. It won't cost the pros as much to play in Charlotte, North Carolina as it does in New York, but it is all one thing, a thing called the tour, a great long caravan that starts in Janu-ary, ends in November without missing a week, and begins all over again the next January. It is the purest of road shows. It has no home base, a different Barnum in every bailiwick. It is not a business in any conventional sense, yet is very much a business, worth over $8 million in prize money in 1973.

The Triumvirate

by **BERNARD DARWIN**

Bernard Darwin was the grandson of Charles Darwin, and like everyone in the Darwin family, a man of multiple talents. One gift was writing about golf in such an inimitable manner that, among golf writers, he is considered "The Master, one who went beyond reporting to create some of golf's greatest stories. Three of Britain's greatest players, Harry Vardon, James Braid and J.H. Taylor, known together as "the Triumvirate," are the subjects of this Darwin essay.

THERE is a natural law in games by which, periodically, a genius arises and sets the standard of achievement perceptibly higher than ever before. He forces the pace; the rest have to follow as best they can, and end by squeezing out of themselves just a yard or two more than they would have believed possible.

During the last year or two we have seen this law at work in billiards. Lindrum has set up a new standard in scoring power and our players, in trying to live up to him, have excelled their old selves. The same thing has happened from time to time in golf, and those whom we call the Triumvirate undoubtedly played their part in the "speeding up" of the game.

Taylor, though by a few months the youngest of the three, was the first to take the stage, and it has always been asserted that he first made

people realize what was possible in combined boldness and accuracy in playing the shots up to the pin. Anything in the nature of safety play in approaching became futile when there was a man who could play brassie shots to the flag in the manner of mashie shots. Mr. Hilton has suggested that this raising of the standard really began earlier and was due to another great Englishman, Mr. John Ball. It may well be so, for it is hard to imagine anything bolder or straighter than that great golfer's shots to the green, but Taylor, being the younger man and coming later, burst on a much larger golfing world than had Mr. Ball. Moreover, he was a professional who played here, there and everywhere, and so was seen by a large number of golfers, whereas the great amateur, except at championship times, lay comparatively hidden at Hoylake. Time was just ripe when Taylor appeared: golf was "booming" and the hour and the man synchronized. Though in the end he failed in his first championship at Prestwick, he had done enough to show that he was going to lead golfers a dance to such a measure as they had not yet attempted. In the next year he won, and for two years after that the world struggled to keep up with him as best it could.

Then there arose somebody who could even improve on Taylor. This was Harry Vardon, who tied with him in the third year of his reign (1896)

63

and beat him on playing off. There was an interval of one more year before the really epoch-making character of Vardon was appreciated. Then he won his second championship in 1898 and was neither to hold nor to bind. He devastated the country in a series of triumphal progresses and, as in the case of Lindrum, there was no doubt that a greater than all before him had come. To the perfect accuracy of Taylor he added a perceptible something more of power and put the standard higher by at least one peg.

And, it may be asked, did Braid have no effect? I hardly think he did in the same degree though he was such a tremendous player. He took longer to mature than did his two contemporaries. Of all men he seemed intended by nature to batter the unresponsive gutty to victory, and he won one championship with a gutty, but his greatest year, his real period of domination, came with the rubber core. He cannot be said to have brought in a new epoch except to this extent perhaps, that he taught people to realize that putting could be learned by hard toil. He disproved the aphorism that putting is an inspiration for, after having been not far short of an execrable putter, he made himself, during his conquering period, into as effective a putter as there was in the country. By doing so he brought new hope to many who had thought that a putter must be born, not made, and had given it up as a bad job.

Presumably everybody thinks that his own youth was spent in the golden age, and that the figures of that period were more romantic than those of any other. At any rate I can claim romance and to spare for my early years of grown-up golf, for I went up to Cambridge in 1894 and that was the year of Taylor's first win at Sandwich. Moreover, the Triumvirate were then, I am sure, far more towering figures in the public eye than are their successors of today. It was their good fortune to have no rivals from beyond the sea. They were indisputably the greatest in the world. Then, too, they had so few ups and downs. Today a professional is in the limelight one year and in almost the dreariest of shade the next, but these three, by virtue of an extraordinary consistency, always clustered round the top.

Finally their zenith was the zenith of the exhibition match. They were constantly playing against one another and no matter on what mud-heap they met, the world really cared which of them won.

It is partly no doubt because I was in the most hero-worshipping stage of youth (I have never wholly emerged from it), but it is also largely due to the personalities of those great players that I can remember quite clearly the first occasion on which I saw each of them. It is a compliment my memory can pay to very few others. Taylor I first saw at Worlington (better, perhaps, known as Mildenhall) when he came almost in the first flush of his champion's honors, to play Jack White, who was then the professional there. I can see one or two shots that he played that day just as clearly as any that I have watched in the thirty-seven years since. I had seen several good Scottish professionals play before that, including my earliest hero, Willie Fernie, most graceful and dashing of golfers. I thought I knew just what a professional style was like, but here was something quite new to me. Here was a man who seemed to play his driver after the manner of a mashie. There was no tremendous swing, no glorious follow-through. Jack White, with his club, in those days, sunk well home into the palm of his right hand, was the traditional free Scottish slasher. He was driving the ball as I imagined driving. Taylor was altogether different and his style reminded me of a phrase in the badminton book, which I knew by heart, about Jamie Anderson and his "careless little switch." One has grown used to J.H. long since, but the first view of him was intensely striking, and I am inclined to think that in his younger days he stood with his right foot more forward than he does now, so that the impression of his playing iron shots with his driver was the more marked. He was not appallingly long, but he was appallingly straight, and he won a very fine match at the thirty-fifth hole. Incidentally, the memory of that game makes me realize how much the rubber-cored ball has changed golf. The first hole at Worlington was much what it is today, except that the green was the old one on the right. Now the aspiring Cambridge undergraduate calls it a two-shot hole and is disappointed with a five there. On that day—to be sure it was against a breeze—Taylor and Jack White took three wooden club shots apiece to reach the outskirts of the green, and Taylor with a run up and a putt won it in five against six.

My first sight of Vardon came next. It was on his own course at Ganton, whither I went for the day from Whitby, and he had just won his first championship. He was playing an ordinary game and I only saw one or two shots, including his drive to the first hole. Two memories vividly remain. One was that he was wearing trousers and that from that day to this I have never seen him play except in knickerbockers, an attire which he first made fashionable amongst his brother professionals. The other is that his style seemed, as had Taylor's on a first view, entirely unique. The club appeared, contrary to all orthodox teaching, to be lifted up so very straight. Even now, when I have seen him play hundreds and hundreds of shots, I cannot quite get it out of my head that he did in those early days take up the club a little more abruptly than he did later. The ball flew away very high, with an astonishing ease, and he made the game look more magical and unattainable than anyone I had ever seen. For that matter, I think he does so still. In view of later events it is curious to recall that a good local amateur, Mr. Broadwood, who was playing with him, talked then of his putting as the most heartbreaking part of his game, and said that he holed everything. I only saw one putt and that he missed.

It must have been a year later that there came the first vision of the third member of the Triumvirate, who had hardly then attained that position. This was at Penarth, where there was a Welsh championship meeting, and Taylor and Herd were to play an exhibition match. Taylor could not come; at the last moment Braid was sent for to take his place and arrived late the night before. I remember that he did in his youthful energy what I feel sure he has not done for a long time now; he went out early after breakfast to have a look at the course and play some practice shots. His enemy, by the way, had come a whole day early and played a couple of rounds. I have almost entirely forgotten the Penarth course, and the shots I played on it myself; the one thing I can vaguely remember is the look of the first hole and of Braid hitting those shots towards it. Here was something much more in the manner that one had been brought up to believe orthodox, but with an added power; save for Mr. Edward Blackwell, with whom I had once had the honor of playing, I had never seen anyone hit so malignantly hard at the ball before. Mr. Hutchinson's phrase about his "divine fury" seemed perfectly apposite. One imagined that there was a greater chance of some error on an heroic scale than in the case of Taylor and Vardon, and so indeed there was, but I remember no noble hooks that day, nothing but a short putt or two missed when he had a winning lead so that Herd crept a little nearer to him.

From the time when I was at Cambridge till I sold my wig in 1908, my golfing education was neglected for, if I may so term it, my legal one. I played all the golf I could, which was a good deal, but watched hardly any. Therefore I never—sad to say—saw Vardon in his most dominating era, nor the great foursome match over four different courses in which he and Taylor crushed Braid and Herd, chiefly through one terrific landslide of holes at Troon. However, in the end I managed to see each of the three win two championships, Braid at Prestwick and St. Andrews in 1908 and 1910, Taylor at Deal and Hoylake, 1909 and 1913, Vardon at Sandwich and Prestwick, 1911 and 1914. I suppose the most exciting was in 1914 when Vardon and Taylor, leading the field, were drawn together on the last day, and the whole of the West of Scotland was apparently moved with a desire to watch them. Braid, too, played his part on that occasion, for had he not designed the bunker almost in the middle of the fairway at the fourth hole? And was it not fear of that bunker that drove Taylor too much to the right into the other one by the Pow Burn, so that he took a seven? No wonder J.H. said that the man who made that bunker should be buried in it with a niblick through his heart. Yes, that was a tremendous occasion, and Braid's golf in 1908—291 with an eight in it at the Cardinal—was incredibly brilliant; and Vardon's driving when

Courtesy United States Golf Association

In the history of sport a "stunning upset" often heralds a new era. Such was the case of Francis Ouimet when he won the 1913 U.S. Open title, aided by his now famous caddie, Eddie Lowery, by defeating Britain's great champions Harry Vardon and Ted Ray. Ouimet's win signaled American golf's coming of age.

he beat Massy in playing off the tie at Sandwich was, I think, the most beautiful display of wooden club hitting I ever saw; but for sheer thrilling quality give me Taylor at Hoylake in 1913. There was no great excitement since, after qualifying by the skin of his teeth, he won by strokes and strokes; but I have seen nothing else in golf which so stirred me and made me want to cry. The wind and the rain were terrific, but not so terrific as Taylor, with his cap pulled down, buffeting his way through them. There are always one or two strokes which stick faster in the memory than any others, and I noticed the other day that my friend Mr. Macfarlane recalled just the one that I should choose. It was the second shot played with a cleek to the Briars hole in the very teeth of the storm. I can still see Taylor standing on rocklike feet, glued flat on the turf, watching that ball as it whizzes over the two cross bunkers straight for the green. There never was such a cleek shot; there never will be such another as long as the world stands.

It is surely a curious fact that, though these three players dominated golf for so long, and the golfer is essentially an imitative animal, no one of them has been the founder of a school. They made people play better by having to live up to their standard, but they did not make people play like them. Here are three strongly marked and characteristic styles to choose from, and yet where are their imitators? Vardon had one, to be sure, in Mr. A.C. Lincoln, an excellent player who belonged to Totteridge; he had at any rate many of the Vardonian mannerisms and a strong superficial likeness. There is George Duncan, too, with a natural talent for mimicry; he remodeled the swing he had learned in Scotland after he first saw the master. Imagine Duncan slowed down and there is much of Vardon. Beyond those two, I can think of no one in the least like him. It is much the same with Taylor. His two sons, J.H., Jr. and Leslie, have something of the tricks of the backswing, but nobody has got the flat-footed hit and the little grunt that goes with it. Braid, with that strange combination of a portentous gravity and a sudden, furious lash, seems the most impossible model of all. I know no one who has even copied his waggle, with that little menacing shake of the clubhead in the middle of it. Each of the three was so unlike the other two that the world hesitated which model to take and ended by taking none. American players look as if they had all been cast in one admirable mold. Ours look as if they came out of innumerable different ones, and as if in nearly every mold there had been some flaw. It was part of the fascination of the Triumvirate that each was extraordinarily individual, but now it seems almost a pity for British golf. If only just one of them could have been easier to imitate! In other respects, of course, they did all three of them leave a model which could be imitated. By all the good golfing qualities of courage and sticking power and chivalry, by their modesty and dignity and self-respect, they helped to make the professional golfer a very different person from what he was when they first came on the scene. Their influence as human beings has been as remarkable as their achievements as golfers.

Pine Valley: Golf's American Shrine

by JOE SCHWENDEMAN

Pine Valley is a unique creation, the apex of penal course design. It yields without too much trouble to the superior player, but the high handicapper will find it purgatorial. Joe Schwendeman's award-winning and delightful account of the Pine Valley mystique explains why.

A few years ago a number of elderly gentlemen from several nations gathered at Pine Valley Golf Club to compete in a tournament that was planned to promote goodwill among men. One of the players, an Englishmen, strode briskly from the clubhouse toward the first tee and turned to look down the fairway. An expression of amazement froze his face.

Stretching before him for some 170 yards was a jumble of sand and underbrush that appeared to be more like the untamed seaside of Scotland than a parcel of the Garden State of the colonies. Beyond the sandy wastes was a lush fairway, closely protected on each side by tall pines. The fairway turned right and disappeared between the trees. There was nothing else in sight.

In one quick glance, the eager golfer saw a beautiful but forbidding hole and he reacted like many an English visitor to this country. He exclaimed: "By Jove, where are all the Indians?"

No one goes to Pine Valley unacquainted, but nearly everybody is surprised. There is no other golf course in the world just like the spread at Clementon, New Jersey. Its unusual design and large, baffling greens have earned for Pine Valley a subtitle: the world's toughest golf course. It is a label that stands without virtual dispute.

Only fifteen miles southeast of Philadelphia's City Hall, Pine Valley is the Mount Everest of golf. Its lofty rating would be sufficient enough to make the course distinctive, but the fifty-four-year-old layout is more than golf's most demanding challenge.

Pine Valley is a living monument to the Philadelphian who conceived it and almost single-handedly started to build it. It is a shrine to the spirit of the game. The condition of its fairways and greens has long been the standard of comparison for our clubs. It is a borough with its own police and fire departments, its own political office-holders. It is, horticulturally, one of the most unusual areas in the East. It is one of the last havens of masculinity. And membership at Pine Valley is a status that only 700 possess.

To thousands of new golfers in Greater Philadelphia, who do not have access through the fence-enclosed, 700-acre property, the question is, what makes Pine Valley tough? Like playing a

68

round there, it is not a question easily answered.

On paper Pine Valley's 6,442 yards, 6,749 from the back tees, are not intimidating. Its par, thirty-five–thirty-five—seventy, sounds rigid and it is. Significantly, its course rating is seventy-three. It is not incorrect to say that par is one of golf's most elusive figures because the course was open twenty-five years before the standard was bettered. Pro Craig Wood turned the trick with a sixty-nine on October 29, 1938.

Pine Valley's unbending backbone is its basic design which George A. Crump visioned before he began transforming the wild pine lands in 1912. Crump, who sold his Philadelphia hotel interests and lived in a tent on the property for six months before a small home was built, leveled only enough land to build the kind of course he wanted. Crump once said he stopped counting after hauling out 22,000 tree stumps.

Although he was a good golfer, Crump was not an engineer, and, after designing and constructing five holes, he secured the services of H.S. Colt, an English architect whose ideas of rugged courses matched those of the Philadelphian. Colt made few changes in Crump's overall design. When he died, January 24, 1918, Crump had fourteen holes in play, with the other four ready to be opened that fall. He had spent $250,000 of his own fortune on the course.

In the cleared avenues between the pines, Crump built islands of green for tees, fairways and greens just as the original links of Scotland had been formed by nature. Between these fragments of turf, he left vast natural stretches of sand, a creek or a pond. These verdant islands, and the arid areas between them, make Pine Valley what it is today.

On many courses a golfer keeps an eye on the sand traps—and if he plays Merion Golf Club he soon learns there are 120 bunkers on the Ardmore, Pennsylvania, track—but at Pine Valley the reverse is true. It's one sprawling sand trap and the golfer counts the links of green.

"Pine Valley's not so tough," said Arnold Palmer, with a wry smile, recently, "if you can hit the ball straight, keep it out of the sand, and putt reasonably well." Some years ago when Palmer was single he played Pine Valley with friends and

scored an unofficial sixty-eight. The score wasn't important, but the outcome was. He picked up $800 in bets and bought an engagement ring for Winnie Walzer, of Coopersburg, Pennsylvania.

A golfer who can keep his drives on line and airborne for at least 175 yards has an advantage over a stronger but more erratic hitter because he can reach all fairways on the driving holes. If he is lucky enough to get on the fairway, then he faces a second shot which must carry more sand or water to reach greens that appear to have as many dips as potato chips.

Fairways were designed so that no two are alike and no two are parallel. They may be as wide as fifty yards in some places, but flat lies are the reward of the control artists or the lucky. As the green is approached on par fives, the fairways narrow.

Pine Valley has a distinction which adds to the woes of all but the consistently straight hitters. The club's scorecard spells it out so briefly that it sounds harmless: "All sand is playable as a hazard."

All areas but the fairways, therefore, come under that section of the rules of golf which prevent one from improving his lie. Though littered with a healthy growth of scrub pines, Scotch broom and an assortment of underbrush, the golfer must play the ball as it lies.

This can be testy to even the most skilled shotmaker. Moreover, this floor of an ancient ocean has a modern characteristic that compounds a golfer's headaches—footprints. Unlike other clubs, Pine Valley does not ask its members to rake the sand.

On the contrary, rakes are conspicuously missing and the sand is as pockmarked as the moon. And there are other signs of a golfer's shame—gouges where he was unable to pick the ball cleanly off the sand. Somehow footprints and gashes seem to attract golf balls like magnets.

Henry McQuiston, Bala Golf Club's pro, said of Pine Valley's sand: "Even if you take an unplayable lie penalty and move the ball two club lengths, you can have no shot . . . there is that much stuff growing all around. Usually you have to play out from where you are and sometimes that means hitting sideways. It's easy to run up your score . . . if you count every stroke."

Pine Valley's greens are rated among golfdom's best in design, trueness of line, and growth. They average 9,000 square feet with the eighteenth being the largest at 15,000 square feet and the eighth the smallest at 3,000. Hitting an approach close to the pin is vital if the golfer wishes to avoid three-putting. Covered with a thick growth of German bent, the greens hold a well-struck shot. They putt true, but it is not unusual to see a ball roll off the green because of bold contours.

Championship-rated courses, no matter where they are located, have one thing in common: They are so designed that a golfer swings every club in his bag during a typical round. Pine Valley fits into this classic mold and sports the added distinction of having four superb parthree holes.

Each of the Clementon par threes presents the golfer with the necessity of making a different type shot than he did on the last short hole. The targets vary in shape and topography. One, the tremendous 217-yard fifth, also has been immortalized in verse.

It occurred during the 1936 Walker Cup matches, the only major championship to be played there. That meeting between the best amateurs of the United States against their British counterparts resulted in a 9–0 victory for the Americans. Both teams had difficulty mastering the course, and the fifth was particularly hard on the players.

Jack McLean, of Scotland, and Charlie Yates, of Atlanta, got together one evening and composed the following doggerel with the fifth in mind:

We think that we shall never see
A tougher course than Pine Valley.
Trees and traps wherever we go
And clumps of earth flying through the air.
This course was made for you and me,
But only God can make a THREE.

Former U.S. Open champion Gene Littler probably agrees, for during a television match at Pine Valley nearly four years ago, Gene took a seven on the fifth.

The club learned a lesson from the '36 Walker Cup competition: That the layout is not suitable for handling galleries. Consequently, it has not played host to any tournaments since. And now, according to club rules, only 100 golfers may play in a single day. But this has not stopped the spread of its fame or dimmed men's desire to play there.

Golfers are a gregarious lot and while Pine Valley maintains a hard-to-crack exclusiveness, men whet the playing appetite of others by telling of their combat with the Jersey devil. Pine Valley has inspired more stories and quips than perhaps a dozen other courses combined.

One of the earliest one-liners, dating back to the club's first decade, has been repeated countless times and applied to holes all over the golf world. An awestruck newcomer finally reached the seventh tee and stared out at the par five. He asked meekly: "Do you play this or photograph it?" The seventh has a Saharalike tract between its first and second fairway links that is called Hell's Half-Acre. Most everyone who tries to hit a ball out of this disaster area agrees that both the adjective and measurement are conservative.

Variety is endless at Pine Valley, adding to a golfer's pleasure and/or his problems. No two tees turn to the same point of the compass and almost every one offers a scenic view that resembles any place but suburban Philadelphia. There are no unnatural hazards, no out-of-bounds and no hidden bunkers. Every bit of trouble is alarmingly in view, just as Mother Nature, in her most devilish mood, might have placed it.

The challenge of the course is a lure that only golfers can understand if not explain. It must have taxed Jack Nicklaus's ability to explain to the utmost when he interrupted his honeymoon to play at Pine Valley. Since club rules bar women from the clubhouse, Jack's bride of a few days had to sit in their car while her husband scored a seventy-four. Women are not allowed on the course except Sundays after noon.

To those who have never played at "the Valley," as it is referred to by the in-golfers, the course might sound like an outdoor penal institution. In an earlier era it was called just that by sportswriters of the day. But Pine Valley's members rarely speak of their course in any terms other than with respect and affection.

"We believe Pine Valley is the toughest course in the world," said club president John Arthur Brown the other day. Then Mr. Pine Valley added the inevitable: "It's tough but fair. It's the kind of course that rewards a good shot but penalizes a poor one. It's a rugged course and that's exactly the way golf courses should be."

It is precisely the tough-but-fair qualities that have made Pine Valley a renowned course, and it is a rare collection of great golf holes that does not include at least one from Clementon. Most frequently named are the second, third, fifth, seventh, thirteenth, fifteenth and eighteenth.

Robert Trent Jones, recognized as today's leading golf course architect, said not long ago: "Pine Valley is replete with classic golf holes, great in the sense that they would be magnificent holes even without its horrifying footprinted sandy wastes." For the record, Jones rates ten Pine Valley holes as "great," five "outstanding" and two "good." Most clubs are proud to have an "outstanding" hole among its eighteen.

Although power hitters have dominated the game since World War II, forcing many clubs to change holes to keep pace with the sluggers, Pine Valley has withstood the years with little change. It is another testimony to its greatness that the course which Crump laid out in 1912 has made only minor modifications since its beginnings.

Two new tees have been built in the last three years, adding forty yards to the twelfth hole and eighteen yards to the fourteenth. Brown recalls playing with Sam Snead some years back and watching the pro drive over the twelfth green. Now the added yardage has made the twelfth into a 330-yarder and the second shot has assumed greater emphasis.

Brown expressed an opinion recently which might surprise some of today's golfers, to say nothing of the Walker Cuppers of '36 and the players of Chick Evans's era. It was in 1916 that Evans, one of golf's biggest-winning amateurs,

played his first round at Clementon and immediately called Pine Valley "the greatest golf course in the world."

Brown was going over the course and said: "Pine Valley is tougher now than when it was built. The reason? Because it has matured so well. The natural growth down there is just marvelous and this makes it play harder. We have more trees and bushes now than at any time in the club's history."

Brown knows Pine Valley better than anyone. An eighty-two-year-old Philadelphia attorney, he has been a Pine Valley member since 1916, its president since 1929. Brown is more than a president, he is a one-man operating committee and nothing happens at the club or on the course that does not bear his approval. According to Pine Valley's members, Brown has made Pine Valley golf's American shrine, just as St. Andrews is considered hallowed ground abroad.

Even this aspect of the club provokes respect among golfers that is best expressed for chuckles. Onetime sportswriter Ed Sullivan once said: "Pine Valley is the shrine of American golf because so many golfers are buried there."

Of course, this is not true though some members have requested that their ashes be spread over the course. Others have remembered the club in their wills.

A New York physician, who had spent many pleasant weekends at Pine Valley and particularly at the beautiful fourteenth, left a will that directed his executor to erect a bench-monument on the fourteenth tee, suitably inscribed to the memory of his constant failure to reach the green. The club's board respectfully denied the request. It was fearful of starting a series of monuments commemorating the unsuccessful play of deceased members.

The fourteenth—a lovely, 167-yard "drop" hole—is statistically noteworthy. In spite of all the longer and more difficult holes on the course, the fourteenth is where the highest number of strokes were taken by one player. The late John Brookes, a club member who also was a former president of Burning Tree Country Club in Washington, once took forty-four strokes on the fourteenth.

Pine Valley's resistance to assaults on par is best told by a few printed lines on a big wooden shield that hangs in the clubhouse. It shows that par was equaled for the first time August 19, 1922, by member George V. Rotan. It stood as a course record until Craig Wood scored his sixty-nine in 1938, and a year later pro Ed Dudley, then of Philadelphia Country Club, lowered that figure by a stroke.

Dudley's sixty-eight seemed to be an unassailable figure, but on July 8, 1961, George Rowbotham scored an amazing sixty-seven. The former city champion, now of Palm Beach Gardens, Florida, scored birds on the fourth, tenth, eleventh and sixteenth holes.

"All I can remember now of that round," said Rowbotham on the phone the other day, "is a three-foot putt I had for a bird on the fourteenth. I remember that because I three-putted it for a bogey!"

Before World War II, Pine Valley members held a series of pro-amateur events to which the country's leading professionals were invited. The field was dotted with the names of Byron Nelson, Sam Snead, Gene Sarazen, Ben Hogan, Vic Ghezzi, Tom Armour and others. In more than 450 rounds played by the pros over a number of years, only Wood and Dudley cracked par.

No mention of course records is made without retelling the start made by J. Wood Platt. Woodie was a seven-time winner of the Philadelphia amateur title and one of the top half-dozen players ever produced there. One day he walked out on the Clementon course and started with a birdie three on the first. On the difficult second he scored an eagle two. The third is a 172-yard three and he scored a hole-in-one there. The fourth was completed with a birdie three.

The fourth green is aside the clubhouse and the friendly confines of the building are only a few steps off the path to the fifth tee. Woodie and his friends felt the need to celebrate such an amazing start. Unfortunately for golf, Woodie and his friends never left the clubhouse until long after dark.

Another kind of round is still another criterion of Pine Valley. In 1950, Bryan Field, then vice-president and general manager of Delaware Park, was challenged to play golf again. It had been twenty years since he was on a course and someone bet he couldn't break 200 at Pine Valley. For eighteen holes, that is. To make the round interesting, the sum of $2,000 was posted, but Bryan said that was pennies compared to all the side bets.

Field borrowed clubs and a pair of golf shoes from his son, Tom. Two pairs of heavy socks filled out the shoes, but Bryan couldn't round out his time-withered game as easily. Pars eluded him all the way around, but he stunned the small gallery with bogeys on the third and seventeenth. His worst hole was the par-four eleventh where he took twelve.

"Never mind, sir," said the caddie, "the captain of the British Ryder Cup team once took a seventeen here."

On the eighteenth, Field bucketed a three-footer to end the two-hour fifty-minute ordeal. His score read seventy-three–seventy-five—148! He had won and, ever the horseman, Bryan said: "Take a quick look and see if I've been claimed."

Monterey: How I Was Seduced by a Peninsula

by CAL BROWN

For many of his golf-writing years Cal Brown roamed America compiling Golf Digest's *list of 100 greatest courses. After seeing them all, Brown set down these thoughts on his favorite golf spot, the Monterey Peninsula.*

IN the Bible it says that God made the world in six days and on the seventh, rested. But I think that on the seventh day he created the Monterey peninsula. There cannot be another place on earth quite like it, nor another place that has three golf courses of such quality in so small a space.

It is as though every thundering emotion, every subtle line had been withheld from the rest of creation and then dumped in this one place to test our understanding of the superlative. One's response to this angular chunk of land, shaped like the snout of a rhinoceros and jutting into the Pacific about ninety miles south of San Francisco, is instant and elemental. Even on a gray, overcast day or during a winter storm, it is compelling and seductive.

Hills and craggy bluffs tumble into the sea which ebbs and crashes against copper-brown rocks, casting huge white plumes and mist into the air above dozing seals and an occasional solitary beachcomber. Gray-boled and winter-green cypress trees cling to the soil in clumps or in stark individuality, bent and twisted by the wind and spray. Here and there the headland splashes down into uneven, white-faced dunes. Surmounting everything is a sense of quiet, a curious intimation of settled spirit on the raging coast.

Here are three of the world's greatest golf courses, and how could they be otherwise. Their names alone stir the juices—Pebble Beach, legendary, rugged and for all of its fame still a bridesmaid to U.S. Open competition; Cypress Point, shy and mysterious, splendidly proportioned and artful mistress; and Spyglass Hill, diabolical, controversial and maddening in its newness.

Within 5,200 acres of private land known as the Del Monte Forest, the late Samuel F.B. Morse founded and developed some of the most expensive real estate and one of the most magnificent resorts in the world. The Del Monte property is encircled by a seventeen-mile drive over which visitors may travel, at three dollars per car. No overnight camping is permitted, and no plant or animal may be "disturbed, injured or removed." Deer roam freely through the forest and across the golf courses.

There are signs of stress on this priceless plot of ground. One hears grumbling about pol-

73

The gnarled cypress trees of the Monterey Peninsula stand sentinel along the golfer's way.

lution in Monterey Bay, and about segregation in public accommodations (including golf courses). Someone at Del Monte has allowed a house to be built behind the fifth green at Spyglass Hill which, while architecturally impressive, intrudes on the natural beauty of the hole. But with few such exceptions, there is little to remind one that life is anything but a succession of aesthetic fulfillments and magnificent golf holes.

PEBBLE BEACH—Rugged

"It is wicked to think of making this course much tougher than it is already, but for the 1972 Open, they will, and God help the pros."

Although the Bing Crosby National Pro-Am is held on all three of Monterey's great courses,

people are most familiar with Pebble Beach, where play is seen on television, even though obscured, at times, by the rain and fog that regularly visit the peninsula.

Like many of our greatest courses, Pebble Beach was designed by amateurs. Jack Neville and Douglas Grant, both California amateur champions, laid out the 6,777-yard course in 1919. It has held three national amateur championships, the first in 1929. That was the year Johnny Goodman, then an unknown, came out from Omaha to beat Bobby Jones in the first round. The winner was unheralded Harrison Johnston of Minnesota, who bested a field that included Francis Ouimet, Chick Evans, Lawson Little, Chandler Egan and Cyril Tolley. In 1947 the cast included Dick Chapman, Bud Ward, Smiley Quick, Bob Rosburg and Frank Stranahan, but the winner was Skee Riegel who walked like a fighter and played like a machine, smoking two packs of cigarettes per round, to beat Johnny Dawson in the finals. In 1961, Jack Nicklaus took the second of his amateur crowns here, beating Dudley Wysong eight and six in the final.

Pebble Beach opens like a lamb, with four easy, very ordinary holes. The fifth is a short, quick thrust up through a sliver of light between the trees and then, suddenly, you are upon the ocean riding two terrifying shots along the crest of a massive bluff to the sixth green. To the right, nothing but emptiness and, far below, thrashing surf and rocks.

The sixth hole, a 515-yard par five that Byron Nelson thinks is the toughest hole on the course, begins a stretch of five of the most spectacular holes in golf, three of them on a narrow; craggy split that overhangs the ocean. The seventh is a tiny, 120-yard downhill pitch that looks almost like a miniature golf hole. But when the wind blows, it can require a solid four-iron into the gale. The eighth is a marvel, one of the great two-shotters in the world. After a blind tee shot to a plateau, you are faced with hitting 180 yards over a sheer cliff, across a chasm that resembles a shark's maw and to a green that is pitched into a depression and completely surrounded by bunkers.

The ninth stretches 450 yards along the ocean, its right margin eaten away by the surf. When the wind is up, the biggest hitters cannot get home even with two wood shots. During the 1963 Crosby, Dale Douglass took nineteen blows here after landing on the steep bank, an even worse place to be than the rocky beach below.

There are many who believe the inland stretch from eleven through sixteen is inferior and not at all in keeping with the hair-raising ocean holes. This is only partially true. Certainly eleven and twelve are routine holes, but thirteen, a straightaway par four of 400 yards, is perhaps the most underrated hole on the course. The second shot must fly true to avoid bunkers and trees guarding the green.

The fourteenth is a marvelously deft par five that curls away from the sea to the right and has been the scene of a few miserable encounters.

Here Arnold Palmer, who has never won the Crosby, came a cropper in 1964. In going for the green on his second shot, Palmer hit a tree on the right and went out of bounds twice. He made nine on the hole and dropped from contention. The next day, a storm knocked the tree down.

The seventeenth, a par three surrounded by sand and ocean, looks more beatable in real life than it appears on television—until you play it. The eighteenth, a journey that ends happily only after three very strong shots and two good putts, is among the most ballyhooed finishing holes in golf, and quite rightly.

In 1972 Pebble Beach will finally get the U.S. Open, which incidentally will be the first time in history the blue-blooded event has been held on a nonprivate course. It is wicked to think of anyone making the course much tougher than it is, but change it the U.S. Golf Association will. It is doubtful that anyone will break Billy Casper's course record of sixty-five. Remodeling will be completed by June of this year, and then the brave can play the course as it will look for the Open.

SPYGLASS HILL—Maddening

"Not long ago two doctors started out with three dozen golf balls. They had to send the caddie in for a new supply after six holes."

Spyglass Hill is a Robert Trent Jones layout that opened in 1966 and ever since has been the target of stronger words than Spiro Agnew at a gathering of New York Republicans. Most of the abuse comes from touring pros, who are not accustomed to shooting in the eighties.

Spyglass, in its youthful striving for greatness, is too new to be finally judged. Several things about it are evident, though. It is ruthlessly tough and on windy days almost impossible. In 1970 it was rated at 76.1 from the back tees (6,972 yards) but it has never been played in competition over its full length.

The course record is seventy, two under par, made by Forrest Fezler, a California amateur who played the ball "as it lies." The best professional score in competition was also seventy, made by Bob Murphy in the 1968 Crosby. But he played from the middle tees (6,609 yards, which carries a rating of 74.1), and was improving his lies.

"People can't believe it's so tough," chortles Spyglass Hill's home professional, Frank Thacker. "The first five holes are more a case of fright than anything else." The first hole sweeps 604 yards through the pines down to the ocean, and the next four holes are played on the dunes from one island of grass to the next. The second, though a lay-up hole, is nevertheless an appealing two-shotter that wants a thoughtful golfer and is, for the medium hitter, a fearsome journey past waist-high spikes of pampas grass. The third and fifth are sand locked par threes sandwiched around the par-four fourth, a partially blind hole.

These psychological thrillers are among the easier holes. Once the course turns inland it gets narrower and longer, and your breath and shoulder turn get shorter. Spyglass Hill's greens are huge, and you can three-putt all day long. Putts of 150 feet are possible. A lot of the criticism of the course centers around the greens, which have since been remodeled. The first time the course was used in the Crosby, on the fourteenth hole, a gem of a par five with an angled green perched on the left above a pond, one of the contestants putted off the green and into the water. On the same green, Jack Nicklaus once four-putted from fourteen feet.

Is Spyglass tougher than Pebble Beach? Probably. Not long ago two doctors teed off at Spyglass Hill with three dozen golf balls between them and had to send the caddie in for a new supply after six holes. But though Spyglass is rated a stroke tougher, it lacks the wild, undisciplined spirit of Pebble Beach. Spyglass is a more refined article, with a harder, more sculptured look than either of the other two courses here. Jones was not given the kind of elemental terrain with which to work that is to be found at Pebble and Cypress yet he has made a great deal of what he was given. One suspects that it is a course whose character is exposed more deeply the more it is played.

CYPRESS POINT—Artful

"By the time you reach the sixth hole you are caught up in the pure joy of the place. You feel that each shot you face is just what you always knew golf should be."

"If I were condemned to play only one course for the rest of my life, I would unhesitatingly pick Cypress Point."

So says Joe Dey, former executive director of USGA and commissioner of the PGA Tour. Dey, no mean judge of courses, is not alone in this choice. Golfers fortunate enough to play this little masterpiece more often than not come away feeling that Cypress Point is more to play than any other on the peninsula.

Its length alone—6,464 yards—makes it the easiest of the three Crosby courses. Still, the course record is the same as at Pebble Beach, sixty-five, set by Bill Nary at the 1949 Crosby. Ben Hogan shot the course in sixty-three during a practice round in 1947 for the unofficial mark.

The course was conceived in 1926 by Marion Hollins, the women's national amateur champion of 1921, and Roger Lapham, who was president of the California Golf Association and a member of the USGA executive committee. They bought property from Del Monte and commissioned Alister Mackenzie to design the course. Mackenzie, a Scot and former doctor in the British Army, later did the Augusta National course in Georgia with Bobby Jones.

Cypress is strictly a golf club, and its members *golfers*. There are no pools, tennis courts or other distractions. Nonmembers are not permitted in the house, even during the Crosby tournament. For years, the pros had to change their shoes outside. No separate room has been added for this purpose. The use of golf carts is discouraged as are other modern frills. The caddies here—many having plied the trade for forty years—are considered by some visitors the best in the world. When you tee it up at Cypress Point, the game is on.

The first hole is a lazy dogleg to the right and, at 407 yards, long enough to loosen the muscles. Until recently the tee shot had to negotiate an old, dead pine tree that blew down in a storm and had been called "Joe DiMaggio"—it caught everything. The second is a properly menacing par five of 544 yards that angles left and thus courts the gambling tee shot. The third is a slender one-shot hole, no more than a middle iron, the fourth a shortish par four that carries you deep into the woods past little bands of deer and half a dozen beautifully placed bunkers. The fifth, a short par five, 490 yards, swoops left abruptly up a hill literally covered with bunkers to a tiny green on top.

By the time you reach the sixth hole you are caught up in the pure joy of the place. You feel that every shot is just what you always knew golf should be. Soon you are heading toward the distant ocean over the rugged dunes from holes eight through thirteen. At fifteen, a mere 139 yards, you play across a narrow gorge where the water boils angrily as it cuts its way into the cliff. The ball must reach the putting surface, for there are trees, sand and clutching ice plant all around. The ice plant, thick, fleshy stuff, is like trying to escape from a vat of marshmallow.

Then comes the sixteenth, which has been called the ultimate test of golfing courage. From the back tees it is 233 yards of carry across the Pacific to a large green on the tip of the point. The average golfer must lay up short to the fairway on the left and then pitch to the green. Only on windless days do the pros try for it. The late Porky Oliver made sixteen after going in the water four times, and Henry Ransom picked up after sixteen attempts to move his shot from the beach up the sheer cliff to the green. Another

pro, Hans Merrill, has the all-time record of nineteen. He made it all on the same ball, going from ice plant to ice plant for nearly half an hour.

The seventeenth is another heroic hole, a par four that runs along the cliff for 375 yards to a green that lurks behind a fat, sprawling cypress tree. The tee, set next to the sixteenth green on the point, looks into the cliff and you can see as much of the barrier as you like. Once in the fairway you must play either left or right of the tree and stop the ball very quickly. You can easily hit over it—and just as easily into it. Jimmy Demaret once played this hole in the wind by hitting two drives; he aimed the second out over the ocean and let it blow back.

After the excitement of the ocean holes, the eighteenth is a soft dissolve swinging gently up through scattered trees to a flagstick silhouetted against the sky next to the clubhouse, of simple Spanish California style that looks so natural on the site it seems to have grown there among the cypress trees.

Opinion about a golf course can be a fragile thing. But taken all as a piece, the Monterey Peninsula and its three courses are something to behold. There is enough variety to sate the most demanding golfing spirit. It is a special place where the tendons and mind can meet on equal terms. In fact, if heaven isn't like Pebble Beach, I won't be going.

Sam Snead with Hair

by DAN JENKINS

In The Dogged Victims of Inexorable Fate *one of golf's wittiest and most perceptive writers,* Sports Illustrated's *Dan Jenkins, has collected his best stories, which include this portrait of life on the pro tour during the colorful decade of the thirties.*

Louise, we've got to hide this $600 before we hit the road. Since we're rich, we're bound to get robbed. But if we hide it, maybe they won't get it all.
— BYRON NELSON
to his wife after winning his first big check in the thirties

TO the hordes of people who feel that Arnold Palmer invented golf on television around, oh, 1960, and who no doubt think the game is played over just four holes, from the fifteenth—where Jim McKay is—through the eighteenth—where Chris Schenkel is—the professional tour probably looks colorful today. Sure it does. After all, there goes Arnold again, streaking back to Latrobe for the evening in his twin-booster, partly deductible rocket ship *PGA One.* And there is Billy Casper eating baked buffalo tongue, or sea-lentil casserole, or whatever, for his diet and allergies. And there's Doug Sanders in his latest lemon-lime ensemble, a

cluster of bell-bottomed lovelies foraging after him. And here comes Lionel Hebert on his way to the cocktail lounge to work his handicap down from eight to six on the trumpet. Jack Nicklaus isn't around this week, they say. He's off in Addis Ababa filming a TV series with the president of the United States, the Soviet premier, the shiek of Kuwait and eight former fraternity brothers from Ohio State. But all he does is win anyhow. This tour is splashed with color without him, boy. You look down that list of entries in our $500,000 Lucky Desert Cajun Festival and you'll see more excitement than the linoleum salesmen caused when the waiter brought the dinner check.

Well, perhaps not to some of us. The sixties had their giddy moments, of course, give or take a Julius Finsteraaron. But there is another period in the history of golf that keeps coming back to haunt those who remember the cleek with a certain fondness. The thirties. Maybe you have to be a little overaged for the discotheques to appreciate that decade. It would help if you could remember who Uncle Fletcher was on *Vic and Sade,* or if you could still set *One Man's Family* defensively: Paul's in the library, Clifford and Claudia are down on the seawall and Hank and Pinky are up at the Sky Ranch, right? If you can handle that and also identify a Russ Columbo, a Filipino

Twirler, a black cow, a Ken Maynard, a sinking of the *Panay* and a Ky Laffoon—well, then. You certainly know that anyone who thinks the pro tour is fun now would have gone right out of his Spalding Dot in the thirties.

For it was the thirties that gave us Sam Snead with hair, right there on his head, parted on the left, and a brooding runt in a snapbrim hat and a wild hook: Ben Hogan. It was the thirties that gave us Jimmy Demaret's pink shoes and polka-dot slacks—outfits that would make Doug Sanders look like a Bond's window today. It was the thirties that gave us Lloyd Mangrum's mustache, Dutch Harrison's drawl, and Ky Laffoon anointing the greens with tobacco juice. It was the thirties that gave us Byron Nelson throwing up between his dazzling rounds, Jug McSpaden's sun goggles, Horton Smith's ominous squint, Jimmy Thomson's booming tee shots, the sand wedge and steel shafts. It was an era in which Ruby Keeler and Dick Powell in their starched sailor suits couldn't do the Big Apple much better than Joan and Paul Runyon, or Emma and Harry Cooper, or Mabel and Frank Walsh. It was a decade with more individuals in professional golf than there were hominy wagons on the streets. And if the pro couldn't make the most of the spirit and hilarity of these struggling times, and if the fan couldn't enjoy them, then the pro could go back to raking cottonseed-hull greens, and the fan could go back to his radio serials.

One of the things that made it special is that golf, looking back on it, still belonged to the amateurs in the early thirties, to aristocratic young men with hyphenated names, blonde sisters and portraits of whaling skippers over their fireplaces. A pro was anyone who had caddied beyond the age of fourteen, who knew how to run a mowing machine, who could wrap leather grips and who frequently had to take his meals in the kitchen of a country club. If he happened to be personable and didn't look *too* Italian, he might be very fortunate. He could give a few fifty-cent lessons each week to some kindly gentleman who owned a railroad or the state of New Jersey. Or if the pro looked like he could really play, a kindly gentleman might lend him $300 to go out and see what this tour was all about, what

those chaps Tommy Hagen and Walter Armour were up to.

The exact date is not recorded when people first realized that a pro could make a niblick back up with more spin than an amateur, but it occurred somewhere in the thirties. At about the same time Walter Hagen was finally about to convince everyone that you could let a pro in the front door of your club and he wouldn't steal the crystal. Hagen had been working at it for a long time—outdressing, outspending and outtraveling the rich. These two circumstances began to combine in the years of the Depression, and this is what actually led America into today's age of the alligator shoe. This was the beginning of the big-money tour that has put Conni Venturi in Balenciagas, made Dave Marr a bon vivant along 52nd Street, transformed Arnold Palmer into a permanent, floating, corporate crap game and made a worldly, theorizing, hardcover author out of every ex-caddie who can chip from sand.

One of the more obvious results of this progress is that going on the tour now is as easy as getting into the University of Houston if you can shoot sixty-five. You birdie four holes in a row at Bending Wedge Country Club and some automobile dealer with a coat of arms on his blazer will step up and hand you $12,000, plus an air travel card. A day later, you're standing on a putting green near Bert Yancey. You're on the tour. To say it was somewhat more of an adventure in the thirties would be like saying Valerie Hogan has seen a clubhouse veranda or two.

You could get to the tour, all right, by hitchhiking or riding a freight if necessary. But to *stay* there, that was the challenge. To put enough chuckburgers down your neck to fend off the hunger from Flagstaff to West Palm. If you shot a seventy-four in the first round somewhere, forget it. Fifteenth place was the last pay spot in any tournament, and of the thirty to forty regulars who were out there trying to beat you Ben Hogan was the least known. "We used to figure $160 a week was the break-even figure," Byron Nelson remembers. So if you shot seventy-four you loaded it and yourself into somebody's Graham-Paige or Essex and drove until the connecting rod made a double bogey. Air travel? That

Courtesy Golf Magazine

Most people think that the only reason Sam Snead wears his familiar hat is to camouflage his baldness. The truth is that Snead always wore something on his head, even in the early days of touring and exhibitions when he entertained people with his fluid swing.

was fantasy, something you saw in the movies for a dime. Air travel was for Noah Beery, Jr., up there flying the mail in the sleet without any de-icers, while Jean Rogers wept softly in the control tower.

The tour began in Los Angeles, just as it does today, but little else is similar. There was none of this 300 guys teeing off on both nines of a public course, everybody trying to finish a nervy twenty-ninth. The L.A. Open was held at the class clubs, Riviera, L.A., Lakeside. Nor were the players scattered everywhere from the Polo Lounge at the Beverly Hills to the cheapest motel in Santa Monica. Everyone piled into the Hollywood Plaza for a dollar a day, single, or five dollars a day for a suite, the hotel providing a whole private floor for the competitors. And at night the established stars congregated at Musso

Franks, or the Brown Derby, or Clara Bow's It Cafe, to drink with Richard Arlen, Clark Gable, Randolph Scott, the serious golfers of Hollywood who also entered the tournament. There, they contemplated the happy fact that L.A. offered the biggest purse on the tour. First place was worth $3,500, and that, for example, was five pay windows higher than the U.S. Open.

L.A. also lured the largest galleries of the year, crowds sparkling with movie celebrities and rising starlets. There were so many one year, in fact, that Dick Metz had to park two miles from the course before the second round and buy a ticket to get in. This would not have been so embarrassing for the sponsors if Metz hadn't been leading the tournament at the time.

"We knew everybody in Hollywood," says Jimmy Demaret. "It was pretty impressive to be hanging around Bing Crosby and folks like that all the time. And there were an awful lot of dandy little old gals around. We didn't know who they were. They had different names then. But we realized later that they were Susan Hayward and that kind of thing."

The tour might stay on the Coast for a month. It would go from L.A. to a Riverside Open, where the players would stuff their golf bags with fruit from the citrus trees in the rough, or it might go to a Pasadena Open, where they scooped niblicks around the Rose Bowl. It might go to an Agua Caliente Open. And one they certainly didn't miss was the Bing Crosby Pro-Am at Rancho Santa Fe, which was only thirty-six holes. It would also head north to a weird thing called the San Francisco Match Play championship. The pros would get into the Sir Francis Drake Hotel, dine at Vanessi's and Nujoe's with a wealthy host and work up the pairings in the locker room. "You figured out who you thought you could beat and challenged him," Demaret says. "And you hoped you didn't get Leonard Dodson because he'd pay a guy to follow you around with a camera and click it on your backswing."

After the flamboyant times on the Coast, fanbelts permitting, the tour moved lazily through the Southwest, the South, the East and the Midwest, until, quite sensibly, it came to a dawdling end as football season began. It embraced a variety of tournaments, many of which sounded as if they ought to be on a billiard circuit, namely, the Miami-Biltmore Four-Ball, the Goodall Round Robin, the Westchester 108-Hole Open, the Dapper Dan and the Vancouver Jubilee.

It was not always easy getting from one place to another. Hogan and Nelson would be more intent on reaching a destination than some of the others because they wanted to practice. They would form a mini-motorcade, Byron and Louise following Ben and Valerie, and dart for shortcuts like Bonnie and Clyde. "Ben wanted to get there and start hittin' golf balls," Demaret says, with a slight trace of bewilderment. "Nobody ever practiced. First guy I ever saw do it was Bobby Cruickshank, about 1932. I didn't know what he was up to. But Ben *really* practiced. I'm sure he invented this business of spending two and three hours hitting balls."

Demaret, of course, would be late because he would still be throwing a party from the previous week. And Lloyd Mangrum, with Buck White or Leonard Dodson, would have found a card game—seven-card low, pitch, auction bridge, casino—while Sam Snead would have to sit around and wait for them in the car. Johnny Bulla's car. "For a while, we traveled in Bulla's Ford sedan. Can you imagine anyone loaning Lloyd Mangrum, Sam Snead and Buck White his car?" Mangrum says. Some cars made the next stop easily, like Walter Hagen's front-wheel drive Cord, or Denny Shute's Graham-Paige. But others didn't. Johnny Revolta has vivid memories of a fanbelt going out somewhere in the infinity of a Texas horizon. His companion at the time, Henry Picard, sat in the car and held his head while Revolta hiked twelve miles, got rescued by a Mexican family, finally found a belt to fit and, six hours later, returned.

This would have been on the way to San Antonio for the Texas Open, the oldest of the winter events (1922). The tournament was distinctive for a number of reasons, not the least of which was that it was usually played among the willows and pecans of Brackenridge Park, a short, tight little public course featuring rubber mats for teeing areas. It was on this course that the most headlined practice round of the era was played one year. In a group with Hogan, Nelson and Paul Runyan, the easygoing Jug McSpaden, wearing sun goggles as always and putting with a mallethead, shot a stunning fifty-nine. The round was accented by the fact that Nelson had a sixty-three, Hogan a sixty-six and Runyan a seventy-one. And it was also at Brackenridge Park one year that Wild Bill Melhorn, who made most of his expenses at the bridge tables, finished with a seventy-two-hole score that looked as if it might win, provided Bobby Cruickshank didn't par the last hole. Melhorn climbed a live oak and tried to heckle Cruickshank into a three-putt on the eighteenth, but when Bobby survived, Melhorn toppled off the branch and into the crowd, without backspin.

From San Antonio, the tour normally frolicked onward to New Orleans, which was both a good and bad town for a riverboat gambler like Lloyd Mangrum. He once arrived on Mardi Gras eve with the town so crowded—and himself so busted—that he joyfully bunked in the city jail for two days. "The only hard part was going without cigarettes," says Mangrum. "Try that course sometime."

Mangrum went on the tour with a $250 stake he got from John Boles, the singer. Cards kept him on it when his golf didn't. "I never won as much as everybody thought at the card tables," he says. "But the first time I ever got enough money to afford it, I bought me a big LaSalle with a couple of four-foot chrome horns on the front fenders, and folks thought I was rich." Stories would spread on him. And grow. When he won $4,000 at gin rummy in Arizona it would be $25,000 by the time it reached Toots Shor's in New York. "The public thought you got thousands from the club companies," he says. "But all I know is I thought it was a big lick to get $300 and some clubs and balls out of MacGregor."

There was usually a way to get something out of somebody. If Mangrum couldn't do it with cards, Leonard Dodson would think of something else. "We're in Niagara Falls, I think it was," says Lloyd, "and I've got about $1.35 and Dodson's got $1.25. Together we can't buy

enough gas to get halfway where we're going. So Dodson scares up this Canadian millionaire and bets him $500 he can outrun his automobile at 100 yards. Now we can't get $500 up if we rob everybody on the tour, and I don't think Dodson can outrun me if I got a heart attack. But Leonard takes the guy out in the country to an old dusty farm road where the tires can't get any traction in the deep soft sand, and damned if Leonard doesn't win the race on his start."

The tour had its elegant stopovers where the foolishness gave way to a more formal atmosphere. Pinehurst was one, the North and South Open was held. You had to have a tux and your wife needed a gown for dinner or it was off to a roadhouse for pork and beans. The same was true at the Masters when everyone stayed at the old Bon Air Hotel and went to millionaire Bill Wallace's antebellum mansion for ham cooked in wine, biscuits, barbecue and corn whiskey in a pitcher. There was also the fanciness of Palm Beach—golf amid the lockjaw accents—a place where Paul Runyan had a fascinating partner in the Seminole Pro-Am one winter.

"He drove 310 yards off the first tee and hit his approach about eighteen inches of the flag," says Runyan. "Now, I'm thinking to myself, we've got this thing all wrapped up. Nobody told me this guy could play like that." But then Runyan's partner took out the putter and tapped his gimme roughly eighteen feet past the hole with all of the gifted feel of a coal miner. His name: Gene Tunney.

It was in Florida that the pros first began to suspicion that they might be semi-celebrities—and all because of the Miami-Biltmore Four-Ball. This was a partnership tournament sponsored by a hotel, which guessed correctly that a lot of sports-page stories with the word Biltmore in them could give ideas to tourists. The Four-Ball tournament also invented "appearance money," for it paid the current U.S. Open and National PGA champions $1,000 each to show up, as if they had somewhere else to go. Promoters were everywhere. Each birdie scored won a bottle of White Horse Scotch for a player plus a tin of Lucky Strikes. Daily, for those willing, players and wives were hoisted by autogyros over to Miami Beach for a swim. Occasionally, when the sponsors grew lax at providing entertainment, some of the players would take over. Such as the evening that Walter Hagen and Joe Kirkwood came back from fishing in the Everglades and dumped their entire catch in the hotel lobby, including an alligator.

Early in the thirties not much was made of the identity between a pro and the club where he spent at least part of his summer or winter teaching. Ben Hogan would later make this a profitable thing through his connection with the Hershey Country Club in Pennsylvania. But before that only a few of the stars were closely associated with certain clubs—Vic Ghezzi with Deal, New Jersey, Craig Wood at Winged Foot, Tommy Armour at Medinah and Sam Snead at Greenbrier, to list a few. Being dragged to his first promotional breakfast by the tour manager, Fred Corcoran, back in '37, Snead told Corcoran, who became Sam's manager as well, "Would you mention that I'm from Greenbrier? Those folks pay me a nice forty-five dollars a month to say so."

The Miami Four-Ball, being publicity conscious, helped promote the clubs to which many of the pros were attached, and it also helped to convey the idea, through its partnership format, that there were certain cliques and friendships on the tour. Hogan and Demaret were nearly always partners, for instance, as were Nelson and McSpaden, Snead and Ralph Guldahl, Horton Smith and Paul Runyan, Johnny Revolta and Henry Picard. The teams, few realized at the time, were mostly formed by the club manufacturers.

As the tour moved through the South the players would note from time to time the emergence of a strange, squealing species that came to be known—Denny Shute is credited with the name—as "Sammy's Lambies." These were the crowds that traipsed after Snead, a prewar Arnie's Army, so to speak. The South was quail and wild turkey country as well, and part of the fun of the Thomasville, Georgia, Open was being permitted to shoot as much game in the fields and thickets as you could between rounds, no limit.

Trying to cook quail and turkey gave the wives something to do besides compare veran-

das. Hettie and Denny Shute liked to think that the wives broke up into three categories, and they named them: ramblers, setters and shadows. The ramblers walked about the course, chose vantage points, and viewed the tournament distantly, sunning, gossiping and getting exercise. The setters were generally older and clung to the porches or lawns with their embroidery or played cards or pondered the possibility of getting a permanent wave like Carole Lombard's. The shadows never left their husbands. They tied bandannas on their heads and did the full eighteen holes, shot for shot.

Potential sponsors for all of these tournaments were mostly where Fred Corcoran could find them, and they came in all shapes and sizes and bankrolls. A sponsor was usually the first to leap in front of a camera, putting his arm around a Snead, a Hogan or a Nelson, buddy-buddy. But not all of them were like that in Corcoran's day. There was this one gentleman, quite amiable, who put up a good portion of cash for the 108-hole Westchester Classic in 1938. Except no photographs, please. Corcoran himself had to present Snead with the victory check so the sponsor could hide from the press. Four years later everyone discovered why. The gentleman was convicted of printing bogus whiskey labels. And no one has yet, to anyone's knowledge, tracked down one of the sponsors of the Indianapolis Open of 1935. It took Al Espinosa, the winner, three years to get his $1,000 prize money from the PGA because the Indianapolis fellow skipped town with the purse.

In all there were no more than twenty-five tournaments a year, compared to forty-five today. If the total prize money added up to $150,000, that was sensational. It looked as good as the $5.5 million of 1968. And a player in the thirties knew that if he could reach most of those tournaments, if he could attach the clubheads, which were made in Scotland, to the shafts, that were made in Tennessee, if he could assemble a set he liked, and if he could survive the card games and the parties and the fan belts, he could bank as much as $6,000 for the year and rate as high as fifth on the money list.

Of course if he *practiced*—that odd ritual Ben Hogan originated—hitting old balls into a vacant lot for Stepin Fetchit to pick up, there was no saying how affluent he could become. It could lead to victories, which could lead to exhibitions, which could lead to club affiliations and on and on, conceivably into movie contracts. A man might become good enough to make some of those marvelously plotted instructional shorts, like Bobby Jones did with W.C. Fields or Buddy Rogers. ("Say, Bobby, since my car seems to have broken down right here by the golf course, how about a tip on playing the mashie-niblick?") It might even help a man get one of those incredible deals that Johnny Farrell had: smiling and holding a pack of cigarettes on the back cover of a magazine. Farrell got $1,000 for that, somebody said.

Sam Snead saw the ad one day and took it to Fred Corcoran, his agent.

"What they call that there?" Sam asked.

"That's an endorsement," said Fred.

"How come you don't git me some of those?" Sam said.

"You don't smoke," Corcoran explained.

Snead thought for a moment and said, "Reckon them folks know that?"

Winning had been outrageously simple for Snead. His big, graceful, natural swing and his hillbilly personality made him an instant star, and Corcoran sold him well. Almost oversold him, in fact. Snead had no sooner begun to earn money on the tour when reporters were phoning Corcoran long distance to ask if this West Virginia guy was real. "He has the finest swing since Jones," Fred would reply. And a few days later Corcoran would see a headline proclaiming: SNEAD PICKED TO WIN U.S. OPEN. That, of course, was something Snead never did, although he gained a negative fame for coming close.

While it was never a problem for Snead, winning that first pro tournament is still, even today, one of the most difficult things for a young player, regardless of how talented he may be. Byron Nelson's baptism in the hazards of near victory makes one of golf's better horror stories. Unknown and unsure, thin, young, broke, nervous, married, armed only with a good, quick, upright swing, Nelson learned the hard way. He was playing along in the General Brock Open at Niagara Falls when, suddenly, at the end of the third round he was the leader.

On Sunday morning it took Nelson a while to adjust to the headlines in the papers. That was Byron Nelson they were talking about. Guy from Fort Worth. Then he looked closer at the stories, at the pairings for the last round. Good God. He was paired with Walter Hagen. He turned to his wife, Louise, and in something akin to a death rattle, he broke the news.

"I, uh, I have to play with, uh, Hagen today," he said, as if to apologize for the eighty-eight he was bound to shoot and the no-money they would leave with.

Now in a situation like that a pro got to the course early, and Nelson did. He chipped awhile, putted awhile and worried awhile. He blushed a lot and hung his head and hid and kept checking to see if his trousers were buttoned. Finally it was time to tee off, but Walter Hagen, naturally, had not arrived yet. "Looks like Mr. Hagen is late again," sighed the starter, unconcerned.

"Late?" Nelson said. Of course. Late was part of it then, what a real pro did to a rookie without penalty or disqualification; in fact, what Hagen usually did to everybody. Didn't he once send to the clubhouse for a folding chair so that Gene Sarazen, the man who introduced the sand iron and steel shafts, could sit down and rest while he, that cunning Hagen, studied a simple chip shot? Wasn't it Hagen who liked to psych guys out by strolling over to their bags, peeking in at their clubs, shaking his head mournfully and walking away? Others, like Horton Smith, just squinted peculiarly at the rookies until the sad young men worked themselves into incurable hooks. And still others, like Dutch Harrison, would sweet-talk a rookie out of his game. "Man, can you massage that ball," Dutch would say. "I ain't seen a swing that good since Mac Smith." But prince of the Slow Plays, that was Hagen.

And so it went for Nelson, the starter telling him, "Go ahead and tee off with Willie Goggin, Byron, or with Ed Dudley. We'll pair Mr. Hagen with someone else when he arrives."

"But Walter Hagen's my idol. I've wanted to play golf with him all my life," Byron said, torn between high privilege and dire necessity.

"Well, we're very sorry."

"But I'm leading the tournament," Nelson said.

"Yes, we know."

Nelson practiced some more and paced and sat and paced and putted, his slacks ballooning in the Niagara breeze like the Graf Zeppelin, his wide-bottomed tie whipping past the curled-up collar tips of his $1.19 shirt and on around his neck.

Fidget, pace, putt, stroll, throw up went Nelson until, thanks a million, two hours later along came Hagen in his white-on-white silk shirt, his gold cuff links and more oil on his hair than they were pumping out of the East Texas fields.

"Hi, boy," he said.

"It's—it's a real big honor," said Nelson in a trance, a trance he did not recover from until forty-two strokes later on the front nine holes.

The disaster was not total. Nelson somehow rallied himself, shot a thirty-five on the back for a seventy-seven and salvaged second place in the tournament. He won $600, which was almost as much money as Andrew Mellon had, he thought.

"Louise, we've got to hide this $600 before we hit the road. Since we're rich, we're bound to get robbed. And if we hide it, maybe they won't get it all," Byron told his wife. She agreed. So $50 went in the glove compartment, $100 in the suitcases, some more in the purse, some in the pockets, a little more under the seats, until it was neatly put away where the Dillinger mob would never find it. As a matter of fact, it took the Nelson mob a couple of hours to find it all when they reached a motel down the road.

If Jimmy Demaret had won the money he would have been eight to five to leave it in a bar or blow it on a handmade pair of orange and purple saddle oxfords. The man who single-handedly led golfers out of neckties and into knit shirts had little trouble getting rid of money. On the contrary, Demaret's problem was that he destroyed it with the same ease of the wealthy people he loafed with.

When Demaret left his native Houston to become a tour rookie in 1935 he had a set of clubs, a car and $600 loaned to him by Sam Maceo, a Galveston nightclub operator, D.B. McDaniel, an oilman, and Ben Bernie, the bandleader. He also had the fervent hope that he could drive through Juarez without stopping. But no such luck. All it took to nearly ruin him during what he hoped would be a brief stopover was for a man to ask him a question.

"Hey, señor, you want to shoot a leetle pool?" the man asked.

Demaret lost the car the first day, the clubs the second and the $600 the third. The only reason he didn't lose the River Oaks Country Club of Houston was because nobody in Juarez would take an IOU for it. The only thing he did right was save the pawn slip for the clubs so his brother, Milton, could retrieve them and ship them to the West Coast where Demaret hoped to wind up on the freight train he boarded.

Jimmy got there, and he did squirm through the first couple of weeks on a diet of sandwiches and muscatel. But as destiny often ordains for free spirits, especially if they can fade a high two-iron, he cashed in for a few hundred the third week, and Demaret has been throwing a party ever since.

From almost the instant he arrived Demaret's quipping nature, his friendliness and his passion for clothes that screamed made him golf's unofficial publicity agent. If the sports pages ever nurtured a grander cliché than "Navy won the toss and elected to receive," it was "colorful Jimmy Demaret, golf's goodwill ambassador."

Demaret wore lavender, gold, pink, orange, red and aqua slacks; yellow, emerald, maroon, plaid, checked, striped and polka-dot coats; and more than 500 hats—berets, Tyroleans, straws—importing all of it from Europe. He paid $250 for the coats as soon as he could and $125 for the slacks in an era when that kind of money could avert a bonus march. He ordered ladies' pastel fabrics from abroad and had them tailored in the U..S. His idea about shoes was to give a factory swatches from his slacks and have matching saddle oxfords made.

Not only did Demaret have a color for every occasion, he also had a quip. Some of the more classic were these:

To an L.A. radio announcer who asked him which player on the tour had the most even disposition: "Clayton Heafner. He's mad *all* the time."

To a sportswriter who asked him if Ben Hogan had said much to him while they were winning the Inverness Four-Ball: "Once I think he said, 'You're away.'"

To Robert Trent Jones, the golf architect with a reputation for building monster courses: "Saw a course you'd really like, Trent. On the first tee you drop the ball over your left shoulder."

To Roberto de Vicenzo at the Masters: "Play good, Roberto. I'm betting on you to be low Mexican."

When the thirties didn't have Demaret for comic relief, they had Ky Laffoon. He was a portly, balding part-Indian who got his start by caddieing for Titanic Thompson, the famed hustler who liked to bet on this and that and usually won. Titanic liked to say to an opponent, "Hell, my caddie could beat you," and Ky Laffoon could.

Except on the tour. Laffoon never won as much as he probably should have, and his temper was largely responsible. It wasn't a legendary temper, the kind which caused earth tremors or broke up a party. It was more of a lovable temper, they say. Almost. Kind of.

Laffoon would wander off into the rough and discreetly, or not so discreetly, flog all of the leaves off of a small tree. He would miss a short putt and spurt tobacco juice into the cup, enough so that a man putting next would reach for his ball rather gingerly. And he would sometimes curse so audibly around a gallery that his wife, embarrassed, would stalk to the clubhouse and call a lawyer.

Once Laffoon had three putts from five feet to win the Cleveland Open. He missed the first, missed the second and thereupon became so violent that he slammed the putter down on top of the ball, not caring whether he finished first or eighth. But the ball ricocheted up in the air and —truly, truly—plopped right into the cup. Seeing it in the newsreel later, Laffoon is said to have let out a screech that cleared three rows.

Lloyd Mangrum remembers being paired with Ky when the Indian threw away one club per hole, finishing with Mangrum's clubs from the fifteenth in. Paul Runyan was with him one day when he broke the head off of his putter out of anger, but stepped up to putt again with the jagged shaft. When he realized what he was doing Laffoon, who had a tendency to stutter when he grew mad, said, "W-what the h-hell h-happened here?"

To appease his wife during a rare period of resolution, Laffoon decided he would play through a whole tournament without cursing. Surprisingly enough he scored fairly well in the first round and succeeded in doing it. He then started decently the second day, but he soon played himself into the lead and things got touchy. He held back for a while. But when an approach shot soared over a green on the back nine and landed in a bed of honeysuckle, that did it.

A jungle guerrilla with a machete could not have attacked the ball more furiously. One swing. Two. Three. And out came a torrent of get-even words that had spectators blushing as far away as the parking lot, which was precisely where his wife headed. Ky chased after her, caught up and began a panting, futile plea.

"I-I w-wasn't cussing," he said. "N-no k-kidding, d-darlin'. It w-wasn't a-anything to d-do w-with the g-golf. I just don't like honeysuckle."

The group to which Ky Laffoon felt the most philosophical kinship was a self-confessed pack of wolves acutely aware that prize money was not the only means of supporting oneself on the golf course.

Dutch Harrison, the Arkansas Traveler, eventually became a consistent money-winner, but he spent his first six years without earning a single penny of official cash. He lived off the fat of other men's golfing egos. In this respect he was much like Leonard Dodson, or better still, the brilliant trickshot artist, Joe Ezar, from Waco, Texas, who could make a golf ball sit up and speak. Ezar would stow away on freighters to Europe and hustle his way back on the Queen Mary balancing golf balls on top of each other on a bet. He could balance one ball on top of another—Lord knows how—hit the bottom ball onto a green and catch the other in his hand before it reached the ground. For money. Ezar would turn up at a tournament armed only with a derby hat, an overcoat and a pair of street shoes. "Loan me the equipment, and I'll pay you back double," he would say, and do it.

Dutch was never greedy. All he and his pal, Bob Hamilton, wanted was a couple of "nine-dollar pigeons" a day, enough to make expenses. Harrison had that splendid talent of being able to name his score. If his opponent shot seventy-one, Dutch shot seventy. If his opponent shot eighty, Dutch squeezed out a seventy-nine and convinced the guy how unlucky he was.

One afternoon on the Coast in 1937, as Dutch and Hamilton negotiated on the first tee for a game, a stranger asked if he could play along. He had a raw swing and a country voice, like Dutch, which mean the couldn't be all bad.

Hamilton, ever eager with loot in sight, said something subtle like, "How much you want to play for?"

"Well, I don't know much about betting," the man said.

"You come along with us," said Hamilton.

No more than a few holes had been played before Dutch and Hamilton were distracted from their game with the nine-dollar pigeons. For every good shot they hit, the stranger hit one better.

"My, my, son, you sure got yourself a pretty swing there," Dutch said. "That old hook grip don't bother you none at all, does it?"

Birdie, birdie went the innocent fellow.

Presently, Harrison lashed a spoon shot into a green—a career shot—and he thought to himself, "Now we see who the men are."

To which the stranger put a two-iron inside of him.

"Bob," Harrison said to Hamilton. "We done got ourselves ahold of something here."

Later on, after Dutch and Hamilton had paid off, the young stranger said, "Sure do thank you fellers. Say, what time you gonna be here tomorrow?"

"Son," Harrison said, "you work your side of the road, and we'll work ours."

"That," Dutch says today, "is how I met Sam Snead."

The tour had no sooner become acquainted with Sam than along came another newcomer who would help fill the glamorous void that had been created by Bobby Jones's retirement. Fellow named Hogan. He was a loner and a brooder, weighing in at 130 pounds with an uncontrollable hook off the tees. No one thought he would ever make it. And he warmed up to only a few of his contemporaries—Demaret, whose humor he admired, and Henry Picard, a gracious and helpful veteran who loaned money and advice, and Harrison, whose ability to survive he found intriguing.

Harrison discovered one evening when he was rooming with Hogan just how determined the Texan was. As Dutch tried to sleep, Ben gently beat his fists against the bedposts in their hotel quarters.

"You done gone crazy?" Dutch said.

"I'm strengthening my wrists," said Hogan.

The thumping continued until the manager arrived, having been summoned by an annoyed guest next door.

"I'm through," Hogan explained, contentedly. "I just figured out what's wrong with my grip."

He almost had. Hogan struggled through the thirties by settling for such stunning successes as third place in the North American Long Driving Contest behind Jimmy Thomson and Porky Oliver at Niagara Falls. He would get a check here and a check there. It wasn't until 1940 at Pinehurst that he finally won a tournament, the North and South. He found it so much to his liking that he quickly won two more, at Greensboro and Asheville—three in a row. And for the next twenty years there never lived a better golfer.

Throughout the thirties only one player came on the tour in absolute comfort, unfettered by financial worries. That was Lawson Little, golf's first bonus baby. He was a handsome, husky, carefree Californian with a square face, curly hair and white duck trousers. He had been the greatest amateur since Jones, winning both the U.S. and British Amateur championships in

1934 and again in 1935—a feat that sportswriters called, rather clumsily, the Double Little Slam.

Little's decision to become a touring pro was final proof that amateur golf was minor league. And when he signed up with Spalding for $10,000 and all expenses to play golf and be a public relations man, it was the most amazing thing the pros had heard of since beltless slacks. Not until twenty-five years later, when Jack Nicklaus made a deal twenty times as big, did amateur golf produce so dazzling a celebrity.

Once Little was in the Spalding stable a group was formed that became known as the "trained seals." They were Little, Horton Smith, Thompson and Harry Cooper, and they were a popular exhibition team. They traveled together, mostly by luxurious train, and staged their own pre-tournament matches and clinics. "Can you fellows really balance golf balls on your nose?" Demaret would ask them.

Horton Smith was the boss and the bookkeeper. At the clinics he demonstrated the short game, Thomson hit the woods, Cooper, a nervous man who had a habit of jingling coins in his pocket, especially when someone stood over a putt, displayed the mid-irons and Lawson Little hit the long irons, the strength of his game.

Gallery ropes were nonexistent in the thirties. Spectators literally formed a barricade around their favorite players; a golfer hardly had room to take a backswing. Self-appointed officials would stand in the middle of the fairways, puff on their pipes and say, "You're away, Byron." During one match Harry Cooper, who carried up to twenty-six clubs in his bag before the fourteen-club limit was set in 1936, kept finding a spectator's shadow over his ball when he addressed it. "Very unethical," Cooper would mumble and hit a fine shot. It happened all the way around the course until about the sixteenth hole when the shadow disappeared. Cooper then hit a ball roughly ten feet. "You bum," he called out. "Why'd you step on those leaves just as I was swinging?"

There were occasions when the fans were permitted to be so indelicately close to the players that a championship could be settled by them. Very nearly. A spectator almost cost Little the U.S. Open. The Californian never became the big winner that everyone expected, possibly because he was so well-fixed, but he did achieve a week of glory at Canterbury during the Open of 1940. He tied with Gene Sarazen for the championship, and they played off over eighteen holes the next day. It was a duel of different personalities. Little was friendly, outgoing, a fine socializer, particularly when he had Jimmy Thomson to drink with. Sarazen was grim, independent. When the pros switched to knickers, Gene introduced slacks. When they switched to slacks, he went back to knickers.

Little took an early lead in the playoff, but even as he led Sarazen he public-related. At the fifth hole a fan came up to him and wanted to ask a question. Sure, said Little.

"What I want to know is whether you inhale or exhale on your backswing?"

"Are you serious?" Little said.

"Quite," said the fan. "As for myself, I think I inhale, but I'm not sure."

Little duck-hooked his next series of shots, trying to figure out if he inhaled or exhaled. He managed to recover, however, and shoot a seventy to defeat Sarazen by three strokes. He was the U.S. Open champion, regardless of how he breathed, and the Spalding Dot was once again guaranteed to give you extra distance.

But that was 1940. The thirties were gone—sunk slowly in the background like the wooden shaft. A wonderfully unpredictable and rather remarkable era of golf had passed, but the legacies it left were many. Among others it left us the fond memory that somewhere around every dogleg there lurked an individual—a Snead, a Hogan, a Nelson, a Demaret. A Laffoon, a Harrison, a Little, a Mangrum. And all of the others. Individuals is what they had to be, really, to last it out.

And what none of them would ever have guessed at the time is that out there on the tour in the sixties a pro could hardly scrape by at all without an agent, a manager, a copilot, a secretary, a valet, a tax consultant and a corporate jet.

Ben Hogan, Carnoustie, 1953

by **MICHAEL MCDONNELL**

Michael McDonnell travels the world covering golf for the London Daily Mail, *and has the uncanny knack of getting inside the minds of the golfers he describes, to the point where his readers experience the winning—or losing—of a championship from the player's viewpoint. McDonnell's account of Ben Hogan's single British Open victory, in 1953, is an exceptional portrait not only of a tournament but of the man himself.*

H E had come to Carnoustie to win. Of that, he had no doubt. That was the job, pure and simple, and fate, destiny, good fortune were discounted from his calculations. What faced him was a practical task requiring industry and planning. It was the attitude of craftsmen who build houses. With the right materials, plans and labor there is no mystery or surprise about the result. And if it is to be the best, then these ingredients have to be superior.

Nobody but Hogan could think of a championship in these terms. But then nobody but Hogan had ever reached that degree of awareness of the game. At some point in his life he had withdrawn from the world so that he was left with himself, a club, a ball and a course to conquer.

Perhaps it was a terrible price to pay for that degree of skill, because Hogan forced something from himself that went beyond diligence, fervor and even obsession. It took him into a lonely world where only he and the golf course existed —he and the task that he had to accomplish. Nobody else lived in that world.

It was not arrogance nor gross presumption of his destiny, because Hogan's vision never stretched that far, never beyond exerting complete mastery over the stroke that confronted him. The only judgment that mattered was his own, and there was none harsher.

He could never share himself with others since he, Hogan, existed only with a club in his hands. He had nothing else to offer, and if others pitied his loneliness then it was a mistake, because within him there was a fullness of life which excited him so much that each day he could not wait for the hours of sleep to pass so that he might return to his beloved clubs and his foe, the golf course.

The compulsion in the beginning may have been a simple desire for affluence or at least a better quality of life than that he had known as a caddie in Fort Worth, Texas. But at some time the original motive had been lost in what became a pilgrimage towards perfection—which seemed, at times, to make both money and titles superfluous.

He strove for absolute mastery of his mind and his body. He was tormented by its logical

Courtesy of Wide World Photos, Inc.

Like Caesar who came, saw and conquered, Ben Hogan made one journey to Scotland for the British Open and won at Carnoustie in 1953. Added to his victories that same year in the Masters and PGA, it became part of the Triple Crown, the closest a player has come to equalling the Grand Slam.

possibility since degrees of excellence were but evidence of mechanical efficiency of the body. From that, it was impossible to escape the theoretical conclusion that the human frame could be drilled, each muscle harnessed, to a repetitive flawless discipline.

To this impossible purpose Hogan devoted his life, and he came closer to it than any other man. He reached an awareness and understanding of the golf swing that went beyond mechanics and, with his interminable drill on the practice ground, he acquired an exhaustive self-knowledge. He would tire himself deliberately to study his swing and attitudes in a state of fatigue. It was objective observation, as if he were studying some other specimen.

In the early days this obsession did him little good and served only to frustrate him because at times it was possible to lose sight of the game's object and be distracted by the quality of strokes played. The successful man has few weaknesses, but those he possesses, he protects and ensures that they are never exposed. Hogan could not tolerate a weakness and would pick at it.

It took him ten dispiriting years before he was adequately equipped to become a champion, and by then he could drill the ball to whatever sector of the sky he wished, to whatever blade of grass he selected. That was the art and the satisfaction. Its application would bring the rewards.

It seemed that most of his triumphs were simply the balance of this equation, in which rewards equaled work done. But that had changed at Oakland Hills because that U.S. Open title was always more than a question of superiority. There, the doubt was whether he was to be robbed by fate of the achievements that his lonely years of dedication had promised.

Just a year earlier, in 1949, he had been invincible and collected thirteen tournament wins, including the U.S. Open and the U.S. Masters titles. Then out of the fog on his way home from Phoenix, a bus crushed his body and forced all but the last breath of life from it.

But the body refused to die. The legs and pelvis were shattered and might never function again and, at best, the doctors suspected he would end his days in a wheelchair, plagued by the thoughts of what should have been. It was

not until then that the earlier frustrating years of Hogan, when he sought absolute mastery of his body, took on their real significance. Hogan had already decided that these shattered pieces would function again; that this body which now trapped him with its frailty would not only stand and walk again—but also that it would play golf as well as before.

That resolution had been made in his darkest moment, when he was capable only of a slight turn of his head. Had he wanted to scale Everest in that condition, the task could not have been greater. Yet he held a furious intolerance of his infirmities which was made even stronger by the memories of what he had achieved.

Not even his wife realized the extent of his will, nor did she know that when he was left alone in his room in later days he would force himself out of bed and drag himself, through blinding agony, in an effort to walk. Nor did she know that he had concealed a putter under his bed, and would practice the stroke when nobody was around.

This secret work with his putter was a sign to himself that the recovery was inevitable and that already he should begin working on what had been his only incurable weakness—his putting. Whatever Hogan had achieved had been despite his putting, and some remarked that his phenomenal accuracy with other clubs was but compensation for this inability to putt to even a reasonable standard.

In truth he considered putting a different game and one that held no interest for him. It must just as well have been baseball or football, so far removed was it from what he considered the fundamental art of golf. His disdain for the gifted putters of this world was clear enough, and he was once to remark to Bill Casper, a genius with that club: "If you couldn't putt you'd be selling hot dogs outside the ropes."

But, imprisoned in that room with his infirmities, Hogan was already intent that his putting should have the longest recuperation. During this period, hundreds of letters began to arrive, from people he had never known, wishing him a quick recovery and offering the clear message that they cared.

It was a new experience for Hogan, and one

which nonplussed him. It was not that he disliked people, but rather that he was totally unaware of them outside his own small circle, and even there friends were accepted only on Hogan's terms. There was, for example, only one bedroom at Hogan's home because he did not like overnight guests.

People, or rather the public, were totally irrelevant to Hogan's view of his life and his work. At a golf course, they were eavesdroppers and, as far as he was concerned, unwelcome guests. His task was to conquer the golf course, and he disliked people looking over his shoulder so much that it would not have mattered to him if nobody turned up. In fact he would have preferred it that way.

He remained aloof from the crowds, and if he deigned to speak then the conversation would be monosyllabic, and he insisted,most times that he played, on being protected by a man carrying a banner which ordered "no cameras!" If they must watch, then it could be only on his terms. He had no need of the crowd.

But Hogan had misjudged them, and while his public accepted that he was a dour, gray, unapproachable man they saw also the overpowering dedication of a man towards his art. As much as the outstanding achievements this brought, it was this strength of will power for which they respected—and perhaps loved— Hogan.

Now he was discovering this truth, yet he was baffled by it. He had been locked too long within himself to change or soften, too tightly bound in his own character to mellow into a warm-hearted idol. But now he was aware of this deep affection and could never again shut the public out of his life. It was as if then, when he was most helpless, that he realized his obligations to the public that his talent imposed. The truth was that any achievement needed a judgment other than one's own.

The close brush with death, the threat of infirmity, the time away from golf and now this unabashed national esteem, certainly brought a new dimension to Hogan's life. But it also served to drive him more desperately towards the only way he could justify himself—by playing golf.

At first he had moved to the quiet parts of his local golf course and ensured that nobody but the caddie could see his first pathetic efforts at a golf swing. He had to build afresh, because the bones had healed his frame to a new physique and there was the pain which would rarely leave him.

His first blows brought tears to the caddie's eyes, because this man remembered the real Hogan, not this bent cripple who was vainly trying to lift a sledge hammer of a golf club. But if the caddie was not prepared for these pathetic efforts, then Hogan certainly was, and once again the ruthless demands he had always made of himself began to piece together a golf swing through the pain of a thousand strokes. He could feel life flooding back into him, as the silent affinity between himself and a golf ball began to exist again.

Within a year, his legs strapped for strength, he filed his entry for a tournament, and if the old Hogan might have thought the crowds had arrived to see a freak, he knew now that they were with him and not against him.

Though his stamina was weak and his competitive shell still fragile, he emerged after four rounds with the best score, but realized that Snead might equal it. He prayed that Snead would beat it, because he felt weak at the prospect of a playoff. As far as Hogan was concerned he had already passed the test and winning did not really matter that much now. But Snead forced him into a playoff and Hogan lost.

Before the U.S. Open at Oakland Hills, he felt restored enough to match anybody and even during that week, although he was assailed by crippling cramps which any number of hot baths and massages could not subdue, he remained among the leaders as they moved into the last round.

For a period in that last round his body was so racked with pain that he was on the verge of giving up. There was too much confusion, too many people with an equal chance, that he might force himself back into hospital without even the consolation of the title.

Yet, though his will was weakening, it still fought to retain the discipline of a lifetime over his body, and it prevailed long enough to force Hogan into a playoff the next day. Then he won, and this time he did not resent sharing his triumph with the thousands who came to watch.

Within three years, he came to Carnoustie, and the task was to win the British Open, because so many of his friends had urged him to extend the evidence of his talent by proving that he could win in alien conditions as other great men —Hagen, Jones, Sarazen—even Snead—had done.

It had never occurred to him before, because it was not an ambition that bothered him. But that year he already had the U.S. Masters and the U.S. Open, and once he had allowed himself to be persuaded about the British title, he pursued the task with scrupulous diligence.

He walked into a hotel in Carnoustie ten days before the championship was due to start, then, a minute later, walked out again because there was no bathroom attached to his bedroom. It proved to be a fortunate deficiency since it meant that Hogan was installed in a house in Dundee, away from the crowd. He could now devote himself fully to the process of preparation, and nobody would ever go into a championship better prepared than Hogan.

At first he simply gazed at the course as if assessing its character and strength. He studied every bunker and walked round them studying the texture and the shapes. He walked the course in reverse order—from greens to tees—to acquire a different perspective of each hole.

Then he went to work on his golf swing, working and working, to become accustomed to the new feel of the smaller British golf ball on his club blade, learning to accept the tightness of these seaside lies, and knowing within inches the precise range of each club, no matter what the conditions.

He would play countless shots to every green, learning the safe routes and avoiding the dangers. He would fire drives to various points on the fairway to discover the best angle of attack for each hole. Nothing was left to chance, since winning was a calculated process of producing the lowest score.

He was to be seen many times during those ten days, just standing on a tee, sometimes for a quarter of an hour, looking down the fairway as if trying to imprint the vision of the perfect strokes on his brain, like an actor learning his lines.

By the time that he was summoned to the first tee for the opening round he had a detailed vision of his route around Carnoustie, and he seemed to tread somewhere between the vision of that perfection and the reality of the day with all its marginal variations. He had learned his lines well and had drilled himself into a repetitive efficiency in which each stroke had been rehearsed a thousand times between his mind and the practice ground. It was as if the real act of judgment for each stroke had been taken long before he reached that first tee.

Yet this scale of preparation seemed preposterous, since it was impossible for a man to handle all the perils of Carnoustie for three days on his own terms. Hogan had rehearsed every move to near-perfection but what would happen if that machine backfired? Had he the flexibility to cope with a crisis, and perhaps produce a stroke that had never been part of his campaign plan? Certainly he would have to fight hard, at some time, for his scores. He would be compelled to exert his powers of escape from the countless ambushes that this course had waiting for all of them, and it would be this ability to maintain his excellence when other forces were dragging him down that would weigh as heavily as that excellence itself.

On the first day, it was not perfection that he offered against Carnoustie, and the battle had been a long one. When it was almost over he faltered slightly, and was trapped twice by the bunkers he had studied so assiduously. It left others at the front of the field to live in hope of taking this title.

It did not bother Hogan, since he had now focused on his foe, the course, and if it were beaten thoroughly enough it was logical to assume that the title would follow. In any case it was the achieving, the process itself more than the result, which drew him. Afterwards there was only satisfaction and pride, none of which could equal the thrill of the act itself, the fashioning of the strokes to conquer each hole.

Thus, by lunchtime on the third day, with one round left to play, Hogan considered himself to be alone, even though Rees, Thomson, de

Vicenzo and Cerda were pressing close. The mathematics did not tell the true story because that lunchtime de Vicenzo already knew that he had lost, and sobbed quietly in his hotel room. Some fatalistic insight told him that, with his pathetic putting, he could not possibly withstand the pressures to come.

Hogan moved upon that course in the afternoon as though he already knew he had an appointment with the trophy, and was in complete command of himself and Carnoustie. Each round had been progressively lower, more incisive, as if it had always been his plan to inflict slow torture on the reputation of the great golf course.

If that was the case, then the victim made one final defiant thrust in its death throes, when his approach shot towards the fifth green began to drift slightly from its planned route and the 15,000 people who had gathered to see Hogan win gasped in horror as they saw the fate of the ball.

The penalty was grossly out of proportion to the error, because he was no more than twenty-five yards from the green yet his ball hung on an upslope, half in sand and half in grass. That next stroke would require a blend of so many skills—the adjustment for an uphill stroke, the precision of a bunker stroke but the correct strength to hit through grass . . . he had to judge the distance to the pin and assess the amount of halting spin he could impart on the ball. Each demand was formidable in itself, but now Carnoustie had conspired to present all of them to Hogan in a single stroke.

The cigarette smouldered, he squinted intensely at his problem and walked between the ball and the green countless times, looking at both. His eyes and his brain had already seen the stroke needed and this information was now being passed to every muscle in his body. It took him four minutes before he was ready.

He took his nine-iron knowing that his brain and hands had to be aware of every fraction of space the clubhead covered on its path to the ball; that the grass must be grazed only slightly with the descending blow; that the force of it all must be precisely judged. He settled, and glowered a few more times at the flagstick.

The act itself, for it was not really a swing, began gently, then he was moving down towards the ball. Such was the gentleness of the caress between club and ball that the union seemed protracted like a lingering kiss. But then the ball rose, touched the green and stayed low. Then it moved onwards and disappeared down the hole.

It should have been, if not disaster, then at least a setback which demanded some penalty. But it was neither, since Hogan had turned that crisis into a simultaneous declaration of skill and dedication to the annihilation of a golf course. He emerged at the end of the round with a course record which was perhaps the real satisfaction that day at Carnoustie for Hogan. He won the British Open. He had done what they asked. He would not come back, because what else was there to prove?

The Maddening First Hole

by ARNOLD PALMER with WILLIAM BARRY FURLONG

Most golfers know of Arnold Palmer's dramatic final-round sixty-five which won the 1960 U.S. Open and catapulted golf into the national consciousness. Few people are aware, as this chapter from Palmer's book reveals, that it was his intention to drive the first hole each day of the Open. His bold plan was a measure of the competitive daring that characterized Palmer's greatest years.

THERE was a sharp bite and sparkle in the mountain air. The Rockies loomed clearly in the distance—immense, clean, barren. I remember on the first hole at Denver, the sun was so bright that it hurt your eyes to look down the fairway. Standing on the tee, it was difficult to see the green without a pair of dark glasses. It took me four rounds to find it— but when I did, the whole thrust of my life was altered.

The time was 1960. The place was Cherry Hills Country Club. The event was the U.S. Open.

On the fourth round of that tournament, I tried a shot that I'd missed three times in three rounds. I tried it again not because I'd failed— or because I like failure—but because I was convinced that it was the shot necessary to win the tournament.

A bold shot?

Yes.

But you must play boldly to win. My whole philosophy has been based on winning golf tournaments, not on finishing a careful fifth, or seventh, or tenth.

A reckless shot?

No.

In eighteen years of tournament golf I feel that I've never tried a shot that I couldn't make.

On that summer day in 1960, I was young in what the world calls fame, but I was ripe in golfing experience. I'd been a professional golfer for five years, and up to then I'd won twenty tournaments. In those years, I'd learned something about the strategy of the game and its psychology and rewards. If there was any reward I treasured most, it was the way that the game responded to my inner drives, to the feeling we all have that—in those moments that are so profoundly a challenge to man himself—he has done his best. That—win or lose—nothing more could have been done.

My own needs were deeply driven ones: I could not retreat from a challenge. If the chance was there and if—no matter how difficult it appeared—it meant winning, I was going to take it. It was the "sweetness" of risk that I remembered, and not its dangers.

In looking back, I feel that in these years I was learning something of the subtle dimensions of all this—I was learning the *meaning* of boldness as well as its feeling.

For boldness does not mean "recklessness" to me. Rather it involves a considered confidence: I *know* I'm going to make the shot that seems reckless to others. I also know the value of the risk involved: A bold shot has to have its own rewards—winning or losing the match, winning or losing the tournament.

But perhaps it was not until the U.S. Open at Cherry Hills that I put it all together, philosophically as well as physically. For not until that summer day in 1960 did it become apparent to me how boldness might influence not just a hole but an entire round, an entire tournament, and even an entire golfing career.

It began, really, on the first tee of the last round at Cherry Hills. On the face of it, there was nothing terribly subtle about this hole: You could see every mistake you made. It was downhill to the green; the tee was elevated perhaps 150 feet above the green. It was only 346 yards long, not a terribly long par four—and a terribly tempting birdie three . . . to me. It was guarded on the left by an irregular line of poplars and pines and on the right by a ditch that the membership had practically paved with golf balls. A nice direct hole for the strong driver, somebody who could—in that thin, mile-high air—get the ball out there 300 yards or so.

But there *was* one nasty little afterthought that had been provided for the U.S. Open: The grass was allowed to grow very long and become a "rough" right in the fairway, about fifty or sixty yards in front of the green. Moreover, the hazard was heightened by a treacherous bunker guarding the gateway to the green. It had grass in it that looked like it was three feet deep. If you got in there, you might never be found again. I mean it was the kind of place where you hunted buffalo—not par.

The idea, of course, was to penalize the strong driver, to threaten him with capture by the rough—and a difficult second shot—if he played to his own best game (a powerful drive) on his first shot.

The safe way to play that hole, for most golfers, was not to invite trouble—not to challenge the rough or the bunker in the first place. In that sense, the first hole was an authentic mirror of the entire course. For Cherry Hills was long in yardage (7,004) but not in reality: The thin air gave most tee shots a much longer carry than on a sea level course. But its greens were small and well guarded by bunkers and water hazards; there was an added danger that under the hot, direct sun and the afternoon winds they would become so dried out that it would be all but impossible to get the ball to stop on them. If you hit those greens with power, the ball would roll right over and off them on the far side. So it was a course that took accuracy, touch, and an unflagging concentration. It *looked* to many like a course whose yardage beckoned to power—Mike Souchak, a powerful golfer, led at the halfway mark of the 1960 Open with a remarkable sixty-eight–sixty-seven for a thirty-six-hole score of 135. But it was, in reality, a course that catered to placement more than to power—in that opening round of sixty-eight, Souchak had only twenty-six putts, nine or ten short of normal for an eighteen-hole round. So he wasn't up there scattering power shots; he was getting good placement with everything he did.

To focus on the first hole: It was the kind of hole that shaped your entire approach to the course in that it could reward you for power or for placement.

To the pretty good amateur golfer, it was an opportunity for a par four. He might put the ball out in the fairway pretty much where he could—far short of the rough—and then hope to get close to, or onto, the green with his second shot.

To the venturesome pro, it was an opportunity for a birdie. He'd use an iron to hit his shot off the tee, expecting to get enough accuracy from it (which he would less likely get from a driver) to drop the ball precisely in the fairway, where he'd have the ideal second shot. In short, he intended to place his first shot so that he could hit his second shot precisely to the cup—not just any old place on the green but *specifically* to the cup. For this was the kind of shot where the pro prefers—where he *intends*—to get his second shot so close to the cup that he'll need only one putt to "get down." So if he emphasized placement over power, he hoped to wind up with a birdie three, not a par four.

From my angle of vision—somewhat singular, I'll admit—this was an eagle hole, not a birdie hole. I figured that, with boldness, I could get down in two strokes, not three or four.

That meant being on the green in one shot, not two.

That meant getting into the cup in one putt, not two.

That meant emphasizing power over placement.

That meant using my driver, not my iron.

My intention was simply to drive the ball hard enough and far enough so that it would bound through the rough in front of the green and run up on the putting surface to a good position near the cup. To get a ball to stop precisely on a green, you must give it backspin, so that it bites into the grass when it hits and then stops short, or even hops backward. That's fairly easy to do when you're using an iron from the fairway that is fairly close to the green; you merely strike straight downward at the ball, taking a divot after making contact with the ball, and take a normal follow-through. But it is difficult to do while driving off the tee and ramming the ball through the rough. For one thing, on tee shots you may be hitting the ground a microsecond before you make contact with the ball. At least that's what I was doing with my driver back in 1960 (though since then I've changed my style somewhat). Then you normally give the ball a considerable overspin when you hit the ball dead center (or thereabouts) and make the big follow-through. Normally you want to give the ball some overspin when hitting off the tee with a driver. Overspin will cause the ball to roll a little farther after it hits the ground. So my tee shot would, I expected, be hitting those small greens without backspin. And if the greens were dry and hard, as I expected, the ball might never stop rolling this side of the Continental Divide.

So I was proposing to use a power club—the driver—rather than a placement club—the iron —on a hole that demanded placement as well as power. And I was accepting overspin, not backspin, on a green that threatened to be faster than the Indianapolis Speedway on Memorial Day.

"Boldness" is what my friends called it. "Insanity" is what they meant.

But I figured to have two things going for me when the ball hit the green.

If the ball went through the rough, not over it, the thick grass would cut down significantly on the ball's momentum, and very likely on how far it would roll, once it hit the green. Also, I'd be playing this hole relatively early in the morning on the first three rounds. (On the fourth and last round—because of the way the U.S. Open was run in those days—I'd be playing it in the early afternoon.) I knew that every green was being heavily watered at night, simply because the tournament officials were afraid that otherwise the greens would be hard and dry by the afternoon. So in the morning, the first green—obviously the first to be played—would likely be heavily laden with the water from the all-night sprinkling, and the water residue would slow down any ball hit onto it. That's another reason why the roll of the ball would be reduced.

(You didn't *really* think that I just went out there and hit the ball hard, without giving any thought to what would happen to it once it came down—now did you?)

The way I looked at it, all I had to do was pound the ball bouncingly through the rough and onto the heavily watered green. Then I'd one-putt and have an eagle. I'd have that course by the throat, and—as my fellow pro, Jerry Barber, once said—"shake it to death."

Only it didn't happen. Not on the first three rounds. That green was tough to reach with a rifle, much less a driver. In my first round I sent my tee shot into the ditch on the right. I didn't get an eagle or a birdie or a par on the hole. I didn't even get a bogey, for that matter. I got a double-bogey six—two over par, instead of the two under par that I'd aimed for. After that, things got better—but not much. I got a bogey five on the second round and a par four on the third round. So in the first three rounds, I'd taken fifteen strokes on that hole, instead of the twelve strokes that playing it safe might have given me. And instead of the six strokes that—in wild flights of genius—my boldness might have given me.

More than that, starting off every round with a deep disappointment damaged my whole pattern of play. After three rounds, I had a total of thirteen birdies in the tournament, but they were so scattered that I'd never gotten any momentum out of them—no "charge," so to speak. The result was that I was in fifteenth place with a 215 after three rounds.

Just before lunch, and the start of my last round, I paused outside the vast white scoreboard outside the rambling, neo-Tudor clubhouse at Cherry Hills. There in the elaborate black and red numerals of golf, written in a manner as highly stylized as medieval script, I saw how the field lay. I was seven strokes behind the leader, Mike Souchak. But Mike wasn't the only hurdle. Between me and the leadership lay such great golfers as Ben Hogan and Sam Snead, Julius Boros and Dow Finsterwald, Dave Marr and Bob Goalby, and a twenty-one-year-old amateur named Jack Nicklaus.

By the time I sat down to a sandwich in the clubhouse, my mood was about as black as a witch's heart. Ken Venturi and Bob Rosburg, who also seemed to be out of contention, joined me, and a couple of newsmen stopped by our table to offer solace to the newly bereaved.

One of them was an old friend, Bob Drum, then of the *Pittsburgh Press*. He knew of my tribulations with that first hole and of my conviction that it was an eagle hole that would unlock the entire course to the player bold enough to attack it. He also knew that my failure in a daring power approach had—in an era of golf when meticulous precision was most admired—given a certain satisfaction to a few older hands around professional golf. "There are some guys out there who think you're just an upstart, a flash-in-the-pan," he'd told me. So when he began to console me, and hint that maybe it was time to play it safe and try to pick up some good also-ran money in the U.S. Open—since it was obvious I couldn't go from fifteenth place to first place in one round—the chemistry began working in me. Explosively.

"What would happen if I shot a sixty-five on this last round?" I asked, perhaps more aggressively than in the thirst for pure knowledge.

"Nothing," said Bob. "You're out of it." He was an old friend but a realistic one. Only one man had *ever* shot a sixty-five in the final round of the U.S. Open: Walter Burkemo in 1957.

But that got to me. And to my pride. Realism—and pessimism—I did not need.

"Well," I said, my voice lowering into my don't-tread-on-me tone, "the way I read it is that a sixty-five would give me 280 for the tournament. And 280 is the kind of score that usually wins the U.S. Open."

Bob gave me a startled look, as if he just noticed I had two heads.

"Sure," he said, "but you won't do it by taking another double-bogey on the first hole."

So there it was: I still looked at the first hole as a chance for triumph; Bob—and a great many others—looked at it as a place for patent disaster. I suppose they were right. If I'd played it safe on the first hole and teed off with my iron, instead of the driver, and gone for placement and par, I'd be three shots closer to the leaders after the first three rounds. If I'd picked up a birdie or two along with it, I might even be right on their necks. So the thing to do now was admit that the first hole had me beaten and go back to playing it like the other pros did—with an iron off the tee—and figure that by placing the ball and playing it safe, I might pick up enough strokes in the standing to avoid further shame.

But that's not the way I saw it. I wasn't playing golf to avoid shame. I was playing it to win championships. And the last round of a National Open is no place to start changing your whole style and philosophy of golf.

The way I looked at it, being fifteenth made it more *imperative* that I play boldly. It couldn't cost me much: The difference between being fifteenth or twenty-fifth or fifty-fifth is not terribly meaningful—at least to me. It's the difference between first and second that has meaning. And a considered boldness might—I was sure—still win me the tournament.

So when I got to the first tee, I reached for my driver. Even though it was now one-forty-five in the afternoon and the green figured to be

Motionless, waiting, the ball is the elusive object of each golfer's swing, and only with the proper caress does he coax it into the hole.

The lashing style of Arnold Palmer displays the fiery confidence that made him into a legend.

For longevity no one beats Sam Snead, who has competed successfully as a pro for almost fifty years.

An ecstatic Jack Nicklaus kicks up his heel after sinking a crucial putt on his way to a memorable fourth U.S. Open victory at Baltusrol Golf Club.

Spain's dashing and daring Severiano Ballesteros has won the British Open and Masters Tournament, and promises to challenge the dominance of U.S. players.

New Mexico's Nancy Lopez is the latest phenomenon on the women's circuit.

Royal County Down is one version of the Irish style course.

The mystifying and subtle contours of St. Andrews Old Course have set the mold for every great golf course ever designed.

Torrey Pines North Course, located near San Diego, is one of America's finest public golf facilities.

A windmill is one hallmark of an early American course masterpiece, the National Golf Links, designed by Charles Blair Macdonald and located on Long Island.

Augusta National's 10th hole is a prelude to the famous series of holes known as Amen Corner.

One of the shortest, but most beautifully engineered par three's in the world is the 7th at Pebble Beach.

The challenge of playing the game is almost equalled by the strain of trying to see tournament action.

Courtesy United States Golf Association

Arnold Palmer's final round 65 in the 1960 U.S. Open at Cherry Hills in Denver climaxed with Palmer hurling his visor into the air to the cheers of the gallery. It was one of Palmer's greatest "charges" and helped start the golf explosion of the Sixties.

dried out and it would take incredible accuracy to hit the green and hold it. One of my luncheon companions (not Bob Drum) had come along, and he looked as if there were nothing wrong with me that brain surgery couldn't cure. I addressed the ball as if it were my enemy—or my slave—and hit it with everything I could get into it. The ball went up and hung in the sharp, clear air as if it had been painted there. When it came down—with overspin—it leaped forward and ran through the rough and right onto the middle of the green.

Twenty feet from the hole.

Three hundred and forty-six yards and I'd not only driven the green but drilled it right in the heart!

Just like I'd been planning it all along.

Right? Right!

Okay—two putts. A birdie, not an eagle. But that didn't much depress me. For I'd shown that my idea *did* work—that boldness could conquer this hole. And that if it made the first hole yield, then the whole course could be conquered with boldness.

Suddenly my whole spirit, my entire attitude changed.

I charged onto the second hole—a 410-yard par four with an elevated green and trees right in the fairway. In two shots I was not quite on the green. But I chipped the ball from off the green right into the cup for another birdie three. I charged onto the 348-yard third hole and birdied it. I charged onto the fourth hole and birdied it with a twisting forty-foot putt. Four holes: four birdie threes. A par on the fifth, a birdie on the sixth, a birdie on the seventh: six birdies on seven holes. I finished the first nine holes in thirty strokes, just one short of a record.

"Damn!" I said to Bob Drum when he finally caught up to us. "I really wanted that twenty-nine." Bob exhibited deplorable self-control: "Well," he murmured consolingly, "maybe next time."

By the tenth hole, I was tied with Mike Souchak. By the twelfth, I was ahead of him. But it was not all over: There had been fourteen men between me and the lead, and before the afternoon was over, a half dozen or more held or challenged for the title. "This was, to put it mildly, the wildest Open ever," said *Sports Illustrated.* For me, the birdies disappeared, but the pars survived. The final five holes at Cherry Hills are a punishing finishing stretch: Ben Hogan, then forty-seven, felt it, and he faded here; Nicklaus was twenty-one, and so did he. I managed to play each of those last five holes in par and to come in with a sixty-five for the eighteen-hole round. Boldness had paid off: That surge at the start was, in the words of golf writer Herbert Warren Wind, "the most explosive stretch of sub-par golf any golfer has ever produced in the championship. . . ." I finished the tournament with a seventy-two-hole score of 280. That was enough to give me the U.S. Open championship and, as it developed, a certain hold on history.

For the "charge" didn't stop there. It was not, in the long perspective, to be confined solely to one round or one tournament. It became a sort of phenomenon that marked my career: In the period 1960–1963, I was to win thirty-two tournaments—and go on to become the first million-dollar winner in golf history.

The 1964 United States Open: The Third Man, Ken Venturi

by HERBERT WARREN WIND

Among American golf writers, Herbert Warren Wind occupies a preeminent position. Author of the definitive history, The Story of American Golf, *he was the original golf writer for* Sports Illustrated *and his graceful prose has appeared in the* New Yorker *for many years. Wind has crafted many wonderful stories and one of his best is the following portrait of the valiant Ken Venturi, the 1964 U.S. Open champion.*

THERE is no question at all in my mind but that the 1964 United States Open Championship, which Ken Venturi won last month at the Congressional Country Club, in Washington, will be remembered as one of the greatest Opens. Such an assertion takes in a good deal of territory, I know, because over the years since 1895, when ten professionals and one amateur teed off in the inaugural U.S. Open, the national championship has, far more often than not, produced climaxes that have outfictioned fiction. Probably no Open can ever match the 1913 championship at the Country Club, in Brookline, Massachusetts, when Francis Ouimet, then an unknown twenty-year-old amateur up from the caddie shack, tied the regal British professionals Harry Vardon and Ted Ray and then went on to defeat them in a three-man playoff, but that is the only Open I would con-sider more stirring than the one that has just taken place. I am not for a moment forgetting the 1960 Open, at Cherry Hills, near Denver, when Arnold Palmer came dashing out of nowhere to birdie six of the first seven holes on his final round and go driving on to a sixty-five and vic-tory—or, to cite just one more example, the 1950 Open, at Merion, outside Philadelphia, which Ben Hogan captured only sixteen months after an all-but-fatal auto accident had made it ex-tremely doubtful whether he would be able to walk again, let alone be a force in competitive golf.

The 1964 Open was notable for much more than a powerful third act. From the morning of the first round, when Sam Snead, the ablest golfer who has never won our national cham-pionship, ensured his twenty-fourth failure in the event by four-putting the fourth green and then three-putting the sixth (after which he flung his ball in disgust into a convenient water hazard), the tournament was charged with exceptional golf and exceptional human intest, and both kept building until we were presented with the im-probable spectacle of a winner emerging from golf's deepest limbo to stagger ashen-faced down the long incline to the final green after beating off not only his last challengers but the threat of heat prostration. To my knowledge, there has never been anything like this in golf history.

A hundred and fifty qualifiers started the Open this year, as usual, but the championship is really the story of three players—Venturi, Palmer, and Tommy Jacobs. Thursday, the day of the first round, belonged almost completely to Palmer. He was a comparatively late starter, going off at twelve-twenty-five, when two-thirds of the field were out on the course or already back at the clubhouse. One of the first men out, Bill Collins, who had the advantage of shooting to greens that hadn't yet been baked hard by the fierce sun, had succeeded in matching par—seventy—but in general the scores were running high, and so was the feeling among the golfers that once again an Open course had been made a bit too severe. For a change, the chief complaint was not that the United States Golf Association, which conducts the Open, had narrowed the fairways too drastically and allowed the rough to grow impossibly high and lush; in fact, it was agreed that the fairways were wide almost to the point of generosity, and that the rough, emaciated by a prolonged dry spell, was eminently playable. Since there was also a minimum of fairway bunkering, Congressional undoubtedly constituted the easiest examination in driving of any Open course in at least a decade. What, then, was giving everyone so much trouble? Well, a number of things. To begin with, Congressional, at 7,053 yards, was the longest course in Open history, and some of the Brobdingnagian par fours—particularly two holes that are ordinarily played by the club members as par fives but had been converted into par fours for the championship—were breeding all kinds of bogeys. On these holes, some of the shorter hitters were unable to reach the greens with two-woods, and the longer hitters, who could get home with an iron, found that their low-trajectory approaches were bounding off the greens. Another complaint—and again a legitimate one—was that the greens, a blend of grasses known as Arlington bent and Congressional bent, were exceedingly grainy. On long approach putts against the grain, it took a real rap to get the ball up to the hole, and on sidehill putts it was hard to judge how much to allow for the break—sometimes the ball didn't break at all.

Just when the conviction was setting in that, under the existing conditions, no one would be able to score below seventy, Palmer went out and brought in a sixty-eight. He was not in his most impressive form, either—especially on the first nine, where he hooked several drives badly. Palmer is a resourceful scrambler when he has to be, though, and he bailed himself out of trouble with deft chipping and putting until he got his driving under control. He paced himself shrewdly, picking up his birdies on the short drive-and-pitch par fours, and coming through with his best tee shots on the long par fours, where his tremendous power enabled him to play his approaches to the hard greens with lofted medium irons. (For example, on the thirteenth, 448 yards long and with the green lying at the top of a fairly steep rise, he got home with a five-iron on his second.) Still, his most conspicuous assets were, as usual, his huge confidence and poise. Whereas the awareness of participating in an important championship like the Open rattles most players, even the seasoned ones, Palmer thrives on the pressure, the crowds, the noise—the whole charged-up atmosphere. As he put together his sixty-eight, to take a two-shot lead, he seemed more relaxed than a man strolling around his own back yard, and one got the feeling that he might very well be on his way to repeating his classic performance in the Masters last April, when he jumped into a tie for the lead on the first day and then pulled farther and farther away.

Friday, the day of the second round, was humid and breezeless, with the temperature hovering around ninety, but the course played a shade more easily, because, for one thing, a rainstorm shortly after daybreak had taken some of the starch out of the greens. For another thing, a threat of more rain during the day had prompted the officials to place the pins in high spots that would drain well and were less exacting targets. Palmer, one of the earlier starters, reached the turn in thirty-four, one under par. He was playing very well. When he rolled in a curving thirty-five-footer for a birdie three on the tough thirteenth, to go two strokes under par for the round and four strokes under par for the tournament, it looked as if he would be holding such a comfortable lead at the end of the first thirty-six holes that on Saturday, when both the third and the fourth rounds would be played, a pair of steady, unfancy seventy-twos would be all he would need to wrap up his second victory in the Open.

Only one other player was making any substantial headway against par. This was Tommy Jacobs, a twenty-nine-year-old Californian who was appearing in his seventh Open. One of the most mature young men on the professional circuit, Jacobs is quite an interesting golfer. Essentially more of a swinger than a hitter, he has a tendency to become a little erratic when the tempo of his swing goes awry, but he can get awfully hot, particularly on long, punishing courses. He plays a much bolder game than most of his all-too-odds-conscious colleagues, and , in addition, he has streaks when he holes putts from all over the greens. On his first round at Congressional, Jacobs had been two strokes under par after the first eleven holes, only to finish weakly with four bogeys on the remaining seven holes, for a seventy-two. On his second round, playing two threesomes in front of Palmer, he was once again two under par after eleven holes, but this time, instead of faltering, he started to take Congressional apart as if it were a hotel course in Switzerland. Having birdied the thirteenth just before Palmer did, he proceeded to birdie the fourteenth, by planting a six-iron approach five-feet from the cup, and then birdied the par-five fifteenth with a fourteen-foot putt. This burst put him five shots under par for the first fifteen holes, and spectators from all over the course, including a few Palmer men on detached service from what is known as Arnold's Army, raced to the sixteenth hole to see if Jacobs could hold on the rest of the way. Jacobs occasionally becomes a bit nervous under the strain of competition, but there was not the slightest suggestion of tension about him as he parred the next two holes and then confronted the eighteenth, a par four an intimidating 465 yards long,

on which the last 400 yards of the fairway sweep down to a thumb-shaped green that juts well out into a sizable pond. After driving down the left side of the fairway, Jacobs, rejecting a more cautious shot, fired a five-iron right at the pin. The ball had perfect line, but after plummeting down onto the front edge of the green it stopped dead, a full sixty feet from the cup. Jacobs stepped up and coolly holed that monstrous putt. His sixty-four did several things. It gave him a halfway-mark total of 136 and catapulted him into the lead, a stroke in front of Palmer, who added a splendid sixty-nine to his opening sixty-eight. It equaled the record low score for an Open round, set by Lee Mackey, Jr., at Merion in 1950. (Mackey, incidentally, had an eighty-one on his next round.) It demonstrated that Congressional, like the first-class course everyone was beginning to realize it was, required excellent golf but would yield to brilliance. Furthermore, as all the facts of Jacobs's round became known—that he had missed the fairway only twice with his tee shots, for example, and that in hitting all but two of the greens on the regulation stroke he had eleven times put his approach twenty feet or less from the pin—there was much speculation as to whether his sixty-four might not be the finest round ever played by a man in serious contention in a major championship. For my part, I would place it ahead of Palmer's sixty-five in 1960 at Cherry Hills, Gene Sarazen's sixty-six in 1932 at Fresh Meadow, on Long Island, and Henry Cotton's sixty-five in the 1934 British Open at the Royal St. George's, in Sandwich, for all three of those courses were far less demanding than Congressional. Indeed, Hogan's sixty-seven in 1951 at Oakland Hills, near Detroit, is the only round that seems to me to be in a class with Jacobs's sixty-four. (It should, however, be noted that Palmer's sixty-five, Sarazen's sixty-six, and Hogan's sixty-seven all came on the fourth round and carried all three to victory.)

Ever since 1898, when our Open, taking its cue from the older British Open, was extended to seventy-two holes, the final thirty-six have been played in one day. Once, most seventy-two-

Courtesy Wally McNamee/ The Washington Post

The 1964 U.S. Open was played in four days of sweltering, heart-sapping heat over the difficult Congressional Country Club. In a dramatic comeback effort, Ken Venturi, pictured here after sinking his final putt, won the title and wrote one of golf's most emotional stories.

hole tournaments were set up this way, but in the years after the Second World War there was a trend to a less demanding (and more lucrative) arrangement—one that called for four days of play, with a single round each day. Today, the Open is the only tournament of any consequence in this country that still adheres to the climactic double round. It does so because the United States Golf Association remains convinced that endurance as well as skill should be a requisite of a national champion. Certainly only the soundest swings can stand up under the attrition of thirty-six holes in one day, and that is what the USGA has in mind when it speaks of endurance. On Saturday morning at Congressional, however, with the temperature climbing into the nineties, it was apparent that sheer physical endurance would also be necessary. For this reason, most veteran observers felt that Palmer, who is probably the strongest man in golf, would outlast and outplay Jacobs. Another point in Palmer's favor was that the two leaders were paired, as is customary on Open Saturday, and it was thought that Jacobs would find the stress of a head-to-head duel harder to take than Palmer. No other golfer was given more than an outside chance of catching the front-runners. The nearest man, Collins, stood at 141, four shots behind Palmer and five behind Jacobs. Venturi and Charlie Sifford, the outstanding Negro professional, were next, at 142.

The first surprise of the long, scorching day was Palmer's rocky start. Obviously impatient, he went aggressively for the pin on his approaches from the very first hole. Despite the fact that the greens had been soaked by a heavy rain during the night and were holding well, these were questionable tactics—or at least they seemed so after Palmer missed the first five greens. He hit the sixth, but when he then three-putted it, he fell four shots behind Jacobs, who was playing placidly and well. At this point, a third man most unexpectedly entered the picture—Venturi. Paired with Ray Floyd two twosomes in front of Palmer and Jacobs, Venturi had birdied the eighth at about the time Palmer was three-putting the sixth. It was his fourth birdie of the day.

He had begun his rush on the first green, when his ten-foot putt for a birdie had hung on the lip of the cup for almost a minute and then toppled in. After that happy augury, he had gone on to birdie the fourth, the sixth and the eighth and to par the other holes, and so, as he moved with his habitual splay-footed stride down the ninth fairway, wearing his habitual white cap and frown of concentration, he was no longer on the periphery of contention, he was in the thick of it. He had actually overtaken and passed Palmer.

The ninth hole, a par five measuring 599 yards, is the longest hole at Congressional. It is called the Ravine Hole, because, about 110 yards from the green, the fairway, after ascending a gentle hillside, plunges abruptly down some forty feet and then rises as sharply to a relatively small, well-trapped green. It is doubtful if any player in the field could have reached the ninth green in two shots, and , in any event, no one was of a mind to try it; on both banks of the ravine, the fairway had been allowed to grow up into rough, so there was nothing to be gained by taking the gamble. The sensible way to play the ninth, and the way every man in the field attempted to play it, was to lay up short of the ravine on the second shot (usually with a long iron) and hope to put the third shot close enough to the pin to have a crack at a birdie. On his third round, Venturi did precisely this, punching his third, a firm wedge shot, eight feet from the pin. He got the putt down to reach the turn in thirty, five shots under par. (His irons to the green had been so accurate that his score could have been even lower; he had missed holeable birdie putts on both the third and the seventh greens.) Venturi kept on going. After getting his pars on the tenth and eleventh holes, he hit what was possibly his best iron shot of the morning on the 188-yard par-three twelfth—a full-blooded four-iron, which stopped hole-high about sixteen feet to the left of the pin. He played the sidehill putt to break down some three inches, and it fell into the middle of the cup. That birdie put Venturi six under par for the round and four under par for the tournament. A glance at a nearby scoreboard brought the news that Jacobs had meanwhile bogeyed both the eighth and the ninth and was now only three under par for the distance. It was hard to believe, but it was a fact: Venturi was leading the Open.

If any golfer in the field had swept to the front on Saturday in such a fantastic fashion, his surge would naturally have excited the galleries at Congressional, but the fact that it was Ken Venturi who was working this miracle made the air incalculably more electric. Venturi's rapid rise to fame and subsequent tumble back into obscurity are familiar to all who follow golf. The son of the manager of the pro shop at the Harding Park public course, in San Francisco, he first achieved national recognition in 1953, when, a slim, handsome twenty-two-year-old amateur, he was selected for our Walker Cup team. In 1956, still an amateur after completing a tour of duty in the army, he confounded the golf world by decisively outplaying the whole field in the first three rounds of the Masters at Augusta and entering the final round with an authoritative four-stroke lead. Then he shot a jittery eighty, and lost the tournament by a stroke. It should be remarked, I think, that his play on that last round was not the utter collapse it has since been called, for he hit no really bad shots; rather, he kept missing the greens on his approaches by small margins, and he failed to hole any of the five- and six-foot putts that his chips left him. In two subsequent years, he came very close to winning at Augusta. In 1958, when Palmer first broke through in the Masters, Venturi, who was paired with him on the final round, was only a shot behind as they entered the stretch, but Palmer shook off his challenge by making a memorable eagle on the thirteenth. In the 1960 Masters, Venturi fought his way back into the battle after a spotty first round, and had the tournament apparently won when Palmer, the only man he still had to worry about, caught him by birdieing the seventy-first hole and beat him by birdieing the seventy-second.

After this third disappointment in the Masters, something went out of Venturi's game, and in a relatively short time it was apparent that he was no longer the superb golfer he had been

between 1956, when he turned professional, and 1960. In those days, he had been not only one of the leading money-winners on the professional tour but probably the most proficient shotmaker in the country. I believe that the Venturi of that period was the finest iron-player I have ever seen —not excepting Byron Nelson, Venturi's teacher. Venturi's style with the irons was not particularly graceful. He took the club back in an upright arc with three rather distinct segments to it, but he arrived at the top of his backswing with his hands in an ideal position and his body perfectly balanced, and it seemed that all he had to do then in order to come into the ball just as he wanted to was to move his hips a notch to the left at the start of the downswing. Moreover, he possessed a rare instinct for iron play; he adapted his shots not only to the wind and the weather but also to the terrain he was playing from and playing to. For example, he would feather one approach in to the flag with a little left-to-right drift and burn his next approach in low and hard and dead on the target. By 1961, though, as I say, he was no longer playing golf of this caliber, and in the succeeding years his game continued to disintegrate. A succession of physical ailments, ranging from a back injury to walking pneumonia, contributed to this decline, but even when Venturi was feeling fit he played unimpressively. His confidence seemed completely shot. He failed to qualify for the Open in 1961, 1962 and 1963, and last year his total winnings on the professional tour came to less than $4,000. This spring he suffered the crowning humiliation of having to watch the Masters at home on television, because he had not qualified for an invitation to the 1964 tournament.

Venturi's behavior during his protracted ordeal was exemplary, and it won him the admiration of his fellow professionals. He never bellyached about his lot, he was not envious of his friends' successes, and he quietly kept trying to put his game together again. This display of character came as a surprise to a number of people around golf. As a young man and one of Hogan's heirs presumptive, he had shown himself to be pleasant and very likable, but, perhaps because his honors had come to him so quickly and easily, there seemed to be large areas in which he lacked perception and tact. After a low round at Augusta, for example, he would come sweeping up the stairs of the clubhouse, the reporters and photographers at his heels, and, sailing by the likes of Hogan and Snead, he would scale his cap halfway across the players' lounge as if he owned the world. He was not arrogant, though; he was simply very young. In adversity, he grew up, and revealed himself as a man of fiber. Late this spring he suddenly began to play quite well again. In June, in the two weeks preceding the Open, he tied for third in the Thunderbird Open and then tied for sixth in the Buick Open. Though his putting stroke remained somewhat unsound, which it always had been, and though he hit a few wild shots in each round, he was setting himself up far more comfortably before the ball than he had done in years, he was playing with a new vigor, and he was concentrating well.

At Congressional, I watched a good part of Venturi's first two rounds, for, like everyone else, I wanted very much to see him do well. His opening seventy-two could easily have been several shots higher, for he played a number of holes very loosely. He topped one bunker shot cold, fluffed another bunker shot completely, and, on a hole where his heeled drive wound up deep in the rough, did not even reach the fairway with his recovery. On his second round, he played much more surely, en route to a seventy. Early in the round, he sank a few bothersome putts, which did his morale a great deal of good, and he was rifling his irons like the Venturi of old. At the same time, not even his warmest supporters would ever have dreamed that on Saturday he would have the shots, the fire, and the emotional composure to birdie six of the first twelve holes and go out in front.

Venturi did not stay out in front very long. Jacobs, summoning up some fine attacking shots, played the second nine in thirty-four—one under par—to post a seventy and a fifty-four-hole total of 206. Venturi, after taking a thirty-six in for a sixty-six, stood at 208. Near the end of the morning round, he had wavered discernibly. On the seventeenth green, he had missed a putt of just eighteen inches, and on the last green he had missed one of thirty inches, in both cases also missing his par. We could only give him all credit for his gallant dash and conclude that apparently he had just run out of gas. Perhaps, after all, that was inevitable for Venturi. Strangely, everyone at Congressional, I think, felt a bit better about things when, shortly after he returned to the clubhouse at the luncheon interval, it was announced that he had been near collapse from the heat on the last five holes. His seemingly imminent failure could at least be attributed to forces beyond his control. On the advice of a doctor, he spent the bulk of the fifty-minute interval resting. He drank some tea but ate no solid food. Then he took some salt tablets and headed for the first tee, accompanied by the doctor, who walked the final round with him.

The leaders had hardly begun the final round when, for the first time in hours, Palmer got back into the picture. In the morning, harried by his wretched putting, he had never really recovered from his poor start and had ended up with a seventy-five, giving him a total of 212 at the three-quarters mark and putting him six shots behind Jacobs and four behind Venturi. All morning long, Palmer had not made a single birdie, but he started his afternoon with a flamboyant one. Jacobs then double-bogeyed the par-three second, after pulling his tee shot into deep trouble, and Palmer closed to within three shots of him. It now looked very much as if we might be seeing one of Palmer's patented whirlwind finishes. However, when he failed to make even his pars on two of the next four holes it became clear, tardily, that the significant thing about Jacobs's double bogey was that it had thrust Venturi back into a tie for first. Playing two holes ahead of Palmer and Jacobs, Venturi looked drawn and pale, and he was walking slowly on stiff, old man's legs, but he was executing his shots with poise and hitting the ball with an astonishing sharpness. He came to the ninth, the 599-yard Ravine Hole, after parring seven of the first eight, still tied for the lead with Jacobs.

I arrived at the ninth too late to see Venturi play his drive or his second shot. His drive must not have been very long, for, I was told, he played a full one-iron on his second. What a shot that must have been! There was his ball sitting up in the middle of the fairway a mere five yards from the edge of the ravine. Only an extremely confident golfer would have attempted to lay up so daringly close to the brink, and as I gazed at the ball it occurred to me for the first time that Venturi could win the Open. In any event, that audacious one-iron put him in position to birdie the hole. The flag was set far to the back of the green, so that there was a menacing trap only about twenty feet directly behind it, but Venturi went for the pin and stopped his wedge nine feet past it. Faced with a delicate downhill putt that broke to the left, he played it exactly right; his ball caught the high corner of the cup and spun in. When it dropped, I felt for the first time that Venturi *would* win the Open. With this beautifully engineered birdie four, he had regained the undisputed lead, and, as it turned out, he not only held on to it the rest of the way but widened it—eventually to four strokes—for he played par golf in, and both Jacobs and Palmer, forced to gamble at this stage of the game, ran into a succession of bogeys.

Indeed, after the ninth it became increasingly evident that only the possibility of physical collapse stood between Venturi and victory. The sun was still beating down furiously, and on the fourteenth hole, where he had started to wobble in the morning, his slow walk decelerated into a painful trudge and his head began to droop. Into my mind's eye, as I watched him, came a photograph from old sports books showing Dorando Pietri, the little Italian marathon runner, being helped by his countrymen across the finish line in the 1908 Olympic Games after he had crumpled in exhaustion only a few yards from his goal. Venturi hung on tenaciously, however, and, while he hit at least one very tired shot on each hole after that, some fortunate bounces and his own tidy work around the greens saw him safely through to the eighteenth hole, the long par four

sloping gradually down to the peninsula green. He needed only a seven there to win. His tee shot was weak but straight. He blocked out his five-iron approach to the right, away from the water, and went into a bunker about forty yards from the pin. He played a much braver recovery than he had to—a beautiful, floating wedge shot that sat down ten feet from the cup. He holed the putt. He had done it.

While I think that the thousands encamped the length of the eighteenth fairway will always treasure that moment when Venturi walked triumphantly off the final green, a champion at last, I am sure they would agree with me that the Open reached its dramatic peak a few moments earlier, when, after hitting his second shot, he came walking shakily down the long slope. He was going to make it now, he knew, and in response to the tumultuous ovation he received as he descended the hill he removed his cap, for the first time that day. A little sun would not hurt now. I shall never forget the expression on his face as he came down the hill. It was taut with fatigue and strain, and yet curiously radiant with pride and happiness. It reminded me of another unforgettable, if entirely different, face—the famous close-up of Charlie Chaplin at the end of *City Lights,* all anguish beneath the attempted smile. Venturi then put his cap back on and hit those two wonderful final shots.

Few things repair a man as quickly as victory. At his press conference back in the air-conditioned clubhouse, Venturi, who has a bright wit, made a number of trenchant remarks. Since we live in an age when every golf hero's band of supporters bears a catchy alliterative name, such as Arnold's Army, Nicklaus's Navy, and Lema's Legions, the new champion got perhaps his biggest laugh when, as he was commenting on how much the cheering of the crowds had helped him all day long, he interrupted himself to say, "For years, all I ever had was Venturi's Vultures." Perhaps he had said this before, but if he had no one was listening.

The Professional, Walter Hagen

by FRED CORCORAN with BUD HARVEY

The mechanism of pro sport was created by men like Fred Corcoran, an agent, official and promoter who truly loved the game. Corcoran is enshrined in the World Golf Hall of Fame. His work lives in the success of the PGA and LPGA tours, which he helped set up, and the World Cup, which was his favorite project until his death. It was Corcoran, along with the flamboyant Walter Hagen, who created the foundations for the media-rich PGA tour and the player management empire of a Mark McCormack.

LET'S make an important distinction right here. There are golf professionals and there are professional golfers. The two terms are not necessarily synonymous. The golf professional is a man who sells you golf balls and, when the occasion calls for it, prescribes for your golfing ills. The professional golfer plays golf for money.

Walter Hagen was a professional golfer, although he may not have been the greatest professional golfer who ever drew breath. I'd have to go along with Ben Hogan in this department, because he owns just about every record in the book, plus a dozen you won't find there. But Hagen was the first professional to make a million dollars at the game—and the first to spend it. If Hogan was the king, Hagen was the prince, and the darling of the people. Where Hogan walked the fairways looking neither to the left nor right, Hagen—in his own words—met a million persons.

He was the corporal of the color guard. No question about it. He had that magnetism, the electric quality, that fired the imagination. He lived the life lesser men dream about as they plod back and forth every day between their offices and the subway.

I suppose I've told more stories about Walter Hagen than about any other sports figure I've ever known. And not because I was that close to Hagen. I wasn't. But only because Hagen himself is a living legend and the sports world is filled with curiosity about him.

The strange part of it is, the legend has distorted the actual portrait. True, Hagen loved life and people. And he hated to go to bed because sleeping seemed like such a waste of time. But the picture of Hagen flashing through life with champagne bubbling out of his ears is a false one. The Hagen of his golden years took excellent care of himself. He was the world's champion hider of drinks. Walter always had a full glass in his hand. But after the ball was over, the sweeper would find a dozen drinks lined up behind the piano where Hagen had slyly stashed them during the revels.

That first year on the PGA tour, I met Walter at San Francisco during the Oakland Open. He was embarking on a world exhibition tour and I had just been named manager of the American Ryder Cup team. We discussed arrangements for handling the team which would be selected that year to play in England. Walter, who was named the nonplaying captain of the American side, said he was planning his itinerary to reach London in time to meet us.

True to his word, Hagen was standing on the station platform in London when the boat train arrived from Plymouth at 2 A.M. And I remember so clearly the picture he made standing there as fresh and debonair as if it were 9 A.M.

While the luggage was being sorted and the hatboxes were being loaded aboard taxis, he drew me aside.

"You'll have to help me identify these wives," he said. "Some I know, but most of them I've never met."

He didn't offend any of them. As they stepped off the train he gave each one a little hug and called her Sugar.

This was so typical of Hagen, this thoughtfulness. He always seemed concerned for the sensibilities of others. I'll never forget his acceptance speech at the end of the matches. When the American team won, Walter began writing memos to himself and stuffing them in the pocket of his polo coat.

"We want to make sure we don't forget anyone," he kept repeating, and down would go another note, perhaps a reminder not to forget an accolade for the assistant greenskeeper.

So he had a pocketful of paper when he took his seat for the presentation ceremonies. Unfortunately, he tossed his polo coat over a chair at the far side of the dais and when the time came for him to accept the Ryder Cup, he reached in vain for his verbal ammunition. Walter sighed and stood up.

"You have no idea," he began, "how proud I am to captain the first American Ryder Cup team to win on home soil . . ."

Several voices in the throng interrupted him at this point to shout: "You mean *foreign* soil, Walter!"

Hagen shrugged. His face broke into a wide smile and he said:

"You can't blame me for feeling completely at home over here, now can you?"

That was all he had to say. The crowd loved it, and loved him for it.

The matches were played at Southport where Hagen saw Snead for the first time. Sam, you'll recall, burst on the golf scene that year like a meteor and had played his way onto the Ryder squad. Walter watched Snead for a few practice holes and marked him immediately as a great player. Yet, he didn't play Sam in the foursome matches and he told me why.

"He's never played an alternate shot affair, has he?" Walter said. "I don't believe I'll play him the first day. It wouldn't be fair to him. He's strange to the game and not familiar with the rules."

So he limited Sam to the singles matches and Sam crushed Richard Burton by six and five.

I first saw Hagen play in the U.S. Open at Brae Burn in 1919 when he beat Mike Brady in a playoff. I was working the scoreboard for the USGA, my first assignment of that kind. Hagen was only twenty-seven years old, but already a sports page celebrity and well on his way to becoming the legend he is now, a bronzed fine specimen of a man who strode down the fairway with his head high. Hagen always walked with his head in the air as if, subconsciously, looking over the heads of ordinary mortals.

He came up to the last hole of regulation play needing a pretty good putt to tie Brady who was already in. Impeccable as always in his traditional white silk shirt and silk tie, Hagen lazily drew his putter and surveyed the putt. Then he looked up with a smile and called, "Where's Mike?"

He wanted Brady out there watching while he stroked home the tying putt. It would give Mike something to think about for the next twenty-four hours.

The playoff round wasn't much of a golfing exhibition. Neither played well. But the turning point came at the seventeenth hole where Hagen took command with a typical Hagen combination

Sir Walter Hagen, as he was known, poses in his 1920s prime, when he was winning all the major titles of the day and capturing the fancy of golfers in both America and England. Hagen became the game's first international superstar.

of brains and skill. He put his tee shot into a peat pocket where it lay virtually buried. Then, as now, there was a penalty for playing the wrong ball, so equity permitted the lifting and cleaning of the ball for purpose of identification. Hagen asked the officials to have the buried ball identified. Naturally, when it was dropped again, the lie was improved considerably. Hagen then put his next shot on the green, holed out in four, and went on to win—a patented Hagen finish.

In 1940 I met Monsignor Robert Barry, a low handicap golfer himself, who was having lunch at the famed Thompson's Spa, across the street from the *Boston Globe*. He said, "Tell me, how is Walter Hagen?" I told him Walter was fine when I had last seen him.

"You know," said the priest, "when I was going to the monastery I would drive a couple of hundred miles on a weekend just to watch him play. There was something about the man I found fascinating. I enjoyed watching him . . . the way he dressed . . . his actions . . . his wonderful golf . . . everything he did was so dramatic. Tell me about him."

Well, what do you tell one man about another? I suppose, instinctively, you try to relate him to the mainstream of the other's life.

"You know," I said, "Walter is not a religious man. I know he believes in God, but if I ever wanted to go looking for him I wouldn't start with a church." I thought a little and added, "I have an idea he's broken eleven of the Ten Commandments, but I'll tell you something else, father, I think I'd like to be with Hagen wherever he goes when he dies . . ."

Monsignor Barry's eyes were following me closely and he was nodding silently. I went on.

"Now, another thing. He's done more for people than anyone I know. For instance, he always takes good care of his caddie. If the boy needs a lift into town, Walter remembers. He always remembers to give the boy a little gift. And he's like that with the other players. Always giving . . . not only his money, but himself . . ."

"Now," I said, "I'd like to ask you this: How are we going to be judged?"

The monsignor didn't hesitate a moment.

"I'll answer you, Fred, by saying the Walter Hagen you have just described has the quality we all must have to earn heaven. That's charity."

Faith, hope and charity, he pointed out, abideth. And the greatest of these, as the Gospels tell us, is charity.

Well, I found this conversation very interesting and, the next time I saw Walter, I reported it. Hagen sat quietly for a moment, looking down at his feet, then he said softly:

"I'm not a very saintly person, I know, but I've tried my best to go through life without deliberately hurting anyone . . ."

Hagen was the first true American golfing internationalist. He enjoyed meeting new people and seeing new places. He was an authentic citizen of the world.

In 1942 I was going to England as a Red Cross volunteer and Hagen made me promise to stop at the Savoy, his favorite London haunt.

"And be sure to ask for Karl Hefflin," he said. "He's the manager. Give him my regards and tell him I asked him to take good care of you."

So I arrived at the Savoy in due time and asked for Mr. Hefflin who met me in the lobby with a puzzled frown. When I identified myself and extended greetings from Hagen, the puzzled frown vanished.

"Oh," he said, "the boy must have misunderstood you. He thought you said *you* were Walter Hagen. And, you know, we've had three bombing raids in the past month and, as I was coming down to meet you, I was asking myself, 'How can I take these air raids *and Walter Hagen, too?*'"

But he said it with affection, and went on to inquire about Walter who, over the years, had become his favorite American guest.

Until Hagen and Gene Sarazen came along, American golf existed in a vacuum. American golfers stood with their backs to the Atlantic and either didn't know or didn't care that the game had any roots. Hagen and Sarazen turned our faces back to the wellspring of golf. Walter was never happier than when, as a player or a captain, he was leading an American team of professionals over to Britain. He believed every American professional worthy of the name owed it to himself and to the game to play in at least one British Open championship. Or *the* Open, as he called it.

Sam Snead, with the other American Ryder Cuppers, had played in the 1937 Open at Carnoustie, following the matches that year. But he hadn't played well at all, and he never went back. In 1946 I entered Sam in the British Open which was going to be played at St. Andrews, shrine of golf and home of the Royal and Ancients.

But during the last round of the Inverness Four-Ball tournament and on the eve of his scheduled departure for Britain, Sam came to me at the ninth hole and said, "Fred, I'm not going. I'm just not putting well and there's no point in me going over there if I can't get the damn ball in the hole . . ."

Well, our plans were all made. He was supposed to fly that evening to New York and take off for England the next day. I remember going into the clubhouse and the first person I met was Walter Hagen. I told him Snead had decided not to play in the Open.

"What's the matter with him?" asked Walter.

"He says he isn't putting."

Hagen said, "Oh, what a shame! And with his touch he'd putt those greens at St. Andrews as if they belonged to him."

When Snead came off the course, Walter was waiting for him. He drew Sam off to the far end of the locker room and said, "Sam, let me see you putt." He watched Sam stroke a few balls, then he stopped him.

"Raise your blade just a little, Sam," he told him. "Try to slap that ball just above the equator. All you want to do is get it rolling . . . rolling . . . rolling . . ."

Over and over, he had Sam stroke balls on the carpet until Sam was snapping his putts with a new crispness. Then he stopped him and said, "All right, you've got it now. Go ahead over there to St. Andrews and win it."

I duly told the newspaper boys about the episode in the locker room and the next morning the local paper carried a sports page headline: "Snead to Play in British Open—Takes Putting Lesson from Walter Hagen." This was all right. But, at the same time, Snead was syndicating a series of instruction pieces and the gospel for the day was set up in a two-column box next to the main golf story. The headline over here read: "How to Putt, by Sam Snead"!

Any good story has to have a happy ending, and this one does. Snead went to St. Andrews and won the Open. He never putted better.

The only time I can recall Walter Hagen losing his poise was in his epic match with Gene Sarazen for the 1923 PGA championship. This might well be classed as the match of the century. Hagen and Sarazen were great rivals. There were unquestionably the two outstanding professional golfers of their day, and I suspect Gene always felt Hagen got the better of it in their daily battle for sports page space. This gnawed at him, and he took a special delight in whipping Hagen.

The 1923 PGA final dingdonged along through thirty-seven well-played holes. On the thirty-eight, Sarazen pulled his tee shot and it appeared to go out of bounds. In fact, to this day, Hagen insists it *did* go out of bounds and was tossed back in play by "an outside agency"—one of Gene's partisan fans who lined the playing limits at the Pelham Country Club, in the heart of "Sarazen country."

Satisfied that Gene's ball was out of bounds, Hagen played his tee shot comfortably down the middle of the fairway. Under the penalty code of the day, a ball out of bounds at this point would spell complete disaster. Sarazen could never have recovered from the penalty and all Hagen had to do was play his ball safely to the green and hole out.

But Gene's ball was found lying in the tall grass, well within the boundary stakes. Sarazen, playing with icy courage, hit a magnificent gambling second shot that carried across a dangerous elbow to the green, within a foot or two of the hole. Hagen stared at Gene in dismay and shook his head in disbelief. Then, obviously shaken, he proceeded to put his second shot in a trap, short of the green, and that was the match.

The Hagen legend has created a myth of invincibility. This isn't so, of course. Hagen lost his share of matches and tournaments and, in fact, was beaten pretty badly on occasion. I remember especially his International match with Archie Compston in 1929. Hagen had just stepped off the boat and was pretty rusty. He hadn't swung a club in weeks. Compston defeated him in a seventy-two-hole match by eighteen and seventeen!

After the first couple of holes, it became clearly apparent that things weren't going well for Hagen. Then he seemed to chuck it entirely, apparently totally unconcerned about the outcome. He seemed more interested in making adjustments in his swing. It was a curious attitude, but he explained it later and I'll never forget his words.

"If you're going to get beaten," he said, "it doesn't make any difference if you lose by one hold or by ten. It was a wonderful chance to get a lot of bad shots out of my system at once."

Two weeks later, at Muirfield, Hagen won the last of his four British Open championships with a 292, matching his best score in this championship which he cherished above all others.

Walter never showed any great enthusiasm for the marathon practice sessions that have become part of the working day for the modern tournament pros. I remember standing with him at the Colonial Club in Fort Worth, watching the players hammering away on the range. We watched Byron Nelson for several minutes while he hit a steady barrage of flawless iron shots. Hagen sighed.

"What a shame to waste those great shots on the practice tee," he said. "What are they doing out there anyway? Those guys already know how to hit a golf ball. They don't have to do that. I'd be afraid to stand out there and work at my game like that. I'd be afraid of finding out what I was doing wrong."

We turned back to the club and Hagen talked on.

"You know," he said, "I used to go out to the practice tee and hit four or five balls—just to relax and get the feel of it. I always planned to make any adjustments on the course. I always figured to make a couple of mistakes on the first few holes. But mistakes don't hurt you at this stage. It's those mistakes you make on the last few holes that kill you. I always figured to have

my game under control by then . . ."

He jerked his head back to the firing line.

"That," he said, "is nothing but corporal punishment."

I'm reminded of the time at Augusta, when Sam Snead spent an hour on the practice tee. When he came in I asked his caddie how Sam was hitting them. The boy grinned and said, "I dunno if we're gonna win the tournament, but man! we sure won the practice tee championship!"

A typical Hagen story is an account of his match with Joe Turnesa at Dallas in 1927. Hagen was the master of applied psychology and always said he liked the head-to-head character of match play. He said he always knew exactly where things stood.

On this occasion, Walter arrived at the clubhouse thirty minutes late and was sharply scolded by the tournament officials. Hagen knew he was wrong. He apologized humbly and hurried off to dress.

On the first three holes he grandly conceded putts of varying lengths and Turnesa quickly went three up. Then Hagen said, "There, that makes up for the thirty minutes I was late. Now we'll play . . ."

Well, the match rocked along until they reached the seventeenth hole—the thirty-fifth of the match—and Joe had a fairly easy putt. But Hagen made no gesture of conceding it. In fact, he was elaborately helpful to Joe in lining it up. Joe missed it and the match was all even.

They came to the last hole and Hagen put his second shot off to the right in some tall grass, partially screened off from the green by some trees. Turnesa was in good position in the middle of the fairway. Walter studied the line of flight, paced back and forth several times, tentatively drew three or four clubs from his bag. Then he turned and waved Turnesa back into the gallery.

"Joe," he called, "I may have to play this safe." Later he chuckled, "I could have driven three Mack trucks up to the green through those trees."

Then he settled down and played his shot, sticking the ball within twelve feet of the flag.

Turnesa, kept waiting and watching this strange performance, finally stepped up to his easy shot and dunked it in the trap flanking the green—and Walter had won his fifth PGA championship.

Curiously, Hagen's grandstand performance thoroughly delighted Turnesa, as it did the gallery. One of the remarkable things about Walter Hagen was the fact that, even in their defeat, his opponents all had a tremendous affection for him. In fact, Joe Turnesa tells this story with complete admiration for Hagen.

There's the famous story about Walter turning up in the lobby of the hotel in the wee small hours before his championship match with Leo Diegel. Somebody remarked to Hagen that he shouldn't be on the town at that hour with a big match staring him in the face in the morning.

"Look at that Diegel," argued the well-intentioned adviser. "He's been in bed asleep for five hours."

To this Hagen replied, "Diegel may have been in bed for five hours, but he's not sleeping . . ."

Hagen, on the other hand, could sleep like a kitten—literally. That's how he slept, all curled up in a ball. I was with Ty Cobb early in the evening in Detroit and he wanted to visit Hagen. So we went over to the Detroit Athletic Club where Walter lived, and asked for him. The clerk said Hagen was sleeping. Cobb refused to accept such a preposterous answer and said he'd see this phenomenon for himself.

So upstairs we went to Hagen's room. His door was open and we walked in. There was Hagen in bed. Cobb shouted, "Walter! Walter! Wake up!" But Hagen didn't move a muscle, just went on snoring peacefully. And Hagen, incidentally, snores pretty good. Cobb studied the sleeper and shook his head in admiration.

"There's the most relaxed man I ever saw," he commented. "See how he sleeps all rolled up in a ball? Any time you have trouble sleeping, just try it. It's complete relaxation . . ."

Bob Harlow, who played full-time manager to Hagen, used to say, "One thing about Walter, he wouldn't spend your money any faster than he spends his own . . ."

I'm reminded of this remark by stories

Tommy Armour tells about Hagen. Armour, a great champion in his own right (U.S. Open champion in 1927, PGA championship in 1930 and British Open champion in 1931), loved and admired Walter Hagen as he did no other player in the game, unless it be Jones. But Armour's natural Scottish instinct for financial responsibility was outraged at times by Walter's extravagance.

He and Hagen traveled to England together in 1929 to play in the Open.

"I gave Walter $200 before we landed," Tommy recalled, "and we went directly to the Savoy where we unpacked and I took a bath and shaved. When I came out of the bathroom there was a case of Scotch, a case of gin and a case of champagne neatly stacked against the wall. A *case* of champagne, mind you! You don't buy champagne by the case. You buy it by the bottle—chilled!

"I turned to Walter and said, 'What's all this for? Are you expecting Parliament to declare a national prohibition law overnight?'"

"Hagen spread his hands and smiled. 'But we'll be having people in and out.'"

Hagen got ready for the warm-up match with Compston we spoke of a few pages back, and Armour pleaded with him to cancel out. Walter hadn't swung a club in a long time and one practice round left his hands blistered. But Hagen insisted on playing. He met the inglorious eighteen and seventeen defeat we have already described, after which he went on to win the Open.

"After that," Armour relates, "we crossed over to France where we split up. I went down to the south of France where I had a couple of exhibition matches at Aix-les-Bains and somewhere else. Hagen stayed in Paris to play in the French Open and in some exhibitions. We met again a couple of weeks later to return to the United States.

"Now Walter had picked up about $2,800 for his exhibition with Compston," he went on, "and he took first money in the Open. He got a couple of exhibition fees in France and won that tournament purse over there. But, do you know something? I had to loan the son of a gun another $200 to get off the ship in New York!"

Typical of Hagen's legendary disregard for basic bookkeeping is what happened when the Hagen memoirs were published several years ago. The press run was 15,000 copies. Of these, Walter ordered several thousand for personal distribution. He was giving books away faster than the booksellers could find customers!

Walter was amazed and indignant when he received a bill from the publisher. He flatly refused to pay it. The idea of paying for copies of his own book struck him as the height of absurdity. The disillusioned publisher finally had to bring Hagen in for an accounting.

But that was typical of golf's most majestic and beloved personality. The daily scramble for coins in the marketplace wasn't for Walter. He lived above the tumult and the shouting. And the pixie in him wouldn't let him have any special regard for the formalities of social banking. There was the grand party he and a dozen Hollywood personalities tossed for themselves in San Francisco one year. When the waiter finally trotted around with the reckoning, Richard Arlen, the actor, demanded to pay it. But Hagen wouldn't hear of it. He snatched the tab and strode over to the cashier's desk where, with a flourish and a broad wink to several others in the party, he signed Arlen's name to the check!

Meanwhile, back at the table, the movie star was delivering an oratorical tribute to the boundless generosity of Hagen, pausing in midsentence to throw a salute across the room at Walter, who smiled broadly and waved back.

I remember, along in the early 1940s, I met the Duke of Windsor, then serving as Governor-General of the Bahamas. I proposed, in the course of a Florida conversation with him, that I would bring to Nassau for a Red Cross benefit exhibition match the four men he had seen win the British Open: Hagen, Armour, Sarazen and Jones. The duke was delighted with the prospect.

I flew to Nassau in advance of the match to complete the arrangements and we sat on the lawn of the Government House, the duke and I, chatting about golf and golfers. He asked especially about Walter and I told him one story after another.

Then I mentioned Hagen's philosophy of life. It went like this: Never hurry and don't worry. You're here for just a short visit. So don't forget to stop and smell the flowers along the way.

The duke's eyes widened and he snatched a pencil from his pocket.

"Oh, I, say," he exclaimed, "this is just priceless! Priceless! Let me write that down . . ." And he scribbled it on the back of an envelope. Then he jumped up.

"I've simply got to read this to the duchess," he said, excusing himself. "I'll be right back."

With that he sprinted for the house and went bounding up the stairs, waving the envelope and shouting for the duchess.

Somehow, every time the name of Walter Hagen comes up in a conversation I always think of that afternoon on the lawn of the government residence at Nassau—and of the king who had given up his throne, racing off to recite the Hagen philosophy to his duchess.

Elements of Greatness—
A Classic Course

by PAT WARD-THOMAS

Every golfer has an idea of what he perceives as a great hole or course. Given all the courses in the world to choose from, Pat Ward-Thomas, who has seen most of those worth remembering, assembled eighteen which combine to make a classic layout.

A great hole may be an architect's dream fashioned in a setting of rare beauty; it can have acquired greatness by constant usage and exposure; it may be a creation from the drawing board; or, like many of the old Scottish links, it may simply have evolved from use down the centuries. Whatever its origins or its claims to greatness, to support them it must be a challenge and an enjoyment to every golfer, no matter how meager or mighty his talents. It must pose problems that can be strict for the masters and yet readily leavened for the humble; it must require thought and reward those who think; its playing values must be high but not unfair. In the words of architect Robert Trent Jones, it should be a demanding par and a comfortable bogey.

No two holes anywhere in the world are precisely similar in any respect but length. The contours of the land, the setting and the architect's ideas are bound to differ, and so the manifestations of his skill are infinite. His creation may inspire admiration from one golfer, dislike from another. Golfers are highly egocentric where their own game is concerned and their judgment of a hole frequently is conditioned by personal experience alone.

With all the world to choose from, selecting the eighteen holes which will best combine to create a golf *course,* with all the considerations of balance and variety that the word implies, can be an endless challenge to memory, research and imagination. Some will inevitably find fault, claiming that this seventh, fifteenth or whatever is not the finest in the world, but who could claim without fear of contradiction that any particular hole was? Far too many imponderables are involved, but all will stand fair comparison and all embrace uncommon qualities of design and natural beauty—and surely few would disagree that together they make a classic course.

No. 1	Royal St. George's		415 yards	par 4
No. 2	Scioto		436 yards	par 4
No. 3	Durban Country Club		506 yards	par 5
No. 4	Baltusrol		194 yards	par 3
No. 5	Mid Ocean		433 yards	par 4
No. 6	Royal Melbourne		428 yards	par 4
No. 7	Cajuiles		195 yards	par 3
No. 8	Pine Valley		327 yards	par 4
No. 9	Muirfield		495 yards	par 5
		Out	3,429 yards	par 36

117

No. 10	Muirfield Village	441 yards	par 4
No. 11	The Country Club	445 yards	par 4
No. 12	Augusta National	155 yards	par 3
No. 13	Harbour Town	358 yards	par 4
No. 14	St. Andrews	567 yards	par 5
No. 15	Oakmont	453 yards	par 4
No. 16	Carnoustie	235 yards	par 3
No. 17	Cypress Point	375 yards	par 4
No. 18	Pebble Beach	540 yards	par 5
	In	3,569 yards	par 36
	Total	6,998 yards	par 72

In creating this classic test of golf, faith has been kept with the number of each hole: thus the ninth is the ninth at Muirfield, and the eighteenth is the tremendous climax to Pebble Beach. To devise a course otherwise would be false to the concept, since the quality of a hole may be indisputable, but its lasting greatness in the minds of golfers owes something to its position in the round and the imprint of history upon it. Would the twelfth at Augusta have been as famous, or infamous according to experience, had it been the seventh and not the Machiavellian centerpiece of Amen Corner? Would the fourteenth at St. Andrews have influenced the course of so many events had it been earlier in the round? Obviously not.

The features that make a great hole depend to some extent on their play on courage and fear. A golfer will take risks early in the round which he would not take towards the end. In creating closing holes the architect usually tries to present challenges that will strike fear into the hearts of the frail, inspire the accomplished player, and possibly cause indecision for those protecting a favorable position.

The eighteen holes come from courses as far apart as California and Carnoustie, Melbourne and Muirfield, Durban and the Dominican Republic. Their settings range from the timeless linksland of Britain, where the influence of man and machine on their creation was minimal and nature was the original architect, to verdant countryside where artifice and nature, tranquil or savage, have been gloriously combined, and to rock-bound ocean coasts where, as Jack Neville and Douglas Grant could not fail to perceive, the great holes of Pebble Beach, now famous the world over, were begging to be made.

The preservation of natural beauty, or an imitation of it, is crucial to the fashioning of a great hole. The impact of a formidable task is leavened if its background is appealing. Whose heart would not quicken, however apprehensive he may be of making the stroke, on the tee of the fifth at Mid Ocean, with Mangrove Lake gleaming far below him, or on the seventeenth tee at Cypress Point with that enticing sweep of fairway across the curve of a bay, where the ocean forever pounds and the gnarled old cypress trees writhe in the distance?

More often than not architects have pleasing landscape for their work, but the great expansion of golf has made it necessary to build courses where space is available, even though, as in Florida or the western deserts of America, there may be a lack of agreeable features. Then the machine and the imagination of the architect come into their own and miracles are wrought. But on this course the setting of every hole, and many of its basic features, are natural.

All the holes fulfill Robert Trent Jones's philosophy that a par must be hard-won but a bogey easily scored, it even being possible to skirt the lake at Baltusrol's short fourth. The other tee shots are not uncompromising. Demands on straightness may be fairly severe on holes like the ninth, tenth, fourteenth, fifteenth and eighteenth if there is to be lively hope of a par, but the handicap golfer has no fearsome task to keep the ball in play.

Increasingly on modern courses water is being used for penal and strategic purposes, and in differing degrees the golfer could not fail to be aware of it on seven of the holes. At the fifth and seventeenth it serves to lure him into attempting overmuch; at the short fourth and seventh holes those in hope of a par must carry it; and on the eighteenth the Pacific acts as a fairly substantial lateral water hazard. Rae's Creek, protecting the twelfth green, is an insidious, mind-torturing menace, even for the greatest players, but the quiet pool on the eleventh serves both to please and to threaten. Such can be the variety of water's uses.

Every great course should be balanced in its demands on the player's skill. Ideally, it should have two par fives and two par threes in each half, and the par fours should be varied in length and difficulty. Some holes should be straight, like the first at St. George's, and others curve left or right without overly favoring one shape of shot. The pronounced movement to the right of the sixth is balanced at the eleventh where, after driving to a rising crest of fairway, the hole swings left and flows across a gentle valley. The lake at the fifth destroys the hook; the ocean at the seventeenth punishes the slice.

The growing number of golfers who power their drives away has diminished the effect of numerous long holes. Many, like the beautiful thirteenth at Augusta, have become par four-and-a-half or less to the masters. Even for lesser mortals, unable to make the carry over the creek to the green, the demands on the second shot are far from severe. A famous old player once said, somewhat irreverently, that he could make pars on all the long holes at Augusta using a putter for his second shot. This may be true of many other par fives, but not of these; they have stood the test of time.

Few golfing aspects are more discouraging than a long toil up from the tee, and the best architects avoid them wherever possible. Aside from the gentle rise of the eleventh and fifteenth fairways the one uphill drive is the tenth at Muirfield Village, the only one on Jack Nicklaus's superb course, and it is not forbidding because the shot is over a valley.

The course is not overly long but it provides the perfect rebuttal to those who would argue that no course of less than 7,000 yards is of championship caliber. Balance and variety are maintained within the par fours. Whereas, for example, long, accurate driving is essential to evade fairway bunkers and set up a good position for an attacking approach on the second, tenth and fifteenth, restraint of length from the tee can be crucial playing the thirteenth at Harbour Town, one of Pete Dye's gems of creation. Again on the eighth at Pine Valley the cruel beauty of the hole lies in the taxing nature of the pitch.

Many may disagree with the composition of the course, but nobody could fairly dispute that it would call upon a golfer to demonstrate skill in every department of the game; that it embraces the qualities of exceptional design, and

much of the beauty with which golf is blessed; that it would command respect from the mighty and be a great deal of fun for anyone to play.

1st Royal St. George's: 415 yards, par four

The paramount requirement for an opening hole is that it should enable play to flow from the outset—that golfers should not be delayed waiting for a green to clear, as on a par five within range of two shots. It should also whet the golfer's appetite for the test ahead, a mission more easily accomplished should its prospect be instantly appealing. To stand on the tee on a summer morning, with the breeze fresh from the sea and the larks in full voice—as they always seem to be at Sandwich—and look down the crumpled spread of fairway, would make any golfer rejoice. The drive is not demanding, but the stance for the second shot, usually a medium iron, may be uneven in the classic links fashion. A cross-bunker, steeply faced and cut deep into a gentle upslope, protects the approaches to a green that falls away from the striker, although the bold shot is not unduly punished. Any golfer still in need of encouragement will delight in the trueness of the green.

2nd Scioto: 436 yards, par four

At Scioto's second hole the golfer is immediately brought face to face with stern reality. In anybody's language the hole is the severest par on the course, and it reflects something of the beauty of Donald Ross's design. It might have been created for Jack Nicklaus, who learned his golf there, because of the demand on the tee shot; unless it carries to the crest of a fairway rising out of a valley there is no clear sight of the green. If the drive is smothered or hit with a diving hook it can vanish in a stream hidden behind a screen of sycamore and fir trees, and those who press for distance risk two large fairway bunkers, trees, or the out-of-bounds that pursues the hole throughout its length. The entrance to the green is narrowed between spreading bunkers; trees stand sentinel on either hand and, as usual with Ross, the green is slightly elevated and subtly contoured. In the 1928 PGA, then a matchplay event three matches went to extra holes: all were decided at the end.

3rd Durban Country Club: 506 yards, par five

The prospect from a tee poised high above the fairway is at once dramatic and, to a handicap golfer, disturbing. The valley unfolds below, rising through a series of mounds and undulations to a green in the shadow of a tree-covered dune. Off to the right the Indian Ocean tumbles silver on a shining beach, but it is of no concern to the golfer, whose line is narrowed by dense shrubs. Contrary to expectation the drive will not be deflected off the valley walls, where the spongy grass tends to smother the bounce. But the drive is not the most difficult shot and the degree of difficulty encountered thereafter relates directly to the ambition of the golfer. A second which is intended merely to open the green is fairly straightforward, but for the man trying to get home in two a mass of bush on the left will devour the hook. The approach itself must be precise, for the dead ground in front and the pronounced shoulders of a raised green do not favor the run-up shot.

4th Baltusrol: 194 yards, par three

The tee shot at Baltusrol's short fourth is over water to a green that begins abruptly atop the stone retaining wall of a lake. The green is large but well trapped to the left and the rear. The problems of this hole are really psychological. The easiest way to threaten the peace of mind of most golfers is to confront them with a stretch of water that must be carried. The handicap golfer may mishit into the water simply because he has a faulty swing and therefore frequently mishits, but more often failure to make the carry is bred in fear. The expert is concerned only with the pin placing, choosing the right club and deciding which part of the tilted green he should aim for to give him the most favorable putting position. The joy of seeing the ball fly safely across water and nestle near the flag is instantaneous, the satisfaction total. Every course should have one hole where the basic challenge is uncompromising—the thrill of being equal to it is unsurpassed in golf.

5th Mid Ocean: 433 yards, par four

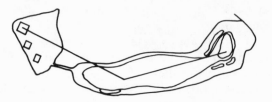

Once again water is the heart of the matter, but not as threateningly as at Baltusrol. The shining expanse of Mangrove Lake lies between tee and green, but no golfer could make the carry even with a hurricane behind him and so the hole is a nice exercise in bravery or caution. Experience tells how much of the lake can be carried to reach the fairway; the longer the better, for then the second shot between guardian bunkers to the green is shorter. The flanking bunkers are long and narrow, that on the left side snaking the entire length of the green. The hole is classic in the simplicity of its challenge: there is nothing devious or subtle about it. Either you make the carry or you do not, but the frail of heart or swing do have an alternative: the green then is out of range in two, but at least the bogey is not difficult to make. In this Charles Blair Macdonald, who designed the course in 1924, observed one of the basic principles of good golf course architecture.

6th Royal Melbourne: 428 yards, par four

The beauty of the hole is the perfect balance of its challenge, a quality of which its creator, Alister Mackenzie, was always deeply aware. However the hole is approached it is never mastered until the final putt is down, and yet it is beautiful rather than alarming to contemplate. From a tee amid the tea-trees, the fairway swoops downhill then swings to the right, mounting to a green set on a hillside against a backdrop of trees. A huge bunker is cut in its left flank, and an abundance of sand awaits the overcorrected shot to the right. Within the curve of the hole lies dense rough and a clustered nest of bunkers; if these can be carried the next shot is appreciably shortened, but the ball will need to fly some 220 yards. A commercial shot straight down the fairway leaves a demanding stroke, usually from a downhill stance. Unless the distance is judged perfectly the danger of three putts is acute because the fast green slopes steeply up from front to back.

7th Cajuiles: 195 yards, par three

Occasionally an architect comes across a situation in the land which clearly begs the making of a golf hole, especially if he is as devoted to making the finest use of natural settings as Pete Dye. A rock-bound curve of the southeastern coast of the Dominican Republic must have jumped to his mind as the setting for a glorious short hole that is less forbidding than it looks and, because of the prevailing trade winds, usually plays some two clubs shorter than its length suggests. The mishit can leap to perdition from the rocks or be trapped in acres of sand, but forward tees help diminish the perils of a shot to a green more receptive to the iron shot that is feathered rather than driven. Any apprehension felt by the golfer standing on the tee above the frothing surf of the azure Caribbean is considerably assuaged by the sheer beauty of the setting. This aspect of golf architecture can be overemphasized, but it is always present to some degree in the great holes.

8th Pine Valley: 327 yards, par four

No great course would be complete without at least one hole where length is of no account but accuracy is all. The eighth at Pine Valley is just such a hole. Although the fairway slopes gently down and a good drive will finish within a hundred yards of the green, the approach must be one of the most taxing pitch shots in the world. The green is shaped like a slender pear and is protected on all sides by deep bunkers, unraked as is traditional for all bunkers at Pine Valley. A pitch is the only shot, its margin of error is minimal and, more often than not, it is played from a downslope with the striker standing above the ball. It is therefore the shanker's nightmare. Legion are the tales of disaster, not least that of the Walker Cup player who took sixteen despite a good drive. The virtue of the short par four cannot be exaggerated, and all good architects are aware of it. A player's skill and nerve can be as thoroughly examined on a hole of 320 yards as on one of the full length of 470 yards.

9th Muirfield: 495 yards, par five

A true five must be a continuing test of control and thought. Many examine the tee shot and the final approach, but often the second shot is simply a matter of making forward progress. Not so at Muirfield's ninth, where into a prevailing wind there is no question of relaxing after hitting a safe shot. This in itself can be demanding, for the fairway becomes a narrow waist between bunkers and uncommonly tenacious rough. Whether going for the green or not, according to the strength and direction of the wind, the rippling lawn of the approaches may look inviting and not too difficult to find. But pull, and out-of-bounds lurks over the gray stone wall; fade or block the shot overmuch, and a whole series of bunkers is waiting. Quite apart from testing to the very last shot the player intent on a good score over the front nine, the hole comes as a timely reminder to the golfer who, having reached the turn, cannot now be in any doubt as to the sternness of his task.

10th Muirfield Village: 441 yards, par four

The second nine begins on a sterner note than the first. Although the immediate prospect of the tenth at Muirfield Village is appealing rather than formidable, it is a hole demanding of excellence and comparable with the splendid tenth holes common to most of the great championship courses. The first essential is a well-placed tee shot where water lurks but hardly threatens. The drive that drifts to the right will be fortunate to escape bunkers, and if it is pulled while striving for undue length, a gathering of trees and more sand await. The green, which is comparatively small, is protected on the right by a multifingered bunker, while another will snare the shot held up overmuch. The hole reveals an admirable aspect of design common to the whole Muirfield Village course, in that Jack Nicklaus uses separate tees of varying shapes and does not rely on the single long strip, which can make the golfer playing from forward markers feel inferior.

11th The Country Club: 445 yards, par four

There has been no undue insistence on length on the par fours on the back nine, but it is none the less demanding for that. Indeed, the most challenging part of the Country Club course at Brookline, as used on its recent great occasions, is the outset of the homeward journey, the heart of which is the beautiful rise and sweep of the eleventh fairway and the lovely shot that follows. The hole tempts—and dangerously so, because of deep woods—a pull from the tee in order to shorten the second shot, which is usually a long iron over a lake in a valley to the inviting green, a small target tightly ringed by trouble. Water protects the front, sand the right side and trees enclose the whole in a stately but potent embrace. Conceivably, the hole cost Arnold Palmer the 1963 Open. In spite of dropping several strokes there to par, including a seven when a hooked drive finished against a tree stump, he tied with Jacky Cupit and Julius Boros; Boros won the playoff.

12th Augusta National: 155 yards, par three

As Masters follows Masters, the fame of the twelfth at Augusta grows apace. No short hole (and rarely is it more than a six-iron) has caused greater uncertainty as to choice of club, and more apprehension as to the fate of the shot. At the peak of its flight the ball is at the whim of the breeze that ever stirs amid the tall trees. The slightest change can mean the difference between a putt for a two or a desperate struggle for a four. Every golfer who ever challenged for the Masters has known tribulation there. Every golfer, regardless of handicap, is greatly relieved to have made the green at the first attempt. It is not deep and the tee shot, slightly overhit for fear of falling short in Rae's Creek, can leave a frighteningly delicate sand or chip shot back. Judgment and finesse are qualities more important to the making of fine golf shots than the ability to power the ball a long way, so a hole of this length is essential to any great course.

13th Harbour Town: 358 yards, par four

For the short par four to be effective it must have well-nigh unassailable defenses, such as the thirteenth at Harbour Town, where precision rather than power is the essence. Many will refrain from using a driver in order to avoid the bunker on the left of the fairway and to finish in a good position for the pitch to the heart-shaped green—guarded by a huge bunker, at some points as deep as a man is tall and faced with boards in the manner of many of the famous old links courses. Tall, stately pines, clothed in Spanish moss line the fairway, creating a delightful feeling of calm seclusion without in any way inhibiting the play. However, two large oak trees stand sentinel some seventy yards before the green, which is only opened up by the truly accurate tee shot, frequently made with a three-wood. Together with the massive bunker that encircles the front half of the green, the shape of which makes for some tough pin positions, this matches any trial posed by sheer length.

14th St. Andrews: 567 yards, par five

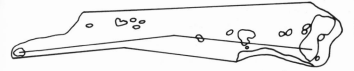

The greatness of the Long Hole at St. Andrews lies in the almost boundless extent of its problems. They can vary from hour to hour according to the wind and the state of a golfer's game and nerve, and can swiftly damn the unknowing or unthinking stroke. After the drive has survived the perils of out-of-bounds and the Beardies bunkers, and found brief sanctuary in the Elysian Fields, comes the time of trial when a decision must be made. Aside from the obvious danger of Hell straight ahead—can it be carried or not?—there is the invisible menace beyond of the Grave and Ginger Beer bunkers. Those who take too cautious a line to left or right are as-

sured of a testing third, frequently from an uneven stance, to the shelf of green tilting away from a steep bank. Surmounting this can demand a shot of fine touch, whether putting, chipping or pitching. In a helpful breeze the strong will hope for a birdie; but rare is the man who is unhappy to settle for a five.

15th Oakmont: 453 yards, par four

If the comparative failure of Ben Hogan to master a hole is a fair indication of its quality then the fifteenth at Oakmont must stand high in the company of long par fours. In the 1953 Open he had a six and a five there in his last two rounds, but won the championship by six strokes. The drive must mount the long rise of fairway to a narrow landing area between church pew bunkers on the left and bunkers and ditches on the right. The fairway then falls gently towards an enormous long green slightly offset to the right and embraced by bunkers; the longest stretches ninety-five yards. The essence of the second shot is in judgment of length, since the greens are normally slippery as ice and those who misjudge the approach can be in lively danger of three putts or more. In 1973 Johnny Miller, soaring to the peak of his incomparable sixty-three, played the hole to perfection: a vast drive, a four-iron to ten feet and a one-putt. But rarely does the hole yield so lightly.

16th Carnoustie: 235 yards, par three

In any finish on a championship course the more accomplished player should be given the opportunity for his greater skill to take effect. At this point in a round the pressure is at its greatest and this stiffens the already formidable challenge of the sixteenth at Carnoustie. Few short holes anywhere demand a long shot of more exacting straightness. The green, beyond a narrow gap between bunkers, is a plateau, and the shot that leaks a little either way has fair chance of remaining on the putting surface. Tom Watson must have set some sort of record, at least in modern times, by winning the 1975 Open without making a single three there in five attempts (including the playoff with Jack Newton). The importance of thoughtful setting of the tee-markers on a hole of this type was evident in the 1968 Open, when in one round only the supremely powerful Nicklaus, using a driver, was able to hit his ball beyond the flag. However, not even he managed a single birdie in four attempts.

17th Cypress Point: 375 yards, par four

No golf architect was more richly endowed with natural features for his work than Alister Mackenzie at Cypress Point. Majestic woodland, a hint of links and heathland here and there and the savage nobility of the coast made for unforgettable holes. The seventeenth is not as fierce or famous as its immediate predecessor, but in less demanding fashion it asks the golfer how brave he is. The drive from a tee high on a rocky peninsula above the ocean at once is tempting and disturbing according to how much of the bay's curve he tries to carry. The beauty of the hole is the extent to which a great cluster of black cypresses come into play for the second shot.

According to where the drive has finished, the second may be played over or to either side, but gallant or foolhardy is the man who takes the righthand route over the ocean. Even without a strong hole to follow, as is the case at Cypress Point, this is a great seventeenth. With the eighteenth at Pebble Beach it makes for a heroic finish.

18th Pebble Beach: 540 yards, par five

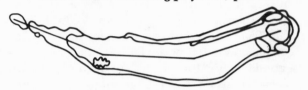

The glory of the eighteenth at Pebble Beach is that its supreme challenge and beauty are entirely natural. The long curve of the coast from tee to green brings the ocean into play as on no other par five in the world, and in so doing emphasizes the essential virtues of a great finishing hole. The man who is down or needs a birdie four has a chance, while the golfer overanxious to protect his lead may be confounded. Forever the golfer is aware that to pull is to die, so the tendency to block the shot is great, although bunkers and trees harass the conservative approach. The farther to the right it is played the longer the hole becomes, and eventually the golfer must turn towards the ocean. The green is so close to it that even the shortest approach cannot be treated lightly; it can so easily scuttle across the green and down on to the rocks beyond. In contrast, meeting the challenge of going for the green needs courage and control of a very high order.

The Grand Slam: 1930-1980

by PETER RYDE

The year 1980 marked the fiftieth anniversary of Bobby Jones's Grand Slam. Peter Ryde, who succeeded Bernard Darwin as golf correspondent at The Times *of London, offers some thoughts on how Jones achieved the slam and why no one will again capture all four of today's major events.*

THE story of the Grand Slam, the jubilee of which we thankfully celebrate this year, started on the stage of an abandoned theater in downtown Atlanta. For this piece of information I have to thank that immensely readable expert, Charles Price, and I choose it for two reasons. One is that so much has been written about the glory of Bobby Jones that another voice raised in simple eulogy would be telling you what no doubt you already well know and cherish.

The other reason is that it brought home to me for the first time that Jones had a sense of predestination about that year when he won the Amateur and Open championships on both sides of the Atlantic. The Grand Slam was something that right from the start he thought he might achieve and 1930 was the year which offered the best chance. The Walker Cup match would take him to Britain anyway as captain of the American team. He would have time in that one trip to play the two British championships and get back for the U.S. Open and for the final act, the National Amateur at Merion, the course that already held so many memories for him.

He was also becoming aware of the toll his championship life was taking of him, far more so than the thousands who mobbed him ever realized. It must have seemed to him that it was now or never, but he kept such thoughts to himself. I can find no evidence of the subject having been raised at that time. In Britain he was already enormously admired and his achievements were well chronicled, but when at last he was victorious in the one championship that had eluded him, one does not read of people thinking "Now he can win the other three." Even after he had notched the second of his four victories in the British Open at Hoylake, when spectators were buzzing with amazement about the seven he had taken at the eighth hole in the final round and when Bernard Darwin was sitting with him in the locker room wondering whether the great man was going to be sick, no one seems to have thought about a Grand Slam.

Nowadays it would be different. We have fabricated a new Grand Slam, as though man has to have a supreme target for his ambition, in which the two Amateur championships have been dropped and replaced by the Masters which did not exist fifty years ago and by the PGA Championship of America. When the press began to think in terms of Arnold Palmer, Gary Player and Jack Nicklaus achieving those four victories in one year, they turned it into headline news, thereby unconsciously making it much less likely that they could achieve it. With marvelous good humor Arnold, Gary and Jack played it down, rightly pointing out that one could only take one championship at a time, and could only start thinking in terms of a Grand Slam when the other three were in the bag.

Jones was spared all that, at least in Britain. It was after his third victory, when he had won the U.S. Open at Interlachen, becoming the first man in the history of that event to break par over seventy-two holes, that things began to happen.

The *London Times* started giving the results day-by-day of the U.S. Amateur championship, something they would not normally have done in those days. It was a sign that something out of the ordinary was going on. The build-up may have been slow but we did not miss the final act. On the day after Jones had triumphed Darwin wrote about it in words that put into perspective the feeling of the golfing public at the time. "For several days past," he wrote, "nongolfers must have been mystified by hearing people say everywhere, in trains and subways and streets and clubs 'I hope to goodness Bobby does it!' Now he has done it." Then in a typical example of Darwinian style which breathed drama into minor incidents but underwrote the great occasions, he added about the man he so affectionately admired "In words that were written of another golfer (Tom Morris) as peerless in his own day, he has held his honors 'without rivalry and yet without envy, his many amiable qualities being no less acknowledged than his golfing achievements.'"

Even so, one is left with the feeling over in Britain that the Grand Slam (or as we with our passion for brevity used to call it the Impregnable Quadrilateral) grew in importance as it became possible to stand back and see his career in perspective. At the time, it seems to me, people were already dazzled by his brilliance, by the number of national titles he had won, by the huge margins by which he destroyed players of the highest class, by the number of records he broke, and by his heroic appearance and behavior, so that the winning of all four in one season must have seemed a natural culmination which was almost inevitable. Nowadays the feat is rightly regarded as a milestone of golfing history, a convenient yardstick of his greatness, but when we really come to think about it, it fades into the background behind all the other amazing single achievements.

Not so with Bobby Jones at the time. We now know that he lived with that secret ambition. He had climbed the highest peaks so often that like the great performers of our time he needed a new incentive to drive his will to the utmost. So this time he set about preparing well before his final ordeal, although normally he laid off in the winter altogether, confining his serious golf to three months in the summer except when it was extended by a visit to Britain. During those years when he was always a national champion, as Price reminds us, he studied mechanical engineering at Georgia Tech, picked up a degree in English literature and another in law. This time he took off weight, a problem he could never entirely ignore, and on that deserted Atlanta stage played "Doug"—a cross between badminton and paddle tennis, to complete his fitness. Then again, and this was something he would not normally have done, he entered for two tournaments. He failed by a stroke to win the Savannah Open, twice lowering the record for the course, and then won the Southeastern in his home town by thirteen strokes. O.B. Keeler's prophetic remark after that "He's going to win the Open and Amateur championships on both sides of the Atlantic; they'll never stop him *this* year," seems to be about as much thought as anyone gave the matter until much nearer the end. Except of course, Bobby himself.

We fail to appreciate the full glory of the Grand Slam unless we accept that inside that sensitive, highly strung mind there ran throughout the season that gnawing, nagging ambition to pull off the greatest challenge of all. He suffered greatly but by an icy self-control and perfect manners concealed from all but his closest friends the extent of that suffering.

If I attach here more importance to his two British victories it is not only that I know more about them, but also because it was in them that he suffered most and came closest to failure. In the last of the four, the U.S. Amateur, having been low qualifier, he never went beyond the fourteenth green in any match, three of which were over thirty-six holes in which he reigned supreme. He never felt safe over eighteen holes from the flash of lightning from an opponent, which is why he took so long to win the British. After a sensational start Jones was taken to the sixteenth in the first round by Sid Roper, a golfer unknown outside Scotland, and he must have been reminded of that terrible day nine years before when, playing in his first British Amateur, he struggled home on the last green against a Mr. Hamlet of Wrexham with a score nearer ninety than eighty.

Other moments of uncertainty occurred on the way to the 1930 final, two of these involving his own countrymen. He lost a five-hole lead against Harrison Johnston and was also taken to the last green by that formidable rival, George Voigt, who was two-up on him with five to play, but drove over the wall at the fourteenth.

In the fourth round came the much-heralded match against the British champion, Cyril Tolley. Volumes have been written about this magnificent dogfight in which each had three times been one up when they came to the seventeenth all square and Jones's second struck a spectator, which stopped the ball running onto the road. No one quite knew what happened—no one ever does on such occasions—and when they asked Darwin about it, the man who watched golf more energetically than anyone before or since, could only say he had no idea, because he was running head down and knees up along with a few hundred others in an attempt to get a ring-side view at the green. When people ask me whether it would be possible for another to complete Jones's Grand Slam, I tell them it is about as likely as it would be for me to go charging along the fairways in an attempt to watch the next shot. We do not do things that way these days, nor do golfers conduct their affairs in such

a way as to make the Grand Slam remotely probable.

At that hole in that match Jones came closest to failing in his great endeavor, but he prevailed by laying Tolley a stymie at the nineteenth which he might not have needed. Jones himself, according to Keeler, and the impression was endorsed by other close observers, felt some spirit of destiny surrounding him during the worst moments of that championship. Faced with horrid putts of eight and twelve feet at crucial moments in different matches, he had the feeling he must hole them because it was his destiny to win the championship at last. Fanciful? Hardly, I think, in a man of that intelligence.

Things were not much better when it came to the British Open at Hoylake. Jones was not playing his best, as he was the first to admit, and one is tempted to believe that having to live day and night with his dream of total victory did not help him to do so. But he knew better than any how to play below his best and still score well. Time and again he started a round badly, time and again his putter saved him so that with one round to go he stood only one stroke behind Archie Compston. Then at the eighth in the final round it was as though all the poison in his system came to a head, and he took seven at that long hole after two cracking good wood shots that left him forty yards from the stick.

I cannot refrain from quoting from an anthology of golf assembled by Peter Lawless. "His third shot" wrote E.M. Cockell, "which just reached the green was worthy of a ten-handicap player not at his best, his fourth, very short, was worthy of a fully blooded rabbit, his fifth would not have got him a club handicap, and his sixth was reminiscent of a ladies' thirty-six. He came to the ninth looking very pale, although his American bodyguard looked much paler, and I must say at that moment my sympathies went out to him. He was right up against it and he knew it, and I knew it. For a hole or two I ceased to watch the ball and could only watch the man. Gradually he became master of himself, but his perfect style cloaked the inward battle that was raging." Such a lapse by such a perfectionist must have cut very deep, and his recovery over those last nine holes

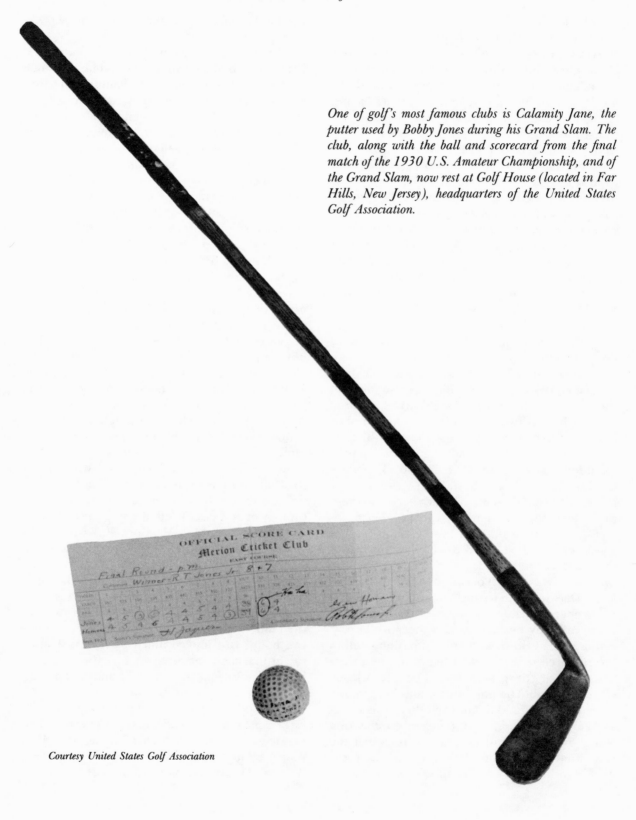

One of golf's most famous clubs is Calamity Jane, the putter used by Bobby Jones during his Grand Slam. The club, along with the ball and scorecard from the final match of the 1930 U.S. Amateur Championship, and of the Grand Slam, now rest at Golf House (located in Far Hills, New Jersey), headquarters of the United States Golf Association.

Courtesy United States Golf Association

was perhaps as fine as anything he did in the whole of that fateful year.

It is not with any desire to belittle his achievement that I draw attention to such incidents. Quite the reverse. Success achieved by mechanical perfection, which he sometimes approached in spite of the artistry of his swing, can be almost unexciting to watch and boring to relate. How much more worthwhile is success that is achieved in spite of oneself, that reveals the struggle against human frailty! What is left to us now of the Grand Slam is not the mechanics of it, not even its value compared with other feats, but the sheer guts that went into the compiling of it.

We know for sure and should never forget that he suffered greatly, even playing the game he loved. He could scarcely eat anything until the day's play was over; on occasions he could not even button his shirt collar for fear the worst might happen; he could lose fourteen pounds in weight during a championship week, and was capable of breaking down to the point of tears from sheer emotional overstrain. Probably he could not have been the supreme champion he was without that degree of sensitivity. But what sporting courage lay behind it! That is the real message of the Grand Slam which makes it worthless to compare what other great players might or might not have done.

That victory in the British Open was the turning point on the path to the Grand Slam, but Jones in the locker-room afterwards was beyond speech, clutching his drink with both hands lest he spill it. Great golfers who have followed him have all made contributed examples for lesser golfers to follow. The example that Jones left behind was surely one of profound encouragement to all highly strung players who are determined to conquer themselves.

The Trial of Dick Mayer

by DAVE ANDERSON

Behind all sports, and golf is no exception, lies the self-destroying agony of those who cannot handle the two-edged sword of success. In this award-winning profile New York Times columnist Dave Anderson tells the difficult story of an Open champion who fell from grace.

"I see where the Open is at Inverness again," somebody said. "Isn't that where Dick Mayer won it in 1957?"

"Yeah, the man in the white cap. Whatever happened to him?"

"The last I heard," another said, "he was teaching at Torrey Pines outside San Diego but that was ten years ago. I don't know where he is now. I understand he's had problems."

"He hasn't been here for several years," the voice at Torrey Pines said. "He left to go to the Stardust."

"He used to be here," the voice at the Stardust in San Diego said. "Then one day he went to play in a tournament in the desert and that was the last we saw of him."

"The desert means Palm Springs," another voice said. "Try him at LaQuinta—I think he's an assistant there."

"He's not here anymore but sometimes he comes around," the voice at LaQuinta said. "I'll give him the message."

Three weeks later a letter arrived. "Please excuse the time lapse in getting in touch with you," Dick Mayer wrote in a stylish hand, "but I have been over on the coast off and on looking for jobs." He was living in Palm Springs with Bill Ennis, his longtime pal and a former golf pro now in the auto-leasing business. And late last year a phone call was made to the Ennis home.

"He's not staying with us anymore," Bill Ennis said. "He's got his own place now. He's working here at the Sunrise driving range."

"He gives lessons at twenty dollars an hour," said Chuck Whisenand, the owner of the range. "He'll be here tomorrow. Stop by around two o'clock."

And there he was, Dick Mayer, the man in the white cap. Only he wasn't wearing a white cap. Or any cap. But it was unmistakably him—still slim at 5–11 and 155, still stylish. His blondish brown hair was shaggily long. From a distance he had not looked much different than when he won the 1957 U.S. Open in a playoff with Dr. Cary Middlecoff. But at a white wooden table in the shade of a yellow-and-white umbrella, his darkly tanned face betrayed his age. It also betrayed his struggle—his drinking problem, his three divorces, his frustration as one of golf's lost souls.

All of Dick Mayer's struggle was chiseled into the crevices of his face, crevices that resemble the dry cracks in the nearby desert. But his eyes were as blue as the sky that hangs over Palm Springs like a dome. His voice was deep and firm.

"Some people bring up the Open and I think back on it once in a while," he was saying now. "Those were fun days. I was young. I could play a little. But then the alcohol and the playboy years . . . they sort of killed a career somewhere along the line. I wonder where it's all going. I keep lying about my age as long as I can."

He said he was fifty-four years old. But when he won the Open he was reported to be thirty-four, which would make him fifty-six now.

Of his present situation he said, "This is a good range to hit balls. Bob Hope comes over here sometimes. But the lessons are slow."

"How about the people who hit balls," he was asked. "Don't they remember you as the man who won the 1957 Open?"

"Some yes, some no. Mostly no. Mostly they just remember a white cap and a guy who used to play a lot of golf."

Dick Mayer was much more than that. In his career he won over $200,000 when the prize money was paltry (only $7,200 as the U.S. Open champion) and he was the leading money winner in 1957 with $65,835. That was his year—he won the Open, he won the old World championship at Tam O'Shanter with its $50,000 bonanza, he made the Ryder Cup team, he was the player of the year. In other years he won five tour events, including the 1965 New Orleans Open with a thirty-five-yard wedge shot into the cup on the final hole. And in the 1962 Bob Hope Desert Classic he made a hole-in-one that was worth $50,000.

That's a career to be proud of. But at the driving range that day he was virtually invisible.

Near the window where the buckets of balls were sold, a "golf professional" shingle had Chuck Whisenand's name on it. There was no shingle for Dick Mayer.

"He didn't feel that was necessary," Whisenand explains. "He was so much on top it's difficult when he's not."

"He has that fear," Bill Ennis says. "That fear, or that shame, of people asking, 'Isn't that the guy . . . ?'"

Maybe it would have been better for Dick Mayer if he had never won the Open, if he had never attained the identity that follows anyone who wins the Open all the way to the headline on his obituary.

"I wasn't Ben Hogan," he was saying now. "I was just another guy who played."

Ben Hogan was his idol. Ben Hogan wore a white cap while winning four U.S. Opens, so Mayer started wearing a white cap. He ordered them by the dozen from a San Antonio, Texas, manufacturer.

"Maybe it was an image thing," he reflected. "I assumed it made me look like a golf professional."

But as much as Mayer wanted to look like Hogan, he was intimidated by Hogan's skill. "I felt Ben was a true professional, I could only mimic him." And perhaps significantly, in the Open that Mayer won, Hogan was not a factor. Not even a contestant. The morning of the first round Hogan suddenly withdrew because of a pleurisy attack that restricted his backswing. Without the spectre of Hogan, the Open over the 6,919-yard Inverness course was wide open.

Mayer had a seventy in the first round, two shots behind both Jimmy Demaret and Chick Harbert, then he fired a sixty-eight to share the thirty-six-hole lead at 138 with amateur Billy Joe Patton. In those years the final thirty-six holes of the Open were played on Saturday, and after the morning round, Demaret was at 211, Mayer at 212 (after a four-over-par seventy-four), Middlecoff and Julius Boros at 214.

In the afternoon, Demaret's seventy-two made him the leader in the clubhouse at 283, but Mayer and Middlecoff, who had won the Open in 1956 and also in 1949, were still in contention.

With two holes remaining, Mayer needed a par-par finish to tie. But at the seventeenth, a dogleg left 451-yard par four with the tee in a chute of trees, he hooked his drive into the rough. He had about 180 yards to the small tilted green.

"The gallery had knocked the rough down," he remembered. "I was just trying to get it on the green."

"The ball was setting on clay," recalls Ennis, who was there. "If he doesn't hit it clean, he's not close to anything. He didn't study it any more than thirty seconds, then he put a perfect swing on it with a five-iron that left him about thirty feet above the cup. What hands he had. He and Demaret had the greatest hands in golf."

Mayer got down in two putts for his par but as he moved to the eighteenth tee he remembered what happened on eighteen in the last round of the 1954 U.S. Open at Baltusrol.

That day he needed a par five for the lead in the clubhouse. But at the top of his backswing on the eighteenth tee, someone in the gallery unthinkingly yelled. Startled, Mayer pushed his drive into a forest. "I needed a seeing-eye dog to find it," he said then, "and I needed an ax to get it out." Playing a provisional ball, he finished with a double-bogey seven for 286. With a par he would have had 284, which is what Ed Furgol shot to win.

"You have to learn to play in the Open—there's too much drama, too much largeness," he was saying now. "I think my experience at Baltusrol left a scar on me."

On the eighteenth tee at Inverness he ignored the scar. To avoid the fairway bunkers on the tight 330-yard finishing hole, he hit a four-wood. Then he lofted a wedge to within nine feet and holed the birdie putt. Now he was the leader at 282 after a par seventy, but Middlecoff was still out there.

In his methodical manner, the Memphis dentist birdied the sixteenth and eighteenth holes for his second sixty-eight that windy day, creating an eighteen-hole playoff the next day.

"The shot that put Dick in the playoff was the five-iron on the seventeenth" Ennis says. "The morning of the playoff, I think Dick psyched Middlecoff out. He kept telling him, 'When I hit a shot like that, Doc, no way you can beat me.'

Between that and the 98° heat that day, Middlecoff never got himself together."

After the eighth hole, Mayer had a four-stroke lead. He won breezing, seventy-two to seventy-nine.

"Winning the Open didn't fulfill me," he acknowledged. "Maybe if I had won it two or three times, that would've said what I was. But looking at it another way, I consider myself lucky. They can't take that Open away from me."

"Ever since then you hear people say he was stiff that whole week he won the Open but he wasn't," Ennis says. "He behaved himself beautifully."

Walking from the driving range office to the tee area, at least a dozen golfers passed nearby without even a glance at the 1957 U.S. Open champion.

"I had a few drinks that week, but I was drinking with intelligence," Mayer said. "But afterward I found out you can't live off winning the Open—I found out the hard way. Alcohol is a drug, a slower drug than some, but it's still a drug. I started drinking like a lot of people around golf do. My family was very soberly social, and after you played golf, it was always, 'Let's have a drink.' "

He grew up in Greenwich, Connecticut an affluent suburb of New York City, where his late father was a prosperous auto dealer and a good amateur golfer. Together they twice won the Westchester County Golf Association's father-and-son title. As a youngster he had learned to play at Innis Arden; later he polished his game at Winged Foot where Craig Wood and Claude Harmon tutored him. But during World War II, his golf was interrupted while he served as an Army tank driver in Europe.

"I got to be a sergeant," he once said, "but then I made the mistake of telling a lieutenant they didn't know how to run the Army, so I wound up back as a private."

After his discharge, he was a stockbroker trainee on Wall Street but he tired of "running to get the train to get to work on time." Concentrating on golf, he won the 1947 New York State Amateur, then turned pro two years later.

"I don't think he really wanted to become a golf pro," Ennis says. "I think his ability put him into it. And he wasn't too popular. With his father's money behind him he was eating steaks when the other young pros were eating hamburgers."

His first tour title was the 1953 Eastern Open, then he won the Miami Four-Ball with Tommy Bolt in 1954, the Kansas City Open in 1955 and the Philadelphia Daily News Open in 1956 before becoming the first U.S. Open champion to have used fiberglass shafts.

Until he signed with Golfcraft several months before his Open triumph, he had spurned offers from equipment manufacturers. Typical of his independence as a free spirit, he had preferred to choose his own equipment and alter it to fit his swing. To lighten his irons, he often ground the top edges down to a sharp point.

Mayer was not an especially long hitter, depending more on accuracy than power for his fine scoring. His swing pace was deliberate, smooth from start to finish, befitting a man who never seemed to be in a hurry.

After 1957, his only tour victory occurred in 1965 at New Orleans—his last hurrah.

"I think winning the Open made the pressure greater, you had to live up to this plateau," he was saying now. "You have a tendency to get two-faced out there. You have one personality on the course, trying to make people say 'he's a nice guy.' But privately, you're more reserved, you're inhibited, you withdraw."

"And when he withdrew, he drank," Ennis says. "And after a while, he drank too much."

"I think it was an escape, a way out," Dick Mayer went on. "Who knows what I was escaping from—to take the pressure off, to create happiness. What made it easier for me to drink is that the golf club life is a drinking life. And we're a country of too much money. With all this money, people are moving faster than they're capable of

moving. It would be nice for the country to slow down."

But he did not slow down until early last year, after he failed to receive an invitation to compete in the inaugural Legends of Golf tournament.

"They had some guys in there who never won what I won," he snapped. "Guys who had been pretty good players—but I won the United States Open."

"They didn't want to take a chance on him," Bill Ennis says. "It got to him. And he had run out of people except for me. Ever since I first met him at the Crosby in 1947 we've been like brothers. He wouldn't ever listen to anybody but his dad and me. He's very contrary when he's drunk, but he's one of the wisest when sober. I had seen him drunk one night about a year ago and I told him if he ever needed me, give me a call. Three days later he called.

"He told me, 'I've had it.' I asked him how bad he was and he said, 'I'm pretty low.' I wanted him to come to me on his own, I didn't want to go get him so I told him, 'All right, get in your car and drive slowly and wisely and get over here.'

"He moved in with my wife and me and he drank every drop we had in the house. But by then I was in touch with two Alcoholics Anonymous people here in Palm Springs—a doctor and a businessman. They suggested a place in Tustin, over near the coast, where he could dry out. I told him about it, but he had to do it himself. And he did. In three weeks there he was dry. I brought him back to my house and my wife and I took care of him for six months. We got him to go to the AA meetings. It wasn't easy. He made me cry, he made my wife cry, but I think I drilled it into his head that if he did it again, he would have nobody else in the world except me to bury him."

At the driving range that day late last year, Dick Mayer watched the sun slide behind the purple mountains.

"I don't know," he said slowly. "Maybe I'll be able to hold myself together. Or maybe I'll fall apart."

Not long ago he appeared to be holding himself together. Invited to this year's Legends tournament, he was preparing for it by hitting balls at the Sunrise range. The twilight deepened the crevices in his face.

"My problems are in the past," he was saying between shots. "I just hope people realize that."

In the driving range office were brochures and small business cards identifying him as a "former United States Open and World champion—lessons by appointment." Similar cards were on the pro shop counter at the nearby Clarkston Golf Center's executive course where he also was available for lessons.

"He's thanked me," Bill Ennis was saying outside the range office. "He has humility. He's one of the softer people in the world. Anything he's accrued, he's given away."

Inside the office Chuck Whisenand peered through the open window toward the far end of the range. Dick Mayer was not wearing a white cap but it was unmistakably him—hitting balls with the shadow of a swing that once won the Open. "For all his problems," the range owner said, "I don't think he's ever hurt anybody."

Except himself.

PART III

The Secret of the Game

"Every golfer scores better when he learns his capabilities."
—from *How to Play Your Best Golf All the Time*
by Tommy Armour

Developing a Style, Finding the Orthodox, Taking the Breaks in Stride

by ROBERT TYRE JONES

Possessed of a fluid, seemingly effortless swing, Bobby Jones is a model all golfers can imitate. After his retirement, Jones authored an instruction series which was eventually edited into the book Bobby Jones on Golf. *The following are three pieces of wisdom from that collection.*

Developing a Style

More than fine-spun theories, the average golfer needs something to give him a clearer conception of what he should try to do with the clubhead. The golf swing is a set or series of movements that must be closely correlated. The smallest change in any one will make a difference in one or more of the others, and although for consistent, high-class performance there can be only a small deviation in any particular, it still is a fact, and always will be so, that there are more ways than one of swinging a golf club effectively.

I do not intend to argue against the development of a good sound method, but I do believe that this method should be put together with due regard for the requirements and swing preferences of the individual. I think also that before a player should begin to worry about the finer points of form, he should play enough to know what his preferences are.

When we speak of a sound swing or of good form, we mean nothing more than that the possessor of either has simplified his swing to the point where errors are less likely to creep in, and that he is able consistently to bring his club against the ball in the correct hitting position. We talk, think, and write so much about the details of the stroke that we sometimes lose sight of the one thing that is all-important—hitting the ball. It is conceivable that a person could perform all sorts of contortions and yet bring the club into correct relation to the ball at impact, in which case a good shot must result. The only reason for discussing method and form at all is to find a way to make it easier for the player to achieve this correct relationship. In a crude way, he might do it only occasionally; in a finished, sound, controlled way, he will be able to do it consistently and with assurance.

Ultraslow motion pictures made by the Professional Golfers Association show one point of comparison of the methods of Harry Vardon and myself that demonstrates how one motion or position depends upon another, and how after all, it is only the contact between club and ball that matters. The pictures show that at the instant of impact, Vardon's hands are perceptibly behind the ball, and that he has whipped the clubhead forward to make contact, whereas at the corresponding instant in my swing, the hands are

136

Courtesy United States Golf Association

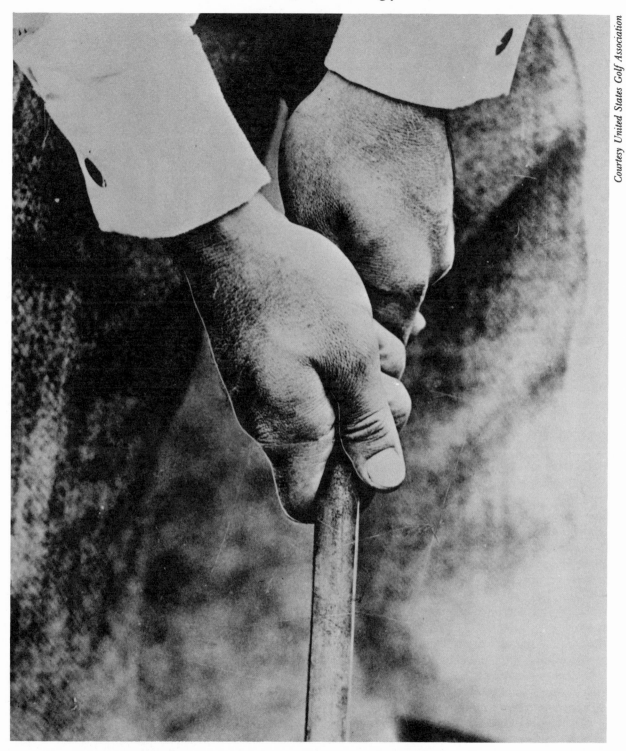

Every teacher agrees that the grip is the foundation of the golf swing. Any golfer can take as a model for holding the club the grip of Bobby Jones.

slightly in front of the ball and the clubhead is being pulled through. Years of play and experience had told each of us that we must handle the club in this way in order to bring the club face into the correct position; and while we may be thinking of some other part of the stroke, subconsciously, through our sense of touch, we bring the clubhead around in the way we have learned produces a good shot. The reason for this difference is found in the slightly different positions of our hands on the club, my left hand being slightly more on top of the shaft than Vardon's. If either should meet the ball in the same way as the other, a bad shot must inevitably result.

This is the sense every golfer must develop. The beginner ought to keep always before him the determination to put the club against the ball in the correct position. It is not easy when form is lacking, but it is the surest way to cause form to be more easily acquired. The expert player corrects subconsciously; some instantaneous telegraphic system tells him, just as he begins to hit, that something is wrong; and at the last instant a muscle that may not always function perfectly will do so in a sufficient number of cases for it to be well worth its keep.

Finding the Orthodox

Golfing methods differ from each other in many particulars. Each good player presents an appearance so unlike any other that he can be recognized from great distances merely by the manner in which he swings the club. The inexperienced observer often fastens onto these differences, concludes that each man employs a radically different swing, and sets about modeling his form upon that of a player he will select; this one he will ape faithfully and exactly to the last detail.

A closer study of the better players reveals that although no two are alike, or even nearly so, still there are certain things that all do. Not only are we justified in regarding these unanimously accepted practices as sound, but it would seem that every golfer, large or small, fat or lean, would do well to adopt them as his own. The fact that almost every effective swing displays certain

things in common with all others is evidence enough that these things ought to be parts of every method. Indeed, these are about the only details of the stroke the instructor is able to give to a rank beginner; these are the only things that he can tell him positively to do. The rest of the teacher's job is to correct faulty movements and to fit together a stroke upon the proper foundation already supplied; but the stroke as a whole is not developed upon any set lines. Fundamentals must be observed, but much latitude is allowed for accommodating individual needs.

A thorough understanding of the fundamentals of the stroke should be the first aim of the beginner. It may be said, of course, that there is a fundamentally correct swing from which everyone should vary only slightly. But that is not what I mean, for a thorough understanding of this sort of swing, and the ability to produce it, are the two things that all of us have been seeking and so few have ever attained. I have reference only to the obvious things that are easily seen and accomplished by the average inexperienced player, things that an ordinarily good player learns for himself, and an expert never has to think about. Nevertheless, these points can be noted by everyone to his advantage.

One reason for the consistency of the best players is the possession of a sound swing; meaning nothing more than a swing in which the successive positions are taken in accordance with accepted practice among expert players. It will be found that the man who departs far from what we call the orthodox, even if he is at times effective, is yet an erratic and unreliable player. He who starts in an unexciting position, and commits no unwarranted extravagance, is usually the more consistent player, because he places himself in positions and moves his club in paths from which, and through which, other successful players have found the going easier. All men are enough alike to make it safe to follow examples proved effective by others.

Taking the Breaks in Stride

Uphill and downhill lies, instances when the player must stand above or below the ball, close lies in swales and the like, when the ball must be gotten up quickly, these are the exacting situations of golf that offer opportunities for the skillful player to profit. At the same time, the certainty of frequent encounters with shots of this nature, in endless variety, accounts in large measure for the eternal fascination of the game.

It is for this reason, more than any other, that seaside terrain is regarded as the best for golfing purposes. There the undulating fairways furnish difficulties that bunkers do not provide, and, without punishing, call for the refinements of skill that an inland course rarely demands. Golfers who play these links learn to appreciate these difficulties and to enjoy trying to overcome them. Encountering lies of this kind so very often, they come to consider them desirable features of a proper course, instead of complaining of bad luck every time the ball is found in such a situation.

I think I first gained an understanding of this attitude upon my first visit to St. Andrews. Playing a practice round before the Open Championship with two American pros and a fellow member of the American amateur team of that year, we were accompanied by a small gallery of club members and townspeople, golfers all. I remember being puzzled when our shots from ordinary fairway lies were greeted with perfect silence, only occasionally broken by a discreet "well played" or "well done," when the ball stopped a little closer to the hole than usual. This was so different from the attitude of spectators in our own country. But when one of us from a tricky lie brought up a shot with a spoon, or brassie, our gallery became quite enthusiastic. Finally I realized that our golfwise friends were refusing to become excited over what were merely good shots any first-class player would be expected to make with some regularity. I suppose they figured we would not have come so far to play in a championship if we could not play these; but

they were most appreciative of the skillful execution of strokes of particular difficulty.

Incidentally, by cultivating the habit of accepting difficult lies as part of the game, we can derive for ourselves more pleasure from the playing of it. It will help us to remember that we tire of banging balls from a practice tee, where for each successive shot the lie of the ball and the problem is the same as for the preceding stroke. We must have a change of scenery, but when we get too much of it, we curse our luck.

One of the reasons Walter Hagen was such a great competitor was his habit of accepting readily any problem the breaks of the game may have tossed his way. Once a spectator, standing by Walter's ball after it had taken a wicked kick into long grass, remarked to him as he came up that he had had bad luck. "Well," said Walter with a smile, "here it is and from here I have to play it."

The continual striving to improve our score, although entirely natural, nevertheless does detract to some extent from our ability to enjoy golf. When we become slaves to the card and pencil, we become inclined to regard as total losses those rounds in which our score mounts beyond our reasonable expectancy. When we take pleasure in the game only according to the scorecard, a bad start is likely to put entirely away the possibility of an enjoyable afternoon.

The real way to enjoy playing golf is to take pleasure not in the score, but in the execution of the strokes. A brassie shot to a green can be just as interesting when played after a recovery from trouble as when it follows a perfect drive. By cultivating this attitude, one finally comes to welcome unusual situations, in which there is the possibility of pulling off something a little out of the ordinary. And again, such an attitude in itself brings better results because it sustains interest and keeps one trying to the end.

When a Player Hits the Ball— What Actually Happens?

by ALASTAIR COCHRAN and JOHN STOBBS

Scientists—and golfers at large—are fascinated by the search for the perfect swing. Whether there is such a phenomenon is still in question, but Alastair Cochran and John Stobbs set out to measure and define it. Their experiment involved basic analysis of what happens when a golf ball is hit.

TO look at the golf swing scientifically, to analyze what exactly happens in it and what sort of movement causes what sort of stroke, and then to build up the model of a perfect swing—that was what the Golf Society of Great Britain team was set up to do. From all we know of golf and golfers, a tall order it obviously was from the beginning.

For hundreds of years, the best of players and the most enthusiastic of pundits and instructors had proved, experimented, theorized, looked at things from different angles and stated their theories in different ways. Over different eras, the manner of make and the characteristics in play of both clubs and balls had changed very widely; and with them the outward appearances of the methods most successfully used to grip the club and to swing it at the ball.

In our own times, fashions and theories have repeatedly varied and swung; and as the team set out on their job the air was thick with controversy about, for instance, the "square method," and the "long right arm," and the "long left arm," and "hitting with the back of the left hand," and "driving" as opposed to "flicking." Although there did perhaps seem to be certain general trends in the development of what was accepted as the ideal game from decade to decade, there remained still almost as many opinions as there were "professors"; and those who knew most about the game were perhaps the most conscious that today's great new discovery was likely all too soon to become yesterday's exploded theory.

Scientists don't work by arguing speculative, unverifiable theory. They approach a new task or line of investigation in a rather more disciplined way. First, they look at what facts they can find about it, or can fairly quickly discover and prove for themselves. Then, working on the basis of these facts, they think up a hypothesis to explain or, more strictly, to describe the whole operation governing them. They can then usefully go ahead to test the hypothesis by further experiments. Further facts thus established either carry it forward, or force them to modify it. If the original hypothesis is off the mark, in due course some unexpected results show where its weakness lies; and may even compel the scientists to rethink it again from scratch.

140

The United States Golf Association, which sets standards for the construction of golf clubs and balls, uses this testing machine to measure overall distance allowed for golf balls. Modeled on the swing of Byron Nelson, the device is affectionately known as "Iron Byron."

First of all, then, scientists need facts. They need to step back, look carefully and decide what exactly it is they are talking about anyway. That applied to this investigation just as fully as to any other line of research.

The first thing the team had to do was to ask themselves what exactly happens when the club strikes the ball; then what is going on while the player swings at it.

It would have been possible, of course, to have set off on the opposite tack by analyzing the game at large: the nature of a "golf course," the structure of the ball and of the clubs used to strike it, and the different flights and trajectories the golfer imparts to it (a gloriously wide field of research in itself, incidentally). All this, of course, comes into a full study of the game, and some of it is reported in the latter part of this book.

But whatever else may be involved in it, or has developed around it, golf still consists in essence of a man or woman making a ball fly through the air by hitting it with a club. Everything else hinges upon that, and has developed, however imperfectly, to suit the possibilities it offers. You can change course, clubs, balls, the rules—at least in theory—as much and as widely as you like. But you cannot change the structure nor the human nature of the player.

Golf begins and ends with a man hitting a ball with a club.

The team, then, first set themselves to answer two questions, phrased simply but carefully like this:

1. What are the essential things a player is trying to do with his club when he swings at a golf ball?

2. What is the essential structure of the physical movement he develops to do them?

What makes a good golf shot?

The first question they could answer immediately from existing knowledge about golf and about physical science. What it boils down to is that, to hit any full-length straight shot, the golfer has to:

—swing the clubface straight through the ball towards his aiming point,

—make the clubface aim square towards his target as he does so—or at least during that part of the swing when it is in contact with the ball,

—swing the clubhead through impact as fast as he can manage to while still achieving both the first two prerequisites of a straight shot,

—hit the ball more or less in the middle of the clubface.

This really is all that is involved. The fact that the good golfer may swing slightly up at the full drive with the ball perched on a high tee, or slightly down at the ball he is forcing out of a divot-hole with a six-iron, does not really affect the essentials of striking a straight shot. Variations of this kind, like variations of swing direction and clubface alignment to produce draw or fade (or, come to that, quick hooks or wild slices) are only modifications of emphasis he may apply, intentionally or unintentionally, to particular strokes within a round. All he is trying to do, on typical shots, is to hit the ball hard, straight and square.

That much is common ground amongst all golfers. So far, so good.

But even the above simple and obvious requirements begin to show faint undertones of assumption. And the second question, about the working of the swing itself, cannot begin to be answered by mere surface appearances, or by the subjective sensations which we all experience as we play the game.

Before they went any further, then, the team had to establish a good deal more in the way of quantitative fact about what exactly happens while a man swings a club and strikes a ball. The experiments put in train to do this produced the most thorough collection of basic established facts about the game of golf ever obtained in one exercise.

Since these facts formed the sure basis upon which the first stages of constructive analysis and thesis could go ahead, it may be of interest to the reader, before we go any further into the account of the team's work, to set some of them out, at least in their bare detail.

Here, then, in outline, is what the team established about some of the main points in the structure of the golf swing, as it works on the course, and as it strikes the ball.

Power

During his downswing, a good golfer can generate up to four horse-power. This is a surprisingly high power; and must need at least thirty pounds of muscles, working flat-out, to produce it. This figure excludes those muscles which merely stabilize his joints in action; and it leaves no doubt that the big muscles of the legs and trunk must play a greater part in the top-class player's striking of the ball than those of his arms and hands.

Impact

Time: During a full drive, the face of the driver is in contact with the ball for only half a thousandth of a second. (For convenience, a thousandth of a second is commonly called a "millisecond." We shall call it that from now on. Contact in a drive thus lasts "half a millisecond.") *Distance:* From the moment it first touches the ball until the moment the ball springs clear of it, the face of the club in a full drive travels forward only three-quarters of an inch. *Force:* The force applied to the ball by the clubhead during impact in a full drive rises to a *peak* of about 2,000 pounds—nearly a ton. The *average* force applied at all stages during the half millisecond contact, that is to say during the compression and springing away again of the ball, is around 1,400 pounds. The time, distance and force involved are very much the same for either the British size of ball or the American size.

"Feel" reaction time

It takes about two-thirds of a millisecond for the shock of impact to travel up the shaft from the clubface to the hands. By this time the ball is about half an inch *clear* of the clubface, and already in flight; but the hands have still not yet "felt" the stroke. At least a further ten milliseconds must elapse before the message gets to the golfer's brain and he can be said to "feel" the reaction. By this time the ball is a foot or more clear of the clubhead. It would be at least another fifth of a second (200 milliseconds) before orders from the golfer's brain could cause his hands to take any action to modify the stroke. Certainly nothing could be done to affect the ball, which by this time would be fifteen yards away.

Speeds

During the downswing, the top-class golfer may accelerate his clubhead about 100 times as fast as the fastest sports car can accelerate: from rest at the top of the backswing, to 100 miles per hour at impact, all in as little as one-fifth of a second!

Travelling at 100 miles per hour, a driver head of the usual weight, seven ounces, sends a top-class ball away at about 135 miles per hour. If the head could be swung at 200 miles per hour, it would send the ball away almost twice as fast, at 250 miles per hour. (Not quite twice as fast, because with all golf balls the faster the impact the less resilient the ball.)

Weight

The principles of mechanics tell us that a heavier head swinging at the same speed of 100 miles per hour will not send the ball away proportionately faster. One of fourteen ounces, twice the normal weight, would send the ball away at 149 miles per hour. A hugely heavy one of sixteen pounds would push the speed up only to 165 miles per hour. Even one weighing 10,000 tons traveling at the same 100 miles per hour would only send the ball away at 166 miles per hour.

Reducing weight, on the other hand, does not add proportionately to the speed at which the head can be swung either. Since the golfer has to swing the club shaft, his arms, and other parts of his body, as well as the clubhead, a ten percent reduction in clubhead weight usually only enables him to swing it about two percent faster; and consequently gains him little, if any, distance. There is, in fact, a very wide range of clubhead weights which will give any player much the same length from the tee if he strikes the ball squarely. What weight of clubhead he should choose is thus much more a matter of what combination of weight and swinging speed best suits his own individual characteristics and abilities in the practical matter of swinging consistently at the ball.

Long hitting

Outstandingly long drivers get their length simply by being able to swing the clubhead faster than the majority. For instance, to carry 280 yards before the ball hits the ground, a player has to send the ball off at 175 miles per hour. To do this he would have to swing:

a six-ounce clubhead at 134 miles per hour;

a seven-ounce clubhead at 130 miles per hour;

an eight-ounce clubhead at 127 miles per hour.

Temperature

A warm golf ball is more lively than a cold one. A drive which carries 200 yards through the air with the ball at 70°F (21°C), would carry only 185 yards if the ball were at freezing point.

Loft and spin

A seven-ounce driver head with a loft of 11° or 12°, swung at 100 miles per hour, normally sends the ball away at 9° or 10° above the horizontal, with a backspin of sixty revolutions per second. A good player's stroke with a typical seven-iron, which has a loft of 39°, sends the ball away at about 26° elevation, with a backspin speed of about 130 revs per second.

These are examples. The actual elevation and spin-speed from any stroke with any club will depend very much upon the precise manner in which the player makes the stroke. "Chopping" or "hitting down" increases spin. "Hooding"—that is playing the stroke with the hands ahead of the ball—tends to start the ball off at a lower angle.

Crooked shots

Pulls and pushes are straight shots in the wrong direction. They fly straight because at impact the clubface is at right angles to the direction in which it is being swung. They go off in the wrong direction because the clubhead is being swung in that direction, instead of straight on target.

For every 1° the swing itself is off-line, the pull or push will pitch only three-and-a-half yards from the intended line, at 200 yards from the tee. To pitch the ball into the rough, which usually means about twenty yards off-line, the player's direction of swing in a pull or push must thus be nearly 6° off-line—quite a big error of swing in fact.

Hooks and slices, are curving shots caused by the clubface aiming, at impact, in a different direction from that in which it is being swung. They go more than twice as far off the correct line as pulls or pushes for the same amount of basic striking error at impact. If, for instance, the clubface points only 1° off the direction in which it is swung, then by the time the ball carries 200 yards through the air it will have curved enough in its flight to end up seven to eight yards off the line it set out on. To hit the rough, twenty yards off-line, needs an error in clubface alignment of less than 3°. The effects of hooking and slicing, moreover, are more spectacularly magnified by long hitting.

The implication of golf's basic facts

Some of the facts above are quite surprising in themselves, and may easily be new to many golfers. To the team they had some pretty obvious, if important, practical implications. The more you look at them, the clearer it becomes that they cast a great deal of light on the real nature of the good golf swing; and even make it quite clear that it doesn't by any means work in a number of ways most golfers have always assumed it did.

Take first that odd fact about impact: that the ball is in contact with the club for less than half a millisecond, that it takes longer than that for the clubhead's reaction to the blow to travel up the club shaft to the hands, and another twenty times the total length of impact before the player becomes aware of the 'feel' in his fingers.

This means, in plain language, that what we all feel while making a stroke is not how we are hitting the ball, but how we have already hit it. This in its turn can only mean that, in hitting a full drive, the player in effect puts his clubhead into orbit at 100 miles per hour around him and —perforce, because he can't do anything else— leaves the clubhead to hit the ball entirely on its own, in the path and at the speed he has already given it.

The clubhead's orbit is then settled by the plane and method of the player's whole downswing, its speed by the power he puts into it, together with how effectively he has applied it. *At the moment of impact,* the clubhead might just as well be connected to his hands by a number of strings holding it to the rough circle of its orbit, for all the effect he can have on it.

Another point of interest is the remarkable accuracy achieved by any top-class player in his swinging of a club. To play the sort of golf he does play most of the time, he must consistently manage to align his clubface at impact within 2° of the direction of his swing. If he didn't, he'd never drive the ball within fifteen yards or so of the middle of the fairway, nor strike it on to some part of the putting surface, in the way most good players do.

He achieves, in fact, outstandingly consist-ent accuracy in alignment and striking, as the illustration of his 2° margin of clubface error shows.

Pretty narrow bounds within which to confine natural human errors in swinging for a full-length shot.

We can also take note that, in order to apply as accurately as this the four horse-power which he may generate in accelerating his clubhead to 100 miles per hour in a fifth of a second, the golfer is not only going to have to use the strength of pretty well his whole body, but also to apply it through a very effective system of mechanical leverage of limbs and joints.

To achieve the accuracy required, any such system just has to be as simple as possible. If it isn't, no player can begin to control it consistently enough to produce anything like championship-standard golf.

One key to the perfect golf swing, then— and, in all probability, to the differences between top-class players and duffers—must be the maximum possible simplicity in operation compatible with generating full power from almost all the active muscles the human body has at its call.

This is the starting-off point for the analysis of the perfect swing.

On Learning

by **PERCY BOOMER**

Percy Boomer is acknowledged as one of the century's leading teachers. One reason Boomer succeeded was that he knew how the learning process worked and accentuated positive gifts, as he explains here.

I want to say a few things about learning the game and about teaching it. I ought to know something about these subjects for I have been learning golf for forty-five years—and teaching it as well for the last thirty of them.

Now I claim that the right way of learning golf has almost nothing in common with the "learning" we did at school; it is an entirely different process. Memorizing the capitals of Europe or a Latin declension, or "learning" chemistry or mathematics, are purely mental feats and depend exclusively upon *mental memory,* whereas I contend that to learn to play good and consistent golf you need *muscular memory.*

What you need to learn (or memorize) are not the technical or mathematical details of a good shot but *the feel of it.* If you and every component muscle in you can remember the feel of a good shot, *you can make it*—and you have become what I term a reflex golfer. That is to say, the good shot has become your "reflex," or *automatic response* to the sight of the ball. But please remember that this golf memory is *a memory of a cycle of sensations* which follow and blend into one another quite smoothly. Each sensation must be connected up with those which precede and follow it; it cannot be considered independently. The truth is that it cannot even be *felt* independently. You cannot, to take a crude example, *feel* the top of your swing as such; you can only feel a sensation between the sensations of the backswing and those of the downswing.

For that reason you must never in golf say, "I've got it!" when you think you have found the secret of some shot that has been evading you—unless what you have "got" fits into your cycle of sensations or, as we shall now call them, *controls.* Because, unless it does so fit in, it cannot become a reliable part of your game. And why do I call sensations controls? Simply because I want you to control your golf by these sensations instead of by *thought.*

There is another reason why your memory of a golf shot must be a memory of a cycle of sensations, not of a number of separate sensations. It takes an exceedingly skillful juggler to juggle with six glass balls at once, but if the six balls were threaded onto a string most of us could manage them—and the memorizing of sensations as a cycle (instead of as independent items) does *thread them up* for us very much in this way.

146

To turn for a moment from learning to teaching. Most of the teaching of golf is completely negative—and a purely negative thing can have no positive value. Why do I say that golf teaching is negative? Well we can all find faults in each other's game, millions of them, and we all start off to teach golf by pointing out these faults and "curing" them. I did this for twenty-five years, but I have now discovered that the right way to get a pupil to hit the ball satisfactorily is *to watch for any good natural qualities* that may be there and to build up the swing around them.

We all hit a good ball sometimes. Maybe with the beginner this is an accident, but the good teacher will use such an accidental shot, photographing it in his mind and starting away to build up controls around the qualities which made it possible.

In this way the beginner can retain his natural capacity to hit the ball and will gain confidence in his ability to do it—and so go on enjoying his game and improving it. But if the teacher merely points out to him a dozen or more faults in his swing he will become perplexed, confused, and fed up. For that reason I never tell a pupil his faults (which is negative teaching). I notice the faults, of course, *and suggest the necessary corrections* (which is positive). So I never tell a pupil that he overswings and breaks his left arm, I explain width to him. That is to say I give him a positive conception and by working on it he actually cures his faults without even being aware that he had them.

Now there is another point about teaching which I would like to emphasize. You will find that in this work I have not tried to set down a set of controls in one way and leave it at that. I have tried to set the same things down and explain them in many different ways. So when you find me repeating myself do not think it is carelessness! All good teachers must repeat, but never in exactly the same words or with just the same connections. I want to give you a clear idea of the controls which will enable you to produce an effective swing, and I do not mind if I have to say the same thing in a dozen different ways so long as one of the twelve gets home with you. I hope you will not mind either, because you should be able to pick something new out of the other eleven also.

I learned golf by the long way—trial and error—and I want to lead you away from that to a method which is methodical and is effective whatever your age or your handicap may be. If you accept my method of learning you do not need a lot of practice on the course to improve; you can assimilate the principles in your armchair and put in useful practice on the hearth rug —where you need no club because you can *feel* your muscular movements without it. You must learn to feel the sensations through your intellect and then forget them intellectually and leave them to your muscular memory or control system.

How long does it take to "learn golf"? Well I am still learning after forty-five years of it! I have known pupils who hit the ball very well after only four lessons and others who have taken a year or more to do even moderately well, but time is apt to level things out a lot. Golf is a curious game in being easy of comprehension but (sometimes) very long in realization. There is much darkness in the early stages, and it is only after a few years at the game that we really come out into full daylight and can assess our own possibilities.

Early difficulties are often emphasized by age or physical make-up. While I was writing this I had just started two young ladies—one of sixteen who is still at college but weighs about 170 pounds and another in the early twenties who weighs less than half that. Apart from the weight of their clubs the conditions will be the same for both, yet obviously their problems will work out very differently. And we have all got our physical individuality and peculiarities in the layout of bones and development of muscles. But I have found by long experience that these things usually level themselves out in the end—I have seen many gifted and precocious beginners fail simply because they would not put in the hard work which is essential before the elementary stage is passed, and only when the elementary stage is passed can golf genius come to the surface.

On the other hand I remember one pupil of mine who started very young and at times could hardly get the ball off the ground; yet at eighteen she was scratch and champion of France. And as I have already told, I started another lady at forty and though she was not gifted she was a worker and ten years later she eliminated Mme. Lacoste from the French Open!

So do not despair if you are trying to learn golf, or better golf, and getting no results. It may be that you have been trying to learn too many things (like juggling with too many balls) and when you have tried to add just one more, your whole game has broken down on you. We will simplify the things you have to learn by stringing them together into cycles of sensation because they are then easier to remember and easier to *add to.*

If you work in this way your golf will be *progressive.* You will still (being human) get bad patches, but each bad patch will tend to be less bad and each good patch will tend to be better, because you are *building up* your game.

The foundation upon which it must be built up is the *feel of the swing;* so in the first practical chapter I give you an idea of the whole swing— just as I do in the first lesson when personal teaching is possible.

The subsequent chapters are what a musician might call "variations on the theme"! Hence the apparent repetition. Because I believe that all golf shots should be made with the same controls, you will not find anything fundamentally different in the chapter on putting than that which you will find in the chapter on the full swing. Yet you might quite possibly get a control for your driving out of the putting chapter; it depends on your make-up and on what you read into what I have written.

Some years ago I told a pupil, in the course of a lesson, "I drive as I putt." Three years later he said to me, "You once told me you drove as you putted—what you meant was that you putted as you drove." I let him have his own way! The great thing was that we had got the two associated in his mind and controls and so proved my system to be teachable and workable in others. I have had plenty of confirmation of this since.

In finishing this chapter I will return again to the need to make your learning *positive.* Don't go out to find out what is wrong with your swing, go out to improve it. You will be none the worse if you start with a really big idea—to learn (or relearn) the golf swing at your first try. If that is your ambition do not tie yourself up with theories; stand up and give the ball a crack—that is the most positive thing in golf.

What Can Your Best Golf Be?

by TOMMY ARMOUR

Realism, unhappily, is not part of the average golfer's playing arsenal. He dreams too high and is brought low. Tommy Armour was a superb teacher who worked on the principle that each player must quickly learn his limitations and work within them—for only then can progress begin.

A discovery I've made as a contestant, observer, and student at innumerable professional and amateur golf championships is a simple fact that undoubtedly will improve your scoring. Here it is:

It is not solely the capacity to make great shots that makes champions, but the essential quality of making very few bad shots.

Watch at the practice tee of any major tournament and you will see many players hit a very high percentage of perfect shots with every club in the bag. Then watch them as they play. They will make superb shots, but they will make too many bad ones.

Their bad shots may be because of faulty execution or the less pardonable reason of bad judgment. But regardless of the cause, they've exceeded the limit of allowable error. In major championship golf the margin of error is narrow.

It's wide in the club competitions between higher handicap players, but there, as well as in expert competitions, you'll note that what distinguishes the winner is that he made fewer bad strokes than the rest.

The champion is the fellow who can make the fewest poor shots. What first vividly impressed me with that fact was an experience I had with Walter Hagen.

Walter and I were playing the final round of a North and South Open. I was leading the field when that fourth round started at Pinehurst. I played the first three holes of that round four-four-three. Hagen had begun six-six-five.

As we walked to the fourth tee, Hagen in his high drawl said to me: "I've missed all I can spare today; now I'm going to work."

He went to work—and on me.

He didn't miss any more shots that round.

He rubbed out my lead, finished with a sixty-eight, and won the tournament.

That lesson cost me plenty, but although I fancied myself as a very keen scholar of golf, I hadn't known what I learned then. That was when I discovered the secret that the way to win was by making fewer bad shots.

Now let's go from that lesson to an application I made of it at Boca Raton. Among my pupils there is a prominent steel man. In lessons and in practice he hits many excellent shots. He's a good hitter but a bad player.

In a moment of high confidence in the grill room, he expressed his conviction that he could break ninety. There were numerous differences of opinion. The outcome was as is customary when there are differences of opinion regarding sports events.

It was agreed that as I had risked a bold wager in support of my pupil, I could accompany him as counselor during the round.

He hit a long, strong drive off the first tee, but in the rough, to the right.

He walked up to make his second shot and picked out a five-iron to go for the green.

"Put that back in the bag," I told him.

"I've got a chance to go for a birdie," he protested.

"You've got a bigger chance of missing the shot, then having another tough one to make before you get on," I explained. "Play an easy eight-iron shot out to the left to where you have another easy shot through the opening of the green. Then you may get yourself a one-putt par."

So that's the way he played the hole, and that's the way it showed on the card . . . par four.

To his and my amazement and delight—and profit—he went around in seventy-nine.

Hole after hole I'd had to argue with him and explain to him that there are two sound rules for low scoring that apply in 999 out of 1,000 cases.

These rules—or practical principles, are:

Play the shot you've got the greatest chance of playing well, and
Play the shot that makes the next shot easy.

If it's mystified you to see fellows with worse swings than yours score better than you do, the mystery will be cleared if you'll note how, instinctively, or by deliberately using their heads, they've applied the two tactical principles I've just set before you.

When you get that lesson in your head, you will greatly improve your scoring. There are plenty of other lessons about making golf shots,

but the main lesson about playing golf is the one I've just given you.

There are variations of this lesson in playing. The variations are determined by match and stroke play and by the player's proficiency. The expert can take more chances with less risk than can the average or high handicap golfer.

Some never learn to play the type of game that fits their capabilities. Countless times I've seen ordinary players try to play courses in ways that would require the shot-making techniques of the most highly gifted stars. Such players may know something about grip, stance and swing, but they don't know the first thing about playing golf.

That mistake isn't made by the champions. Walter Travis knew his weak points. He couldn't get much distance. And he also knew that he was superior in accuracy and in the short game. His winning tactics were to fit his game to the course he was playing.

Lawson Little was an excellent shot-maker before I ever saw him, but he wasn't winning as he should. About all I taught him was tactics. When he learned tactics, he won four American and British national amateur championships in two consecutive years, and later won the American National Open title and other events against fine professional fields.

Julius Boros was a very good shot-maker before he started winning major events. He wasn't winning because he didn't have a tactical plan of play that fitted his game. He was playing in a cautious way that fitted neither his ability nor his temperament.

I suggested to him that since he was one of the best I'd ever seen in playing out of traps, he could change from his plan of trying to steer shots and boldly let them fly. Then if a shot came to rest in a trap around a green he had nothing to worry about, as he could come out close enough to the cup to sink his putt.

He had been unnaturally cautious as a putter. When it was impressed upon him that he very, very rarely missed much to either side of the cup but often failed to get up to the hole with putts that were precisely on the line, he began putting with more confidence and by daring to

Courtesy United States Golf Association

Tommy Armour, known as "The Silver Scot," won both the U.S. and British Open champion-ships. Noted for his mastery of iron play, he is famed also as a great teacher. Here he demonstrates a balanced finish, proof of a good swing.

get the ball to the hole, or even past, improved his putting.

Boros is a strong player who'd been trying to play with a tightening fear of being wild with his long shots. When he learned to swing freely rather than steer in making his long shots and to depend on the precision of his short game, he became a champion.

Every golfer scores better when he learns his capabilities.

This is the first time I've ever mentioned what I am certain is my greatest value to my pupils. I learn about them before I try to teach them. I determine, pretty closely, what is the best golf each individual can possibly play.

It is utterly illogical to expect a person with physical, temperamental, and manner-of-living limitations to become able to play par or sub-par championship golf. One might as well expect to become a great master of painting, sculpture, the violin or piano, become a scientific genius, or even to become rich, simply by taking lessons and practicing.

I've taught some of the greatest golfers a few of the polishing details that have helped them get as near to perfection as is possible. That has been comparatively easy because they have an aptitude for learning, sound basic ability, and fine physical qualifications. But the utmost demands on my own capabilities as an instructor have been made by those who are shooting the courses in eighty-five or up into three figures, discovering what would be their best games and teaching them to perform consistently to the limit of their capacities.

Golf is a comparative game. That is the marvelous merit of golf's handicapping system.

Ellsworth Vines pointed out this attraction of golf when he told me that in tennis, when he was starring, there were less than a dozen who could give him an exciting and entertaining game, but in golf he could get a fine, close match with a dub or an expert because of the handicapping.

Certainly a game that permits many thousands all over the United States to play against champions, with the handicaps making all contestants equal at the start, has a feature of enjoyment that makes it unique.

At Boca Raton, in the winter, and at northern courses in the spring, summer and fall, I play many rounds with players whose average scores range from eighty-five to 110, and we have very close games on the handicaps.

You might think I'd be bored playing with a real duffer, but I don't find that to be the case. In the first place he interests me by being so bad when he might well be so much better. He will hit some excellent shots, but they're hit by accident and I wonder how I might make such accidents become consistent.

The principal error in viewpoint of a majority of golfers is failure to understand that if they play to a uniform standard that is well within their capabilities, the handicapping system will take care of the rest. They'll probably take money from many proficient professionals and amateurs to whom the handicaps allow an extremely small margin of error.

But they all want to be stars when they just simply haven't got it in them. As the Bard might have said, "Ambition is a grievous fault and grievously doth the duffer pay."

You see overvaulting ambition at its dirty work when the ninety-five-shooter gets an eighty-two with twenty-five putts and ten lucky bounces. He thinks he is an eighty-two performer, whereas he actually has a game of about eighty-seven under best normal circumstances. If he has once shot an eighty-two, he rarely realizes that in scoring eighty-seven, considering his limitations, he's doing as well comparatively as the gifted player who goes around in sixty-eight.

The most difficult part of my responsibility as a teacher is to determine what is the best my pupil could consistently score. Then I can teach him to do that. If he shows unexpected promise after reaching that goal, we can advance together toward the next higher plateau of learning.

Heaven knows I want every pupil to become as good as is humanly possible, but the more realistic part of my work is to make reasonably certain that he never gets more than a few strokes worse than he should be.

The fact that at least ninety percent of the millions of golfers score in the nineties—or approximately a stroke a hole over par—is highly significant. It is a plain indication of their inherent limitations. Few of them are reconciled to their limitations. Fortunately, practically all of them can learn to reduce many of the faults that are preventing them from getting as close to par as nature will allow them.

But they must be willing to learn.

There are at least six people who want to be taught golf to every one who wants to learn.

My task with those six is to make them understand primarily their attainable objective, the rational method of achieving their aim, and the relationship that must exist during a lesson.

The very best I can do for them—or for anybody else—is to get them started correctly on the most solid and lasting basis of improvement; a basis on which they establish the best game they ultimately can play.

Harry Vardon, the Master Mold

by KEN BOWDEN

Although he didn't invent it, Harry Vardon, the British genius who won six of his country's Opens, popularized what is called the overlapping grip. His style of play influenced the development of the swing and the game in general.

PROMINENTLY displayed in the foyer of the South Herts Golf Club, north of London, is a commanding bronze sculpture of a golfer's hands gripping a club. Because this was the course where Harry Vardon ended his days—he is buried a few paces away in the Toteridge parish churchyard—every visitor knows or quickly guesses whose hands they are. But take those hands of golf's first true superstar out of their commemorative setting, and not one golfer in 10,000 would be able to identify their owner.

The sheer size and muscular power of the hands would surely prompt a strong vote for Arnold Palmer. To the more intense student of technical nitty-gritty, the fairly "strong" placement of the left hand might suggest Billy Casper or Lee Trevino. Perhaps the purposeful "short-thumbed" snugness of the overall grip would even bring Jack Nicklaus to mind. But it would be a guessing game at best because the fact is that this grip, for all practical purposes, is the grip of just about ninety-nine percent of today's top professional and amateur golfers the world over.

It won't, of course, be news to anyone who can break ninety that Harry Vardon popularized the principle of "wedding" (to use his word) the hands together by wrapping the little finger of the bottom hand around the forefinger of the top hand. What may be news is that he didn't actually invent this overlapping technique: His fellow member of the "Great Triumvirate," J.H. Taylor, developed it simultaneously but independently, and a fine Scottish amateur, John E. Laidlay, had used it in winning the British Amateur championship in 1889, the year before Vardon played his first round of tournament golf. What may be even bigger news to the modern golfer is the exceptional degree of influence that Vardon had on the golf swing as a whole, far beyond his popularization of a grip style.

Harry Vardon's achievements were awesome—every bit as overwhelming in his own time as Nicklaus's are today. But, looking back now, what impresses most about him is not so much his inevitably mist-shrouded victories as the method through which he achieved them. The deeper one gets into his technique, the more dramatically apparent it becomes that he was the greatest technical innovator in the history of golf. The swing style of his predecessors is so foreign to the form we know today as to be

Courtesy of United Statse Golf Association

One of the five greatest players of the game, Harry Vardon helped popularize what is known as the overlapping grip. In spite of the restrictive clothing he wore at the turn of the century he managed a fine swing. His position at the top shows how it's done by a master.

almost unrecognizable—indeed, if we didn't know better, its practitioners would often seem to have been playing an entirely different game. But when one watches Vardon on film, one sees, in essence, the swings of Gene Sarazen, Walter Hagen and Bobby Jones—even the timeless Sam Snead. In basic principles at least, here is the swing with which countless good senior golfers —and others who cannot physically or temperamentally accommodate the stressful body-con-

trolled actions of the game's young lions—still continue to win golfing prizes and pleasure. Here, in short, is the master mold; the mold from which Byron Nelson built in initiating the method now so successfully refined on the U.S. professional tour; but a mold which remains, almost in its original form, a wonderfully valid swing pattern for the purely recreational golfer.

Harry Vardon was born the son of an artisan in the spring of 1870 in Grouville, Jersey, one of the Channel Islands between England and France at the gateway to the Atlantic Ocean. Almost from the time he could walk he would occasionally swing a homemade club in rudimentary backyard golf games with his five brothers and two sisters, but he had slight interest in the sport. When he began work at twelve, in domestic service, cricket and soccer consumed most of his sparse leisure time, and the rest was spent supplementing family income by such means as collecting and selling sea shells. Between the ages of thirteen and seventeen, when he worked as a pageboy and waiter, he played virtually no golf at all. In 1887 he took a position as under gardener in the household of a member of the Royal Jersey Golf Club and would play on the four annual British national holidays and occasionally with his employer at other times. But the game was certainly no more than a casual pastime for him during adolescence. He never had a lesson, never formally studied technique, never consciously copied anyone's swing. His clubs were a ragbag of discards and homemades, and he ferreted his gutta-percha balls out of Royal Jersey's wiry sea grasses. In 1922 he wrote: "Up until I was twenty years of age, I played so little golf that even now I can remember every round as a red-letter event of my youth. In later days people often said to me: 'I used to know you when you were playing golf as a boy at Jersey.' In point of fact, it was my brother Tom they knew, for he obtained a good deal of golf, whereas I was not far from being a stranger to the game."

By the time he was twenty, Vardon had, by his own estimate, played no more than twenty full rounds of golf, and the closest he had come to practicing shots had been hitting balls around a cultivated field to scare away crows in the course of his gardening duties. Then, while still in his twentieth year, he entered a tournament at the local workingmen's club and won the first and only prize—a vase—with ease. Simultaneously news arrived that his brother Tom had won a professional tournament in Scotland and with it a prize of twenty dollars. Said Vardon later: "This seemed an enormous amount to me and I pondered long and intently over it. I knew that, little as I had played, I was as good as Tom. If he could win that vast fortune, why shouldn't I?"

So began a career that was not only to immortalize the name Vardon but was massively and permanently to alter the character of the golf swing.

Prior to Vardon's appearance on the professional tournament scene, such as it was in the mid-1890s, golf was played at every level with what had become known as the "St. Andrews swing." As today, there were individual variations on its basic theme, but fundamentally the St. Andrews swing consisted of a long, flat, slashing action deriving from an ultraloose grip, a huge swaying body turn away from and through the ball, and an uninhibited slinging of the clubhead through the ball with the hands, wrists, and shoulders. Unquestionably the equipment of the day—the long, whippy, wooden-shafted clubs and the stonelike, rise-resistant guttie balls—had helped father this freestyle formula. The few action paintings and prints, and the limited amount of technical exposition in the golf literature of the era, indicate that one or two outstanding players—notably young Tom Morris—employed a somewhat more compact style. But basically the St. Andrews swing predominated, both in achievement and aesthetically.

Vardon changed all that. His first three British Open wins in 1896, 1898 and 1899 severely dented confidence in the old Scottish style, even though many leading Scots vigorously defended their invention, often to the point of bad-mouthing the "English" method that was beating them so soundly. By the time Vardon won his sixth and last British Open in 1914, the St. Andrews swing—at least in its most extreme form—had disappeared. And its demise would probably have come even sooner had two bouts of tuberculosis not forced Vardon out of competition and into sanatoriums for long spells between 1904 and 1911.

At a time so far removed, and in a world where excellence of strike is commonplace at the highest levels of the game, it is difficult today to fully appreciate the brilliance of Vardon's shotmaking, especially during his halcyon years before the long battle with tuberculosis. His greatest victories were won with the guttie ball, which he always preferred to the rubber version because of the thoughtfulness and precision it demanded in conceiving and executing every shot. From tee to green he was in his day totally without peer. He flew the unresponsive guttie appreciably higher than his rivals, thus gaining the twin advantages of long carry and soft landing that have so aided Nicklaus. He drove straight and, when necessary, extremely far. No one before—and probably no one since—played more majestically with the brassie: Vardon himself said that, on form, he could expect to hit the ball consistently within fifteen feet of the pin with this equivalent of the modern two-wood. With the shorter clubs he grew, if anything, even more adept. "No one ever played irons more prettily," eulogized Bernard Darwin, Vardon's equivalent among writers of the game. "He merely shaved the turf and did not take cruel divots out of it." He was an expert manufacturer of special shots with every club in the bag, describing as his best-ever stroke a shot over a clubhouse that was situated just a few feet away from his ball. The ball, struck with an open-faced niblick (eight-iron), appeared to rise almost vertically and then arc forward over the building's roof to fall softly within a yard of the cup! "His play was enough to break the heart of an iron horse," said Andrew Kirkaldy, a demon performer in the big-money challenge matches that interspersed the few tournaments of the day, and a frequent Vardon victim. "In truth, in his great years, no one had any real hope against him," wrote Darwin.

It was only when Vardon reached the green that he sank to the level of his contemporaries. "A grand player up to the green, and a very bad one when he got there," was how Darwin—never a man to mince words—put it. "But then," he added, "Vardon gave himself less putting to do than any other man." Contemporary reports constantly refer to Vardon's ineptitude with the putter as the cause of his either winning by only a smallish margin or actually losing when clearly he should have won, especially during the second half of his career after his illness. Ultimately it was the missed "gimme," caused by a distinct twitch or jerk in the right hand and forearm, that

caused him to give up tournament play. But, although he lost power as he aged, the majesty—the "supreme grace," as Darwin called it—of his long game remained with him to the grave.

The overlapping grip, although Vardon's most famous legacy to golf, was actually one of his least drastic departures from the St. Andrews swing, which featured a mechanically passable if somewhat loose and sloppy ten-fingered hold on the club. Vardon was an average-size man—five feet nine-and-a-half inches and 165 pounds in middle life—but he had unusually large hands and long fingers. Almost certainly, wrapping the little finger of his right hand around the forefinger of his left was originally simply a way of compacting his hold on the club. It took him no time at all, however, to discover the real value of this type of grip, which is the "wedding" of the hands into a single unit, and he strongly advocated it for this purpose for all players very early in his career.

The modern golf teacher would find little fault in Vardon's grip and a lot to praise. The club passed from the inner knuckle joint of the first finger of his left hand across the base of the second and little fingers, which placed it a little more in the fingers than is currently fashionable. But this was essential to the light grip pressure and fluid motion of Vardon's swing, as it is to many good modern "hands" players. In most other respects Vardon's grip could have come right out of the 1970s. His left thumb sat just to the right of the center of the shaft and was snugly covered by the right palm when this hand was added. The club lay at the roots of the fingers of the right hand, and the right thumb rode just to the left of top-center on the shaft. The V's formed by the thumb and forefinger of both hands matched exactly, both pointing somewhere between his right ear and shoulder.

About grip pressure he expressed himself with a bit more flourish than might your 20th century teaching pro, but the message was the same: "In the ordinary way of things, the tight grip creates a tautening of the muscles in the body and when the player is in this condition the chances of executing a perfect stroke are remote. The golfer's muscles should be at once healthy and supple—like a boxer's. When they are encouraged to develop hardness and size—like a weightlifter's—they retard the ease and quickness of hitting, which count so much at the instant of impact." Vardon did vary from modern theory, however, when he added that "it is quite sufficient to grip a little tighter with the thumbs and forefingers. They will prove sufficient to keep the clubhead in position. The other fingers may be left to look after themselves in the matter of the strength they apply."

Modern grip principles call for maximum pressure in the last two fingers of the top hand and the middle two fingers of the bottom hand. But this is much more a matter of feel than mechanics. From photographs of grips only, few average golfers today would be able to distinguish Vardon from seventy percent of present-day tour players.

It is a forgivable human failing to bestow originality on current practice, and nothing more piquantly exemplifies this tendency in golf than three of Vardon's basic grip principles.

The modern golfer is frequently advised to face the back of the left hand and the palm of the right to the target at address. This point was also stressed by Vardon: "The left-hand knuckles should face [down] the line of play and the right-hand knuckles the other way," he instructed many times in his books and magazine articles. Then there is the question of which hand should grasp the club most firmly. Modern teaching favors either equal grip pressure or a slightly softer hold with the bottom hand. Said Vardon: "I grip equally firmly with both hands at the start, but the pressure of the right hand decreases during the backswing." And finally the matter of which is the master hand and arm. Although the very latest theories lean strongly toward "left-sidedness," a consensus of international teaching opinion would probably favor a balanced effort. Wrote Vardon: "I don't believe in a master hand or arm. All should work as a unit, and I believe the overlapping grip best achieves this."

Harry Vardon played all his competitive golf in knickers, fancy-topped stockings, a hard collar and tie, and a tightly buttoned jacket ("A cardigan or jumper permits too great a freedom in the shoulders," he said). Re-dress him in a sport shirt and double knits and he would still look incongruous on today's pro tours because, champion innovator that he was, certain elements of his swing definitely conflict with modern theory.

His manner of starting the club back, for example (although also employed by Jones and Hagen), would create horror at any present-day PGA teaching seminar. Vardon's first move was a pronounced drag backward and inward of the hands, with the clubhead trailing the hands almost until they reached hip height, at which point a free wrist-cock from a cupped left wrist position set the hands very much "under" the shaft and established a wide-open clubface. That is certainly about as far as you can get from the "one-piece" policy of the 1960s and light years away from the "square-to-square" and "set-the-angle-early" edicts of the 1970s!

Conceivably, Vardon's famous bent left arm would be less sinful in principle today than his takeaway, in that a number of top golfers currently play with discernible "give" at the elbow (including Europe's top teacher and former tournament star, John Jacobs). But Vardon's elbow didn't just "give"; it categorically *bent*—during his early years almost at right angles! When teaching, he did not insist on so great a kink, but he strongly advocated relaxation in the elbows to prevent tension and to produce smoothness and rhythm, arguing that centrifugal force would automatically straighten the leading arm at the appropriate moment in the downswing. "I am constantly having to cure patients ruined by the stiff left arm," he wrote in an American golf magazine, and he stressed the bent arm frequently and persuasively in his books.

Vardon's swing contained other departures from what is presently regarded as good form; for example, he allowed his hips to turn very freely in the backswing; his right elbow to rise high and away from his body (into almost the same position as Nicklaus!); his left heel to swing high at the completion of a full backswing (again like Nicklaus!); and he "crossed the line" at the top—pointed the club right of target. But these were minor aberrations compared to his thoughts about the correct way to start the downswing.

Golf instruction over the years has been liberally sprinkled with tips from leading players who inadvertently advocated something they genuinely felt they did, but actually did not do. Vardon was not to escape this trap. To return the clubhead back to the ball, the golfer using the long, flat, floppy St. Andrews swing was forced to make a throwing action with the hands, wrists, and arms as the first move of the downswing. This was the one element of the old Scottish method that Vardon *thought* he retained. In many of his writings he talks of "leading the downswing with the clubhead," of "throwing the club to the right and a little behind the body" starting down, of "only the arms moving until halfway down," of "early uncocking of the wrists"; in short, of what we know today as "hitting from the top."

There is no doubt that Vardon "released" his wrists in plenty of time to deliver the clubhead solidly into the back of the ball, traveling low enough to the ground to catch the ball cleanly with a divotless sweep rather than an abrupt downward hit. Indeed, the smoothness and comparative slowness of his swing, as captured on film, are such that one can actually *see* his wrists beginning to uncock as his hands pass hip height on the downswing—a movement far less visible in films of modern tournament players. There is also no doubt that the pattern of wrist-hand action Vardon employed to release the clubhead would not be regarded as ideal today, in that his left wrist arched inward—became concave—through the impact zone (modern methods call for the left wrist to maintain a firm straight-line relationship to the forearm while turning anticlockwise through impact).

But whatever his stylistic differences and whatever he thought he did, Vardon categorically *did not* "hit from the top." In every one of the scores of pictures of him studied by the authors, it is blindingly apparent that the set, or cock, of Vardon's wrists is at least maintained—and sometimes on a full drive increased—early in his downswing. In fact, in hitting what in his day was a famous specialty of both himself and J.H.

Taylor, a low-flying mashie (five-iron) "push shot," Vardon hit the ball as "late" as any golfer on the tour today.

Whatever Vardon's variations from modern standards, they are vastly outweighed by his similarities. In fact, discovering from Vardon's literature how little is truly new in golf was an educational experience for this writer, despite his long-held suspicion that so-called modern methods draw more from the recycling of old ideas than from solid invention.

See, for example, how many of the following principles, paraphrased from Vardon's writings, you can fault as conflicting with modern practice:

· The body should be easy and comfortable at address.
· The stance should be open, with the rear foot square to the line of play and the leading foot angled toward the target.
· The ball should be addressed opposite the left heel or, if not there, nearer to the left heel than the right—unless you wish to play a low shot.
· I like my ankles to be free, which is why I play in shoes, not boots.
· When the clubface is against the ball, the end of the shaft should reach to the flexed left knee.
· The arms do not touch the body at address, but neither do they reach.
· The weight should be divided equally between both feet.
· It is necessary only to find the correct stance and the shot is certain to be a success.
· The head should be steady throughout the swing because if it moves, the body goes with it, disrupting the club's path.
· The eyes should focus on the back of the ball or on the ground just to the right of the ball.
· An upright backswing offers the shortest and therefore the most efficient route from and to the ball.
· Avoid straining for too wide a backswing, for if you do, you will likely sway your body.
· The backswing is wound up by the swinging of the arms, the hips turning, and the left knee bending as the body pivots from the waist.
· As the backswing proceeds, the right knee holds firm, but does not quite become stiff.
· Don't lift your left heel too much, but let it

come comfortably up as you pivot onto the inside of the foot in response to your body pivot.

· The grip relaxes a little as the backswing proceeds, especially the right hand.

· The right shoulder rises gradually as the body pivots. The body turns on its axis in the backswing and the downswing.

· There is no pause between the backswing and the downswing; they flow into each other.

· Don't jerk or snatch at the top or coming down or let the right wrist get on top of the club.

· The downswing is faster than the backswing, but there should be no conscious effort to make it so.

· At its simplest, the swing is a matter of winding yourself up with your arms and unwinding yourself with your arms.

· The grip automatically becomes firmer as the downswing proceeds.

· Let the shoulder movement be steady and rhythmic, especially in the downswing.

· The club accelerates gradually to impact.

· The wrists should be held fairly firmly as the ball is hit. Do not bend the right wrist toward the target until after the ball has been struck.

· At impact the feet should be flat on the ground.

· As the club goes through, the weight moves to the left, the left leg resists the blow, the right leg bends, the body fronts the line of flight, and the right foot raises almost vertically. At the finish the arms are up, the hands level with the head, the club beyond horizontal, and the body and shoulders face the target.

· I have always preferred an open stance because then I am not in the way of the clubhead as it swings through the ball. Also, an open stance encourages the upright swing that I favor.

· Don't scoop with the iron; thump down on the ball.

· The straight shot is difficult to repeat. Intentional pulls (hooks) and slices are golf's master shots.

· Good driving is the foundation of a good game. Learn to drive first with the brassie, for it is easier than the driver.

· I believe I use lighter clubs than many of my contemporaries. My driver is forty-two inches long and weighs twelve-and-three-quarter ounces; my brassie is the same length but twelve ounces.

· Never throw the clubhead or make a hit with it; swing it all the way.

· There is no such thing as a pure wrist shot in golf, except for putting.

· The shorter the swing or the shot, the narrower the stance, the less the foot and body action, and the more the emphasis on the knees. The length of the backswing determines the distance of the less-than-full shot.

· The most successful way to play golf is the easiest way.

· To play well, you must feel tranquil and at peace. I have never been troubled by nerves in golf because I felt I had nothing to lose and all to gain.

Good action photography of Vardon is scarce today, but what is available of his mature swing depicts a number of strikingly modern features—all of them seminal departures from the St. Andrews swing.

Vardon's "centeredness" throughout the swing is one such. A 1927 commentator graphically described it thus: "Imagine that, as he addresses the ball, a pole is passed downward through the center of his head and body, and into the ground: then his swing is a rotating movement performed by the shoulders and hips, around the pole, while the arms are being lifted up and the left knee is bending inwards." The writer goes on to quote Vardon as saying that his ability to maintain a fixed axis was perhaps the major factor in his accuracy and control—why he "would not be off the fairway six times in six rounds."

Another remarkably modern feature of Vardon was his address posture: knees slightly flexed; upper body angled forward from the waist; back straight; arms hanging easily and freely; head high; hands slightly below a straight line from the clubhead to the left shoulder.

Leg action, the core of the modern golf swing, was little discussed as such by Vardon in his writings, but he did recognize it obliquely, and he certainly employed it, albeit unconsciously, as an effect rather than a cause. As photographs prove, his open stance and speedy return of the left heel to earth immediately on starting his downswing definitely brought his legs and hips into play, even though he felt that he started down by moving the clubhead with his hands and arms. The reason he never thought or wrote much about the legs is, in this writer's view, very simple: His lower-body movement was a natural, unconscious, *reflex* reaction to the winding of his upper body in the backswing (as it is with every golfer who makes a full body turn and free arm swing). Thus, because his legs operated so instinctively and automatically once he'd got to the top of the swing, Vardon never had occasion to think about them consciously— or, if he did, he could quickly put the matter out of mind as being a natural reflex movement not needing or warranting conscious direction.

It would seem that Vardon was definitely way ahead of most of the moderns in at least one respect, that being his swing's appearance of grace, ease, and economy of effort. Today only a handful of tour players, such as Sam Snead and Gene Littler, would seem to come close to matching what Bernard Darwin called the "beautiful free movement of one having a natural gift for opening his shoulders and hitting clean." "Time after time," Darwin extolled, "he [Vardon] would come right through, drawn to his full height, the club round over his left shoulder, the hands well up, the left elbow tolerably high. It was the ideal copybook follow-through, and he did it every time with an almost monotonous perfection." An even better word picture of Vardon's overall motion comes from Walter Cavanaugh, writing in *The American Golfer* in 1924: "The outstanding impression of watching Vardon play is that of utter ease and lack of physical effort. His hands, arms, body and legs appear to work as a well-oiled machine, and there is always present that element denoting complete coordination, ordinarily referred to in golf matters as rhythm."

How many of today's stars, one wonders, will evoke such prose?

A recurring theme is the influence the master golfers' personalities have had on their playing methods. Unquestionably Vardon's swing style and general approach to the game were born of his remarkably placid, easygoing nature. "He had a calm and cheerful temperament," wrote Bernard Darwin. "The game seemed to take little out of him, and he could fight, if need be, without appearing to be fighting at all." This quiet, considerate, and unfailingly courteous nature threaded every facet of Vardon's life. At no time did he make any effort to impose his grip or swing on the world or even to suggest that they were superior to any others. Particularly in his early days he simply let his achievements speak for his technique, which, in the small, clubby golf world of that time, they did with nuclear force. Later, when he came to write about the game, he did so with great modesty and lucidity and only the gentlest chiding of what he regarded as erroneous or befuddled theories. Perhaps his open-minded, nondogmatic approach stemmed as much from his almost happenstance entry into the game as from his easygoing personality. Threading all his writings is the impression that initially he really had little idea about what he did when he swung a golf club and that he found out only when, as a superstar, he was forced to think about technique in order to communicate about it.

In fact, in 1922, reflecting on the "shock" his swing initially created, he wrote revealingly: "My own brother and Edward [Ted] Ray [and other Jersey golfers] all drifted involuntarily into the habit of taking the club to the top of the swing by the shortest route, whereas the popular way before was to swing flat at the start and make a very full flourish. . . . Why we hit upon the other way we do not know. Personally, I never thought about the matter until I obtained my first professional post at Ripon, Yorkshire. And it was only when I was twenty-one and in my second appointment, at Bury, Lancashire, that I began to study and learn golf in real earnest. So you can see that there is every chance for you."

Why Golf Is So Different— And So Difficult

by **DAVID MORLEY**

Psychologist David Morley has looked into the mental side of the game and come up with some interesting—and accurate—observations on why the game is so challenging.

GOLF is a game that is uniquely different from other games men play. For one thing, it doesn't require any exceptional physical gifts. To play golf well you don't have to weigh over 200 pounds, or stand closer to seven feet than six, or be capable of covering 100 yards in less than ten seconds. Nor is the game particularly demanding intellectually. To win the U.S. Open you certainly don't need the kind of brain it would take to win a Ph.D. in nuclear physics. In fact, if the example of quite a number of past champions is anything to go by, you don't even need to have finished high school to become a master of the links.

In short, golf seems to demand few if any of the attributes that are essential to achieve excellence in other games. And yet, as everyone knows who has tried it, golf is incredibly difficult to play well.

Why?

Some of the reasons are certainly physical, in the sense that repeatedly striking a golf ball hard and true takes a lot of dexterity. Some of the reasons are certainly intellectual, in the sense that intelligence is necessary in order to meet the game's strategical and tactical demands. But there is more to it than that, as the champions acknowledge when they so frequently and insistently state that "golf is seventy (or eighty or ninety) percent a *mental* game."

The champions are right, even though they rarely try to explain exactly what they mean. There *are* mental dimensions to golf that either are not present at all or are of comparatively minor influence in other games. That these mental factors are rarely publicly discussed, let alone endlessly dissected and analyzed like the physical elements of golf, is probably due to their complexity and to their highly emotional (and therefore intimate) character. And yet, as we shall see as we look quickly at the most important of them, there can be no doubt that they contribute enormously to the difficulty of golf.

Listening to Two Tunes at Once

Although golf is a game played with other people, it is essentially an individualistic, and therefore a lonely, experience. The presence and demeanor of the other people involved generally inject a spirit of camaraderie into the game. But, at root, this overt show of fellowship is a disguise

161

masking an inherent loneliness of endeavor often so intense as to be almost existential.

Mentally, the golfer is almost always in the position of listening to two orchestras playing two tunes at once. Part of his mind is engaged in the light, warm comradeship of like-minded people taking pleasure in the fresh air, the sunshine, the beautiful scenery, and so on. This part of his mind is bright and cheerful, bathed in the pleasure of that very enjoyable human experience.

At the same time, another part of the golfer's mind is deeply involved in a constant internal monologue involving his actual *performance* of the game. This part of the mind, separated from the other, is inward-looking, brooding, scheming, often worrying—in short, intensely concerned with the personal business at hand. Thus preoccupied, it wants to have very little to do with external factors—doesn't really give a darn about the balmy weather, or the lovely scenery, or being sociable. It is involved in a very private activity, in which there is little room for anyone or anything else.

This inner monologue is a very intimate process, and most golfers—even the best—try hard to conceal both its presence and its intensity. Many try to do so by appearing nonchalant, or at least fairly lighthearted, even when under the most intense competitive pressure.

The compensatory behavior of Lee Trevino, whose approach to the game sometimes seems to be casual almost to the point of frivolity, is perhaps the supreme example of this type of reaction to the threats of the internal monologue. Most of the time Trevino's ebullient facade very effectively masks that dark, somber side of his mind that is totally egocentric and antisocial, and therefore must be kept carefully hidden from the exterior world. It is when the inner monologue becomes so strident that it overpowers the facade that the exterior world sometimes glimpses another Trevino—the Trevino grumpily hurrying straight from the eighteenth green to the private haven of his motel room.

At the opposite end of the scale, a golfer will react to the inner struggle by almost completely excluding himself from the external world, even when operating within it. Ben Hogan reacted thusly, as did Jack Nicklaus in his early days. Hogan, and to a lesser degree Nicklaus, simply drew down the blind on that part of their experience beyond the internal dialogue. As a result, both often came across to audiences as antisocial, brooding, machinelike, and generally unappealing beyond their sheer golfing genius.

Hogan was thought of as a heartless machine programmed for victory at any cost, and ever ready to slam the door in the face of anyone wishing to examine more than his golf scores. Nicklaus's nickname, the Golden Bear, stuck with him not so much, in my view, because of his golden locks, but because he came across as an angry bear who glowered through the bars of his cage at anyone who dared interfere with his intense inner involvement. As he matured and met more and more of his goals, the internal dialogue became easier for him to handle, and he became a warmer, friendlier, more sociable being, increasingly aware of, and responsive to, the crowd and the drama of the spectacle in which he was so often a major actor.

This dichotomy within the mind is something that every golfer has to recognize and deal with. And it is one of the mental peculiarities that make golf such a unique—and difficult—game.

You're on Your Own

In almost all games you play with other people, the actions of your fellow participants are much more than social functions. What they do dramatically affects what you do: the pitcher's moves in baseball determine the behavior of the batter; the action of the man who serves the ball in tennis determines the response of the person waiting on the other side of the net; and so on. But in golf all of the meaningful physical activity is strictly between the golfer and the ball. Even when he is playing a so-called "head-to-head" match, only through what he does with the ball can the golfer influence the play of his opponent. And when the golfer is involved with the ball, he must turn off all other functions of his personality. For these few moments he must shut himself off completely from the rest of the world and become totally preoccupied with the ball and its position on the golf course relative to the hole. What he actually does to that ball depends solely upon his own capabilities. He has no coach, no one to run interference for him, no teammates to help him. All decisions and actions are his sole responsibility.

However, once he has made his physical commitment and struck the ball, the golfer is free to relax and enjoy the company of his companions—and he makes a big mistake if he doesn't do so.

Most great golfers recognize the intervals between shots as periods of relief, when they can clear their minds of tension and other distracting influences, allowing them to recover from the intensity of that brief but lonely experience over the ball. Of course, no golfer can be totally free of some subconscious thoughts concerning the tactics of his game. But, if he is wise, in the intervals of relief between his shots he will turn *off* that internal monologue with as much deliberation as he turns it *on* when he addresses the ball.

Unfortunately, achieving this flexibility demands a mental discipline difficult for most golfers to attain. Some seem to fear losing touch with that seething inner monologue, and their excursions into the social side of the game are thus at best tentative. They appear grumpy, moody, antisocial, giving the impression that the intervals between shots are wasted time. They would do better to utilize these respites by recognizing that the ability to tune in one world and tune out another actually increases the intensity of their mental concentration when they most need it.

The Emotional Impact of Opponents

Most golfers fail to recognize that golf is, in the final analysis, essentially a game played between the golfer and the golf course. Certainly, if more would grasp this, they would avoid a lot of mental pitfalls. However, although this is the *basic* truth, on a more obvious level the golfer is also competing directly against other people and thus is naturally interested in their games to some degree. The risk here is of emotional involvement *in,* rather than detached awareness *of,* the opponents' games. Many golfers, even at the

pro tournament level, have discovered that their own games can be adversely affected by emotional reactions to their opponents' play.

This happens because in golf a participant is not only a performer, but by necessity a spectator as well. And the way the golfer handles this second role can affect the efficiency of his own game as much as the way he holds the club in his hands.

When the first player to tee off hits a booming drive down the center of the fairway, the golfers who follow react in various ways. Many are threatened by such demonstrations of strength. They respond to the challenge by wanting to outdrive the man who has just struck the ball. Thus they immediately regress to the caveman situation of one man proving his superiority to another by some demonstration of brute strength. Their reaction is to swing the club with all the finesse of a Stone Age man smashing a club at a dinosaur. The result is almost always disastrous.

Other golfers allow themselves to be overawed by their opponents' demonstrations of strength. Their minds flood with negative thoughts, their muscles turn to jelly, their knees become weak, and their nerves begin to jangle. As a result, when they step to center stage, they are so filled with doubts that their efforts become just as ineffective as those of the golfer who turns into a gorilla any time he is threatened by superior strength.

Although these two reactions are diametrically opposite, the results are essentially the same: both golfers are victims of internal reactions to something that they have *seen.* In short, their emotional reaction to another's performance has devastating effects on their own game.

Objectivity in spectatorship is therefore another unique difficulty of golf. It is not easy to achieve, but it must be striven for. The successful golfer must not allow himself to identify *emotionally* with the actions of other performers, and the easiest way for him to avoid doing so is to recognize that these actions cannot in any way directly influence his own game. Emotional involvement with sporting performance should be reserved for the stadium or the TV set. It's fine to identify

The meeting of a hole which creates trouble, the 15th at Augusta National, and a player especially adept at trouble shots, produced this explosion from water by Ben Crenshaw.

with Joe Namath as you watch him complete a fifty-yard pass, because you're not expected to get up from the bleachers, or your easy chair, and do the same thing. However, when you see a man hit a long ball from the tee, and you're up next, you have to follow him onto that same stage and try to emulate him. Any time you let your emotions rule how you do so, you're in trouble.

The better pro tournament players solve this problem by watching their rivals with a detachment that allows them to derive, from what they see, certain specific physical information that can be helpful to their own games. For example, they look for such information as the effect of the wind upon the flight of the ball; the distance the ball rolls or kicks to left or right on landing; the speed of the green as revealed by the action of an opponent's ball; and so on.

The trick is never to get into the habit of making judgments about your own game by comparing it with other people's. That kind of emotional approach courts disaster by opening the mind to all kinds of negative feedback.

The Influence of the Ball

Golf is a ball game, of course, but what makes it different from almost every other ball game is that the ball doesn't move until the golfer hits it. This static state of the ball encourages the mind to become passively related to it. In other words, the ball influences the golfer's mind instead of the golfer's mind influencing the ball.

Staring at a motionless object does not stimulate the mind or the body into action. Rather, it invites immobility. For example, when a person stares at a crystal ball, his mind has a tendency to enter into the early stages of hypnosis, in which condition it becomes very open to suggestion—particularly to the kind of negative feedback mentioned a moment ago. The tendency for the mind to slip into a state of passive suggestibility, as a result of being "hypnotized" by the immobile ball, is thus another characteristic contributing to golf's unique difficulty.

To be successful as a player, the golfer must at all times relate to the ball actively rather than passively. *He,* not the ball, must be in control. Once the ball takes over, the mind becomes susceptible to myriad influences that can at best inhibit and at worst totally destroy the mechanics of swinging the club.

The Influence of the Club

Nothing in golf is more unique than the strangely shaped implements with which the player propels the ball. The novelist John Updike referred to the golf club as a "silver wand, curiously warped at one end." Few people have given much thought to the mental effect of this oddly shaped instrument on the player. In most other ball-striking games the hitting surface of the bat or racket extends in a straight line from the shaft. This makes it much easier for the mind and body to execute coordinated movements, because the implement seems like a natural extension of the arm.

The fact that the hitting surface of the golf club is not in the same geometric plane as the shaft can subtly undermine the golfer's belief that it can actually do the job for which it is supposedly designed. The insecurity associated with such a thought is bound to create an appreciable amount of tension, which floods the golfer's nervous system and does all kinds of strange things to the tempo of his swing.

Then there is the factor that the shaft of a golf club is much longer than, for example, the shaft of a tennis racket, or even a baseball bat. Thus the ball is much farther away from the hands in golf than in baseball or tennis, and this factor is accentuated by the tiny size of the ball and the striking surface of the club. Again, more insecurity, and more tension.

Fear and Anger

Golf certainly is a mental game, as all the great players agree, but it is not really an *intellectual* game like, for example, chess. No complicated mental gymnastics are required, nor is there any demand in golf for quick or spontaneous thinking as in games like baseball or tennis.

The golf ball isn't going to take a bad bounce before you hit it.

In a curious way, the mental aspect of the game is in one sense independent of the physical part. Yet, in another way, it is very intimately connected. For example, you can plan precisely the way the shot should be made, and all of that thinking may be flawless. But the actual execution of the shot may fail completely because your physical ability to carry out the stroke has not measured up to your mental ability to conceive it.

The mental activity in golf involves mostly synthesis and control. Synthesis has to do with the planning of the swing. The control factor involves the emotional state of the mind. And, while it is true that there are certain fundamentals about the game that must be learned by every golfer, the understanding of these principles doesn't require any towering intellect. The big mental challenge in golf is thus in the area of *emotional control*. And it is here that many potentially great golfers have been destroyed—destroyed by their inability to handle their emotions.

Two emotions especially are difficult for the golfer to deal with. One is fear and the other is anger.

The fear is generally fear of inadequacy. The demands for precision in golf almost parallel those required in mathematics; these demands are so great that there is almost no margin for error. This kind of pressure is too great for most people, and they crumble under its unrelenting force. That's why it is so important for the golfer to understand as much as possible about *how* he must strike the ball. The more he understands each element of the physical action, the better he can implement the overall swing with absolute confidence, and thus the more easily he can overcome the fear of inadequacy.

It is the same stringent demand for precision that spawns the frustration leading to the anger so often displayed at every level of golf. I think golf causes more self-anger than any other sport, and in most instances this anger is simply the extreme form of a frustration that just can't be expressed in any other way.

Anger has driven people to some remarkable actions on the golf course. I had a professor of surgery in medical school who was said to have been one of the finest athletes in the country during his undergraduate days. One day he hit two successive balls into a water hazard on a short hole. Thereupon, he took his matched set of clubs and threw them one by one as far as he could out into the pond. He never played the game after that. This method of dealing with anger is hardly the most effective one, but it is a classic example of how the game can reduce a highly intelligent, well-controlled, and otherwise emotionally stable human being to a savage beast.

The problem here is the conflict created by two diametrically opposed concepts. You have on the one hand the mental formulation of the easiest way to move the golf ball from A to B, and on the other hand the extraordinary physical precision required to carry out that task. To reconcile the two requires simultaneously a great degree of confidence and an equal degree of humbleness—a mixture present in most of the greatest golfers of the past. Confidence comes from experience and a thorough knowledge of all aspects of the game. Humility also comes from experience, which teaches the golfer that he will always hit some bad shots; that 100 percent technical proficiency is impossible; that the game will win more often than he does.

The Aura of Reverence

There is implicit in the game of golf a deep sense of control that is difficult for many people to adopt or even accept. It is almost a religious quality, as though everyone involved in the game were participating in a sacred ritual. And the ritual *has* to be accepted, because people who depart from it are at first censored by the other participants and finally excommunicated.

Some of the high priests of golf do eventually, through the privileges that grow from success, acquire more liberty in this area than the general run of players. Lee Trevino, for example, clowns like a little boy who has brought his new toy to Sunday school. But how quickly he turns that clowning off when he addresses the ball.

Generally, this peculiar state of religiosity is always present, not only on occasions as celestial as the Masters Tournament, but in all "serious" golf—right on down to the one dollar Nassau. The golfer who reacts against this aspect of the game eventually finds himself playing alone. Indeed, anyone who is not ready to play golf with this peculiar reverence is really not ready to play at all.

Even though this kind of statement infuriates the nongolfer, in that it smacks of fanaticism and elitism, there is a good sociological reason for it. In a modern technocratic society that takes away individual initiatives, this one activity stands firm like a rock, for everyone is equal on the golf course. There, the shipping clerk can for brief moments become superior to the chairman of the board. And if the spirit of the true golfer resides in the heart of the chairman of the board, he humbly bows to the man who may be considerably inferior to him in many other areas of life.

The "hooked" golfer can thus come to feel toward the game the same way that young lovers feel about each other. Golf invades every area of his life, gradually moving to the top of his hierarchy of values, offering an emotional experience that is almost spiritual in its quality. This experience can lock him to golf with an intensity that rarely exists in other games.

The Physical Challenge

Finally among golf's challenges there are the physical factors. Golf is certainly a very physical game, but it is physical in a very special way.

The golfer about to execute his shot is not unlike the diver who stands at the tip of the diving board contemplating the kind of maneuver he will execute. This maneuver is reviewed mentally with great care before execution. The mechanics and timing of all its aspects are fully understood. There is nothing spontaneous about the action itself. It is simply the end result of a final intellectual rehearsal.

But the golfer's experience is more complicated than that of the gymnast or diver. He not only has to perform precisely and with good timing a complex physical maneuver, but he has to perform it in such a way that the face of the club he holds in his hands contacts a very small ball within very fine limits at very high speed. The measure of excellence of the diver or the gymnast lies in the beauty and precision of his own physical maneuver. The excellence of the golfer's physical maneuver is judged by the fate of the ball itself, in that, no matter how beautifully the golfer swings, he has failed if the ball does not go to his intended target.

All of these factors make golf a very demanding game. And for this very different and difficult game, special mental as well as physical techniques are required.

Golf's One Unarguable, Universal Fundamental

by JACK NICKLAUS with KEN BOWDEN

As all great players have attempted to do, Jack Nicklaus has set down the principles that guide his game. Generally, he is not dogmatic, simply indicating how he does it and allowing the reader to choose what is useful. In one area of principle, though, he is adamant, as he explains below.

THE next time you are looking for something to watch on the practice tee at a PGA tour event, study the players' heads as they swing. You'll see a few that swivel —mine included. But I'd be very surprised if you see many that move up, down, or from side to side.

I regard keeping the head very steady, if not absolutely stock still, throughout the swing as *the* bedrock fundamental of golf. It is inviolable as far as I'm concerned, which is why I bring the subject up. If you are hoping to improve your game through these pages, but can't, or won't, learn to keep your head steady throughout the swing, read no farther. There is nothing that I— or anyone else—can do for your golf game.

The reasons the head must stay steady are so obvious to me that I feel a little foolish enumerating them. But since so many handicap players do seem to move their heads around with cavalier abandon, I suppose I'd better. They are as follows:

1. The head, or at least the neck or the top of the spine, is the fulcrum or hub or axis of the swing. As such, any shifting of it up, down, or sideways must inhibit or weaken the springlike coiling of the body on the backswing that is so essential to the generation of proper leverage on the forward swing.

History's "Quiet" Heads
A steady head has certainly been fundamental to the game's finest players. In this century, Walter Hagen would appear to be (I never saw him play) the only superstar who moved his head around during the swing. Personally, I tend to think that this and other swing peculiarities of Hagen's, along with some of his off-course activities, have been exaggerated through the exuberance of the storytellers. But if it's true he moved his head a lot, it probably explains why he missed so many full shots. Certainly no other 20th century champion has been a head-mover. In fact, in one—Arnold Palmer—I believe a "quiet" head has been a premier success factor. With his type of violent swing, I think Arnold's superstill head has often saved his game.

2. Any shifting of the head, at any point from address to impact, will alter the arc and plane of the swing, which, if not a totally destructive fac-

Courtesy Hershey Entertainment & Resort Co.

The young Ben Hogan assumes a steady, perfectly aligned set-up position before making a shot.

tor, is certainly a very complicating one.

3. Movement of the head changes the line of vision, and it tends to force the eyes to alter their image or focus. It is very difficult to hit any object you are not looking at.

4. As the heaviest part of the body, relative to its size, the head has a strong influence on balance. Few people are agile enough to retain their full balance during the exertion of a full golf swing if their head moves.

When you think about these factors it is easy to see why a steady head is the one fundamental of golf that is universal to all "methods" and to all teaching systems throughout history. Hitting the ball as hard as I do, I know I couldn't break eighty if I were unable to keep my head in one place throughout the swing.

That capability did not come easily to me. I believe that keeping the head still is one of the most difficult things a golfer has to learn to do. Certainly it was for me, probably because, in striving for distance through a big arc, it was so easy to sway the top of my body off the ball.

I've told the story before of how Jack Grout finally cured me of head movement. When nothing else would work he had his assistant, Larry Glosser, stand in front of me and grab my hair while I hit shots. My scalp still tingles at the thought of those sessions. I cried tears of pain many a time. But by the time I was thirteen I had learned to keep my head in one place, no matter how hard I tried to hit the ball.

Grout is the least sadistic man you'd ever meet, and this was, of course, a last resort. A less-painful technique of his to get a pupil to keep his head still is one I used in hitting thousands of shots as a kid, and still use today to check myself out periodically. Grout applied this technique because he believed a golfer couldn't keep his head steady if he didn't stay well balanced throughout the swing. He felt the key to balance was footwork, and the later success of what he taught me obliges me to agree with him 1,000 percent.

Before I was ever allowed to hit woods, Grout made me hit thousands of iron shots—usually with a five-iron—with a flat-footed swing. He made me first plant my heels solidly on the ground, then, during the swing, I was allowed to roll my ankles: the left in toward the right on the backswing and the right in toward the left on the forward swing. But I was not permitted to lift either heel off the ground so much as the thickness of this page.

One invaluable benefit of this exercise was the sound, repetitive pattern of footwork it taught me. Rolling rather than lifting the feet is still integral to my game today. But the main objective originally was to keep me centered and balanced over the ball, and it certainly worked, especially when combined with the hair-grabbing act. Unless you have a tough scalp, I recommend swinging without lifting your heels as the finest of all head-steadying exercises.

The commonest kind of head movement I see among amateurs is lateral. The head shifts away from the target with the club on the backswing then stays there, usually causing the player either to fall onto his back foot and spin his body into the forward swing or, less frequently, to jerk his head forward as the club starts down in a vain attempt to regain his original head position.

Probably the biggest cause of the original fault—the lateral backswing sway—is sheer laziness. Swaying is a cheap way to get the club back and up without turning and coiling the torso; without really stretching and working

Stop Head Bobbing

Handicap players often bob their heads up and down during the swing. This is just as fatal, in terms of disrupting the "geometry" of the swing, as lateral movement, but is often even tougher to cure because the movement is usually more difficult for the player himself to detect. As does swaying, I believe bobbing stems mostly from laziness; from making the backswing a lifting action instead of a turning and coiling movement.

A good drill is to get someone to stand in front of you and lay the grip end of a driver lightly on top of your head until you develop the "feel" of a level-headed swing. It might take a while, but it will pay pretty big dividends in the long run.

the back and leg muscles. Thus, if you can improve your body pivot going back, there's a good chance that that will automatically take care of your head movement. If not, the only answer is to consciously practice keeping your head steady, *behind the ball,* until it becomes an ingrained habit. To do so, obviously it helps to "keep your eye on the ball." But be wary of that old golfing maxim as head-steadying medicine. I can sway my head two feet and still "keep my eye on the ball."

A final warning: I've been talking all along about a *steady* head, not a stiff or rigid one. The forward sliding of the legs on the downswing can cause a slight lowering and/or backward movement of the head on the forward swing. Such movements are always slight among good players, and are better not made at all. But if you find such a slight movement hard to eliminate completely, don't force it. The forward and upward head movement is the one you have to worry about most on your forward swing.

Even in trying to eliminate that, however, you should use your common sense. There must obviously be a pulling-up force on your head as the club rises after impact, and a too-conscious determination to prevent it happening can inject tension or rigidity into your forward swing. The trick is to let the head swivel and rise only when the natural momentum of the through-swing forces it to do so. I find in my own game that this happens automatically if I keep my eyes focused on the ball's original position until the club reaches full extension away from me toward the target.

The Inner Game of Golf

by TIM GALLWEY

Presently, investigation into the mental side of the game is still somewhat primitive. Tim Gallwey, who operates Inner Game Resources and has authored books on Inner Tennis *and* Inner Skiing, *is completing a book on* Inner Golf. *Here are some Gallwey ideas on how the game can reveal itself, if you listen to your body and mind.*

FOR most golfers, the real problem is not ignorance of the proper way to swing the club. Information on that subject abounds. No, the most common complaint is, "I know what I've got to do, but I can't do it!"

In other words, there seems to be room for information on how to translate golf knowledge into corresponding bodily action. How to develop this skill is the subject of the "Inner Game of Golf."

The "Inner Game" is concerned with a natural and effective process of learning and doing almost anything. It is similar to the process we all used, but soon forgot as we learned to walk and talk. It uses the unconscious mind more than the "conscious" mind. We don't have to learn this process; we already know it. All that is necessary is to *unlearn* those habits that interfere with it and then *let it happen.*

Self 1 vs. Self 2

A major breakthrough in my attempts to understand the art of control of mind and body came one day when I noticed that most players talk to themselves while they're playing golf, tennis or other sports.

"Keep your eye on the ball, you dope."

"If I've told you once, I've told you a million times—follow through," and so on.

Just who is this "I" and "you"? They seem to be two separate entities; otherwise no conversation—not even a one-sided conversation—could take place. The "I" seems to give instructions, the other, "myself," seems to perform the action. Then "I" returns and evaluates the action. For clarity, let's call the "teller" Self 1, and the "doer" Self 2.

You are now ready for the first major principle of the Inner Game. The relationship between Self 1 and Self 2 is the prime factor in determining your ability to transfer your knowledge of technique into effective action. In other words, the key to better golf is to improve the relationship between the conscious mind, the "teller" (Self 1) and the unconscious, automatic doer (Self 2).

As the examples indicate, the typical relationship between Self 1 and Self 2 is that of Self

172

Today's tournament professional wields the putter like a surgeon.

1 issuing commands to Self 2 and then criticizing the results. It's obvious that Self 1 doesn't trust Self 2. It's as though Self 1 thinks that Self 2 doesn't hear too well, has a short memory and is stupid. Yet Self 2 is anything but stupid, for it includes the unconscious mind and automatic nervous system. It hears everything and forgets nothing. In fact, when Self 2 has hit the ball well once, it knows forever what muscles to contract to do it. That is part of Self 2's nature.

What happens is that, by thinking too much and trying too hard, Self 1 produces tension and muscle conflict in the body. In fact, Self 1 is responsible for errors you make in your swing, yet it blames Self 2. Self 1's condemnation of Self 2 undermines your confidence, your swings get worse and frustration builds.

There is a way to overcome this conflict between Self 1 and Self 2. The first step is to learn to trust Self 2. The ability of the human body to learn, without the "help" of all the verbal instructions that Self 1 wants to give it, is much greater than most people imagine. When you succeed in quieting Self 1, the true potential of Self 2 emerges.

Most golfers have had the experience of hitting a drive that almost literally leaps off the club and flies long and straight. You didn't "try hard," yet it was such a great shot you were amazed and called it lucky. Yet in Inner Game

terms, this is only an example of what your Self 2 can do, *if* your Self 1 does not interfere.

Another example. Sometimes you play "above your head" for a series of holes or a whole round. In Inner Game terms, this means a temporary disappearance of Self 1, and thus you experienced no interference from conscious thought. You lose yourself in the action, your awareness was heightened, while analysis, anxiety and conscious thought were completely forgotten.

The first skill needed, therefore, in the Inner Game is called "letting it happen." Gradually, you (Self 1) build a trust in the ability of your body (Self 2) to learn and perform. This relationship will take a little time, but it can start immediately. Instead of telling your body what to do, let it have its way. Don't scold it for any mistakes, but let it learn from them. Let your body control itself without any nitpicking from your mind. Anyone who does this rediscovers natural learning, the process we used as youngsters.

The second skill needed is quieting the conscious mind (Self 1). The capacity of the body to perform is in direct proportion to the stillness of the mind. When the mind is noisy, anxious or distracted, it interferes with the nervous system's silent instructions to the muscles. It's like static interfering with radio signals. The louder the static from Self 1, the more the messages from the nervous system are drowned out and the worse you perform.

How do you quiet Self 1? By having it totally occupied during the swing, to the point where Self 2 can learn. If Self 1 is given something subtle and interesting enough to hold its attention during the stroke, then Self 2 is left free to perform up to its potential.

Inner Game Drills to Divert Self 1

Thus, the role of the Inner Game teacher is to provide situations where such learning experiences can take place. I will now discuss these situations, or drills, as I call them. As a starting point, assume you're on the practice tee, that you've warmed up your golf muscles with a few shots and you're ready to go. To make it easy, use a seven-iron.

The first drill I suggest is called "Back-Hit." Feel the club swing back, and when it changes directions at the top, you call out loud, "Back." The instant the club meets the ball, say, "Hit." The game is no longer golf—it's simply "Back-Hit." Detach yourself from the results of the shots. You (Self 1) observe yourself (Self 2) doing the drill.

As you get into the swing of "Back-Hit," you will probably surprise yourself by the quality of many shots you hit. And at some point you will probably hit a superb shot, followed by one less good. The superb shot so excites Self 1 that on the next shot, its attention is not on "Back-Hit" but on duplicating the superb shot. As a result you "try harder," tighten unnecessary muscles and get less than a satisfactory result. Often, you may notice that when Self 1 is trying hard, it forgets to say "Back-Hit."

By now you will be beginning to appreciate how reluctant Self 1 is to relinquish control. Whether you hit a good shot or a bad shot, Self 1 is always poised to get into the act. However, don't worry about these interruptions. You'll find that all you have to do to become concentrated again is simply put your attention back on "Back-Hit."

Incidentally, when you're playing a round of golf, I recommend experimenting with "Back-Hit" as your primary focus of concentration rather than simply looking at the ball. In golf, the ball sits there and is not an interesting or subtle enough object to totally occupy Self 1. "Back-Hit," however, if done with relaxed concentration, does fulfill these criteria and will keep Self 1 "out of it" as you swing.

Next, you might try a slightly more advanced concentration drill called "clubhead path." Put your attention on the entire arc of the clubhead as it travels in space, feeling every inch and moment of its path. This focus of attention is more subtle, and for some, more interesting than "Back-Hit." It, therefore, has the potential to command a higher degree of concentration. In this exercise, it is important not to try to exercise conscious control over the path of the club, but to observe it with your fullest attention. If you do this without Self 1 interference, errors in your swing will self-correct, just as your balance self-corrected when you first learned to walk or ride a bicycle.

When practicing "clubhead path" on the practice tee, I recommend you try hitting a number of balls with your eyes shut. With just a little bit of trust, you will soon be making good contact with the ball and your awareness of the "feel" of the club will be noticeably increased. Some of that increased awareness will carry over to your open-eyed swing. You will have learned that you don't really need to put as much of your consciousness on the ball as you may have thought. Yet as much of your attention as possible is needed to increase awareness of feel.

As you work with these concentration drills, you may very well find that your swing is changing, for the better. Let it change—this is Self 2 in action. You'll also find that the quality of learning is in direct proportion to the quality of concentration.

There's an almost unlimited number of focuses for your attention, which will increase club and body awareness and, therefore, increase control. One of the most effective focuses of attention concerns increasing awareness of the way the club swings through impact. Hit some balls with the sole aim being to notice whether the club is swinging through the ball from inside to out, outside to in or inside to square to inside. After you swing, assign number values to the results. For example, the most inside-out swing you could make would be plus five, the most outside-in swing, minus five with zero representing a flush hit. Try to give in-between values across this spectrum. Don't worry if you find difficulty in doing this. Many of our pupils find that their Self 1s have difficulty at first being accurate—yet their Self 2s learn anyway! Just stay with the drill.

Another effective focus is on the clubface at impact. The aim of the drill is to see if you can feel the degree to which the clubface is open or closed at impact or if it is square. Imagine that the ball is teed in the center of a clockface. Square would be 12 o'clock, a slightly open blade 1 or 2 o'clock, and a slightly closed clubface would be 10 or 11 o'clock. Again, assign Self 1 the task of giving values for clubface orientation at impact on each swing. The added awareness of the feel of the clubface will soon result in added Self 2 control.

One important point on all of the foregoing drills is that you should observe the results of each shot, but don't allow Self 1 to sit in judgment of it. Get away from thinking, "That's a bad shot" *or* "That's a good shot." There is no such thing as "good" or "bad." There are simply *results*—the ball went straight or to the left or right. Notice the result attentively but without judgment. As you cultivate the skill of nonjudgmental observation, Self 2 receives increasingly calm and clear input that it can learn from.

Inner Game Drills For Letting Go

Letting go, letting it happen is very important in the Inner Game—letting Self 2 perform/learn without mental interference from Self 1. Here are a couple of drills to help you.

The first is very simple. Hit a series of balls and after every shot, ask the question: To what extent am I really letting Self 2 swing the club? Make the answer on a one to ten basis. After a while, you will notice more clearly when Self 1 is steering, getting tense or trying too hard. Just by noticing the effects of Self 1 on your swing with

nonjudgmental awareness, it will begin to let go more. You will learn from experience that the tightness doesn't feel good and doesn't produce the results you want. As awareness of your body increases you will automatically start swinging with more freedom as well as with more power and accuracy.

The second drill could be called "film star." Imagine you're an actor in a movie and you're playing the role of a famous golfer (pick your own—it can be Jack Nicklaus, Sam Snead, or any fine golfer with whom you identify). In this scene, you will be hitting balls, but the camera will be shooting closeups—only your head and shoulders will appear in the footage. The director will be looking for the same facial expressions of supreme confidence and lack of self-doubt shown by the pro. It's also important to realize that results don't matter—whether the balls are hit straight or not is of no consequence—the ball flight pictures will be shot separately.

Now, step into the shoes of your chosen star. You are he for the period of the drill. This exercise very often has embarrassingly good results, showing us we can actually hit the ball so much better than we normally do. Our image of ourselves based on poor past performance is one of the greatest limiting factors in our game. Many players are in fact only playing the role of hackers because they've convinced themselves that that's what they are, whereas in actuality they have the potential to be much better if they could only let go of their negative self-image.

As you experiment with these drills, it is important to remember that they are not like the usual golf tips—supposed to work immediately. Rather, they're designed gradually to increase awareness and concentration. You will find that the quality of your golf is in direct proportion to the quality of your concentration. Improvement in concentration is not a temporary gimmick. It is the most fundamental and important skill you can learn for improving your golf.

There's a bonus to playing the Inner Game. The skill in concentration you develop on the golf course will automatically be applicable and improve the quality of the different areas of your life off the course.

What It Is All About

No matter how many pieces we break the golf swing into, it is still a swing, like the rhythmic movement of a pendulum or the motion of a penknife tied to a handkerchief. This last image was the famous illustration used by Ernest Jones, one of golf's most influential teachers. His exposition of the swing follows.

BRIEFLY stated, every good golfer displays *control*, *balance* and *timing* in wielding the club. Without these factors no one becomes a consistently good player. Practically all discussions of the game from the instructive side abound in references to these three points, but usually, when one presses for explicit, detailed explanation of just what is meant by any one or all, the answers received are vague and indefinite.

One hears, for instance, that this or that expert player has fine control. But just what is control, how is it achieved, and what does it mean? In brief, what are we trying to achieve in swinging a golf club? Now, questions on fundamentals of any subject frequently sound simple—so simple, in fact, as to appear ridiculous. The above question may strike the reader as just that. We are trying to strike the ball with the clubhead, of course. That's obvious, to be sure—so obvious that a great army of golfers, trying desperately to

remember half a dozen things, or more, at the time of wielding the club, entirely forget the main purpose.

We are trying to strike the ball with the clubhead, so it should be plain that we must have control of the clubhead. Next, what are the dominant factors in the action of the clubhead in striking the ball? The answer to that is *speed* and *accuracy*. To get maximum distance from the effort, the clubhead must be traveling at the maximum speed at the instant of impact. So, also, the higher the speed, the finer the degree of accuracy in the well-made stroke, as I shall explain later on. We want maximum speed, and we want it at the right time and place—the instant of impact.

In approaching the factor of speed and how to attain it, let me first direct your attention to the action of a pendulum. On first consideration, the easy rhythmic movement of a pendulum, of an old-fashioned clock, let us say, back and forth, hardly suggests speed. But reflect a moment; if the arc through which the pendulum is swung is gradually increased, the pendulum must in time move through a complete circle. To move an object in a circular path, the power must be applied at the center. That is centrifugal application of power. It is one of two basic methods of applying power; the other is leverage. In wield-

Before facing the test of a tournament round, touring pros like Johnny Miller spend many hours studying and refining their swings.

Courtesy Educational Films.

Although Walter Hagen and players of his era were portrayed as swing stylists, they could still generate tremendous clubhead speed and power, as this photo illustrates.

ing a golf club, one swings the clubhead with the hands around the center. Centrifugal application of power can and does develop the greatest speed possible from a given supply of power.

Now suppose we look at the movement of the clubhead in a golf stroke by comparison with the action of a pendulum. It does not matter how long or how short the stroke is; this is merely a matter of the size of the angle through which the pendulum or the clubhead is moved. No matter how large or how small this angle may be, the nature of the action remains the same and the movement of the clubhead is always under control. The speed of the movement is dependent on the amount of power applied, but the nature of the response is always uniform.

A swinging action in moving the clubhead is the source of control in a golf stroke, and it is the only reliable and dependable source. Therefore we arrive at the conclusion that, in order to acquire control, we must learn to move the clubhead with a swinging action. This must be the chief aim, first, last, and all the time, if we are to acquire a positive and recognizable base on which to build in developing skill in playing golf. It is the one essential present in the stroke of every good golfer. A swinging action dominates the stroke of the experts, one and all, regardless of how different individuals may seem to vary one from another in outward appearance while playing a stroke.

The problem of how to acquire and apply control calls for much fuller discussion. I want now to turn to a consideration of *balance,* second of the three basic factors. Balance is a state, a condition. It is simple and easily understood. When a person stands erect with his weight evenly distributed on his two feet, he displays a simple form of easy balance in a condition of rest or absence of movement. When he walks, he exhibits balance in motion. In either case he is a ready and simple exhibit of easy balance, maintained entirely without conscious thought or effort.

Balance in playing a golf stroke starts with a condition of rest, and develops into a condition of movement. In both phases it is quite as simple as in standing or walking, if we only cease to look

at it as an end consciously to be attained. Only when we insist on considering it in the light of transfer of weight, as a matter for conscious effort, does balance become a perplexing and annoying problem. Obviously, then, we are dragging in unnecessary grief when we insist on thinking out a plan for keeping balanced as the club is moved first back, then forward. The simplest solution to such a problem is merely to put away any thought of trying consciously to maintain balance.

In swinging a golf club through any considerable arc, the body plainly must do a certain amount of turning. That changing of body posture destroys the condition of balance at rest, unless there is a compensating movement to maintain it. That identical situation is true in walking, yet no conscious thought is given to maintaining balance as you walk along under normal conditions over a fairly level or flat surface. When you walk uphill, you instinctively lean forward. You are maintaining your sense of balance in doing so, but you are quite unconscious of a definite purpose in doing so.

This is exactly what should take place in playing a golf stroke. All movement to maintain the condition of balance should be purely responsive to the main purpose of the action you are consciously trying to execute, that is, wielding the golf club. In no case should there be a conscious action aimed at maintaining balance as an end in itself. You cannot possibly achieve the two actions at the same time through conscious effort.

The main purpose in playing a golf stroke is to strike the ball with the clubhead. The hands hold and control the club. You try consciously to control this action through the use and movement of the hands. Maintaining the condition of balance must be responsive to what you are trying to do with your hands, just as it is when you swing a pair of Indian clubs, for example, or perform any of the innumerable other physical acts common in everyday life. You cannot hope consciously to control what you are doing with the hands and at the same time to direct body contortions in an effort to maintain balance. You strike the ball with the clubhead and you control the clubhead through the manipulation of the hands, not through the conscious turning or twisting of the body. Forget the latter, and let it respond naturally to the main purpose, as it does in walking.

Coming now to *timing*, suppose we submit the simple question: just what are you timing? Why, the striking the ball with the clubhead. Unless you can feel what you are doing with the clubhead, you cannot possibly have any idea or sense of timing. Expressed in one way, timing means producing the maximum speed with the clubhead at the instant of impact against the ball. From the standpoint of those who prefer to approach the problem of learning golf from the analytical angle of identifying the outward appearance of a correct stroke, timing might be defined as the proper coordination of body, arms, and hands to produce this maximum speed at the designated time. But I doubt that this is going to be very helpful to anybody in learning to develop timing in his own stroke.

Perfect timing is the identification of a true swinging action. It is the essence of rhythm, or measured motion. If you swing a weight on the end of a string, the speed at which the weight can be made to move is proportional to the amount of force applied. Regardless of the speed at which the weight is moved, there is always a feel of the presence of the weight at the end of the string, exerting an outward pull on the source of application, due to the basic nature of centrifugal application. Throughout the movement there is complete coordination or uniformity between the amount of force applied and the result obtained in speed at which the weight is moved. Again, a swinging action is the only positive and reliable insurance for producing and maintain-

ing this uniformity of relation. In other words, a true swing cannot fail to produce perfect timing.

Timing is a product of moving the clubhead with smooth rhythm. Consider, for instance, the case of a child jumping a rope. Coordination is achieved by centering the attention on the action of swinging the rope with the hands and not on the jumping. The swinging action with the rope lends itself to timing and rhythm, and the act of jumping is attuned to the swinging of the rope. Consider for a moment the difficulty of trying to reverse the procedure.

Let us review what has been said of the three essentials to a correct swing, control, balance, and timing. Control may best and most easily be assured through the use of a swinging action in wielding the club. Furthermore, balance and timing are natural and logical adjuncts of swinging, which result without conscious action or thought on our part; these two factors become troublesome only when we set out to make them objectives of conscious effort.

Control, combining balance and timing, can be attained through developing a swinging action in wielding the club. We sense control through a feeling in the hands of what is being done with the clubhead. This, I submit, is a positive way to learn golf—to learn what we are doing when we are playing well, instead of worrying about what we are doing when we are playing badly. It affords a definite point of orientation. There can be little satisfaction to a traveler to be told that he is traveling a wrong road to reach an expressed destination, unless he is told also how to find the right road. Learn to swing the clubhead and to know when you are swinging; this is and for many years has been the basic theme in my teaching.

First, Understand What You Are Trying to Do

by JOHN JACOBS with KEN BOWDEN

John Jacobs is the man who brought European golf instruction into the 20th century. His impact in the United States has been equally great. His working principle is that the ball teaches the golfer. By analyzing the flight of the ball Jacobs works backwards to the swing that produced such a shot. Better than anyone, he has described the geometry underlying the golf shot.

"THE only purpose of the golf swing is to move the club through the ball square to the target at maximum speed. How this is done is of no significance at all, so long as the method employed enables it to be done repetitively."

That is my number one credo. It is the basis on which I teach golf. It may sound elementary, but I am certain that the point it makes has been missed by most golfers. Ninety-five percent of the people who come to me for lessons don't really know what they are trying to do when they swing a golf club. Their prime concern is to get into certain "positions" during the swing. Therein, they believe, lies the elusive "secret" of golf. They have either never known or have long forgotten that the only reason such positions are necessary is *to get the club to swing correctly through the ball.*

There are four possible impact variations produced by the golf swing that, in concert, determine the behavior of the ball. They are:

1. The direction in which the clubface looks.
2. The direction of the swing.
3. The angle of the club's approach to the ball.
4. The speed of the club.

Of these four, the alignment of the clubface at impact is the most vital. If it is not reasonably correct, it will cause errors in the other three areas. For example, the clubface being open—pointing right of target—invariably leads at impact to an out-to-in swing path through the ball. This in turn forces the club into too steep an angle of approach to the ball. The clubface *cannot* meet the ball either squarely or solidly. Conversely, a closed clubface at impact generally leads to an in-to-out swing path. That causes too shallow an angle of approach—the club reaches the bottom of its arc before it reaches the ball. Again, the clubface *cannot* meet the ball either solidly or square.

Do one thing right in the golf swing and it will lead to another right. Do one thing wrong and it will produce another wrong. In this sense, golf is a *reaction* game. Never forget that fact.

Most of what you read about curing slicing

181

tells you to do things like "slide the hips as the first movement of the downswing," "stay inside," "tuck the right elbow in," "hit late," "hold back your shoulders," and so on, ad nauseam. Unless you cure the *basic* fault—your open clubface at impact—you'll never do those things. You *can't,* because your *natural reactions* oppose them. That is why the world is full of golfers who say "I know what to do but I can't do it." They can't do it because, whatever their conscious desires, their actual swing actions are *reactions* to basic major faults.

The thing we all react to most is the face of the club. You must realize—and never forget—that incorrect alignment of the clubface at impact on one shot affects the entire golf swing on the next. Any cure is not to be found in swing "positions." It lies in developing a grip and swing that brings the clubface square to your swing line at impact. Do this and all your reactions will be correct ones. Everything suddenly—and miraculously—falls into place. Now, if you swing from out-to-in, the ball will go to the left. You will immediately, *subconsciously,* make an effort to hit more from inside the target line. Your *natural* adjustment to help you do that will be to pull your body around so that you can swing that way. And—bingo!—suddenly you are set up square instead of open. Now you can swing the club so that it can approach the ball at the right level to hit it solidly in the back. Your shots start straight and fly straight. You've got the "secret"! Fantastic! And not one word about "hit late," "slide your hips," "keep your head down"!

Technically, golf is a much simpler game than most people realize. Here's another way to look at it simply. If you are consistently mishitting and misdirecting the ball, it should cheer you to know that there are only two basic causes. Either:

1. *You have an open clubface at impact,* which makes you swing across the target line from outside to inside, which in turn makes the club descend too steeply into the ball and thus not meet it solidly—or

2. *You have a closed clubface at impact,* which makes you swing across the target line from inside to outside, which makes the clubhead descend too shallowly into the ball, thus either catching the ground behind it or hitting the ball "thin" at the start of the upswing.

The perfect impact occurs only when the clubhead at impact travels exactly along the target line and exactly faces the target. This is "square"—the only "square" in golf. This is your aim—the total objective of all you do with a golf club.

There's just one more point I must make. It is my number two credo as a teacher of golf. It is this: "The art of competing is to know your limitations and to try on every shot."

What this really means is that the technique of striking the ball—the thing I personally deal in most of the time—is no more than fifty percent of the game. Temperament, intelligence, nerve, desire and many other mental qualities make up the other fifty percent. So, when we are talking technique, you might like to keep in mind that we are not dealing with the whole game. Unfortunately, even if you can learn to hit it like Jack Nicklaus, you still have to learn to play like him.

Learn—and never forget—golf's basic 'geometry'
If what I said a moment ago makes sense, being able, *yourself,* to analyze errors in your clubface alignment and swing direction from the way your shots behave is obviously an absolute prerequisite to playing better golf.

Learning what I call the "geometry" of the game is a mental, not a practice-ground, process. It isn't difficult, but it involves sitting down and thinking for a few moments.

The behavior of every shot you hit is caused by a specific inter-relationship of the clubface angle and the swing direction at impact. Here is how:

PULL—ball flies on a straight line but to the left of your target.
The club's head is traveling across your intended target line from outside to inside that line at impact. The clubface is square to the *line of your swing,* but not to your *target line.* These shots often feel solid even though they fly in the wrong

direction. The direction the clubface was looking and clubhead was moving "matched," thus obviating a glancing blow.

SLICE—ball starts left of your target then bends to the right.

The club is again traveling across the intended target line from out to in during impact, but this time the face is *open*—facing right—of your swing line. This creates a clockwise sidespin that bends the ball to the right as its forward impetus decreases. The more the clubface and swing path are in opposition, the more oblique the blow, the greater the sidespin and the bigger the slice. Also, the more your swing line is from outside your target line, the steeper will be the club's approach to the ball and the higher up—and thus more glancing—its contact on the ball.

PULLED HOOK—ball starts left of your target, then bends farther to the left.

Again, the club is traveling across your intended target line from out to in, but this time the face is *closed* to the line of swing. This combination of two faults in the same direction sends the ball disastrously to the left—the infamous "smothered hook."

PUSH—ball flies straight but to the right of your target.

Again, the clubhead is traveling across your intended target line at impact, but this time from in to out. Your clubface is square to your line of swing, but *not* to your target line. Obviously the ball flies where both the clubface and swing path direct it—to the right. As with the pull, this shot often feels solid, because the blow is not of the glancing variety.

HOOK—ball starts right of your target, then bends to the left.

The club is again traveling across your intended line from in to out, but this time the face is *closed*, facing left of the line of your swing. This creates counterclockwise sidespin that bends the ball left once its forward impetus decreases. Unless the clubhead's angle of approach is so low that it hits the ground before it gets to the ball, a hooked shot feels much more solidly struck than a slice. This is because the clubface, by moving parallel to the ground instead of sharply downward, contacts the back-center of the ball, not its top as in a slice.

PUSHED SLICE—ball starts right of your target then bends more to the right.

Again, the club is traveling across your intended target line from in to out at impact, but this time the face is *open* to the line of your swing. These two faults combining in the same direction send the ball devastatingly far right.

STRAIGHT SHOT—Ball starts straight and flies straight along your target line.

The clubface looks at the target and your swing line coincides with the target line at impact.

You are now able to analyze your own swing, and I hope you will at last appreciate what "analyze" really means in golfing terms. It doesn't mean standing in front of a mirror and trying to spot whether your left knee bends inwards or forwards, whether your left arm is straight or bent at the top, etc., etc. You can make a complete analysis of your swing while you shave, sit in a train, ride to the office, or lie in bed. *All you have to do is think about the way your golf ball reacts when you hit it.*

It is obvious that, if you hook a lot, you'll probably also push the ball because these two shapes are a *swing-path pair*. Both require a swing-path that is in-to-out during impact. Conversely, if you slice you will also pull, because these two shapes are the other *swing-path pair* (out-to-in).

Every golfer belongs to one of these categories. His off-line shots will *start out* consistently left or right of the target line. A big bending of the shot, left or right, is dependent on the direction his clubface was looking, relative to his swing line during impact. A closed-clubface golfer will be a hooker who pushes the ball when he happens to return the clubface in the same direction he's swinging. An open-clubface golfer will be a slicer who pulls when he happens to return the clubface in the same direction *he* is swinging.

Want to be sure of your category? Here's how to find out.

First, take a driver to the practice ground and hit half a dozen shots. If they bend from left to right in the air, the clubface is open to your swing line at impact. If they curve the other way the clubface is closed. By using a club with very little loft, you will always get an honest picture of your clubface alignment at impact. Why? Because, since the club's loft is minimal, little backspin is created by a back-of-the-ball blow—too little, in fact, to override the sidespin imparted by the oblique contact of an open or shut clubface.

Next, take a nine-iron and hit a few more shots. Because of its greater loft, this club contacts the *bottom* back of the ball, imparting heavy backspin. Consequently, the influence of sidespin is reduced to the point where the direction in which the ball flies accurately reflects the path of your swing. For example, you will almost certainly hit the highly lofted clubs straight, but left, if you are a slicer with the driver.

Before we leave golf's "geometry," there are a couple more factors I'd like you to understand.

The first is that your club needs to swing *along* the target line only just before, during and just after impact—a *matter of a few inches.* You *do not,* as some books suggest, have to swing it along the target line a number of feet in order to hit the ball straight. This leads directly to another point I'd like to clarify. You stand *inside* the arc you make with the club. The only way, therefore, that you can swing the club straight along the target line is to have it coming into the ball from *inside* the target line. Once the clubhead passes outside the target line in the downswing, it cannot swing along this line during impact, *but only back across it.*

By the same token, if your club is to follow a true arc, it will quickly move *inside* the target line again after you have struck the ball. Thus the clubhead path of a golf swing that hits the ball straight is not, as many people seem to believe, inside to out. *It is inside, to straight-through, to inside again.* We will go further into this much-misunderstood piece of "geometry" in discussing the mechanics of the actual swing.

The Fun of the Game

"Q: When and how did golf begin?
"A: Arnold Palmer invented it about eight years ago in a
little town outside Pittsburgh."
—from *Golf Through TV Eyes*
by Frank Hannigan

Golfers and Other Strangers

by ALISTAIR COOKE

Alistair Cooke is a man of letters, television personality and lover of golf, a game he encountered in his middle years and has pursued passionately ever since. In his quest of the game's holy grail—par—he has played some unusual rounds, like those described below.

JUST after dawn on a brisk but brilliant December day a couple of years ago, I was about to ask Raquel Welch if she was all set for a droll caper I had in mind, when the telephone went off like a fire alarm, and an eager voice shouted, "All set?" It was, alas, not Raquel but my golf partner, a merry banker of indestructible cheerfulness who calls all stock-market recessions "healthy shake-outs." I climbed out of my promising dream and out of bed, and in no time I was washing the irons, downing the Bufferin, rubbing resin on the last three fingers of the left hand, inserting the plastic heel cup, searching for my Hogan cap—performing the whole early morning routine of the senior golfer. This was the great day we had promised ourselves ever since I had suffered the shock of hearing Herbert Warren Wind confess he had never played Century, the tough and beautiful rolling course in Purchase, New York, where Ben Hogan had his first job as a teaching pro. It seemed ridiculous that the man who had helped Hogan lay down "The Modern Fundamentals of Golf" should never have played the course on which Ben laid them down. Another telephone call alerted Wind to get the hell out of his own variation on the Welch fantasy. An hour later we were on our way, up the West Side Highway and the Saw Mill River Parkway, and on to Purchase.

Century is the private domain of some very well-heeled gents from Wall Street, but they are so busy watching those healthy shake-outs that none of them has much time for weekday golf. Furthermore, in December, the caviar and hamburgers are stacked in the deep freeze. But, since it is very difficult to close a golf course, the course is open. The caddie master had been briefed about the signal honor that Wind was going to confer on one of the fifty toughest courses in America and he had obligingly mobilized two of his veteran caddies.

As we swung around White Plains and began to thread up through the country lanes of Purchase, we were puzzled to see strips of white cement smearing the grassy banks of the highway. They got thicker as we turned into the club driveway, and as we came out on the hill that overlooks the undulating terrain, we saw that the whole course was overlaid not with cement but with snow. The caddies were already there and looking pretty glum. They greeted us by stomping their feet and slapping their ears and otherwise conveying that, though our original idea was a brave one, it had obviously been aborted by the weather. "You serious about this thing, Mr. Manheim?" one of the caddies asked the banker. "Sure," said Manheim, who would play golf in a hammock if that's what the rules called for.

We started off with three reasonable drives, which scudded into the snow the way Hawaiian surfers skim under a tidal wave. The caddies went after them like ferrets and, after a lot of burrowing and signaling, retrieved them and stood there holding the balls and looking at us, as the song says, square down in the eye, as if to say, "What are you going to do with these damn things?" We had to find little slivers of exposed ground (no nearer the hole) and drop them and swipe off once more. The greens were either iced over or had sheets of ice floating in little lakes. After several five-putts on the first two greens, we decided that anybody who could hold a green deserved the concession of two putts.

This went on for eight holes, at the end of which, however, Wind allowed that Hogan sure loved to set himself problems. Plodding up the long ninth fairway, with Cooke beginning to turn blue and the banker humming happily to himself (it was the two-putt rule that did it), Wind turned and said, "Tell me, Manheim, do you do this because you're nuts or because your p.r. man says its good for your image?" We three-putted the ninth green, which "held" with the consistency of rice pudding, and that was it.

As I recall this Arctic expedition, there is a blustery wind bending the trees in Central Park and a steady rain, a combination of circumstances that fires many a Scotsman to rush out and play a round of golf in what one of them once told me are "the only propair condeetions." But, because this is America, they are conditions that immediately empty the golf courses from Maine to San Diego, forcing the sons of the pioneers to clean their clubs, putt on the bedroom carpet or sink into the torpor of watching a football game. We have it from the Mexican ambassador himself, His Excellency Lee Trevino, that there are Texans who will not play at all whenever the temperature toboggans below 80° Fahrenheit. And there are by now many generations of Dutchmen who gave up the game once it moved off ice onto grass.

It is a wonderful tribute to the game or to the dottiness of the people who play it that for some people somewhere there is no such thing as an insurmountable obstacle, an unplayable course, the wrong time of the day or the year. Last year I took Manheim—whose idea of a beautiful golf course was a beautiful park—to play his first links course. It is the home course of the English golf writer Pat Ward-Thomas (Ward-Thomas's idea of the most beautiful golf course in the world is his home course). It is up in the bleak stretch of southeastern England known as Norfolk, a sort of miniature prairie exposed to the winds whistling out of Siberia. The course is called Brancaster, and you can drive up to the rude clubhouse, a kind of Charles Addams gabled shack, and start asking people where is the golf course. For ahead of you is nothing but flat marshland—which floods at the high tide—and beyond that the gray North Sea and a chorus of squawking gulls. The flags are about two feet high, so as to encourage the notion that man has not been known to tamper with a masterpiece of nature.

When we went into lunch it was spitting rain and when we came out it was raining stairrods. The wind gauge at the clubhouse entrance registered forty-three knots. There was Ward-Thomas; a handsome and imperturbable Englishman named Tom Harvey; Manheim and I. There were also two caddies, aged about ten, already half-drowned and cowering in the whirling sand like two fugitives from Dotheboys Hall.

Nobody raised a question or lifted an eyebrow, so Manheim and I—remembering the good old White House slogan—soldiered on. By about the seventh, Manheim, who wears glasses, had to be guided to the proper tees. We were all so swollen with sweaters and raingear we looked like the man in the Michelin ads. Well, sir, they talked throughout in well-modulated tones about "sharp doglegs" and "a rather long carry" and "it's normally an easy five-iron, but maybe with this touch of wind you'd be safer with a four-iron, even a four-wood, I shouldn't wonder." We were now all water-logged, from the toenails to the scalp, and Manheim came squelching over to me and said, "Are these guys nuts?" I told him that on the contrary this was for them a regular outing: "You know what the Scotsman said—'If there's nae wind, it isn't gawf.' " Manheim shook his head like a drenched terrier and plodded on. The awful thing was that Harvey, a pretty formidable golfer, was drawing and fading the damn thing at will, thus proving the sad truth that if you hit it right, even a tornado is not much of a factor.

Outward bound, we'd been carried downwind. But as we were bouncing like tumbleweed down to the ninth green, Ward-Thomas came staggering over. I should tell you that he is a gaunt and a very engaging gent who looks like an impoverished Mexican landowner (a hundred acres in beans and not doing very well), and he has a vocabulary that would have qualified him for an absolutely top advisory post in the last Republican administration. He came at me with his spiky hair plastered against his forehead and water blobbing off his nose and chin. He screamed confidentially into the gale: "If you think this (expletive deleted) nine is a (expletive deleted) picnic, wait till we come to the (expletive deleted) turn!"

He was right. We could just about stand in the teeth of the gale, but the balls kept toppling off the tees. It was a time to make you yearn for the old sandbox. Manheim's glasses now looked like the flooded windshield of a gangster escaping through a hurricane in an old Warner Brothers movie. Moreover, his tweed hat kept swiveling around, making him stand to the ball like a guy who'd been taught about his master eye by a one-eyed pirate. At this point, Ward-Thomas offered up the supreme sacrifice. He is a longtime idolater of Arnold Palmer and he cried, "Hold it!" and plunged into his bag. He came up with a faded sunhat and tendered it to Manheim with the reverent remark: "It was given to me by Palmer. Try it." As everybody knows, Palmer's head is on the same scale as his forearms, and this one blotted out Manheim's forehead, nose, glasses, master eye and all. What we did from then on was to slop our way down the last nine, pity the trembling caddies and throw murderous glances at Harvey, who was firing beautiful woods into the hurricane.

Very little was said as we retired to Harvey's home, fed every strip of clothing into a basement stove and stewed in baths that would have scalded a Turk. At dinner it came out. All through the first nine, Harvey and Ward-Thomas had been muttering to each other just as Manheim and I had been doing: "They must be out of their minds, but if this is what they're used to. . . ." Harvey said, "We decided that since you were our guests, the only thing to do was to stick it out."

. . . . .

If these are fair samples of maniacal golfers, how about crazy golf courses?

You would not think, looking at the stony rampart of the mountain face back of Monte Carlo, that anyone could plant a one-hole putting green between those slabs of granite. But when you get to the top, there the indomitable British have somehow contrived a course that lurches all around the Maritime Alps. There is rarely a straightaway drive. On the very first tee, you jump up in the air and see the flag fluttering in a depression way to the left. You ask the caddie for the line. He points with a Napoleonic gesture to a mountain far to the right. "La ligne!" he commands. And if you believe him and bang away at the mountain top, you then see the ball come toppling about a hundred yards to the left and going out of sight. Which is the proper trajectory to the green.

The golf "clubu" at Istanbul is, if anything, more improbable still. The banks of the Bosporus are studded with more boulders than Vermont. But when the Scots took Constantinople at the end of World War I and laid in an adequate supply of their *vin du pays*, what else was there to do but build a golf course? The original rude layout is still there in the "clubu" house, and on paper it looks like a golf course. In fact, it is simply a collection of flags stuck at random on a mountainside of boulders. Every ball comes to rest against a rock. The local rule is a free drop on every stroke. You drop it and drop it till it stops, and never mind the fussy business of "no nearer the hole."

In Bangkok, before the natives took to cement and the automobile, the canals looked like irrigation ditches slicing every fairway. Forecaddies, as nimble as grasshoppers, spent the day diving into the canals and surfacing with an ear-to-ear grin while they held aloft a ball drenched with cholera. Once they'd wiped it and dropped it, you were on your way again, and free to enjoy the great game in a dripping temperature of 110°.

A lion, you might guess, is not a normal item of wildlife on your course or mine. But in Nairobi once, a tawny monster strolled out of the woods, sniffed at my ball and padded off again, while my partner, a British native of the place, tweaked his mustache and drawled: "You're away, I think." At about the third hole I pushed my drive into the woods, and when I started after it, the host screamed at me to cease and desist. "Snakes, man, snakes!" he hissed; "leave it to the forecaddies." They plunged into shoulder-high underbrush, and I meekly muttered, "How about *them?*" "Them?" the man said, "Good God, they're marvelous. Splendid chaps; lost only two this year." That round, I recall, was something of a nightmare, what with my pushed drives and the caddies (the ones who survived) chattering away in Swahili. The whole place was so exotic that I began to wonder if any of the normal rules of golf applied. One time, we came on a sign which read, "GUR." I gave it the full Swahili treatment. "What," I said, "does GHOOOR mean?" He gave a slight start, as if some hippo were pounding in from the shade. Then he saw the sign. "That," he said firmly, "means Ground Under Repair." And he sighed and started to hum a Sousa march. After all, you must expect anything in golf. A stranger comes through; he's keen for a game; he seems affable enough, and on the eighth fairway he turns out to be an idiot. It's the rub of the green, isn't it?

Well, it takes more sorts than you and I have dreamed of to make up the world of golf. In Japan, they take a ski lift up to the tee of a famous par three. In Cannes, the club members never bat an eyelid as they board a ferry from one green to the next tee.

But for sheer systematic nuttiness, nothing can compare with an annual ceremony put on by the Oxford and Cambridge Golfing Society, a collection of leather-elbowed oldsters and shaggy-haired youngsters who play for the President's Putter, no less, every year in the first week of January at Rye, on the coast of Sussex, another treeless links course fronting on a marsh which gives out into the English Channel. This tournament is intended to prove the English boast that "we can play golf every day of the year." If they can do it at Rye in January, they can do it at the South Pole, which in some sharp ways Rye resembles. At any rate, under the supervision of Gerald Micklem, a peppery stockbroker in his 60s who is the Genghis Khan of British amateur golf, these maniacs go through with this tournament on the scheduled date no matter what. Snow, hail, wind, torrents—nothing can keep them from the swift completion of their Micklem-appointed rounds.

I was there four years ago. On the first morning, the small town and the course were completely obliterated in a fog denser than anything in Dickens. It seeped into the hotels so you needed a links boy to light your way to your plate of bacon, baps and bangers. I assumed the whole thing was off, till a telephone call warned a few dallying competitors that their tee-off time was about to strike. We crawled out to the course, and the first person I ran into, marching around the clubhouse, was Micklem. I asked him if anyone was out there, and if so, why. "Nonsense," he barked. "they're all out there. Haven't lost a ball yet." He motioned toward the great gray nothingness outside, not fog, not landscape, but what John Milton (thirteen handicap) once called "not light but darkness visible." I hopped off into what might very well have been the edge of the world, as it was conceived by those Portuguese mariners who would have liked very much to discover America but who were afraid to sail out into the Atlantic, beyond sight of land, for fear of falling off. The word, God knows how it got through, was that Donald Steel was doing nicely toward repeating his win of the previous year. He had just teed off on the second nine. I ran into a swirl of nothingness and, sure enough, there emerged, like a zombie on the heath in a horror film, a plumpish, confident figure recognizable at three yards as Steel. He took out an iron for his approach shot, though what he thought he was approaching I have no idea—San Salvador, no doubt. He hit it low and clean, and a sizable divot sailed away from him and vanished. He went off after it and vanished too. I kept following in the gloom, and from time to time a wraith swinging a golf club would loom up, take two steps and be gone.

It was true! They all finished, and nobody lost a ball. I felt my way back to the clubhouse, and at the end the last ghost was in. Within five minutes they were up against the bar, chests out, faces like lobsters, beer mugs high, slapping thighs, yokking it up. Queer fish, the Oxford and Cambridge Golfing Society. They behave just as if they'd been out for a round of golf. What they play every year on that barren fork of Sussex that reaches out to the Channel, and Holland, and eventually to the Bering Strait, is a wholly new game: Invisible Golf.

Golf Through TV Eyes

by FRANK HANNIGAN

The television generation absorbs the world through the tube and its knowledge of golf is no exception. In this now-classic satire, Frank Hannigan profiles the average viewer's perception of golf as gained from a few hours in front of the set.

THE USGA is grateful to the advertising firm of Tension, Nettled and Timorous for granting permission to print the result of its recent Golf TV Audience Survey.

This survey sheds light on that phenomenon of the 1960s, the New Golf Fan, whose knowledge of the game, gleaned from television reports, has transformed golf into a basic American industry.

TNT's trained investigators talked to thousands of viewers. The taped interviews were fed into an electronic computer which digested the material and then spewed out a Master Interview, which purports to represent accurately the average television viewer's thoughts on golf.

The Master Interview is now being weighed carefully by a *TNT* client who contemplates sponsorship of yet another Golf TV Extravaganza next fall. Tentative plans call for a first prize of $250,000, a seat on the New York Stock Exchange, and fifteen acres of real estate in New York's Murray Hill district.

The Master Interview follows:

Q: When and how did golf begin?

A: Arnold Palmer invented it about eight years ago in a little town outside Pittsburgh.

Q: And who was the first woman golfer?

A: I'm not sure, but it was either a tall blonde named Mickey Wright or a little French girl named Brigitte Bardot. Anyhow, they took it up in Portugal and the French girl lost.

Q: Then golf has become more popular recently?

A: Absolutely. Now it is even being played in England, where there is a British Open tournament.

Q: Has this British Open become an important event?

A: It sure has. The winner qualifies for the World Series every year in Ohio.

Q: To what do you attribute the growth of golf's popularity?

A: Are you kidding? It's the cash. Some of these guys make more money than Willie Shoemaker.

Q: What about the rules of golf? Where do they come from?

A: Palmer and a bunch of the other pros sat down and made them up.

Q: Suppose there's a dispute about the rules. How would such a dispute be settled?

A: That's a tough one. I suppose they'd have to go to the sponsor of the program. If the sponsor didn't know what to do, maybe they could

Inside his control booth, CBS director Frank Chirkinian controls his bank of cameras as deftly as Gary Player plays a sand iron.

have a panel discussion with David Susskind.

Q: What is meant by a "golf handicap"?

A: That's something they made up so that Sam Snead can play Johnny Weissmuller and those other movie stars.

Q: Do you know the difference between stroke play and match play?

A: Match play is when they play two on a team on Saturday afternoons and the first prize is $50,000; stroke play is generally played on Sundays with one man against the other, but the money isn't so big.

Q: Who, in your opinion, is the greatest golfer to date?

A: Palmer—the founder.

Q: Has anyone come close to matching his skills?

A: Young Nicklaus, but he hasn't caught up to Palmer yet.

Q: How can you tell?

A: For one thing, there is no Jack Nicklaus building in New York.

Q: What about Bob Jones?

A: I hear it's a great movie, but it hasn't been on television yet.

Q: Does golf have a "czar," like baseball's Ford Frick?

A: Sure. I read that he's a young lawyer out of Cleveland who handles all the business for Palmer, Nicklaus and Player, the little guy with the funny accent who teams up with Palmer on weekends.

Q: Judging from what you've seen and heard, how far would you say the average professional drives a golf ball?

A: Between 325 and 350 yards.

Q: What happens when a tournament ends in a tie?

A: They go back to the fourteenth hole, where the cameras are first set up, and start over again from there.

Q: What role do amateurs play in golf?

A: They are like the minor leaguers in baseball or the college kids in football. The best ones get to turn pro and play the tour.

Q: Have you noticed much difference between the various courses you've seen on television?

A: Not much. All of them seem to have "one of the greatest finishing holes in golf."

Q: Who are your favorite golf announcers?

A: Frank Sinatra and Dean Martin. They go right out on the course in California and say funny things to the players between shots. Phil Harris is pretty good, too.

Q: Just one more question. More than one community lays claim to being "the golf capital of the United States." Which city do you think properly holds that distinction?

A: It must be Las Vegas. There were two tournaments televised live from there last year.

The Golfomaniac

*In the extreme, golf can dominate one's life to the point
where it colors every subject. Humorist Stephen Leacock
portrays one such golf fanatic whose skill, it turns out,
does not equal his enthusiasm for the game.*

WE ride in and out pretty often together, he and I, on a surburban train.

That's how I came to talk to him. "Fine morning," I said as I sat down beside him yesterday and opened a newspaper.

"Great!" he answered, "the grass is drying out fast now and the greens will soon be all right to play."

"Yes," I said, "the sun is getting higher and the days are decidedly lengthening."

"For the matter of that," said my friend, "a man could begin to play at six in the morning easily. In fact, I've often wondered that there's so little golf played before breakfast. We happened to be talking about golf, a few of us last night—I don't know how it came up—and we were saying that it seems a pity that some of the best part of the day, say, from five o'clock to seven-thirty, is never used."

"That's true," I answered, and then, to shift the subject, I said, looking out of the window:

"It's a pretty bit of country just here, isn't it?"

"It is," he replied, "but it seems a shame they make no use of it—just a few market gardens and things like that. Why, I noticed along here acres and acres of just glass—some kind of houses for plants or something—and whole fields full of lettuce and things like that. It's a pity they don't make something of it. I was remarking only the other day as I came along in the train with a friend of mine, that you could easily lay out an eighteen-hole course anywhere here."

"Could you?" I said.

"Oh, yes. This ground, you know, is an excellent light soil to shovel up into bunkers. You could drive some big ditches through it and make one or two deep holes—the kind they have on some of the French links. In fact, improve it to any extent."

I glanced at my morning paper. "I see," I said, "that it is again rumored that Lloyd George is at last definitely to retire."

"Funny thing about Lloyd George," answered my friend. "He never played, you know; most extraordinary thing—don't you think?—for a man in his position. Balfour, of course, was very different: I remember when I was over in Scotland last summer I had the honor of going

194

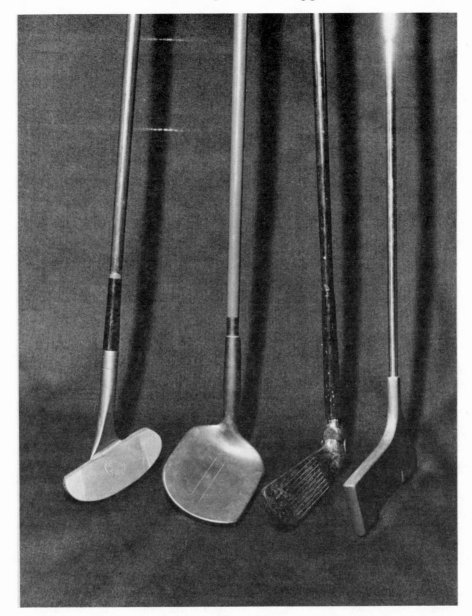

The search for perfection in golf involves not only swing techniques but attempts to create the "perfect club." Here are some illegal putters now displayed at the USGA's Golf House museum.

around the course at Dumfries just after Lord Balfour. Pretty interesting experience, don't you think?"

"Were you over on business?" I asked.

"No, not exactly. I went to get a golf ball, a particular golf ball. Of course, I didn't go merely

for that. I wanted to get a mashie as well. The only way, you know, to get just what you want is to go to Scotland for it."

"Did you see much of Scotland?"

"I saw it all. I was on the links at St. Andrews and I visited the Loch Lomond course and the course at Inverness. In fact, I saw everything."

"It's an interesting country, isn't it, historically?"

"It certainly is. Do you know they have played there for over 500 years! Think of it! They showed me at Loch Lomond the place where they said Robert the Bruce played the Red Douglas (I think that was the other party—at any rate, Bruce was one of them), and I saw where Bonnie Prince Charlie disguised himself as a caddie when the Duke of Cumberland's soldiers were looking for him. Oh, it's a wonderful country historically."

After that I let a silence intervene so as to get a new start. Then I looked up again from my newspaper.

"Look at this," I said, pointing to a headline, "United States Navy Ordered Again to Nicaragua." "Looks like more trouble, doesn't it?"

"Did you see in the paper a while back," said my companion, "that the United States Navy Department is now making golf compulsory at the training school at Annapolis? That's progressive, isn't it? I suppose it will have to mean shorter cruises at sea; in fact, probably lessen the use of the navy for sea purposes. But it will raise the standard."

"I suppose so," I answered. "Did you read about this extraordinary murder case on Long Island?"

"No," he said. "I never read murder cases. They don't interest me. In fact, I think this whole continent is getting over-preoccupied with them—"

"Yes, but this case had such odd features—"

"Oh, they all have," he replied, with an air of weariness. "Each one is just boomed by the papers to make a sensation—"

"I know, but in this case it seems that the man was killed with a blow from a golf club."

"What's that? Eh, what's that? Killed him with a blow from a golf club!!"

"Yes, some kind of club—"

"I wonder if it was an iron—let me see the paper—though, for the matter of that, I imagine that a blow with even a wooden driver, let alone one of the steel-handled drivers—where does it say it?—pshaw, it only just says 'a blow with golf club.' It's a pity the papers don't write these things up with more detail, isn't it? But perhaps

it will be better in the afternoon paper. . . ."

"Have you played golf much?" I inquired. I saw it was no use to talk of anything else.

"No," answered my companion, "I am sorry to say I haven't. You see, I began late. I've only played twenty years, twenty-one if you count the year that's beginning in May. I don't know what I was doing. I wasted about half my life. In fact, it wasn't till I was well over thirty that I caught on to the game. I suppose a lot of us look back over our lives that way and realize what we have lost.

"And even as it is," he continued, "I don't get much chance to play. At the best I can only manage about four afternoons a week, though of course I get most of Saturday and all Sunday. I get my holiday in the summer, but it's only a month, and that's nothing. In the winter I manage to take a run South for a game once or twice and perhaps a little swack at it around Easter, but only a week at a time. I'm too busy—that's the plain truth of it." He sighed. "It's hard to leave the office before two," he said. "Something always turns up."

And after that he went on to tell me something of the technique of the game, illustrate it with a golf ball on the seat of the car, and the peculiar mental poise needed for driving, and the neat, quick action of the wrist (he showed me how it worked) that is needed to undercut a ball so that it flies straight up in the air. He explained to me how you can do practically anything with a golf ball, provided that you keep your mind absolutely poised and your eye in shape, and your body a trained machine. It appears that even Bobby Jones of Atlanta and people like that fall short very often from the high standard set up by my golfing friend in the suburban car.

·   ·   ·   ·   ·

So, later in the day, meeting someone in my club who was a person of authority on such things, I made inquiry about my friend. "I rode into town with Llewellyn Smith," I said. "I think he belongs to your golf club. He's a great player, isn't he?"

"A great player!" laughed the expert. "Llewellyn Smith? Why, he can hardly hit a ball! And anyway, he's only played about twenty years!"

The Whitwams Go to the Masters

by JOLEE EDMONDSON

Many of the people who play and follow golf do not belong to the sophisticated world of the tournament circuit. But they care just as much about the game and surely dream of attending a very exclusive event like the Masters Tournament. Jolee Edmondson, the first woman to win a first prize in the annual golf writing awards, captures the spirit of one couple who sought entrance at Augusta.

FRED Whitwam leered at the broken yellow line—stitches in the asphalt being consumed by the Winnebago at a law-abiding fifty-five miles an hour. It was four in the afternoon, and he had driven a grueling stretch since pulling out of the KOA at dawn. An abrupt transition from the clean sweep of freeway to a two-lane blacktop with rollercoaster curves made his fifty-four-year-old heart thump with apprehension. He was tired. He wanted nothing more than to steer the big domicile on wheels off the road and nap for thirty or forty minutes.

But he resolutely stiffened his posture and stifled a yawn. A hundred more miles to the next campground. He rubbed the back of his neck and sternly told himself that he could make it, because floating at the back of his mind, always, was the vision of his destination: a lush plot of earth where the coloring book pink of azalea explodes

against a blue sky. Where the scent of magnolia mingles with cool spring air to concoct an intoxicating whiff for smog-sore nostrils. Where stately white homes stand out like Tiffany diamonds on green velvet. Augusta National.

Fred looked over at his wife, Ellen, a rather fleshy woman with tightly curled brown hair and tiny eyes that were always merry, laughing, as if she had just heard an acceptably risqué joke. She was in the passenger seat sipping ginger ale through a straw and gleaning instructional information from the pages of *Golf Magazine,* conjuring up the image of a research scientist peering through a microscope. "Pa," she announced without glancing up, "I think I've found a cure for my duck hook . . ."

Fred, stretching his increasingly flabby frame while one hand gripped the wheel, interrupted her, "Well mama, by my calculations we should be rolling into Augusta by eight tomorrow morning if we leave the campsite at 3 A.M. Just in time to watch the boys hit a few practice shots before the first round. I figure if we hit it right, when he's walking from the driving range to the putting green, we just might be able to angle a few tips from Arnie. He's that kind of guy, you know. Down to earth. He'd be real congenial about something like that."

The thought of standing face to face with

197

Arnold Palmer made Ellen dizzy. Her mind was a collage of the legend in varying phases of body language—photos she had glimpsed through the years that had adhered to her psyche like lint to Scotchtape. She turned slowly to her husband, awe on her sun-crinkled face, and murmured, "Papa, I can hardly believe this is happening to us."

"Ha!" chortled Fred, leaning over and jostling her hand. "You will when we get there. Hey honey, why don't you go back and make me a peanut butter and jelly sandwich. I'm hungry as hell."

"One Gei-burger coming up," winked Ellen. An inside joke that they cherished with whimsical pride, snatching it out of their grab bag of homemade golf humor at every opportunity. It was Fred who first quipped the double entendre, and he thought it the cleverest pun this side of Henny Youngman, his favorite comic. He used the little *bon mot* to wow them at backyard barbecues and member-guest tournaments, never quite grasping why, in many instances, a feeble, forced smile was all that it garnered when he anticipated uproarious laughter.

Fred and Ellen Whitwam are to golf what an SRO audience is to a Broadway show; what window shoppers are to windows; what men are to Raquel Welch; what racetrack touts are to Secretariat. Admirers in the purest form. Appreciative, charmed, engrossed, possessed perhaps, authoritative on the subject and slightly intimidated. Some folks in the couple's publinx circle called them fanatics, but Fred and Ellen took that as a compliment. "Fanatic," he would say pompously, "is just another word for elite fan."

The Whitwams met twenty-five years ago on a pitch-and-putt in Culver City, California. Fred was pitching and Ellen was putting. After Fred executed his famous lob twenty feet from the cup, he noticed a lone woman crouched over her ball on a distant green. He liked her form. And to make a long, pretty dull story short, they fell in love and married a year later, moved to Azusa, where Fred became foreman of a fruit-packing plant and bought a mobile home only a few blocks from the municipal golf course. Early in their union they decided not to have children for fear that offspring might interfere with their games. A baby's cry has deterred many a birdie.

And so it was that for twenty-five years the Whitwams shared a bond that was beautiful, impregnable and unbreakable. Golf.

On their fifteenth wedding anniversary, while sipping some bubbly over a lavish cake decorated with a likeness of Pinehurst number 2, Fred toasted his bride with a promise, "In ten years, honey, we're going to the Masters."

Thus began a decade of planning, dreaming and saving. To the Whitwams and legions of devotees, the Masters is the ultimate—the royal event of golf, and Augusta National is Camelot. A realm, not a mere country club. Ellen set aside a cookie jar labeled "Masters Money," and Fred brown-bagged it at work every day instead of splurging at Harry's Bar and Grill. They vowed to all the muny regulars that they would bring home a bounty of newspaper clippings, slides and autographs for their viewing pleasure . . . perhaps Fred could emcee a special dinner program recapping the glory of the Great Happening.

As the departure date drew near they dipped into their savings and leased a motor home and shopped for suitable sportswear. Fred got himself three pairs of Hush Puppies, Hawaiian print Bermuda shorts, checked button-down shirts, sunglasses and straw hats the size of Texas. "If you're going to the Masters," he pronounced, "you might as well go in style."

Ellen indulged herself by purchasing several white canvas caps (for autographs), pastel-colored tennis shoes, stretch capris and blouses with golf patterns. And of course, there was the investment in spectating paraphernalia.

Fred was cruising at a steady clip now. The road was unraveling and he thought he spotted a freeway junction ahead. A peanut butter and jelly sandwich was jammed in his mouth and he said thickly, "Yep, tomorrow we'll be there."

The next morning the Whitwams showed their gallery badges, which Fred had sent for months in advance, to the guard at the entrance of Augusta National. They were quaking with excitement. A mist fell on the grounds, and Fred's bare legs were prickly with goose bumps.

Courtesy Golf Magazine

Hitting a golf ball with a regular club is challenge enough. For trick-shot artists like the legendary Joe Kirkwood, an arsenal of zany clubs and implements was a vehicle to entertain audiences worldwide.

But other than the illogical choice in clothing, he was as well-geared for the occasion as MacArthur was for World War II. Around his neck hung binoculars, an autograph book, a pen and a bottle opener. His hands clutched a portable seat, an umbrella and an ice chest stocked with soda pop and Gei-burgers. And from his back pockets sprouted the pairing sheet and the program.

The initial catatonic elation soon wore off, and the Whitwams were on their merry way, ready to explore and discover. The first item on their agenda was the practice tee, a strip of turf back-dropped by the hallowed clubhouse—a structure that inspires visions of a graying Bobby Jones rocking on the veranda and Walter Hagen walking jauntily to the upstairs gentlemen-only lounge.

A worshipful crowd stood behind the ropes gazing at a string of pros hitting irons with crisp accuracy. It was Ellen who first viewed Palmer. He was at the far end of the tee, conversing with men in green jackets and pulling a cluster of clubs from his bag. "There he is!" she exclaimed. "Oh! He's hitching up his pants!"

Without breathing a word Fred led her toward Arnie, pushing through a group of miffed onlookers and muttering, "Fore please." They leaned against the rope and stared. After the target of their observation finished warming up, Fred beckoned him with his index finger, hoarsly whispering, "Over here, Arn!" Palmer, puzzled, strode over to Whitwam.

Fred flung his arm around him in a hugging gesture and said, "Jeez, it's good to see you, boy. Ha, ha, how're you doing? You going to win this thing? Listen, while I've got you here, the wife and I would like to ask you a few questions. We're both having problems with the old hook, you know, and I personally think the remedy lies in the grip. Would you mind telling us how to place our hands on the club to . . ."

Good natured as he is, Arnie found it difficult to cope with this encounter. "Uh, well, I'd suggest that you ask your club pro about that. He'll straighten it out for you." He shook their hands and walked away.

"Did you hear that, mama? We should ask our pro. How 'bout that? Straight from the mouth of Arnold Palmer. A real gem of advice. Hell of a nice guy . . . hell of a nice guy."

They scurried to the first tee and secured a perfect vantage point only five feet from the markers, where the intermittently Merry Mex was taking a few practice swings. When the starter announced his name he took his stance and smothered one down the middle. Above the polite round of applause billowed Fred's ecstatic war whoops. "Go get 'em, Lee! Murder 'em! Pour on some of that hot sauce! Never fear, the enchilada man is here!"

Obviously pleased with his drive, Trevino spouted, "You'd be surprised what this Mexican can do."

Whitwam poked Ellen and several other spectators, chuckling, "Did you hear that? 'You'd be surprised what this Mexican can do.' Ha! What a sense of humor. Terrifically funny guy. He's wittier than I thought. C'mon let's follow him for a few holes and then we can wait for Player and them down the line."

An hour later they were stationed on the knoll leading up to the fourth tee where Nicklaus was getting ready to hit. Fred studied the Bear's dramatic turn off the ball, the slow slide of the head and the uninhibited right elbow. When Jack completed his swing Whitwam dropped his gear, gripped an invisible club and tried to imitate the blonde bomber's form. He stood there, his arms swishing back and forth, while the throng moved past him.

"Ellen," he intoned, "I'm convinced that the secret is in the pivot. Jack's got it down to a fine science. Man I wish I had his teacher."

Fred and Ellen absorbed as much of the Masters aura as possible. In an authorized picnic area they spread a tablecloth under a sprawling tree, devoured their lunch and marveled at Ellen's autograph cap, black and blue with hurried signatures.

Toward evening they trooped back to the camper where Ellen did a light wash and prepared dinner while her husband, sublimely content over his panache as a spectator, dozed.

It was a peaceful night, the kind of noiseless eve that precedes calamity. For indeed, the following morning after the sputter of the alarm clock and a quick breakfast, the golf balls would hit the threshing machine, so to speak. The Whitwam's euphoric little world would explode. Ellen would discover that she had accidentally discarded their badges along with other odds and ends while washing. She would report what had happened to Fred. He would let out a glass-shattering "Whhhaaaaattttt???!!!" And there would be a mad hunt for the laminated jewels in the trash bins throughout the campsite, to no avail.

"We'll just have to explain the whole situation to the guards at the gate and see if they'll let us in."

So they drove to Augusta National and accosted the first man in uniform they saw. "Hi," greeted Fred weakly. "The name is Whitwam as in wigwam." He began to plead, "Look, we're all the way from Azusa. Over 2,000 miles we traveled for the Masters. And we lost our passes. We're honest, decent golf fans. Please. Give us a break. Let us in." Perspiration streamed down his red face and he was constricting the circulation in the guard's forearm.

"You don't know what this means to us, officer," whimpered Ellen.

But the guard shook his head, "Sorry."

"It's no use," said Fred. "I can tell he won't budge. Our last resort is with the scalpers. You look on this side of the street and I'll search for one on the other side. Pay whatever they want."

They paced up and down the traffic-jammed byway for hours, but the usual parade of rip-off artists had disappeared—the law had no doubt dispersed them.

Finally, at the end of his rope, Whitwam started confronting those privileged wearers of badges and proclaiming with the theatrical gestures of a Shakespearean actor, "Please. We're all the way from Azusa. Let me buy a pass for me and the wife. Name your price. I'll pay anything. Here, here's a hundred dollars. Please, I ask only for a drop of your milk of human kindness."

But no one succumbed.

Fred crossed the street and called Ellen. "Mama," he said wearily, "I don't know. It looks pretty hopeless. I've been wracking my brain about what to do. But I can't come up with a solution. We better try and get a room someplace and at least we can watch the rest of the tournament on TV."

There were no vacancies in Augusta, so the Whitwams crossed the state line to Aiken, South Carolina, where they roosted in a motel called the Walk-On Inn with green phosphorescent lights over the doorways. Aside from a few cockroaches and the stench of tobacco in the linen, it was a luxurious room because it had a black and white set with a twenty-four-inch screen.

On Saturday and Sunday Fred and Ellen propped themselves up in bed, flanking their ice chest and gazed at the network splendor before them. Fred wore his Hawaiian shorts and straw hat and peered through his binoculars at the action to simulate the feel of actual spectating.

And it wasn't long before they believed that they were in the midst of it all, in the majestic green yonder clapping and laughing and slapping the backs of their favorite pros between shots. Fred swallowed another sandwich and commented, "Yeah, that Jack's got a helluva pivot."

The Whitwams had been to the Masters.

Mr. Frisbie

by **RING LARDNER**

Famous for sports writing of all types, Ring Lardner knew golf—and the wealthy—well enough to produce this tale of romance on a very private course.

I AM Mr. Allen Frisbie's chauffeur. Allen Frisbie is a name I made up because they tell me that if I used the real name of the man I am employed by that he might take offense and start trouble though I am sure he will never see what I am writing as he does not read anything except *The American Golfer*, but of course some of his friends might call his attention to it. If you knew who the real name of the man is, it would make more interesting reading as he is one of the ten most wealthiest men in the United States and a man who everybody is interested in because he is so famous and the newspapers are always writing articles about him and sending high salary reporters to interview him but he is a very hard man to reproach or get an interview with and when they do he never tells them anything.

That is how I come to be writing this article because about two weeks ago a Mr. Kirk had an appointment to interview Mr. Frisbie for one of the newspapers and I drove him to the station after the interview was over and he said to me your boss is certainly a tough egg to interview and getting a word out of him is like pulling turnips.

"The public do not know anything about the man," said Mr. Kirk. "They know he is very rich and has got a wife and a son and a daughter and what their names are but as to his private life and his likes and dislikes he might just as well be a monk in a convent."

"The public knows he likes golf," I said.

"They do not know what kind of a game he plays."

"He plays pretty good," I said.

"How good?" said Mr. Kirk.

"About eighty-eight or ninety," I said.

"So is your grandmother," said Mr. Kirk.

He only meant the remark as a comparison but had either of my grandmothers lived they would both have been over ninety. Mr. Kirk did not believe I was telling the truth about Mr. Frisbie's game and he was right though was I using real names I would not admit it as Mr. Frisbie is very sensitive in regards to his golf.

Mr. Kirk kept pumping at me but I am used to being pumped at and Mr. Kirk finally gave up pumping at me as he found me as closed mouth as Mr. Frisbie himself but he made the remark that he wished he was in my place for a few days and as close to the old man as I am and he would then be able to write the first real article which had ever been written about the old man. He called Mr. Frisbie the old man.

He said it was too bad I am not a writer so I could write up a few instance about Mr. Frisbie from the human side on account of being his

202

caddy at golf and some paper or magazine would pay me big. He said if you would tell me a few instance I would write them up and split with you but I said no I could not think of anything which would make an article but after Mr. Kirk had gone I got to thinking it over and thought to myself maybe I could be a writer if I tried and at least there is no harm in trying so for the week after Mr. Kirk's visit I spent all my spare time writing down about Mr. Frisbie only at first I used his real name but when I showed the article they said for me not to use real names but the public would guess who it was anyway and that was just as good as using real names.

So I have gone over the writing again and changed the name to Allen Frisbie and other changes and here is the article using Allen Frisbie.

When I say I am Mr. Frisbie's chauffeur I mean I am his personal chauffeur. There are two other chauffeurs who drive for the rest of the family and run errands. Had I nothing else to do only drive I might well be turned a man of leisure as Mr. Frisbie seldom never goes in to the city more than twice a week and even less oftener than that does he pay social visits.

His golf links is right on the place an easy walk from the house to the first tee and here is where he spends a good part of each and every day playing alone with myself in the roll of caddie. So one would not be far from amiss to refer to me as Mr. Frisbie's caddie rather than his chauffeur but it was as a chauffeur that I was engaged and can flatter myself that there are very few men of my calling who would not gladly exchange their salary and position for mine.

Mr. Frisbie is a man just this side of sixty years of age. Almost ten years ago he retired from active business with money enough to put him in a class with the richest men in the United States and since then his investments have increased their value to such an extent so that now he is in a class with the richest men in the United States.

It was soon after his retirement that he bought the Peter Vischer estate near Westbury, Long Island. On this estate there was a nine-hole golf course in good condition and considered one of the best private nine-hole golf courses in the United States but Mr. Frisbie would have had it plowed up and the land used for some other usage only for a stroke of chance which was when Mrs. Frisbie's brother came over from England for a visit.

It was during while this brother-in-law was visiting Mr. Frisbie that I entered the last named employee and was an onlooker when Mr. Frisbie's brother-in-law persuaded his brother-in-law to try the game of golf. As luck would have it Mr. Frisbie's first drive was so good that his brother-in-law would not believe he was a new beginner till he had seen Mr. Frisbie shoot again but that first perfect drive made Mr. Frisbie a slave of the game and without which there would be no such instance as I am about to relate.

I would better explain at this junction that I am not a golfer but I have learned quite a lot of knowledge about the game by caddieing for Mr. Frisbie and also once or twice in company with my employer have picked up some knowledge of the game by witnessing players like Bobby Jones and Hagen and Sarazen and Smith in some of their matches. I have only tried it myself on a very few occasions when I was sure Mr. Frisbie could not observe me and will confide that in my own mind I am convinced that with a little practice that I would have little trouble defeating Mr. Frisbie but will never seek to prove same for reasons which I will leave it to the reader to guess the reasons.

One day shortly after Mr. Frisbie's brother-in-law had ended his visit I was caddieing for Mr. Frisbie and as had become my custom keeping the score for him when a question arose as to whether he had taken seven or eight strokes on the last hole. A seven would have given him a total of sixty-three for the nine holes while a eight would have made it sixty-four. Mr. Frisbie tried to recall the different strokes but was not certain and asked me to help him.

As I remembered it he had sliced his fourth wooden shot in to a trap but had recovered well and got on to the green and then had taken three putts which would make him a eight but by some slip of the tongue when I started to say eight I

Courtsey of Photograms.

Golf forces players to manufacture unusual shots. Here a master of improvisation, Rube Goldberg, engineers a tree shot.

said seven and before I could correct myself Mr. Frisbie said yes you are right it was a seven.

"That is even sevens," said Mr. Frisbie.

"Yes," I said.

On the way back to the house he asked me what was my salary which I told him and he said well I think you are worth more than that and from now on you will get twenty-five dollars more per week.

On another occasion when nine more holes had been added to the course and Mr. Frisbie was playing the eighteen holes regular every day he came to the last hole needing a five to break 112 which was his best score.

The eighteenth hole is only 120 yards with a big green but a brook in front and traps in back of it. Mr. Frisbie got across the brook with his second but the ball went over in to the trap and it looked like bad business because Mr. Frisbie is even worse with a niblick than almost any other club except maybe the number three- and four-irons and the wood.

Well I happened to get to the ball ahead of him and it laid there burred in the deep sand about a foot from a straight up and down bank eight foot high where it would have been impossible for any man alive to oust it in one stroke but as luck would have it I stumbled and gave the ball a little kick and by chance it struck the side of the bank and stuck in the grass and Mr. Frisbie got it up on the green in one stroke and was down in two putts for his five.

"Well that is my record 111 or three over sixes," he said.

Now my brother had a couple of tickets for the polo at Meadowbrook the next afternoon and I am a great lover of horses flesh so I said to Mr. Frisbie can I go to the polo tomorrow afternoon and he said certainly any time you want a afternoon off do not hesitate to ask me but a little while later there was a friend of mine going to get married at Atlantic City and Mr. Frisbie had just shot a 128 and broke his spoon besides and when I mentioned about going to Atlantic City for my friend's wedding he snapped at me like a wolf and said what did I think it was the xmas holidays.

Personally I am a man of simple tastes and few wants and it is very seldom when I am not satisfied to take my life and work as they come and not seek fear or favor but of course there are times in every man's life when they desire something a little out of the ordinary in the way of a little vacation or perhaps a financial accommodation of some kind and in such cases I have found Mr. Frisbie a king amongst men provide it one uses discretion in choosing the moment of their reproach but a variable tyrant if one uses bad judgment in choosing the moment of their reproach.

You can count on him granting any reasonable request just after he has made a good score or even a good shot where as a person seeking a favor when he is off his game might just as well ask President Coolidge to do the split.

I wish to state that having learned my lesson along these lines I did not use my knowledge to benefit myself alone but have on the other hand utilized same mostly to the advantage of others especially the members of Mr. Frisbie's own family. Mr. Frisbie's wife and son and daughter all realized early in my employment that I could handle Mr. Frisbie better than anyone else and without me ever exactly divulging the secret of my methods they just naturally began to take it for granted that I could succeed with him where they failed and it became their habit when they sought something from their respective spouse and father to summons me as their adviser and advocate.

As an example of the above I will first sight an example in connection with Mrs. Frisbie. This occurred many years ago and was the instance which convinced her beyond all doubt that I was a expert on the subject of managing her husband.

Mrs. Frisbie is a great lover of music but unable to perform on any instrument herself. It was her hope that one of the children would be a pianiste and a great deal of money was spent on piano lessons for both Robert the son and Florence the daughter but all in vain as neither of the two showed any talent and their teachers one after another gave them up in despair.

Mrs. Frisbie at last became desirous of purchasing a player piano and of course would consider none but the best but when she brooched the subject to Mr. Frisbie he turned a deaf ear as he said pianos were made to be played by hand and people who could not learn same did not deserve music in the home.

I do not know how often Mr. and Mrs. Frisbie disgust the matter pro and con.

Personally they disgust it in my presence any number of times and finally being a great admirer of music myself and seeing no reason why a man of Mr. Frisbie's great wealth should deny his wife a harmless pleasure such as a player piano I suggested to the madam that possibly if she would leave matters to me the entire proposition might be put over. I can no more than fail I told her and I do not think I will fail so she instructed me to go ahead as I could not do worse than fail which she had already done herself.

I will relate the success of my plan as briefly as possible. Between the house and the golf course there was a summer house in which Mrs. Frisbie sat reading while Mr. Frisbie played golf. In this summer house she could sit so as not to be visible from the golf course. She was to sit there till she heard me whistle the strains of "Over There" where at she was to appear on the scene like she had come direct from the house and the fruits of our scheme would then be known.

For two days Mrs. Frisbie had to console herself with her book as Mr. Frisbie's golf was terrible and there was no moment when I felt like it would not be courting disaster to summons her on the scene but during the third afternoon his game suddenly improved and he had shot the first nine holes in fifty-three and started out on the tenth with a pretty drive when I realized the time had come.

Mrs. Frisbie appeared promptly in answer to my whistling and walked rapidly up to Mr. Frisbie like she had hurried from the house and said there is a man at the house from that player piano company and he says he will take fifty dollars off the price if I order today and please let me order one as I want one so much.

"Why certainly dear go ahead and get it dear," said Mr. Frisbie and that is the way Mrs. Frisbie got her way in regards to a player piano. Had I not whistled when I did but waited a little longer it would have spelt ruination to our schemes as Mr. Frisbie took a twelve on the eleventh hole and would have bashed his wife over the head with a one-iron had she even asked him for a toy drum.

I have been of assistance to young Mr. Robert Frisbie the son with reference to several items of which I will only take time to touch on one item with reference to Mr. Robert wanting to drive a car. Before Mr. Robert was sixteen years of age he was always after Mr. Frisbie to allow him to drive one of the cars and Mr. Frisbie always said him nay on the grounds that it is against the law for a person under sixteen years of age to drive a car.

When Mr. Robert reached the age of sixteen years old however this excuse no longer held good and yet Mr. Frisbie continued to say Mr. Robert nay in regards to driving a car. There is plenty of chauffeurs at your beckon call said Mr. Frisbie to drive you where ever and when ever you wish to go but of course Mr. Robert like all youngsters wanted to drive himself and personally I could see no harm in it as I personally could not drive for him and the other two chauffeurs in Mr. Frisbie's employee at the time were just as lightly to wreck a car as Mr. Robert so I promised Mr. Robert that I would do my best towards helping him towards obtaining permission to drive one of the cars.

"Leave it to me" was my bequest to Mr. Robert and sure enough my little strategy turned the trick though Mr. Robert did not have the patience like his mother to wait in the summer house till a favorable moment arrived so it was necessary for me to carry through the entire proposition by myself.

The sixteenth hole on our course is perhaps the most difficult hole on our course at least it has always been a variable tartar for Mr. Frisbie.

It is about 350 yards long in lenth and it is what is called a blind hole as you can not see the green from the tee as you drive from the tee up over a hill with a direction flag as the only guide and down at the bottom of the hill there is a brook a little over 225 yards from the tee which is the same brook which you come to again on the last hole and in all the times Mr. Frisbie has played around the course he has seldom never made this sixteenth hole in less than seven strokes or more as his tee shot just barely skins the top of the hill giving him a down hill lie which upsets him so that he will miss the second shot entirely or top it and go in to the brook.

Well I generally always stand up on top of the hill to watch where his tee shot goes and on the occasion referred to he got a pretty good tee shot which struck on top of the hill and rolled half way down and I hurried to the ball before he could see me and I picked it up and threw it across the brook and when he climbed to the top of the hill I pointed to where the ball laid the other side of the brook and shouted good shot Mr. Frisbie. He was overjoyed and beamed with joy and did not suspect anything out of the way though in reality he could not hit a ball more than sixty yards if it was teed on the summit of Pike's Peak.

Fate was on my side at this junction and Mr. Frisbie hit a perfect mashie shot on to the green and sunk his second putt for the only four of his career on this hole. He was almost delirious with joy and you may be sure I took advantage of the situation and before we were fairly off the green I said to him Mr. Frisbie if you do not need me tomorrow morning do you not think it would be a good time for me to learn Mr. Robert to drive a car.

"Why certainly he is old enough now to drive a car and it is time he learned."

I now come to the main instance of my article which is in regards to Miss Florence Frisbie who is now Mrs. Henry Craig and of course Craig is not the real name but you will soon see that what I was able to do for her was no such childs play like gaining consent for Mr. Robert to run a automobile or Mrs. Frisbie to purchase a player piano but this was a matter of the up most importance and I am sure the reader will not consider me a vain bragger when I claim that I handled it with some skill.

Miss Florence is a very pretty and handsome girl who has always had a host of suiters who paid court to her on account of being pretty as much as her great wealth and I believe there has been

times when no less than half a dozen or more young men were paying court to her at one time. Well about two years ago she lost her heart to young Henry Craig and at the same time Mr. Frisbie told her in no uncertain turns that she must throw young Craig over board and marry his own choice young Junior Holt or he would cut her off without a dime.

Holt and Craig are not the real names of the two young men referred to though I am using their real first names namely Junior and Henry. Young Holt is a son of Mr. Frisbie's former partner in business and a young man who does not drink or smoke and has got plenty of money in his own rights and a young man who any father would feel safe in trusting their daughter in the bands of matrimony. Young Craig at that time had no money and no position and his parents had both died leaving nothing but debts.

"Craig is just a tramp and will never amount to anything," said Mr. Frisbie. "I have had inquiries made and I understand he drinks when anyone will furnish him the drinks. He has never worked and never will. Junior Holt is a model young man from all accounts and comes of good stock and is the only young man I know whose conduct and habits are such that I would consider him fit to marry my daughter."

Miss Florence said that Craig was not a tramp and she loved him and would not marry anyone else and as for Holt he was terrible but even if he was not terrible she would never consider undergoing the bands of matrimony with a man named Junior.

"I will elope with Henry if you do not give in," she said.

Mr. Frisbie was not alarmed by this threat as Miss Florence has a little common sense and would not be lightly to elope with a young man who could hardly finance a honeymoon trip on the subway. But neither was she showing any signs of yielding in regards to his wishes in regards to young Holt and things began to take on the appearance of a dead lock between father and daughter with neither side showing signs of yielding.

Miss Florence grew pale and thin and spent most of her time in her room instead of seeking enjoyment amongst her friends as was her custom. As for Mr. Frisbie he was always a man of iron will and things began to take on the appearance of a dead lock with neither side showing any signs of yielding.

It was when it looked like Miss Florence was on the verge of a serious illness when Mrs. Frisbie came to me and said we all realize that you have more influence with Mr. Frisbie than anyone else and is there any way you can think of to get him to change his status towards Florence and these two young men because if something is not done right away I am afraid of what will happen. Miss Florence likes you and has a great deal of confidence in you said Mrs. Frisbie so will you see her and talk matters over with her and see if you can not think up some plan between you which will put a end to this situation before my poor little girl dies.

So I went to see Miss Florence in her bedroom and she was a sad sight with her eyes red from weeping and so pale and thin and yet her face lit up with a smile when I entered the room and she shook hands with me like I was a long lost friend.

"I asked my mother to send you," said Miss Florence. "This case looks hopeless but I know you are a great fixer as far as Father is concerned and you can fix it if anyone can. Now I have got a idea which I will tell you and if you like it it will be up to you to carry it out."

"What is your idea?"

"Well," said Miss Florence, "I think that if Mr. Craig the man I love could do Father a favor why Father would not be so set against him."

"What kind of a favor?"

"Well Mr. Craig plays a very good game of golf and he might give Father some pointers which would improve Father's game."

"Your father will not play golf with anyone and certainly not with a good player and besides that your father is not the kind of a man that wants anyone giving him pointers. Personally I would just as leaf go up and tickle him as tell him that his stance is wrong."

"Then I guess my idea is not so good."

"No," I said and then all of a sudden I had a idea of my own. "Listen Miss Florence does the other one play golf?"

"Who?"

"Young Junior Holt."

"Even better than Mr. Craig."

"Does your father know that?"

"Father does not know anything about him or he would not like him so well."

Well I said I have got a scheme which may work or may not work but no harm to try and the first thing to be done is for you to spruce up and pretend like you do not feel so unkindly towards young Holt after all. The next thing is to tell your father that Mr. Holt never played golf and never even saw it played but would like to watch your father play so he can get the hang of the game.

And then after that you must get Mr. Holt to ask your father to let him follow him around the course and very secretly you must tip Mr. Holt off that your father wants his advice. When ever your father does anything wrong Mr. Holt is to correct him. Tell him your father is crazy to improve his golf but is shy in regards to asking for help.

There is a lot of things that may happen to this scheme but if it should go through why I will guarantee that at least half your troubles will be over.

Well as I said there was a lot of things that might have happened to spoil my scheme but nothing did happen and the very next afternoon Mr. Frisbie confided in me that Miss Florence seemed to feel much better and seemed to have changed her mind in regards to Mr. Holt and also said that the last named had expressed a desire to follow Mr. Frisbie around the golf course and learn something about the game.

Mr. Holt was a kind of a fat pudgy young man with a kind of a sneering smile and the first minute I saw him I wished him the worst.

For a second before Mr. Frisbie started to play I was certain we were lost as Mr. Frisbie remarked where have you been keeping yourself Junior that you never watched golf before. But luckily young Holt took the remark as a joke and made no reply. Right afterwards the storm clouds began to gather in the sky. Mr. Frisbie sliced his tee shot.

"Mr. Frisbie," said young Holt, "there are several things the matter with you then but the main trouble was that you stood too close to the ball and cut across it with your clubhead and besides that you swang back faster than Alex Smith and you were off your balance and you gripped too hard and you jerked instead of hitting with a smooth follow through."

Well, Mr. Frisbie gave him a queer look and then made up his mind that Junior was trying to be humorous and he frowned at him so as he would not try it again but when we located the ball in the rough and Mr. Frisbie asked me for his spoon young Holt said Oh take your mashie Mr. Frisbie never use a wooden club in a place like that and Mr. Frisbie scowled and mumbled under his breath and missed the ball with his spoon and missed it again and then took a mid-iron and just dribbled it on to the fairway and finally got on the green in seven and took three putts.

I suppose you might say that this was one of the quickest golf matches on record as it ended on the second tee. Mr. Frisbie tried to drive and sliced again. Then young Holt took a ball from my pocket and a club from the bag and said here let me show you the swing and drove the ball 250 yards straight down the middle of the course.

I looked at Mr. Frisbie's face and it was puffed out and a kind of a purple black color. Then he burst and I will only repeat a few of the more friendlier of his remarks.

"Get to hell and gone of my place. Do not never darken my doors again. Just show up around here one more time and I will blow out what you have got instead of brains. You lied to my girl and you tried to make a fool out of me. Get out before I sick my dogs on you and tear you to pieces."

Junior most lightly wanted to offer some word of explanation or to demand one on his own account but saw at a glance how useless same would be. I heard later that he saw Miss Florence and that she just laughed at him.

"I made a mistake about Junior Holt," said Mr. Frisbie that evening. "He is no good and must never come to this house again."

"Oh Father and just when I was beginning to like him," said Miss Florence.

Well like him or not like him she and the other young man Henry Craig were married soon afterwards which I suppose Mr. Frisbie permitted the bands in the hopes that same would rile Junior Holt.

Mr. Frisbie admitted he had made a mistake in regards to the last named but he certainly was not mistaken when he said that young Craig was a tramp and would never amount to anything.

Well I guess I have rambled on long enough about Mr. Frisbie.

Golf in Los Angeles: Part Royal and Ancient, Part Disney

by JIM MURRAY

Nationally syndicated sports columnist Jim Murray has covered golf for over thirty years. As a resident of Los Angeles, he may be the world's greatest authority on the golfing styles of those who live in the nation's movie capital.

GOLF in and around Los Angeles tends to be—like the rest of the landscape—unreal . . . . part Royal and Ancient, part Disneyland. The Good Ship Lollipop with four-irons. You expect a director to come walking out of the woods on eighteen in puttees and with his cap on backward yelling, "Cut!"

The stuffy types at Blind Brook or Old Elm or the Country Club would never understand. There's a gaudy impermanence to Golf Hollywood that would shake the walrus mustaches right off the portraits in those staid old clubs. Remember, we're talking about an area where a chain-saw manufacturer bought the London Bridge and had it shipped over to provide a crossing over desert sand. They bought the Queen Mary and turned it into a chop house. They could buy St. Andrews and stick it up at La Quinta.

You get a running start toward understanding palm-tree waterpipe golf if you listen to that old joke about the sport in Los Angeles. Seems a man named Frank Rosenberg, a Texas oil man, wanted to get into Los Angeles Country Club, the West Coast version of the stodgiest and most exclusive club in the world. It is said eligibility for membership is a Hoover button, a home in Pasadena and proof-positive you never had an actor in the family. Once, when a member proposed Jimmy Roosevelt for membership, they not only black-balled the Roosevelt, they kicked out the member.

Rosenberg was rejected out of hand and the membership committeeman politely suggested he try Hillcrest. Hillcrest is a golf course which was founded by a movie man who was snubbed at a Pasadena course because of his religion. It has fewer gentiles than a kibbutz.

Rosenberg was stunned to be rejected by LACC and he so confided to a friend. "Oh," suggested the friend, "they probably thought you were Jewish. The club is restricted."

So Rosenberg applied at Hillcrest. "Fine, we'll take your application and wait for the first opening," he was told. "Fine," said Rosenberg, "but there's one other thing I want you to know —I'm not Jewish."

The committeeman looked at him and said softly, "Oh, dear. I'm sorry. We don't admit gentiles." "Well I'm an SOB!" exploded Rosenberg. "If you can prove that," the committeeman told him, "you can get in Riviera!"

Riviera may be the most beautiful of the L. A. area courses. But it's a monster. It is the *only* Southern California golf course ever to host the Open. Hogan won it there in 1948. It's a demanding 7,100-yard, par-seventy-one track no weekend player should be abroad on. Its rolls list mostly ruthless golfers, not cardplayers, not social members, but guys who can shoot in the seventies anywhere in the world.

It used to be a hustler's paradise. The stories are legendary (also libelous) of the dentists, Philippine generals, European counts, carefree movie stars and moguls who got fleeced on its not-so-broad fairways. It was Titanic Thompson country. You could get a bet on the color of the next dog coming up the fairway. It is Dean Martin's happy hunting ground as this is written and Dino is usually marauding on its tees and eucalyptus trees in division strength. It looks like Hitler's armor coming down the back side. Martin usually has three or four foursomes (or fivesomes) of pals, usually including one name pro (Devlin, Floyd, Bayer or Bolt), and the bets flow two or three holes back. Barry Jaeckel, French Open winner and son of a movie star, used to *caddie* for Dino, who has a reputation for having lost a fortune at the game. If so, he did it some time ago. Dean now is recognized around Riviera as a guy you give strokes to at your own peril. All the same, the trading is livelier among those golf cars than it is on the Paris Bourse. I know a lot of people who would like to cut ten percent of it and retire to the French Riviera after one season.

So, if golf is your bag, get in Riviera. They don't care what your religion or background is there. But they hope you have money and are willing to risk it. Mac Hunter, the pro there, was once considered a better prospect than Arnold Palmer and may hold the record for a club pro making cuts in the U.S. Open. His dad won the British Amateur and his son just won the California Amateur at Pebble Beach. If a guy says he's from Riviera, be sure to say, "We'll adjust at the turn," or you may go home in a barrel.

L. A. Country Club, apart from its exclusivity, is noteworthy because it sits athwart what must be the most expensive cluster of real estate in the world. It is almost in the center of Beverly Hills and its two golf courses have nearly a mile of front footage along Wilshire Boulevard. It is a two-iron from Saks Fifth Avenue, I. Magnin, Tiffany's and the most expensive furriers and jewelers and boutiques in the world. The Beverly Hilton Hotel hangs over it. Imagine a golf course on either side of Fifth Avenue from 38th Street to the 80s and extending for 250 acres in all directions, and you have a notion of the Big Rock Candy Mountain that is LACC. Some *countries* couldn't afford to buy it.

You can get into L. A. Country Club for about $25,000, but, since you get a piece of the action, that's not as steep as it sounds. With 800 members, this computes out at $2 million for the property. I'd like to get it at that price.

Country clubs are social dinosaurs. Their mores, rules and lifestyles are right out of the 19th century and they might have become as extinct as the sabre-tooth tiger were it not for the ecological uproar. Now they are popularly regarded, even by the fiercest of environmental militants, as "green belts." Even though they are refuges for those other dinosaurs, the entrenched millionaires, they are grudgingly tolerated, even by the anarchists.

But most of the clubs in L. A. suddenly canvassed their rolls and found they read like a headstone count in a cemetery. Something like twenty percent of the memberships in one country club were owned by estates, part of the last will and testament of J. Rotten Rich, who has long since gone to that Great-Fairway-in-the-Sky. Ghosts don't buy drinks or alpacas or patronize the Thursday night dance, and the rigor mortis eventually would hit the club, too. Accordingly, the clubs took to offering $5,000 nonequity memberships to qualified applicants UNDER forty, the fee payable in two installments. All three of the high-priced L. A. clubs, Bel-Air ($13,500 plus $85 a month dues), Lakeside ($11,500 plus $75 dues) and L. A. ($100 a month after the initiation) offer the "youth" memberships.

If Riviera is the club for golfers and L. A. the club for oil, orange and railroad barons, Bel-Air attracts the management end of the broadcast and movie media. There are more station managers, network West Coast brass and their satellite advertising agency account executives (with a sprinkling of used-car dealers) at Bel-Air than at any other club in America.

It once was a club for L. A. Country Club rejects. It, too, sits astride some of the world's richest real estate, and it used to be a sandbox for the movie rich. Bing Crosby once belonged here. Fred MacMurray, Ray Bolger, Andy Williams play here and the show-biz types, the *talent*, shower downstairs. The upstairs locker room is, fittingly, the executive suite. The talent *handlers*—directors, agents, press agents, producers, ad men and network veepees shower up here.

Dean Martin was a daily communicant at Bel-Air until a greens committeeman cut up the greens to "improve" the course, a venture that was to prove long and, therefore, costly, because Dino and dozens of others quit in protest at having to play temporary greens. The departure of a Dean Martin from a golf club is comparable to a nearsighted millionaire leaving a crap game in a smoky room.

Lakeside has a charisma all its own. Here, in the salad years, the movie greats gamboled. . . . Laurel and Hardy, W. C. Fields, Crosby, Hope, Jack Carson, Dennis Morgan, Gordon MacRae and Johnny Weissmuller drank here. Across the street from Warner Brothers, it was a happy hunting ground for Warner's stars, who were not of the same magnitude as MGM's in those years but were a whole lot more festive. A requirement at Lakeside was that you be able to hold your booze. This was the club of the hard-drinking Irish and, the gag was, a standard for admission was that you had to be able to kill a fifth in nine holes.

Disc jockeys, industrial press agents, radio announcers *(radio!)* still dot Lakeside's membership rolls. The Old Guard is almost all gone (Buddy Rogers and Richard Arlen still play, for you trivia buffs). Only Bob Hope remains and fits in a fast nine holes on the infrequent occasions he is at home. Crosby keeps a locker but hasn't

used it in years. The hard core of Lakeside is made up of guys who made it in the Big Band Era. It's THE club to belong to if you live in the lace-curtain sections of the Valley. Like Bel-Air, it has a slightly more modern step to it, as reflected in its clubhouse and dining areas. It's a golf course for the well-heeled suburban types. Unlike the mutton-chop sideburns courses like L. A., it has no trouble making the bar and restaurant pay off but, like them, its club flag is at half-mast too often these days.

Wilshire Country Club is almost in downtown L. A. This makes it accessible to judges, lawyers, business executives, railroad and bank presidents. Color it dull gray.

The city's most celebrated golfers long were Hope and Crosby. Crosby in his prime was a solid two, but he has drifted away from the grand old game in favor of bird-shooting and game-fishing. But not before he was hitting a few practice shots off the tenth tee at Bel-Air one afternoon (Bel-Air has no practice range) and a member of the greens committee came out and stuffily ordered Der Bingle to cease and desist. Crosby looked at him with that cold look a friend once described as "Arctic blue," the look that could stave in the bow of the Titanic. And Crosby gravely packed his clubs, emptied his locker—and has not been seen at Bel-Air since. He occasionally shows up at the more raffish Lakeside (which has a practice range), where the members don't much care where or for what purpose you hit the ball. W. C. Fields was fond of playing the course sideways with his pal, Oliver Hardy. He liked being in the trees where he could drink without scandalizing the natives.

Mickey Rooney holds the unique distinction of being thrown out of Lakeside. The Mick was a solid three in his best days, but he was not only a club-thrower, he threw whole sets. He once played the front nine with a new set and, at the turn, junked them and bought another new one for the back nine.

Playing with Mickey is like playing in the middle of a rehearsal for a Broadway musical. Mickey will sing the score, act the parts. He will do Judy Garland and Professor Labermacher (an old Jessel routine). He showed up on the first tee

The PGA Tour's winter circuit is dominated by tournaments involving colorful characters like Jackie Gleason, engaged here in comic repartee with Arnold Palmer.

one day proudly announcing that Jack Nicklaus, no less, had straightened out his swing. As he moved flawlessly through the first three holes, he purred with praise for the new set of stiff shafts he had purchased. He dispensed tips with a lavish hand for the rest of the foursome. By hole five, the swing began to disintegrate. By hole nine, the Mick was looking darkly at his new set of clubs and beginning to question Nicklaus's credentials to be teaching golf. By the back side, Mickey was holding the clubs aloft to anyone who would listen and demanding, "I ask you! Just look at these things! Look at the hosel! How can a man play with implements like these!" If you're a Mickey Rooney fan, you're rolling behind the trees, helpless with mirth. Mickey's funnier when he's not trying to be. But the members got tired of ducking in the showers when Mickey came through looking for a game, and they told him to empty his locker.

At Hillcrest, the game is "Can-You-Top-This?" and I don't mean a golf ball. There is a table at Hillcrest that is a shrine of show business. George Burns, Jack Benny, George Jessel, Eddie Cantor and Al Jolson used to lunch in a shower of one-liners. Every noon was a Friar's Roast. Danny Thomas represents the Catholics at Hillcrest. In the days of the Dusenberg-Bugatti-leopard-on-a-leash Hollywood, more picture deals were set here than at neighboring Twentieth Century-Fox, which is just across the street and is gradually giving way to a high-rise subdivision. The opulence of Hillcrest is Hapsburgian. The chandeliered dining room makes the Queen Mary foyer look like a lunch counter. The Marx brothers (save for Groucho, who disapproved of golf courses because there weren't enough girls) were the best players in the comedians' flight.

Brentwood, referred to as "Hillcrest East," plays host to the newer crop of comedians—Joey Bishop, Don Rickles, Don Adams (who also belongs at Riviera) and the generation of stand-up comics who came along in the television-Las Vegas era. Brentwood is not as severe a test of golf as LACC's North Course or Hillcrest, but successive renovations have given its clubhouse more and more of a Taj Mahal look.

Brentwood is important historically, because it was to have been the site of the 1962 PGA. The California attorney general threatened legal action because of the PGA's "Caucasian only" clause, and the PGA in 1961 jerked the tournament to friendlier climes at Aronomink in Philadelphia. But later in '61 the offending phrase was removed from the by-laws and the way was paved on tour for the Charlie Siffords, Lee Elders and George Johnsons.

Los Angeles probably has more "celebrity" tournaments per square foot than any golfing area in the world. Any golfing actor worth his marquee value would rather be caught without his makeup on camera than without a favorite charity. As Jerry Lewis once complained, "By the time *I* arrived, all the diseases were taken." George Jessel once observed that all that was left for the newcomers was gonorrhea. Chuck Connors has a tournament. A Tim Conway, a Bob Stack and even character actors have tournaments of their own. Even the tour fixtures have reached out to embrace celebrities. The venerable L. A. Open was the last to capitulate and become the "Glen Campbell L. A. Open." The slightly-less-venerable San Diego Open is now the Andy Williams SDO. The celebrities trade guest appearances at each other's tournaments, and the star power attracts the Kansas City wheat merchant to pay out a grand to tee it up with some crooner or TV tough guy in the pro-am.

Humphrey Bogart, it may surprise you to know, was very nearly a scratch golfer. Once a journalist drinking buddy of his put this reputation down to side-of-the-mouth braggadocio. Bogey, who rarely made one, took his pal down to Tamarisk and proceeded to rip off an impeccable seventy-three after not playing for two months.

It's a game for all seasons in California. You can play golf 365 days a year. Every private club is awash with entertainment giants and sports greats. You might bump into a Jerry West (but not in the rough) at Riviera or a Jim Brown at Western Avenue (a flat muni-type club where the membership is largely black). The Dodgers' Don Sutton will be at Oakmont in the off-season, as will half the franchise. The Rams are addicts.

It's not a game uniquely suited to a community famed for its happy endings. John Wayne ducked the game throughout his career, even though his whole stock company, including Grant Withers and Ward Bond and Forrest Tucker, was scattered around Lakeside, where Wayne had a membership. The official reason was that "a golf ball just isn't Duke's size." The screenwriter, James Edward Grant, had a better explanation: "How could a guy who won the West, recaptured Bataan and won the battle of Iwo Jima let himself be defeated by a little hole in the ground?"

The Heart of a Goof

by P.G. WODEHOUSE

Maybe because he never played all that well, P.G. Wodehouse, who captured the ritual of "the club" better than anyone, could sympathize with others who labored unsuccessfully at golf but found happily—sometimes—that their efforts were rewarded with more than the occasional good score.

IT was a morning when all nature shouted "Fore!" The breeze, as it blew gently up from the valley, seemed to bring a message of hope and cheer, whispering of chip shots holed and brassies landing squarely on the meat. The fairway, as yet unscarred by the irons of a hundred dubs, smiled greenly up at the azure sky; and the sun, peeping above the trees, looked like a giant golf ball perfectly lofted by the mashie of some unseen god and about to drop dead by the pin of the eighteenth. It was the day of the opening of the course after the long winter, and a crowd of considerable dimensions had collected at the first tee. Plus fours gleamed in the sunshine, and the air was charged with happy anticipation.

In all that gay throng there was but one sad face. It belonged to the man who was waggling his driver over the new ball perched on its little hill of sand. This man seemed careworn, hopeless. He gazed down the fairway, shifted his feet, waggled, gazed down the fairway again, shifted

the dogs once more, and waggled afresh. He waggled as Hamlet might have waggled, moodily, irresolutely. Then, at last, he swung, and, taking from his caddie the niblick which the intelligent lad had been holding in readiness from the moment when he had walked on to the tee, trudged wearily off to play his second.

The Oldest Member, who had been observing the scene with a benevolent eye from his favorite chair on the terrace, sighed.

"Poor Jenkinson," he said, "does not improve."

"No," agreed his companion, a young man with open features and a handicap of six. "And yet I happen to know that he has been taking lessons all the winter at one of those indoor places."

"Futile, quite futile," said the Sage with a shake of his snowy head. "There is no wizard living who could make that man go round in an average of sevens. I keep advising him to give up the game."

"You!" cried the young man, raising a shocked and startled face from the driver with which he was toying. "*You* told him to give up golf! Why I thought—"

"I understand and approve of your horror," said the Oldest Member, gently. "But you must bear in mind that Jenkinson's is not an ordinary case. You know and I know scores of men who

215

have never broken 120 in their lives, and yet contrive to be happy, useful members of society. However badly they may play, they are able to forget. But with Jenkinson it is different. He is not one of those who can take it or leave it alone. His only chance of happiness lies in complete abstinence. Jenkinson is a goof."

"A what?"

"A goof," repeated the Sage. "One of those unfortunate beings who have allowed this noblest of sports to get too great a grip upon them, who have permitted it to eat into their souls, like some malignant growth. The goof, you must understand, is not like you and me. He broods. He becomes morbid. His goofery unfits him for the battles of life. Jenkinson, for example, was once a man with a glowing future in the hay, corn, and feed business, but a constant stream of hooks, tops, and slices gradually made him so diffident and mistrustful of himself, that he let opportunity after opportunity slip, with the result that other, sterner, hay, corn, and feed merchants passed him in the race. Every time he had the chance to carry through some big deal in hay, or to execute some flashing *coup* in corn and feed, the fatal diffidence generated by a hundred rotten rounds would undo him. I understand his bankruptcy may be expected at any moment."

"My golly!" said the young man, deeply impressed. "I hope I never become a goof. Do you mean to say there is really no cure except giving up the game?"

The Oldest Member was silent for a while.

"It is curious that you should have asked that question," he said at last, "for only this morning I was thinking of the one case in my experience where a goof was enabled to overcome his deplorable malady. It was owing to a girl, of course. The longer I live, the more I come to see that most things are. But you will, no doubt, wish to hear the story from the beginning."

The young man rose with the startled haste of some wild creature, which, wandering through the undergrowth, perceives the trap in his path.

"I should love to," he mumbled, "only I shall be losing my place at the tee."

"The goof in question," said the Sage, attaching himself with quiet firmness to the youth's coat button, "was a man of about your age, by name Ferdinand Dibble. I knew him well. In fact, it was to me—"

"Some other time, eh?"

"It was to me," proceeded the Sage, placidly, "that he came for sympathy in the great crisis of his life, and I am not ashamed to say that when he had finished laying bare his soul to me there were tears in my eyes. My heart bled for the boy."

"I bet it did. But—"

The Oldest Member pushed him gently back into his seat.

"Golf," he said, "is the Great Mystery. Like some capricious goddess—"

The young man, who had been exhibiting symptoms of feverishness, appeared to become resigned. He sighed softly.

"Did you ever read 'The Ancient Mariner'?" he said.

"Many years ago," said the Oldest Member. "Why do you ask?"

"Oh, I don't know," said the young man. "It just occurred to me."

Golf (resumed the Oldest Member) is the Great Mystery. Like some capricious goddess, it bestows its favors with what would appear an almost fat-headed lack of method and discrimination. On every side we see big two-fisted he-men floundering round in three figures, stopping every few minutes to let through little shrimps with knock-knees and hollow cheeks, who are tearing off snappy seventy-fours. Giants of finance have to accept a stroke per from their junior clerks. Men capable of governing empires fail to control a small, white ball, which presents no difficulties whatever to others with one ounce more brain than a cuckoo clock. Mysterious, but there it is. There was no apparent reason why Ferdinand Dibble should not have been a competent golfer. He had strong wrists and a good eye. Nevertheless, the fact remains that he was a dub. And on a certain evening in June I realized that he was also a goof. I found it out quite suddenly as the result of a conversation which we had on this very terrace.

I was sitting here that evening thinking of this and that, when by the corner of the club house I observed young Dibble in conversation with a girl in white. I could not see who she was, for her back was turned. Presently they parted and Ferdinand came slowly across to where I sat. His air was dejected. He had had the boots licked off him earlier in the afternoon by Jimmy Fothergill, and it was to this that I attributed his gloom. I was to find out in a few moments that I was partly but not entirely correct in this surmise. He took the next chair to mine, and for several minutes sat staring moodily down into the valley.

"I've just been talking to Barbara Medway," he said, suddenly breaking the silence.

"Indeed?" I said. "A delightful girl."

"She's going away for the summer to Marvis Bay."

"She will take the sunshine with her."

"You bet she will!" said Ferdinand Dibble, with extraordinary warmth, and there was another long silence.

Presently Ferdinand uttered a hollow groan. "I love her, dammit!" he muttered brokenly. "Oh golly, how I love her!"

I was not surprised at his making me the recipient of his confidences like this. Most of the young folk in the place brought their troubles to me sooner or later.

"And does she return your love?"

"I don't know. I haven't asked her."

"Why not? I should have thought the point not without its interest for you."

Ferdinand gnawed the handle of his putter distractedly.

"I haven't the nerve," he burst out at length. "I simply can't summon up the cold gall to ask a girl, least of all an angel like her, to marry me. You see, it's like this. Every time I work myself up to the point of having a dash at it, I go out and get trimmed by someone giving me a stroke a hole. Every time I feel I've mustered up enough pep to propose, I take on a bogey three. Every time I'm in good midseason form for putting my fate to the test, to win or lose it all, something goes all blooey with my swing, and I slice into the rough at every tree. And then my self-confidence leaves me. I become nervous, tongue-tied, diffident. I wish to goodness I knew the man who invented this infernal game. I'd strangle him. But I suppose he's been dead for ages. Still, I could go and jump on his grave."

It was at this point that I understood all, and the heart within me sank like lead. The truth was out. Ferdinand Dibble was a goof.

"Come, come, my boy," I said, though feeling the uselessness of any words. "Master this weakness."

"I can't."

"Try!"

"I have tried."

He gnawed his putter again.

"She was asking me just now if I couldn't manage to come to Marvis Bay, too," he said.

"That surely is encouraging? It suggests that she is not entirely indifferent to your society."

"Yes, but what's the use? Do you know," a gleam coming into his eyes for a moment, "I have a feeling that if I could ever beat some really fairly good player—just once—I could bring the thing off." The gleam faded. "But what chance is there of that?"

It was a question which I did not care to answer. I merely patted his shoulder sympathetically, and after a little while he left me and walked away. I was still sitting there, thinking over his hard case, when Barbara Medway came out of the clubhouse.

She, too, seemed grave and preoccupied, as if there was something on her mind. She took the chair which Ferdinand had vacated, and sighed wearily.

"Have you ever felt," she asked, "that you would like to bang a man on the head with something hard and heavy? With knobs on?"

I said I had sometimes experienced such a desire, and asked if she had any particular man in mind. She seemed to hesitate for a moment before replying, then, apparently, made up her mind to confide in me. My advanced years carry with them certain pleasant compensations, one of which is that nice girls often confide in me. I frequently find myself enrolled as a father-confessor on the most intimate matters by beautiful creatures from whom many a younger man would give his eyeteeth to get a friendly word. Besides, I had known Barbara since she was a child. Frequently—though not recently—I had given her her evening bath. These things form a bond.

"Why are men such chumps?" she exclaimed.

"You still have not told me who it is that has caused these harsh words. Do I know him?"

"Of course you do. You've just been talking to him."

"Ferdinand Dibble? But why should you wish to bang Ferdinand Dibble on the head with something hard and heavy with knobs on?"

"Because he's such a goop."

"You mean a goof?" I queried, wondering how she could have penetrated the unhappy man's secret.

"No, a goop. A goop is a man who's in love with a girl and won't tell her so. I am as certain as I am of anything that Ferdinand is fond of me."

"Your instinct is unerring. He has just been confiding in me on that very point."

"Well, why doesn't he confide in *me*, the poor fish?" cried the high-spirited girl, petulantly flicking a pebble at a passing grasshopper. "I can't be expected to fling myself into his arms unless he gives some sort of a hint that he's ready to catch me."

"Would it help if I were to repeat to him the substance of this conversation of ours?"

"If you breathe a word of it, I'll never speak to you again," she cried. "I'd rather die an awful death than have any man think I wanted him so badly that I had to send relays of messengers begging him to marry me."

I saw her point.

"Then I fear," I said, gravely, "that there is nothing to be done. One can only wait and hope. It may be that in the years to come Ferdinand Dibble will acquire a nice lissom, wristy swing, with the head kept rigid and the right leg firmly braced and—"

"What are you talking about?"

"I was toying with the hope that some sunny day Ferdinand Dibble would cease to be a goof."

"You mean a goop?"

"No, a goof. A goof is a man who—" And I went on to explain the peculiar psychological difficulties which lay in the way of any declaration of affection on Ferdinand's part.

"But I have never heard of anything so ridiculous in my life," she ejaculated. "Do you mean to say that he is waiting till he is good at golf before he asks me to marry him?"

"It is not quite so simple as that," I said sadly. "Many bad golfers marry, feeling that a wife's loving solicitude may improve their game. But they are rugged, thick-skinned men, not sensitive and introspective, like Ferdinand. Ferdinand has allowed himself to become morbid. It is one of the chief merits of golf that nonsuccess at the game induces a certain amount of decent humility, which keeps a man from pluming himself too much on any petty triumphs he may achieve in other walks of life; but in all things there is a happy mean, and with Ferdinand this humility has gone too far. It has taken all the spirit out of him. He feels crushed and worthless. He is grateful to caddies when they accept a tip instead of drawing themselves up to their full height and flinging the money in his face."

"Then do you mean that things have got to go on like this forever?"

I thought for a moment.

"It is a pity," I said, "that you could not have induced Ferdinand to go to Marvis Bay for a month or two."

"Why?"

"Because it seems to me, thinking the thing over, that it is just possible that Marvis Bay might cure him. At the hotel there he would find collected a mob of golfers—I used the term in its broadest sense, to embrace the paralytics and the men who play left-handed—whom even he would be able to beat. When I was last at Marvis Bay, the hotel links were a sort of Sargasso Sea into which had drifted all the pitiful flotsam and jetsam of golf. I have seen things done on that course at which I shuddered and averted my eyes —and I am not a weak man. If Ferdinand can polish up his game so as to go round in a fairly steady 105, I fancy there is hope. But I understand he is not going to Marvis Bay."

"Oh yes he is," said the girl.

"Indeed! He did not tell me that when we were talking just now."

"He didn't know it then. He will when I have had a few words with him."

And she walked with firm steps back into the clubhouse.

It has been well said that there are many

kinds of golf, beginning at the top with the golf of professionals and the best amateurs and working down through the golf of ossified men to that of Scotch University professors. Until recently this last was looked upon as the lowest possible depth; but nowadays, with the growing popularity of summer hotels, we are able to add a brand still lower, the golf you find at places like Marvis Bay.

To Ferdinand Dibble, coming from a club where the standard of play was rather unusually high, Marvis Bay was a revelation, and for some days after his arrival there he went about dazed, like a man who cannot believe it is really true. To go out on the links at this summer resort was like entering a new world. The hotel was full of stout, middle-aged men, who, after a misspent youth devoted to making money, had taken to a game at which real proficiency can only be acquired by those who start playing in their cradles and keep their weight down. Out on the course each morning you could see representatives of every nightmare style that was ever invented. There was the man who seemed to be attempting to deceive his ball and lull it into a false security by looking away from it and then making a lightning slash in the apparent hope of catching it off its guard. There was the man who wielded his mid-iron like one killing snakes. There was the man who addressed his ball as if he were stroking a cat, the man who drove as if he were cracking a whip, the man who brooded over each shot like one whose heart is bowed down by bad news from home, and the man who scooped with his mashie as if he were ladling soup. By the end of the first week Ferdinand Dibble was the acknowledged champion of the place. He had gone through the entire menagerie like a bullet through a cream puff.

First, scarcely daring to consider the possibility of success, he had taken on the man who tried to catch his ball off its guard and had beaten him five up and four to play. Then, with gradually growing confidence, he tackled in turn the Cat-Stroker, the Whip-Cracker, the Heart-Bowed-Down, and the Soup-Scooper, and walked all over their faces with spiked shoes. And as these were the leading local amateurs, whose prowess the octogenarians and the men who went round in bath-chairs vainly strove to emulate, Ferdinand Dibble was faced on the

eighth morning of his visit by the startling fact that he had no more worlds to conquer. He was monarch of all he surveyed, and, what is more, had won his first trophy, the prize in the great medal play handicap tournament, in which he had nosed in ahead of the field by two strokes, edging out his nearest rival, a venerable old gentleman, by means of a brilliant and unexpected four on the last hole. The prize was a handsome pewter mug, about the size of the old oaken bucket, and Ferdinand used to go to his room immediately after dinner to croon over it like a mother over her child.

You are wondering, no doubt, why, in these circumstances, he did not take advantage of the new spirit of exhilarated pride which had replaced his old humility and instantly propose to Barbara Medway. I will tell you. He did not propose to Barbara because Barbara was not there. At the last moment she had been detained at home to nurse a sick parent and had been compelled to postpone her visit for a couple of weeks. He could, no doubt, have proposed in one of the daily letters which he wrote to her, but somehow, once he started writing, he found that he used up so much space describing his best shots on the links that day that it was difficult to squeeze in a declaration of undying passion. After all, you can hardly cram that sort of thing into a postscript.

He decided, therefore, to wait till she arrived, and meanwhile pursued his conquering course. The longer he waited, the better, in one way, for every morning and afternoon that passed was adding new layers to his self-esteem. Day by day in every way he grew chestier and chestier.

Meanwhile, however, dark clouds were gathering. Sullen mutterings were to be heard in corners of the hotel lounge, and the spirit of revolt was abroad. For Ferdinand's chestiness had not escaped the notice of his defeated rivals. There is nobody so chesty as a normally unchesty man who suddenly becomes chesty, and I am sorry to say that the chestiness which had come to Ferdinand was the aggressive type of chestiness which breeds enemies. He had developed a habit of holding the game up in order to give his opponent advice. The Whip-Cracker had not for-given, and never would forgive, his well-meant but galling criticism of his backswing. The Scooper, who had always scooped since the day when, at the age of sixty-four, he subscribed to the Correspondence Course which was to teach him golf in twelve lessons by mail, resented being told by a snip of a boy that the mashie stroke should be a smooth, unhurried swing. The Snake-Killer—but I need not weary you with a detailed recital of these men's grievances; it is enough to say that they all had it in for Ferdi-nand, and one night, after dinner, they met in the lounge to decide what was to be done about it.

A nasty spirit was displayed by all.

"A mere lad telling me how to use my ma-shie!" growled the Scooper. "Smooth and un-hurried my left eyeball! I get it up, don't I? Well, what more do you want?"

"I keep telling him that mine is the old, full St. Andrews swing," muttered the Whip-Cracker, between set teeth, "but he won't listen to me."

"He ought to be taken down a peg or two," hissed the Snake-Killer. It is not easy to hiss a sentence without a single "s" in it, and the fact that he succeeded in doing so shows to what a pitch of emotion the man had been goaded by Ferdinand's maddening air of superiority.

"Yes, but what can we do?" queried an oc-togenarian, when this last remark had been passed on to him down his ear-trumpet.

"That's the trouble," sighed the Scooper. "What can we do?" And there was a sorrowful shaking of heads.

"I know!" exclaimed the Cat-Stroker, who had not hitherto spoken. He was a lawyer, and a man of subtle and sinister mind. "I have it! There's a boy in my office—young Parsloe—who could beat this man Dibble hollow. I'll wire him to come down here and we'll spring him on this fellow and knock some of the conceit out of him."

There was a chorus of approval.

"But are you sure he can beat him?" asked the Snake-Killer, anxiously. "It would never do to make a mistake."

"Of course I'm sure," said the Cat-Stroker. "George Parsloe once went round in "ninety-four."

"Many changes there have been since nine-ty-four," said the octogenarian, nodding sagely. "Ah, many, many changes. None of these motor-cars then, tearing about and killing—"

Kindly hands led him off to have an egg-and-milk, and the remaining conspirators returned to the point at issue with bent brows.

"Ninety-four?" said the Scooper, incredu-lously. "Do you mean counting every stroke?"

"Counting every stroke."

"Not conceding himself any putts?"

"Not one."

"Wire him to come at once," said the meet-ing with one voice.

That night the Cat-Stroker approached Fer-dinand, smooth, subtle, lawyerlike.

"Oh, Dibble," he said, "just the man I wanted to see. Dibble, there's a young friend of mine coming down here who goes in for golf a little. George Parsloe is his name. I was wonder-ing if you could spare time to give him a game. He is just a novice, you know."

"I shall be delighted to play a round with him," said Ferdinand kindly.

"He might pick up a pointer or two from watching you." said the Cat-Stroker.

"True, true," said Ferdinand.

"Then I'll introduce you when he shows up."

"Delighted," said Ferdinand.

He was in excellent humor that night, for he had had a letter from Barbara saying that she was arriving on the next day but one.

It was Ferdinand's healthy custom of a morning to get up in good time and take a dip in the sea before breakfast. On the morning of the day of Barbara's arrival, he arose, as usual, donned his flannels, took a good look at the cup, and started out. It was a fine, fresh morning, and he glowed both externally and internally. As he crossed the links, for the nearest route to the water was through the fairway of the seventh, he was whistling happily and rehearsing in his mind the opening sentences of his proposal. For it was his firm resolve that night after dinner to ask Barbara to marry him. He was proceeding over the smooth turf without a care in the world, when there was a sudden cry of "Fore!" and the next moment a golf ball, missing him by inches, sailed up the fairway and came to a rest fifty yards from where he stood. He looked up and observed a figure coming towards him from the tee.

The distance from the tee was fully 130 yards. Add fifty to that, and you have 180 yards. No such drive had been made on the Marvis Bay links since their foundation, and such is the generous spirit of the true golfer that Ferdinand's first emotion, after the not inexcusable spasm of panic caused by the hum of the ball past his ear, was one of cordial admiration. By some kindly miracle, he supposed, one of his hotel acquaintances had been permitted for once in his life to time a drive right. It was only when the other man came up that there began to steal over him a sickening apprehension. The faces of all those who hewed divots on the hotel course were familiar to him, and the fact that this fellow was a stranger seemed to point with dreadful certainty to his being the man he had agreed to play.

"Sorry," said the man. He was a tall, strikingly handsome youth, with brown eyes and a dark mustache.

"Oh, that's all right," said Ferdinand. "Er— do you always drive like that?"

"Well, I generally get a big longer ball, but I'm off my drive this morning. It's lucky I came out and got this practice. I'm playing a match tomorrow with a fellow named Dibble, who's a local champion, or something."

"Me," said Ferdinand, humbly.

"Eh? Oh, you?" Mr. Parsloe eyed him appraisingly. "Well, may the best man win."

As this was precisely what Ferdinand was afraid was going to happen, he nodded in a sickly manner and tottered off to his bathe. The magic had gone out of the morning. The sun still shone, but in a silly, feeble way; and a cold and depressing wind had sprung up. For Ferdinand's inferiority complex, which had seemed cured for ever, was back again, doing business at the old stand.

How sad it is in this life that the moment to which we have looked forward with the most glowing anticipation so often turns out on arrival, flat, cold, and disappointing. For ten days Barbara Medway had been living for that meeting with Ferdinand, when, getting out of the train, she would see him popping about on the horizon with the lovelight sparkling in his eyes and words of devotion trembling on his lips. The poor girl never doubted for an instant that he would unleash his pent-up emotions inside the first five minutes, and her only worry was lest he should give an embarrassing publicity to the sacred scene by falling on his knees on the station platform.

"Well, here I am at last," she cried gaily.

"Hullo!" said Ferdinand, with a twisted smile.

The girl looked at him, chilled. How could she know that his peculiar manner was due entirely to the severe attack of cold feet resultant upon his meeting with George Parsloe that morning? The interpretation which she placed upon it was that he was not glad to see her. If he had behaved like this before, she would, of course, have put it down to ingrowing goofery, but now she had his written statements to prove that for the last ten days his golf had been one long series of triumphs.

"I got your letters," she said, persevering bravely.

"I thought you would," said Ferdinand, absently.

"You seem to have been doing wonders."

"Yes."

There was a silence.

"Have a nice journey?" said Ferdinand.

"Very," said Barbara.

She spoke coldly, for she was madder than a wet hen. She saw it all now. In the ten days since they had parted, his love, she realized, had waned. Some other girl, met in the romantic surroundings of this picturesque resort, had supplanted her in his affections. She knew how quickly Cupid gets off the mark at a summer hotel, and for an instant she blamed herself for ever having been so ivory-skulled as to let him come to this place alone. Then regret was swallowed up in wrath, and she became so glacial that Ferdinand, who had been on the point of telling her the secret of his gloom, retired into his shell and conversation during the drive to the hotel never soared above a certain level. Ferdinand said the sunshine was nice and Barbara said yes, it was nice, and Ferdinand said it looked pretty on the water, and Barbara said yes, it did look pretty on the water, and Ferdinand said he hoped it was not going to rain, and Barbara said yes, it would be a pity if it rained. And then there was another lengthy silence.

"How is my uncle?" asked Barbara at last.

I omitted to mention that the individual to whom I have referred as the Cat-Stroker was Barbara's mother's brother, and her host at Marvis Bay.

"Your uncle?"

"His name is Tuttle. Have you met him?"

"Oh yes. I've seen a good deal of him. He has got a friend staying with him," said Ferdinand, his mind returning to the matter nearest his heart. "A fellow named Parsloe."

"Oh, is George Parsloe here? How jolly!"

"Do you know him?" barked Ferdinand, hollowly. He would not have supposed that anything could have added to his existing depression, but he was conscious now of having slipped a few rungs farther down the ladder of gloom. There had been a horribly joyful ring in her voice. Ah, well, he reflected morosely, how like life it all was! We never know what the morrow may bring forth. We strike a good patch and are beginning to think pretty well of ourselves, and along comes a George Parsloe.

"Of course I do," said Barbara. "Why, there he is."

The cab had drawn up at the door of the hotel, and on the porch George Parsloe was airing his graceful person. To Ferdinand's fevered eye he looked like a Greek god, and his inferiority complex began to exhibit symptoms of elephantiasis. How could he compete at love or golf with a fellow who looked as if he had stepped out of the movies and considered himself off his drive when he did 180 yards?

"Geor-gee!" cried Barbara blithely. "Hullo, George!"

"Why, hullo, Barbara!"

They fell into pleasant conversation, while Ferdinand hung miserably about in the offing. And presently, feeling that his society was not essential to their happiness, he slunk away.

George Parsloe dined at the Cat-Stroker's table that night, and it was with George Parsloe that Barbara roamed in the moonlight after dinner. Ferdinand, after a profitless hour at the billiard table, went early to his room. But not even the rays of the moon, glinting on his cup, could soothe the fever in his soul. He practiced putting somberly into his tooth-glass for a while; then, going to bed, fell at last into a troubled sleep.

Barbara slept late the next morning and breakfasted in her room. Coming down towards noon, she found a strange emptiness in the hotel. It was her experience of summer hotels that a really fine day like this one was the cue for half the inhabitants to collect in the lounge, shut all the windows, and talk about conditions in the jute industry. To her surprise, though the sun was streaming down from a cloudless sky, the only occupant of the lounge was the octogenarian with the ear-trumpet. She observed that he was chuckling to himself in a senile manner.

"Good morning," she said, politely, for she had made his acquaintance on the previous evening.

"Hey?" said the octogenarian, suspending his chuckling and getting his trumpet into position.

"I said 'Good morning!' " roared Barbara into the receiver.

"Hey?"

"Good morning!"

"Ah! Yes, it's a very fine morning, a very fine morning. If it wasn't for missing my bun and glass of milk at twelve sharp," said the octogenarian, "I'd be down on the links. That's where I'd be, down on the links. If it wasn't for missing my bun and glass of milk."

This refreshment arriving at this moment,

he dismantled the radio outfit and began to restore his tissues.

"Watching the match," he explained, pausing for a moment in his bun-mangling.

"What match?"

The octogenarian sipped his milk.

"What match?" repeated Barbara.

"Hey?"

"What match?"

The octogenarian began to chuckle again and nearly swallowed a crumb the wrong way.

"Take some of the conceit out of him," he gurgled.

"Out of who?" asked Barbara, knowing perfectly well that she should have said "whom."

"Yes," said the octogenarian.

"Who is conceited?"

"Ah! This young fellow, Dibble. Very conceited. I saw it in his eye from the first, but nobody would listen to me. Mark my words, I said, that boy needs taking down a peg or two. Well, he's going to be this morning. Your uncle wired to young Parsloe to come down, and he's arranged a match between them. Dibble—" Here the octogenarian choked again and had to rinse himself out with milk, "Dibble doesn't know that Parsloe once went round in ninety-four!"

"What?"

Everything seemed to go black to Barbara. Through a murky mist she appeared to be looking at a negro octogenarian, sipping ink. Then her eyes cleared, and she found herself clutching for support at the back of a chair. She understood now. She realized why Ferdinand had been so distrait, and her whole heart went out to him in a spasm of maternal pity. How she had wronged him!

"Take some of the conceit out of him," the octogenarian was mumbling, and Barbara felt a sudden sharp loathing for the old man. For two pins she could have dropped a beetle in his milk. Then the need for action aroused her. What action? She did not know. All she knew was that she must act.

"Oh!" she cried.

"Hey?" said the octogenarian, bringing his trumpet to the ready.

But Barbara had gone.

It was not far to the links, and Barbara covered the distance on flying feet. She reached the clubhouse, but the course was empty except for the Scooper, who was preparing to drive off the first tee. In spite of the fact that something seemed to tell her subconsciously that this was one of the sights she ought not to miss, the girl did not wait to watch. Assuming that the match had started soon after breakfast, it must by now have reached one of the holes on the second nine. She ran down the hill, looking to left and right, and was presently aware of a group of spectators clustered about a green in the distance. As she hurried towards them they moved away, and now she could see Ferdinand advancing to the next tee. With a thrill that shook her whole body she realized that he had the honor. So he must have won one hole, at any rate. Then she saw her uncle.

"How are they?" she gasped.

Mr. Tuttle seemed moody. It was apparent that things were not going altogether to his liking.

"All square at the fifteenth," he replied, gloomily.

"All square!"

"Yes. Young Parsloe," said Mr. Tuttle with a sour look in the direction of that lissom athlete, "doesn't seem to be able to do a thing right on the greens. He has been putting like a sheep with the botts."

From the foregoing remark of Mr. Tuttle you will, no doubt, have gleaned at least a clue to the mystery of how Ferdinand Dibble had managed to hold his long-driving adversary up to the fifteenth green, but for all that you will probably consider that some further explanation of this amazing state of affairs is required. Mere bad putting on the part of George Parsloe is not, you feel, sufficient to cover the matter entirely. You are right. There was another very important factor in the situation—to wit, that by some extraordinary chance Ferdinand Dibble had started right off from the first tee, playing the game of a lifetime. Never had he made such drives, never chipped his chips so shrewdly.

About Ferdinand's driving there was as a general thing a fatal stiffness and over-caution which prevented success. And with his chip shots he rarely achieved accuracy owing to his habit of rearing his head like the lion of the jungle just before the club struck the ball. But today he had been swinging with a careless freedom, and his chips had been true and clean. The thing had puzzled him all the way round. It had not elated him, for, owing to Barbara's aloofness and the way in which she had gambolled about George Parsloe, like a young lamb in the springtime, he was in too deep a state of dejection to be elated by anything. And now, suddenly, in a flash of clear vision, he perceived the reason why he had been playing so well today. It was just because he was not elated. It was simply because he was so profoundly miserable.

That was what Ferdinand told himself as he stepped off the sixteenth, after hitting a screamer down the center of the fairway, and I am convinced that he was right. Like so many indifferent golfers, Ferdinand Dibble had always made the game hard for himself by thinking too much. He was a deep student of the works of the masters, and whenever he prepared to play a stroke he had a complete mental list of all the mistakes which it was possible to make. He would remember how Taylor had warned against dipping the right shoulder, how Vardon had inveighed against any movement of the head; he would recall how Ray had mentioned the tendency to snatch back the club, how Braid had spoken sadly of those who sin against their better selves by stiffening the muscles and heaving.

The consequence was that when, after waggling in a frozen manner till mere shame urged him to take some definite course of action, he eventually swung, he invariably proceeded to dip his right shoulder, stiffen his muscles, heave, and snatch back the club, at the same time raising his head sharply as in the illustrated plate ("Some Frequent Faults of Beginners—No. 3—Lifting the Bean") facing page 34 of James Braid's *Golf Without Tears*. Today, he had been so preoccupied with his broken heart that he had made his shots absently, almost carelessly, with the re-

sult that at least one in every three had been a lallapaloosa.

Meanwhile, George Parsloe had driven off and the match was progressing. George was feeling a little flustered by now. He had been given to understand that this bird Dibble was a hundred-at-his-best man, and all the way round the fellow had been reeling off fives in great profusion, and had once actually got a four. True, there had been an occasional six, and even a seven, but that did not alter the main fact that the man was making the dickens of a game of it. With the haughty spirit of one who had once done a ninety-four, George Parsloe had anticipated being at least three up at the turn. Instead of which he had been two down, and had had to fight strenuously to draw level.

Nevertheless, he drove steadily and well, and would certainly have won the hole had it not been for his weak and sinful putting. The same defect caused him to halve the seventeenth, after being on in two, with Ferdinand wandering in the desert and only reaching the green with his fourth. Then, however, Ferdinand holed out from a distance of seven yards, getting a five; which George's three putts just enabled him to equal.

Barbara had watched the proceedings with a beating heart. At first she had looked on from afar; but now, drawn as by a magnet, she approached the tee. Ferdinand was driving off. She held her breath. Ferdinand held his breath. And all around one could see their respective breaths being held by George Parsloe, Mr. Tuttle, and the enthralled crowd of spectators. It was a moment of the acutest tension, and it was broken by the crack of Ferdinand's driver as it met the ball and sent it hopping along the ground for a mere thirty yards. At this supreme crisis in the match Ferdinand Dibble had topped.

George Parsloe teed up his ball. There was a smile of quiet satisfaction on his face. He snuggled the driver in his hands, and gave it a preliminary swish. This, felt George Parsloe, was where the happy ending came. He could drive as he had never driven before. He would so drive that it would take his opponent at least three shots to catch up with him. He drew back his club with infinite caution, poised it at the top of the swing—

"I always wonder—" said a clear, girlish voice, ripping the silence like the explosion of a bomb.

George Parsloe started. His club wobbled. It descended. The ball trickled into the long grass in front of the tee. There was a grim pause.

"You were saying, Miss Medway—" said George Parsloe, in a small, flat voice.

"Oh, I'm so sorry," said Barbara. "I'm afraid I put you off."

"A little, perhaps. Possibly the merest trifle. But you were saying you wondered about something. Can I be of any assistance?"

"I was only saying," said Barbara, "that I always wonder why tees are called tees."

George Parsloe swallowed once or twice. He also blinked a little feverishly. His eyes had a dazed, staring expression.

"I am afraid I cannot tell you off-hand," he said, "but I will make a point of consulting some good encyclopedia at the earliest opportunity."

"Thank you so much."

"Not at all. It will be a pleasure. In case you were thinking of inquiring at the moment when I am putting why greens are called greens, may I venture the suggestion now that it is because they are green?"

And, so saying, George Parsloe stalked to his ball and found it nestling in the heart of some shrub of which, not being a botanist, I cannot give you the name. It was a close-knit, adhesive shrub, and it twined its tentacles so lovingly around George Parsloe's niblick that he missed his first shot altogether. His second made the ball rock, and his third dislodged it. Playing a full swing with his brassie and being by now a mere cauldron of seething emotions he missed his fourth. His fifth came to within a few inches of Ferdinand's drive, and he picked it up and hurled it from him into the rough as if it had been something venomous.

"Your hole and match," said George Parsloe, thinly.

Ferdinand Dibble sat beside the glittering ocean. He had hurried off the course with swift strides the moment George Parsloe had spoken those bitter words. He wanted to be alone with his thoughts.

They were mixed thoughts. For a moment joy at the reflection that he had won a tough match came irresistibly to the surface, only to sink again as he remembered that life, whatever its triumphs, could hold nothing for him now that Barbara Medway loved another.

"Mr. Dibble!"

He looked up. She was standing at his side. He gulped and rose to his feet.

"Yes?"

There was a silence.

"Doesn't the sun look pretty on the water?" said Barbara.

Ferdinand groaned. This was too much.

"Leave me," he said, hollowly. "Go back to your Parsloe, the man with whom you walked in the moonlight beside this same water."

"Well, why shouldn't I walk with Mr. Parsloe in the moonlight beside this same water?" demanded Barbara, with spirit.

"I never said," replied Ferdinand, for he was a fair man at heart, "that you shouldn't walk with Mr. Parsloe beside this same water. I simply said you did walk with Mr. Parsloe beside this same water."

"I've a perfect right to walk with Mr. Parsloe beside this same water," persisted Barbara. "He and I are old friends."

Ferdinand groaned again.

"Exactly! There you are! As I suspected. Old friends. Played together as children, and what not, I shouldn't wonder."

"No, we didn't. I've only known him five years. But he is engaged to be married to my greatest chum, so that draws us together."

Ferdinand uttered a strangled cry.

"Parsloe engaged to be married!"

"Yes. The wedding takes place next month."

"But look here." Ferdinand's forehead was wrinkled. He was thinking tensely. "Look here," said Ferdinand, a close reasoner. "If Parsloe's engaged to your greatest chum, he can't be in love with *you.*"

"No."

"And you aren't in love with him?"

"No."

"Then, by gad," said Ferdinand, "how about it?"

"What do you mean?"

"Will you marry me?" bellowed Ferdinand.

"Yes."

"You will?"

"Of course I will."

"Darling!" cried Ferdinand.

"There is only one thing that bothers me a bit," said Ferdinand, thoughtfully, as they strolled together over the scented meadows, while in the trees above them a thousand birds trilled Mendelssohn's Wedding March.

"What is that?"

"Well, I'll tell you," said Ferdinand. "The fact is, I've just discovered the great secret of golf. You can't play a really hot game unless you're so miserable that you don't worry over your shots. Take the case of a chip shot, for instance. If you're really wretched, you don't care

where the ball is going and so you don't raise your head to see. Grief automatically prevents pressing and overswinging. Look at the top-notchers. Have you ever seen a happy pro?"

"No. I don't think I have."

"Well, then!"

"But pros are all Scotchmen," argued Barbara.

"It doesn't matter. I'm sure I'm right. And the darned thing is that I'm going to be so infernally happy all the rest of my life that I suppose my handicap will go up to thirty or something."

Barbara squeezed his hand lovingly.

"Don't worry, precious," she said, soothingly. "It will be all right. I am a woman, and, once we are married, I shall be able to think of at least a hundred ways of snootering you to such an extent that you'll be fit to win the Amateur Championship."

"You will?" said Ferdinand, anxiously. "You're sure?"

"Quite, quite sure, dearest," said Barbara.

"My angel!" said Ferdinand.

He folded her in his arms, using the interlocking grip.

All to Play For/
The Cup and the Lip

by IAN FLEMING

Those captivated by spy thrillers have to love the some-what outrageous adventures of James Bond, Agent 007. His creator, Ian Fleming, endowed Bond with many talents, including a single-figure handicap. In truth, the following match between Bond and master villain, Goldfinger, is one of the best in all golf literature and shows that Fleming knew his golf as well as his intrigues.

All to Play For

"Good afternoon, Blacking. All set?" The voice was casual, authoritative. "I see there's a car outside. Not somebody looking for a game, I suppose?"

"I'm not sure, sir. It's an old member come back to have a club made up. Would you like me to ask him, sir?"

"Who is it? What's his name?"

Bond smiled grimly. He pricked his ears. He wanted to catch every inflection.

"A Mr. Bond, sir."

There was a pause. "Bond?" The voice had not changed. It was politely interested. "Met a fellow called Bond the other day. What's his first name?"

"James, sir."

"Oh yes." Now the pause was longer. "Does he know I'm here?" Bond could sense Goldfinger's antennae probing the situation.

"He's in the workshop, sir. May have seen your car drive up." Bond thought: Alfred's never told a lie in his life. He's not going to start now.

"Might be an idea." Now Goldfinger's voice unbent. He wanted something from Alfred Blacking, some information. "What sort of a game does this chap play? What's his handicap?"

"Used to be quite useful when he was a boy, sir. Haven't seen his game since then."

"Hm."

Bond could feel the man weighing it all up. Bond smelled that the bait was going to be taken. He reached into his bag and pulled out his driver and started rubbing down the grip with a block of shellac. Might as well look busy. A board in the shop creaked. Bond honed away industriously, his back to the open door.

"I think we've met before." The voice from the doorway was low, neutral.

Bond looked quickly over his shoulder. "My God, you made me jump. Why—" recognition dawned—"It's Gold, Goldman . . . er— Goldfinger." He hoped he wasn't overplaying it. He said with a hint of dislike, or mistrust, "Where have you sprung from?"

"I told you I played down here. Remember?" Goldfinger was looking at him shrewdly.

Now the eyes opened wide. The X-ray gaze pierced through to the back of Bond's skull.

"No."

"Did not Miss Masterton give you my message?"

"No. What was it?"

"I said I would be over here and that I would like a game of golf with you."

"Oh, well," Bond's voice was coldly polite, "we must do that some day."

"I was playing with the professional. I will play with you instead." Goldfinger was stating a fact.

There was no doubt that Goldfinger was hooked. Now Bond must play hard to get.

"Why not some other time? I've come to order a club. Anyway I'm not in practice. There probably isn't a caddie." Bond was being as rude as he could. Obviously the last thing he wanted to do was play with Goldfinger.

"I also haven't played for some time." (Bloody liar, thought Bond.) "Ordering a club will not take a moment." Goldfinger turned back into the shop. "Blacking, have you got a caddie for Mr. Bond?"

"Yes, sir."

"Then that is arranged."

Bond wearily thrust his driver back into his bag. "Well, all right then." He thought of a final way of putting Goldfinger off. He said roughly, "But I warn you I like playing for money. I can't be bothered to knock a ball round just for the fun of it." Bond felt pleased with the character he was building up for himself.

Was there a glint of triumph, quickly concealed, in Goldfinger's pale eyes? He said indifferently, "That suits me. Anything you like. Off handicap, of course. I think you said you're nine."

"Yes."

Goldfinger said carefully, "Where, may I ask?"

"Huntercombe." Bond was also nine at Sunningdale. Huntercombe was an easier course. Nine at Huntercombe wouldn't frighten Goldfinger.

"And I also am nine. Here. Up on the board. So it's a level game. Right?"

Bond shrugged. "You'll be too good for me."

"I doubt it. However," Goldfinger was offhand, "tell you what I'll do. That bit of money you removed from me in Miami. Remember? The big figure was ten. I like a gamble. It will be good for me to have to try. I will play you double or quits for that."

Bond said indifferently, "That's too much." Then, as if he thought better of it, thought he might win, he said—with just the right amount of craft mixed with reluctance—"Of course you can say that was 'found money'. I won't miss it if it goes again. Oh, well, all right. Easy come easy go. Level match. Ten thousand dollars it is."

Goldfinger turned away. He said, and there was a sudden sweetness in the flat voice, "That's all arranged then, Mr. Blacking. Many thanks. Put your fee down on my account. Very sorry we shall be missing our game. Now, let me pay the caddie fees."

Alfred Blacking came into the workroom and picked up Bond's clubs. He looked very directly at Bond. He said, "Remember what I told you, sir." One eye closed and opened again. "I mean about that flat swing of yours. It needs watching—all the time."

Bond smiled at him. Alfred had long ears. He might not have caught the figure, but he knew that somehow this was to be a key game. "Thanks, Alfred. I won't forget. Four Penfolds—with hearts on them. And a dozen tees. I won't be a minute."

Bond walked through the shop and out to his car. The bowler-hatted man was polishing the metal work of the Rolls with a cloth. Bond felt rather than saw him stop and watch Bond take out his zip bag and go into the clubhouse. The man had a square flat yellow face. One of the Koreans?

Bond paid his green fee to Hampton, the steward, and went into the changing room. It was just the same—the same tacky smell of old shoes and socks and last summer's sweat. Why was it a tradition of the most famous golf clubs that their standard of hygiene should be that of a Victorian private school? Bond changed his socks and put on the battered old pair of nailed Saxones. He took off the coat of his yellowing black and white hound's-tooth suit and pulled on a faded black windcheater. Cigarettes? Lighter? He was ready to go.

Bond walked slowly out, preparing his mind for the game. On purpose he had needled this man into a high, tough match so that Goldfinger's respect for him should be increased and Goldfinger's view of Bond—that he was the type of ruthless, hard adventurer who might be very useful to Goldfinger—would be confirmed. Bond had thought that perhaps a hundred-pound Nassau would be the form. But $10,000! There had probably never been such a high singles game in history—except in the finals of American Championships or in the big amateur Calcutta Sweeps where it was the backers rather than the players who had the money on. Goldfinger's private accounting must have taken a nasty dent. He wouldn't have liked that. He would be aching to get some of his money back. When Bond had talked about playing high, Goldfinger had seen his chance. So be it. But one thing was certain, for a hundred reasons Bond could not afford to lose.

He turned into the shop and picked up the balls and tees from Alfred Blacking.

"Hawker's got the clubs, sir."

Bond strolled out across the 500 yards of shaven seaside turf that led to the first tee. Goldfinger was practicing on the putting green. His caddie stood near by, rolling balls to him. Goldfinger putted in the new fashion—between his legs with a mallet putter. Bond felt encouraged. He didn't believe in the system. He knew it was no good practicing himself. His old hickory Calamity Jane had its good days and its bad. There was nothing to do about it. He knew also that the St. Marks practice green bore no resemblance, in speed or texture, to the greens on the course.

Bond caught up with the limping, insouciant figure of his caddie who was sauntering along chipping at an imaginary ball with Bond's blaster. "Afternoon, Hawker."

"Afternoon, sir." Hawker handed Bond the blaster and threw down three used balls. His keen sardonic poacher's face split in a wry grin

of welcome. "How've you been keepin', sir? Played any golf in the last twenty years? Can you still put them on the roof of the starter's hut?" This referred to the day when Bond, trying to do just that before a match, had put two balls through the starter's window.

"Let's see." Bond took the blaster and hefted it in his hand, gauging the distance. The tap of the balls on the practice green had ceased. Bond addressed the ball, swung quickly, lifted his head and shanked the ball almost at right angles. He tried again. This time it was a dunch. A foot of turf flew up. The ball went ten yards. Bond turned to Hawker, who was looking his most sardonic. "It's all right, Hawker. Those were for show. Now then, one for you." He stepped up to the third ball, took his club back slowly and whipped the clubhead through. The ball soared 100 feet, paused elegantly, dropped eighty feet on to the thatched roof of the starter's hut and bounced down.

Bond handed back the club. Hawker's eyes were thoughtful, amused. He said nothing. He pulled out the driver and handed it to Bond. They walked together to the first tee, talking about Hawker's family.

Goldfinger joined them, relaxed, impassive. Bond greeted Goldfinger's caddie, an obsequious, talkative man called Foulks whom Bond had never liked. Bond glanced at Goldfinger's clubs. They were a brand-new set of American Ben Hogans with smart St. Marks leather covers for the woods. The bag was one of the stitched black leather holdalls favored by American pros. The clubs were in individual cardboard tubes for easy extraction. It was a pretentious outfit, but the best.

"Toss for honor?" Goldfinger flicked a coin. "Tails."

It was heads. Goldfinger took out his driver and unpeeled a new ball. He said "Dunlop 65. Number one. Always use the same ball. What's yours?"

"Penfold. Hearts."

Goldfinger looked keenly at Bond. "Strict rules of golf?"

"Naturally."

"Right." Goldfinger walked on to the tee

and teed up. He took one or two careful, concentrated practice swings. It was a type of swing Bond knew well—the grooved, mechanical, repeating swing of someone who had studied the game with great care, read all the books and spent 5,000 pounds on the finest pro teachers. It would be a good, scoring swing which might not collapse under pressure. Bond envied it.

Goldfinger took up his stance, waggled gracefully, took his clubhead back in a wide slow arc and, with his eyes glued to the ball, broke his wrists correctly. He brought the clubhead mechanically, effortlessly, down and through the ball and into a rather artificial, copybook finish. The ball went straight and true about 200 yards down the fairway.

It was an excellent, uninspiring shot. Bond knew that Goldfinger would be capable of repeating the same swing with different clubs again and again round the eighteen holes.

Bond took his place, gave himself a lowish tee, addressed the ball with careful enmity and, with a flat, racket-player's swing in which there was just too much wrist for safety, lashed the ball away. It was a fine, attacking drive that landed past Goldfinger's ball and rolled on fifty yards. But it had had a shade of draw and ended on the edge of the left-hand rough.

They were two good drives. As Bond handed his clubs to Hawker and strolled off in the wake of the more impatient Goldfinger, he smelled the sweet smell of the beginning of a knock-down-and-drag-out game of golf on a beautiful day in May with the larks singing over the greatest seaside course in the world.

The first hole of the Royal St. Marks is 450 yards long—450 yards of undulating fairway with one central bunker to trap a mishit second shot and a chain of bunkers guarding three-quarters of the green to trap a well-hit one. You can slip through the unguarded quarter, but the fairway slopes to the right there and you are more likely to end up with a nasty first-chip-of-the-day out of the rough. Goldfinger was well placed to try for this opening. Bond watched him take what was probably a spoon, make his two practice swings and address the ball.

Many unlikely people play golf, including people who are blind, who have only one arm, or even no legs, and people often wear bizarre clothes to the game. Other golfers don't think them odd, for there are no rules of appearance or dress at golf. That is one of its minor pleasures. But Goldfinger had made an attempt to look smart at golf and that is the only way of dressing that is incongruous on a links. Everything matched in a blaze of rust-colored tweed from the buttoned "golfer's cap" centered on the huge, flaming red hair, to the brilliantly polished, almost orange shoes. The plus-four suit was too well cut and the plus-fours themselves had been pressed down the sides. The stockings were of a matching heather mixture and had green garter tabs. It was as if Goldfinger had gone to his tailor and said, "Dress me for golf—you know, like they wear in Scotland." Social errors made no impression on Bond, and for the matter of that he rarely noticed them. With Goldfinger it was different. Everything about theman had grated on Bond's teeth from the first moment he had seen him. The assertive blatancy of his clothes was just part of the malevolent animal magnetism that had affected Bond from the beginning.

Goldfinger executed his mechanical, faultless swing. The ball flew true but just failed to make the slope and curled off to the right to finish pin high off the green in the short rough. Easy five. A good chip could turn it into a four, but it would have to be a good one.

Bond walked over to his ball. It was lying cocked up, just off the fairway. Bond took his number four-wood. Now for the "all air route" —a soaring shot that would carry the cross-bunkers and give him two putts for a four. Bond remembered the dictum of the pros: "It's never too early to start winning." He took it easy, determined not to press for the long but comfortable carry.

As soon as Bond had hit the shot he knew it wouldn't do. The difference between a good golf shot and a bad one is the same as the difference between a beautiful and a plain woman—a matter of millimeters. In this case, the clubface had gone through just that one millimeter too low under the ball. The arc of flight was high and soft

—no legs. Why the hell hadn't he taken a spoon or a two-iron off that lie? The ball hit the lip of the far bunker and fell back. Now it was the blaster, and fighting for a half.

Bond never worried too long about his bad or stupid shots. He put them behind him and thought of the next. He came up with the bunker, took his blaster and measured the distance to the pin. Twenty yards. The ball was lying well back. Should he splash it out with a wide stance and an outside-in swing, or should he blast it and take plenty of sand? For safety's sake he would blast it out. Bond went down into the bunker. Head down and follow well through. The easiest shot in golf. Try and put it dead. The wish, halfway down his backswing, hurried the hands in front of the clubhead. The loft was killed and there was the ball rolling back off the face. Get it out, you bloody fool, and hole a long putt! Now Bond took too much sand. He was out, but barely on the green. Goldfinger bent to his chip and kept his head down until the ball was halfway to the hole. The ball stopped three inches from the pin. Without waiting to be given the putt, Goldfinger turned his back on Bond and walked off towards the second tee. Bond picked up his ball and took his driver from Hawker.

"What does he say his handicap is, sir?"

"Nine. It's a level match. Have to do better than that though. Ought to have taken my spoon for the second."

Hawker said encouragingly, "It's early days yet, sir."

Bond knew it wasn't. It was always too early to start losing.

The Cup and the Lip

Goldfinger had already teed up. Bond walked slowly behind him, followed by Hawker. Bond stood and leant on his driver. He said, "I thought you said we would be playing the strict rules of golf. But I'll give you that putt. That makes you one up."

Goldfinger nodded curtly. He went through his practice routine and hit his usual excellent, safe drive.

The second hole is a 370-yard dogleg to the left with deep cross-bunkers daring you to take the tiger's line. But there was a light helping breeze. For Goldfinger it would now be a five-iron for his second. Bond decided to try and make it easier for himself and only have a wedge for the green. He laid his ears back and hit the ball hard and straight for the bunkers. The breeze got under the slight draw and winged the ball on and over. The ball pitched and disappeared down into the gully just short of the green. A four. Chance of a three.

Goldfinger strode off without comment. Bond lengthened his stride and caught up. "How's the agoraphobia? Doesn't all this wide open space bother it?"

"No."

Goldfinger deviated to the right. He glanced at the distant, half-hidden flag, planning his second shot. He took his five-iron and hit a good, careful shot which took a bad kick short of the green and ran down into the thick grass to the left. Bond knew that territory. Goldfinger would be lucky to get down in two.

Bond walked up to his ball, took the wedge and flicked the ball on to the green with plenty of stop. The ball pulled up and lay a yard past the hole. Goldfinger executed a creditable pitch but missed the twelve-foot putt. Bond had two for the hole from a yard. He didn't wait to be given the hole but walked up and putted. The ball stopped an inch short. Goldfinger walked off the green. Bond knocked the ball in. All square.

The third is a blind 240 yards, all carry, a difficult three. Bond chose his brassie and hit a good one. It would be on or near the green. Goldfinger's routine drive was well hit but would probably not have enough steam to carry the last of the rough and trickle down into the saucer of the green. Sure enough, Goldfinger's ball was on top of the protecting mound of rough. He had a nasty, cuppy lie, with a tuft just behind the ball. Goldfinger stood and looked at the lie. He seemed to make up his mind. He stepped past his ball to take a club from the caddie. His left foot came down just behind the ball, flattening the tuft. Goldfinger could now take his putter. He did so and trickled the ball down the bank towards the hole. It stopped three feet short.

Bond frowned. The only remedy against a cheat at golf is not to play with him again. But that was no good in this match. Bond had no intention of playing with the man again. And it was no good starting a you-did-I-didn't argument unless he caught Goldfinger doing something even more outrageous. Bond would just have to try and beat him, cheating and all.

Now Bond's twenty-foot putt was no joke. There was no question of going for the hole. He would have to concentrate on laying it dead. As usual, when one plays to go dead, the ball stopped short—a good yard short. Bond took a lot of trouble about the putt and holed it, sweating. He knocked Goldfinger's ball away. He would go on giving Goldfinger missable putts until suddenly Bond would ask him to hole one. Then that one might look just a bit more difficult.

Still all square. The fourth is 460 yards. You drive over one of the tallest and deepest bunkers in the United Kingdom and then have a long second shot across an undulating hilly fairway to a plateau green guarded by a final steep slope which makes it easier to take three putts than two.

Bond picked up his usual fifty yards on the drive and Goldfinger hit two of his respectable shots to the gully below the green. Bond, determined to get up, took a brassie instead of a spoon and went over the green and almost up against the boundary fence. From there he was glad to get down in three for a half.

The fifth was again a long carry, followed by Bond's favorite second shot on the course—over bunkers and through a valley between high sand dunes to a distant, taunting flag. It is a testing hole for which the first essential is a well-placed drive. Bond stood on the tee, perched high up in the sand hills, and paused before the shot while he gazed at the glittering distant sea and at the faraway crescent of white cliffs beyond Pegwell Bay. Then he took up his stance and visualized the tennis court of turf that was his target. He took the club back as slowly as he knew how and started down for the last terrific acceleration before the clubhead met the ball. There was a dull clang on his right. It was too late to stop. Desperately Bond focused the ball and tried to keep his swing all in one piece. There came the ugly clonk of a mishit ball. Bond's head shot up. It was a lofted hook. Would it have the legs? Get on! Get on! The ball hit the top of a mountain of rough and bounced over. Would it reach the beginning of the fairway?

Bond turned towards Goldfinger and the caddies, his eyes fierce. Goldfinger was straightening up. He met Bond's eyes indifferently. "Sorry. Dropped my driver."

"Don't do it again," said Bond curtly. He stood down off the tee and handed his driver to Hawker. Hawker shook his head sympathetically. Bond took out a cigarette and lit it. Goldfinger hit his drive the dead straight regulation 200 yards.

They walked down the hill in a silence which Goldfinger unexpectedly broke. "What is the firm you work for?"

"Universal Export."

"And where do they hang out?"

"London. Regent's Park."

"What do they export?"

Bond woke up from his angry ruminations. Here, pay attention! This is work, not a game. All right, he put you off your drive, but you've got your cover to think about. Don't let him needle you into making mistakes about it. Build up your story. Bond said casually, "Oh everything from sewing machines to tanks."

"What's your specialty?"

Bond could feel Goldfinger's eyes on him. He said, "I look after the small arms side. Spend most of my time selling miscellaneous ironmongery to sheiks and rajahs—anyone the Foreign Office decides doesn't want the stuff to shoot at us with.'

"Interesting work." Goldfinger's voice was flat, bored.

"Not very. I'm thinking of quitting. Came down here for a week's holiday to think it out. Not much future in England. Rather like the idea of Canada."

"Indeed?"

They were past the rough and Bond was relieved to find that his ball had got a forward kick off the hill on to the fairway. The fairway curved slightly to the left and Bond had even managed to pick up a few feet on Goldfinger. It was Goldfinger to play. Goldfinger took out his spoon. He wasn't going for the green but only to get over the bunkers and through the valley.

Bond waited for the usual safe shot. He looked at his own lie. Yes, he could take his brassie. There came the wooden thud of a mishit. Goldfinger's ball, hit off the heel, sped along the ground and into the stony wastes of Hell Bunker —the widest bunker and the only unkempt one, because of the pebbles, on the course.

For once Homer had nodded—or rather, lifted his head. Perhaps his mind had been half on what Bond had told him. Good show! But Goldfinger might still get down in three more. Bond took out his brassie. He couldn't afford to play safe. He addressed the ball, seeing in his mind's eye its eighty-eight-millimeter trajectory through the valley and then the two or three bounces that would take it on to the green. He laid off a bit to the right to allow for his draw. Now!

There came a soft clinking away to his right. Bond stood away from his ball. Goldfinger had his back to Bond. He was gazing out to sea, rapt in its contemplation, while his right hand played "unconsciously" with the money in his pocket.

Bond smiled grimly. He said, "Could you stop shifting bullion till after my shot?"

Goldfinger didn't turn round or answer. The noise stopped.

Bond turned back to his shot, desperately trying to clear his mind again. Now the brassie was too much of a risk. It needed too good a shot. He handed it to Hawker and took his spoon and banged the ball safely through the valley. It ran on well and stopped on the apron. A five, perhaps a four.

Goldfinger got well out of the bunker and put his chip dead. Bond putted too hard and missed the one back. Still all square.

The sixth, appropriately called "the Virgin," is a famous short hole in the world of golf. A narrow green, almost ringed with bunkers, it can need anything from an eight- to a two-iron according to the wind. Today, for Bond, it was a seven. He played a soaring shot, laid off to the right for the wind to bring it in. It ended twenty

feet beyond the pin with a difficult putt over and down a shoulder. Should be a three. Goldfinger took his five and played it straight. The breeze took it and it rolled into the deep bunker on the left. Good news! That would be the hell of a difficult three.

They walked in silence to the green. Bond glanced into the bunker. Goldfinger's ball was in a deep heel mark. Bond walked over to his ball and listened to the larks. This was going to put him one up. He looked for Hawker to take his putter, but Hawker was the other side of the green, watching with intent concentration Goldfinger play his shot. Goldfinger got down into the bunker with his blaster. He jumped up to get a view of the hole and then settled himself for the shot. As his club went up Bond's heart lifted. He was going to try and flick it out—a hopeless technique from that buried lie. The only hope would have been to explode it. Down came the club, smoothly, without hurry. With hardly a handful of sand the ball curved up out of the deep bunker, bounced once and lay dead!

Bond swallowed. Blast his eyes! How the hell had Goldfinger managed that? Now, out of sour grapes, Bond must try for his two. He went for it, missed the hole by an inch and rolled a good yard past. Hell and damnation! Bond walked slowly up to the putt, knocking Goldfinger's ball away. Come on, you bloody fool! But the specter of the big swing—from an almost certain one up to a possible one down— made Bond wish the ball into the hole instead of tapping it in. The coaxed ball, lacking decision, slid past the lip. One down!

Now Bond was angry with himself. He, and he alone, had lost that hole. He had taken three putts from twenty feet. He really must pull himself together and get going.

At the seventh, 1500 yards, they both hit good drives and Goldfinger's immaculate second lay fifty yards short of the green. Bond took his brassie. Now for the equalizer! But he hit from the top, his club head came down too far ahead of the hands and the smothered ball shot into one of the right-hand bunkers. Not a good lie, but he must put it on the green. Bond took a dangerous seven and failed to get it out.

Goldfinger got his five. Two down. They halved the short eighth in three. At the ninth, Bond, determined to turn only one down, again tried to do too much off a poor lie. Goldfinger got his four to Bond's five. Three down at the turn! Not too good. Bond asked Hawker for a new ball. Hawker unwrapped it slowly, waiting for Goldfinger to walk over the hillock to the next tee. Hawker said softly, "You saw what he did at the Virgin, sir?"

"Yes, damn him. It was an amazing shot."

Hawker was surprised. "Oh, you didn't see what he did in the bunker, sir?"

"No, what? I was too far away."

The other two were out of sight over the rise. Hawker silently walked down into one of the bunkers guarding the ninth green, kicked a hole with his toe and dropped the ball in the hole. He then stood just behind the half-buried ball with his feet close together. He looked up at Bond. "Remember he jumped up to look at the line to the hole, sir?"

"Yes."

"Just watch this, sir." Hawker looked towards the ninth pin and jumped, just as Goldfinger had done, as if to get the line. Then he looked up at Bond again and pointed to the ball at his feet. The heavy impact of the two feet just behind the ball had leveled the hole in which it had lain and had squeezed the ball out so that it was now perfectly teed for an easy shot—for just the easy cut-up shot which had seemed utterly impossible from Goldfinger's lie at the Virgin.

Bond looked at his caddie for a moment in silence. Then he said, "Thanks, Hawker. Give me the bat and the ball. Somebody's going to be second in this match, and I'm damned if it's going to be me."

"Yes, sir," said Hawker stolidly. He limped off on the shortcut that would take him halfway down the tenth fairway.

Bond sauntered slowly over the rise and down to the tenth tee. He hardly looked at Goldfinger who was standing on the tee swishing his driver impatiently. Bond was clearing his mind of everything but cold, offensive resolve. For the first time since the first tee, he felt supremely confident. All he needed was a sign from

heaven and his game would catch fire.

The tenth at the Royal St. Marks is the most dangerous hole on the course. The second shot, to the skiddy plateau green with cavernous bunkers to right and left and a steep hill beyond, has broken many hearts. Bond remembered that Philip Scrutton, out in four under fours in the Gold Bowl, had taken a fourteen at this hole, seven of them ping-pong shots from one bunker to another, to and fro across the green. Bond knew that Goldfinger would play his second to the apron, or short of it, and be glad to get a five. Bond must go for it and get his four.

Two good drives and, sure enough, Goldfinger well up on the apron with his second. A possible four. Bond took his seven, laid off plenty for the breeze and fired the ball off into the sky. At first he thought he had laid off too much, but then the ball began to float to the left. It pitched and stopped dead in the soft sand blown on to the green from the right-hand bunker. A nasty fifteen-foot putt. Bond would now be glad to get a half. Sure enough, Goldfinger putted up to within a yard. That, thought Bond as he squared up to his putt, he will have to hole. He hit his own putt fairly smartly to get it through the powdering of sand and was horrified to see it going like lightning across the skiddy green. God, he was going to have not a yard, but a two-yard putt back! But suddenly, as if drawn by a magnet, the ball swerved straight for the hole, hit the back of the tin, bounced up and fell into the cup with an audible rattle. The sign from heaven! Bond went up to Hawker, winked at him and took his driver.

They left the caddies and walked down the slope and back to the next tee. Goldfinger said coldly, "That putt ought to have run off the green."

Bond said off-handedly, "Always give the hole a chance!" He teed up his ball and hit his best drive of the day down the breeze. Wedge and one putt? Goldfinger hit his regulation shot and they walked off again. Bond said, "By the way, what happened to that nice Miss Masterton?"

Goldfinger looked straight in front of him. "She left my employ."

Bond thought, good for her! He said, "Oh,

I must get in touch with her again. Where did she go to?"

"I couldn't say." Goldfinger walked away from Bond towards his ball. Bond's drive was out of sight, over the ridge that bisected the fairway. It wouldn't be more than fifty yards from the pin. Bond thought he knew what would be in Goldfinger's mind, what is in most golfer's minds when they smell the first scent of a good lead melting away. Bond wouldn't be surprised to see that grooved swing quicken a trifle. It did. Goldfinger hooked into a bunker on the left of the green.

Now was the moment when it would be the end of the game if Bond made a mistake, let his man off the hook. He had a slightly downhill lie, otherwise an easy chip—but to the trickiest green on the course. Bond played it like a man. The ball ended six feet from the pin. Goldfinger played well out of his bunker, but missed the longish putt. Now Bond was only one down.

They halved the dogleg twelfth in inglorious fives and the longish thirteenth also in fives, Goldfinger having to hole a good putt to do so.

Now a tiny cleft of concentration had appeared on Goldfinger's massive, unlined forehead. He took a drink of water from the tap beside the fourteenth tee. Bond waited for him. He didn't want a sharp clang from that tin cup when it was out-of-bounds over the fence to the right and the drive into the breeze favoring a slice! Bond brought his left hand over to increase his draw and slowed down his swing. The drive, well to the left, was only just adequate, but at least it had stayed in bounds. Goldfinger, apparently unmoved by the out-of-bounds hazard, hit his standard shot. They both negotiated the transverse canal without damage and it was another half in five. Still one down and now only four to play.

The 460-yard fifteenth is perhaps the only hole where the long hitter may hope to gain one clear shot. Two smashing woods will just get you over the line of bunkers that lie right up against the green. Goldfinger had to play short of them with his second. He could hardly improve on a five and it was up to Bond to hit a really godlike second shot from a barely adequate drive.

The sun was on its way down and the shadows of the four men were beginning to lengthen. Bond had taken up his stance. It was a good lie. He had kept his driver. There was dead silence as he gave his two incisive waggles. This was going to be a vital stroke. Remember to pause at the top of the swing, come down slow and whip the clubhead through at the last second. Bond began to take the club back. Something moved at the corner of his right eye. From nowhere the shadow of Goldfinger's huge head approached the ball on the ground, engulfed it and moved on. Bond let his swing take itself to pieces in sections. Then he stood away from his ball and looked up. Goldfinger's feet were still moving. He was looking carefully up at the sky.

"Shades please, Goldfinger." Bond's voice was furiously controlled.

Goldfinger stopped and looked slowly at Bond. The eyebrows were raised a fraction in inquiry. He moved back and stood still, saying nothing.

Bond went back to his ball. Now then, relax! To hell with Goldfinger. Slam that ball on to the green. Just stand still and hit it. There was a moment when the world stood still, then . . . then somehow Bond did hit it—on a low trajectory that mounted gracefully to carry the distant surf of the bunkers. The ball hit the bank below the green, bounced high with the impact and rolled out of sight into the saucer around the pin.

Hawker came up and took the driver out of Bond's hand. They walked on together. Hawker said seriously, "That's one of the finest shots I've seen in thirty years." He lowered his voice. "I thought he'd fixed you then, sir."

"He damned nearly did, Hawker. It was Alfred Blacking that hit that ball, not me." Bond took out his cigarettes, gave one to Hawker and lit his own. He said quietly, "All square and three to play. We've got to watch those next three holes. Know what I mean?"

"Don't you worry, sir. I'll keep my eye on him."

They came up with the green. Goldfinger had pitched on and had a long putt for a four, but Bond's ball was only two inches away from the hole. Goldfinger picked up his ball and walked off the green. They halved the short sixteenth in good threes. Now there were the two long holes home. Fours would win them. Bond hit a fine drive down the center. Goldfinger pushed his far out to the right into deep rough. Bond walked along trying not to be too jubilant, trying not to count his chickens. A win for him at this hole and he would only need a half at the eighteenth for the match. He prayed that Goldfinger's ball would be unplayable or, better still, lost.

Hawker had gone on ahead. He had already laid down his bag and was busily—far too busily to Bond's way of thinking—searching for Goldfinger's ball when they came up.

It was bad stuff—jungle country, deep thick luxuriant grass whose roots still held last night's dew. Unless they were very lucky, they couldn't hope to find the ball. After a few minutes' search Goldfinger and his caddie drifted away still wider to where the rough thinned out into isolated tufts. That's good, thought Bond. That wasn't anything like the line. Suddenly he trod on something. Hell and damnation. Should he stamp it in? He shrugged his shoulders, bent down and gently uncovered the ball so as not to improve the lie. Yes it was a Dunlop 65. 'Here you are,' he called grudgingly. 'Oh no, sorry. You play with a number one, don't you?'

"Yes," came back Goldfinger's voice impatiently.

"Well, this is a number seven." Bond picked it up and walked over to Goldfinger.

Goldfinger gave the ball a cursory glance. He said, "Not mine," and went on poking among the tufts with the head of his driver.

It was a good ball, unmarked and almost new. Bond put it in his pocket and went back to his search. He glanced at his watch. The statutory five minutes was almost up. Another half-minute and by God he was going to claim the hole. Strict rules of golf, Goldfinger had stipulated. All right my friend, you shall have them!

Goldfinger was casting back towards Bond, diligently prodding and shuffling through the grass.

Bond said, "Nearly time, I'm afraid."

Goldfinger grunted. He started to say something when there came a cry from his caddie, "Here you are, sir. Number one Dunlop."

Bond followed Goldfinger over to where the caddie stood on a small plateau of higher ground. He was pointing down. Bond bent and inspected the ball. Yes, an almost new Dunlop one and in an astonishingly good lie. It was miraculous—more than miraculous. Bond stared hard from Goldfinger to his caddie. "Must have had the hell of a lucky kick," he said mildly.

The caddie shrugged his shoulders. Goldfinger's eyes were calm, untroubled. "So it would seem." He turned to his caddie. "I think we can get a spoon to that one, Foulks."

Bond walked thoughtfully away and then turned to watch the shot. It was one of Goldfinger's best. It soared over a far shoulder of rough towards the green. Might just have caught the bunker on the right.

Bond walked on to where Hawker, a long blade of grass dangling from his wry lips, was standing on the fairway watching the shot finish. Bond smiled bitterly at him. He said in a controlled voice, "Is my good friend in the bunker, or is the bastard on the green?"

"Green, sir," said Hawker unemotionally.

Bond went up to his ball. Now things had got tough again. Once more he was fighting for a half after having a certain win in his pocket. He glanced towards the pin, gauging the distance. This was a tricky one. He said, "Five or six?"

"The six should do it, sir. Nice firm shot." Hawker handed him the club.

Now then, clear your mind. Keep it slow and deliberate. It's an easy shot. Just punch it so that it's got plenty of zip to get up the bank and on to the green. Stand still and head down. Click! The ball, hit with a slightly closed face, went off on just the medium trajectory Bond had wanted. It pitched below the bank. It was perfect! No, damn it. It had hit the bank with its second bounce, stopped dead, hesitated and then rolled back and down again. Hell's bells! Was it Hagen who had said, "You drive for show, but you putt for dough"? Getting dead from below that bank was one of the most difficult putts on the course. Bond reached for his cigarettes and lit one, already preparing his mind for the next crucial shot to save the hole—so long as that bastard Goldfinger didn't hole his from thirty feet!

Hawker walked along by his side. Bond said, "Miracle finding that ball."

"It wasn't his ball, sir." Hawker was stating a fact.

"What do you mean?" Bond's voice was tense.

"Money passed, sir. White, probably a fiver. Foulks must have dropped that ball down his trouser leg."

"Hawker!" Bond stopped in his tracks. He looked round. Goldfinger and his caddie were fifty yards away, walking slowly towards the green. Bond said fiercely, "Do you swear to that? How can you be sure?"

Hawker gave a half-ashamed, lopsided grin. But there was a crafty belligerence in his eye. "Because his ball was lying under my bag of clubs, sir." When he saw Bond's open-mouthed expression he added apologetically, "Sorry, sir. Had to do it after what he's been doing to you. Wouldn't have mentioned it, but I had to let you know he's fixed you again."

Bond had to laugh. He said admiringly, "Well, you *are* a card, Hawker. So you were going to win the match for me all on your own!" He added bitterly, "But, by God, that man's the flaming limit. I've got to get him. I've simply got to. Now let's think!" They walked slowly on.

Bond's left hand was in his trousers pocket, absent-mindedly fingering the ball he had picked up in the rough. Suddenly the message went to his brain. Got it! He came close to Hawker. He glanced across at the others. Goldfinger had stopped. His back was to Bond and he was taking the putter out of his bag. Bond nudged Hawker. "Here, take this." He slipped the ball into the gnarled hand. Bond said softly, urgently, "Be certain you take the flag. When you pick up the balls from the green, whichever way the hole has gone, give Goldfinger this one. Right?"

Hawker walked stolidly forward. His face was expressionless. "Got it, sir," he said in his normal voice. "Will you take the putter for this one?"

"Yes." Bond walked up to his ball. "Give me a line, would you?"

Hawker walked up on to the green. He stood sideways to the line of the putt and then stalked round to behind the flag and crouched. He got up. "Inch outside the right lip, sir. Firm putt. Flag, sir?"

"No. Leave it in, would you."

Hawker stood away. Goldfinger was standing by his ball on the right of the green. His caddie had stopped at the bottom of the slope. Bond bent to the putt. Come on, Calamity Jane! This one has got to go dead or I'll put you across my knee. Stand still. Clubhead straight back on the line and follow through towards the hole. Give it a chance. Now! The ball, hit firmly in the middle of the club, had run up the bank and was on its way to the hole. But too hard, dammit! Hit the stick! Obediently the ball curved in, rapped the stick hard and bounced back three inches—dead as a doornail!

Bond let out a deep sigh and picked up his discarded cigarette. He looked over at Goldfinger. Now then, you bastard. Sweat that one out. And by God if you hole it! But Goldfinger couldn't afford to try. He stopped two feet short. "All right, all right," said Bond generously. "All square and one to go." It was vital that Hawker should pick up the balls. If he had made Goldfinger hole the short putt it would have been Goldfinger who would have picked the ball out of the hole. Anyway, Bond didn't want Goldfinger to miss that putt. That wasn't part of the plan.

Hawker bent down and picked up the balls. He rolled one towards Bond and handed the other to Goldfinger. They walked off the green, Goldfinger leading as usual. Bond noticed Hawker's hand go to his pocket. Now, so long as Goldfinger didn't notice anything on the tee!

But, with all square and one to go, you don't scrutinize your ball. Your motions are more or less automatic. You are thinking of how to place your drive, of whether to go for the green with the second or play to the apron, of the strength of the wind—of the vital figure four that must somehow be achieved to win or at least to halve.

Considering that Bond could hardly wait for Goldfinger to follow him and hit, just once, that treacherous Dunlop number seven that looked so very like a number one, Bond's own drive down the 450-yard eighteenth was praiseworthy.

If he wanted to, he could now reach the green—if he wanted to!

Now Goldfinger was on the tee. Now he had bent down. The ball was on the peg, its lying face turned up at him. But Goldfinger had straightened, had stood back, was taking his two deliberate practice swings. He stepped up to the ball, cautiously, deliberately. Stood over it, waggled, focusing the ball minutely. Surely he would see! Surely he would stop and bend down at the last minute to inspect the ball! Would the waggle never end? But now the clubhead was going back, coming down, the left knee bent correctly in towards the ball, the left arm straight as a ramrod. Crack! The ball sailed off, a beautiful drive, as good as Goldfinger had hit, straight down the fairway.

Bond's heart sang. Got you, you bastard! Got you! Blithely Bond stepped down from the tee and strolled off down the fairway planning the next steps which could now be as eccentric, as fiendish as he wished. Goldfinger was beaten already—hoist with his own petard! Now to roast him, slowly, exquisitely.

Bond had no compunction. Goldfinger had cheated him twice and got away with it. But for his cheats at the Virgin and the seventeenth, not to mention his improved lie at the third and the various times he had tried to put Bond off, Goldfinger would have been beaten by now. If it needed one cheat by Bond to rectify the score sheet that was only poetic justice. And besides, there was more to this than a game of golf. It was Bond's duty to win. By his reading of Goldfinger he *had* to win. If he was beaten, the score between the two men would have been equalized. If he won the match, as he now had, he would be two up on Goldfinger—an intolerable state of affairs, Bond guessed, to a man who saw himself as all powerful. This man Bond, Goldfinger would say to himself, *has* something. He has qualities I can use. He is a tough adventurer with plenty of tricks up his sleeve. This is the sort of man I need for—for what? Bond didn't know. Perhaps there would be nothing for him. Perhaps his reading of Goldfinger was wrong, but there was certainly no other way of creeping up on the man.

Goldfinger cautiously took out his spoon for the longish second over cross-bunkers to the narrow entrance to the green. He made one more practice swing than usual and then hit exactly the right, controlled shot up to the apron. A certain five, probably a four. Much good would it do him!

Bond, after a great show of taking pains, brought his hands down well ahead of the club and smothered his number three-iron so that the topped ball barely scrambled over the cross-bunkers. He then wedged the ball on to the green twenty feet past the pin. He was where he wanted to be—enough of a threat to make Goldfinger savor the sweet smell of victory, enough to make Goldfinger really sweat to get his four.

And now Goldfinger really was sweating. There was a savage grin of concentration and greed as he bent to the long putt up the bank and down to the hole. Not too hard, not too soft. Bond could read every anxious thought that would be running through the man's mind. Goldfinger straightened up again, walked deliberately across the green to behind the flag to verify his line. He walked slowly back beside his line, brushing away—carefully, with the back of his hand—a wisp or two of grass, a speck of top-dressing. He bent again and made one or two practice swings and then stood to the putt, the veins standing out on his temples, the cleft of concentration deep between his eyes.

Goldfinger hit the putt and followed through on the line. It was a beautiful putt that stopped six inches past the pin. Now Goldfinger would be sure that unless Bond sank his difficult twenty-footer, the match was his!

Bond went through a long rigmarole of sizing up his putt. He took his time, letting the suspense gather like a thunder cloud round the long shadows on the livid, fateful green.

"Flag out, please. I'm going to sink this one." Bond charged the words with a deadly certitude, while debating whether to miss the hole to the right or the left or leave it short. He bent to the putt and missed the hole well on the right.

"Missed it, by God!" Bond put bitterness and rage into his voice. He walked over to the hole and picked up the two balls, keeping them in full view.

Goldfinger came up. His face was glistening with triumph. "Well, thanks for the game. Seems I was just too good for you after all."

"You're a good nine handicap," said Bond with just sufficient sourness. He glanced at the balls in his hand to pick out Goldfinger's and hand it to him. He gave a start of surprise. "Hullo!" He looked sharply at Goldfinger. "You play a number one Dunlop, don't you?"

"Yes, of course." A sixth sense of disaster wiped the triumph off Goldfinger's face. "What is it? What's the matter?"

"Well," said Bond apologetically. "'Fraid you've been playing with the wrong ball. Here's my Penfold Hearts and this is a number seven Dunlop." He handed both balls to Goldfinger. Goldfinger tore them off his palm and examined them feverishly.

Slowly the color flooded over Goldfinger's face. He stood, his mouth working, looking from the balls to Bond and back to the balls.

Bond said softly, "Too bad we were playing to the rules. Afraid that means you lose the hole. And, of course, the match." Bond's eyes observed Goldfinger impassively.

"But, but . . ."

This was what Bond had been looking forward to—the cup dashed from the lips. He stood and waited, saying nothing.

Rage suddenly burst Goldfinger's usually relaxed face like a bomb. "It was a Dunlop seven you found in the rough. It was your caddie that gave me this ball. On the seventeenth green. He gave me the wrong ball on purpose, the damned che—"

"Here, steady on," said Bond mildly. 'You'll get a slander action on your hands if you aren't careful. Hawker, did you give Mr. Goldfinger the wrong ball by mistake or anything?'

"No, sir." Hawker's face was stolid. He said indifferently, "If you want my opinion, sir, the mistake may have been made at the seventeenth when the gentleman found his ball pretty far off the line we'd all marked it on. A seven looks very much like a one. I'd say that's what happened, sir. It would have been a miracle for the gentleman's ball to have ended up as wide as where it was found.'

"Tommyrot!" Goldfinger gave a snort of disgust. He turned angrily on Bond. "You saw that was a number one my caddie found."

Bond shook his head doubtfully. "I didn't really look closely, I'm afraid. However," Bond's voice became brisk, businesslike, "it's really the job of the player to make certain he's using the right ball, isn't it? I can't see that anyone else can be blamed if you tee the wrong ball up and play three shots with it. Anyway," he started walking off the green, "many thanks for the match. We must have it again one day."

Goldfinger, lit with glory by the setting sun, but with a long black shadow tied to his heels, followed Bond slowly, his eyes fixed thoughtfully on Bond's back.

An Amateur on Tour

by **GEORGE PLIMPTON**

George Plimpton has lived many sporting lives—pro football quarterback, baseball player, boxer and some-time amateur on the pro golf tour. With his eighteen handicap he represents all of us who want to tee it up with Arnold, Jack and Tom.

MY woes in golf, I have felt, have been largely psychological. When I am playing well, in the low nineties (my handicap is eighteen), I am still plagued with small quirks—a suspicion that, for example, just as I begin my downswing, my eyes straining with concentration, a bug or a beetle is going to sud-denly materialize on the golf ball.

When I am playing badly, far more massive speculation occurs: I often sense as I commit myself to a golf swing that my body changes its corporeal status completely and becomes a *me-chanical* entity, built of tubes and conduits, and boiler rooms here and there, with big dials and gauges to check, a Brobdingnagian structure put together by a team of brilliant engineers but manned largely by a dispirited, eccentric group of dissolutes—men with drinking problems, who do not see very well, and who are plagued by liver complaints.

The structure they work in is enormous. I see myself as a monstrous, manned colossus poised high over the golf ball, a spheroid that is barely discernible fourteen stories down on its tee. From above, staring through the windows of the eyes, which bulge like great bay porches, is an unsteady group (as I see them) of Japanese navymen—admirals, most of them. In their hands they hold ancient and useless voice tubes into which they yell the familiar orders: "Eye on the ball! Chin steady! Left arm stiff! Flex the knees! Swing from the inside out! Follow through! Keep head down!" Since the voice tubes are useless, the cries drift down the long corridors and shaftways between the iron ten-dons and muscles, and echo into vacant cham-bers and out, until finally, as a burble of sound, they reach the control centers. These posts are situated at the joints, and in charge are the disso-lutes I mentioned—typical of them a cantanker-ous elder perched on a metal stool, half a bottle of rye on the floor beside him, his ear cocked for the orders that he acknowledges with ancient epithets, yelling back up the corridors, "Ah, your father's mustache!" and such things, and if he's of a mind, he'll reach for the controls (like the banks of tall levers one remembers from a rail-road-yard switch house) and perhaps he'll pull the proper lever and perhaps not. So that, in sum, the whole apparatus, bent on hitting a golf ball smartly, tips and convolutes and lunges, the

Japanese admirals clutching each other for support in the main control center up in the head as the structure rocks and creaks. And when the golf shot is on its way the navymen get to their feet and peer out through the eyes and report: "A shank! A shank! My God, we've hit another shank!" They stir about in the control center drinking paper-thin cups of rice wine, consoling themselves, and every once in a while one of them will reach for a voice tube and shout:

"Smarten up down there!"

Down below, in the dark reaches of the structure, the dissolutes reach for their rye, tittering, and they've got their feet up on the levers and perhaps soon it will be time to read the evening newspaper.

It was a discouraging image to carry around in one's mind; but I had an interesting notion: a month on the professional golf tour (I had been invited to three tournaments), competing steadily and under tournament conditions before crowds and under the scrutiny of the pros with whom I would be playing, might result in five, perhaps even six, strokes being pruned from my eighteen handicap. An overhaul would result. My Japanese admirals would be politely asked to leave, and they would, bowing and smiling. The dissolutes would be removed from the control centers, grumbling, clutching their bottles of rye, many of them evicted bodily, being carried out in their chairs.

The replacements would appear—a squad of scientific blokes dressed in white smocks. Not too many of them. But a great tonnage of equipment would arrive with them—automatic equipment in gray-green boxes and computer devices that would be placed about and plugged in and set to clicking and whirring. The great structure would become almost entirely automatized. Life in the control center would change—boring, really, with the scientists looking out on the golf course at the ball and then twiddling with dials and working out estimations, wind resistance, and such things, and finally locking everything into the big computers; and with yawns working at the corners of their mouths because it was all so simple, they would push the "activate" buttons to generate the smooth motion in the great

structure that would whip the golf ball out toward the distant green far and true. Very dull and predictable. The scientists would scarcely find very much to say to each other after a shot. Perhaps "Y-e-s," very drawn out. "Y-e-s. Very nice." Occasionally someone down in the innards of the structure would appear down the long glistening corridors with an oil can, or perhaps with some brass polish to sparkle up the pipes.

That was the vision I had. I began the overhaul myself. I would obviously have to look the part. A month before I left on the tour, I outfitted myself completely and expensively with new golf equipment. I had played golf since I began (which was when I was twelve or so) with a white cloth golf bag that bore the trade name "Canvasback" for some reason; if the clubs were removed it collapsed on itself like an accordion, or like a pair of trousers being stepped out of. It was light as a feather, and caddies always looked jaunty and supercilious under its weight. I often carried it myself. It had a small pocket with room for three balls and some tees. It had eight clubs in it, perhaps nine—two woods and a putter and the rest, of course, irons with two or three missing—an outfit hardly suitable for tournament play.

So I bought the works. Clubs and a new bag. Sweaters. Argyle socks. A small plastic bag of gold golf tees. I bought some golf shoes with flaps that came down over the laces—my first pair; I had always used sneakers. The golf bag was enormous. It seemed a dull conservative color when I saw it in the late afternoon gloom of a Florida golf shop. But when I took it out on a practice round the next day, it glowed a rich oxblood color, like a vast sausage. It was very heavy with a metal bottom with brass studs around it, and when I first went out I felt guilty seeing it on a caddy's back. But the clubs let off a fine chinking sound as the bag was carried, as expensive and exclusive as the sound of a Cadillac door shutting to, and the fact that porters, caddies, and I myself, whoever carried it, were bent nearly double by its weight only seemed to add to its stature.

It was proper to have such an enormous bag.

Courtesy Golf Magazine

The success of golf owes much to celebrities like Bing Crosby, who started his "Clambake" over 30 years ago. It is now the Bing Crosby National Pro-Am and invitations to play are coveted by amateurs everywhere.

I thought of the caddies coming up the long hills of the Congressional on television, wearing the white coveralls with the numbers, and those huge bags—MacGregors, Haigs or Wilsons, with the pros' names stamped down the front—with the wiping towels dangling, and the bags nearly slantwise across their shoulders, with one hand back to steady it so the weight would be more properly distributed.

Still, I never really got accustomed to my great golf bag. The woods had brown woolen covers on them. In my early practice rounds in the East I used to follow the clubs at quite a distance, and off to one side, as they were carried down the fairway, as one might circle at a distance workmen moving a harpsichord into one's home—self-conscious and a little embarrassed.

I was particularly aware of the big bag on trips—particularly lugging it around in a railroad station or an air terminal, where intense men with briefcases hurry past, and there are tearful farewells going on, and melancholy groups of military people stand around with plastic name tags on their tunics to tell us who they are. A golf bag is such an immense symbol of frivolity in these parlous times, so much bigger than a tennis racket. When I arrived in Los Angeles by plane to head upstate for the Crosby tournament, the terminal seemed filled with soldiers. There had been many on my plane. At the baggage claim counter the gray-green military duffel bags began coming down the conveyor belt, one after another, and the soldiers would heft them off and set them to one side in a great mound. My golf bag appeared among them with its rich ox-blood glow, obscene, jingling slightly as it came toward me on the conveyor.

A porter gave me a hand with it. We got it outside to the traffic ramp with the rest of my luggage and he waited while I arranged to rent a car for the long ride up to Monterey.

"You must be going up to the tournament," the porter said.

"Why, yes," I said gratefully. "The Crosby."

"George Knudson just came through a while ago," he said. "And George Archer. Always tell him 'cause he's, man, *tall.*"

"That's right," I said. "He's as tall as they come."

He hefted the bag into the trunk of the car.

"They set you up with a new bag, I see."

The bag was so new that a strong odor drifted from it—a tang of furniture polish.

"A great big one," I said. "They're getting bigger, it seems."

I fished in my pocket for a tip.

"Well, good luck up there," he said. He wanted me to tell him my name, some name he would recognize from the tour so he could announce to them back in the terminal, "Well, you know, so-and-so just came through . . . on his way up to the Crosby."

"I guess I just head *north,*" I said. I waved an arm, and stepped into the car.

"Yes, that's where it is. Up the coast." He smiled. "Well, good luck," he said. "I play to a five myself."

"No kidding?" I said.

"Well, that's nothing compared to you guys. I play out on the municipal course. And at Ramble Beach."

"A five handicap is nothing to be sneezed at," I said.

"I wish it was a four," he said.

"Sure," I said. "Well . . ." I tried hard to think of an appropriate golf term.

"Well, *pop it,*" I said.

He looked startled.

"I mean really *pop* it out there."

A tentative smile of appreciation began to work at his features. I put the car in gear and started off. As I looked in the rear view mirror I could see him staring after the car.

. . . . .

The easiest book to turn to in the book bag, when I had an hour or so to loll around in my room or out on the terrace that overlooked the eighteenth fairway and the ocean beyond, was a volume called *The Golfer's Handbook.* It is a British publication, thick as an almanac, and in it is every conceivable golfing record. You can find out who won the Isle of Wight Ladies' Championship in 1929 (Mrs. P. Snelling).

The book, for all its statistics, rules and tables, has an odd and refreshing individuality and, indeed, an irreverence about golf which in my difficulties with the game I found very comforting. Most of the character of the book turns up in the section entitled "Miscellaneous," which includes such topics, identified by subheadings, as "Freak Matches"; "Birds and Animals Interfering with Golf Balls and Attacking Players"; "Dark, Playing In"; "Golf Links on Fire"; "Longest Holes"; "Legless Golfers"; "Balls Hit to and from Great Heights"; etc., etc. The paragraphs under such head are sprightly and often, typical of British journals such as *Country Life,* are the ultimate in minutiae. For example, the following item of absolutely no consequence, with a bit of ethnic editorializing, appears under the heading "Miscellaneous Incidents and Strange Golfing Facts": "In a competition at Cragentinny, Edinburgh, 13th May, 1939, a player, when looking for his ball in the rough, found seven others. This incident of golfing treasure-trove is all the more remarkable as it happened in Scotland."

The editors may be interested in little harmless digs of this sort, but there is also a somewhat more Satanic edge to be found—especially under the odd heading, "Hit by Ball—Distance of Rebound." A number of cases are given. The following is representative: "Mr. R. J. Barton . . . was approaching the green of a blind hole 354 yards long. When his ball struck a caddy, named John M'Niven, on the head as he was replacing the flag in the hole, the ball rebounded 42 yards 2 feet 10 inches, which distance was measured twice in the presence of three people." This ends the item, without a word about the caddy whom I've always imagined sitting dolefully on the edge of a bunker holding his head between his hands while the measuring tapes are being stretched out and one fellow is calling, ". . . and 2 feet 10 inches. Got that, Tom?" And the other, holding the tape, is saying, "What's that again?"

"Two feet ten!"

"Right. Got it."

This record took place on September 1, 1913 at Machrie on the Isle of Aran, Scotland. The former record was a rebound of 34 yards off a caddy's noggin conked in August, 1908 on the Blairgowrie Golf Course. The *world's record,* which still stands, happened on September 28, 1913, at the 7th hole of the Premier Mine Golf Course in South Africa. A 150-yard drive by Edward W. Sladward hit a native caddy on the forehead just above the right eye and the ball, which was a "Colonel," bounded back on a direct line seventy-five yards. The tapes were brought out and the distance, as in the case of the John M'Niven affair, was measured. The native's name was not recorded (a sign of those times and perhaps the locale) but it was reported that he suffered no more than a slight abrasion of the skin and was able to continue. The ball's name, though, the Colonel, got into the records, and so does a description of the drive which produced the record: ". . . one so dear to the heart of a golfer—a hard, raking shot."

I have often thought about the scene, just as I have about the John M'Niven rebound—particularly about the Colonel golf ball.

"Charlie, what's that distance again?"

"It's seventy-*five,* seventy-five *yards.*"

"Good Lord. That has it all over the Islay record."

"What? I can hardly hear you."

"It beats the Machrie record."

"I've got the tape absolutely stretched out. Are you holding it at your end?"

"Right! Oh lord, Charlie, I've got the record!"

"Bully! Edward! Bully for you."

"A hard, raking shot, Charlie."

"What?"

"It was a Colonel I hit. A Colonel."

(A side glance at the caddie.) "A what?"

"A Colonel."

"Oh, a Colonel *ball.* Bully for the Colonel. Oh bully," etc.

Violence quite evidently fascinates golf editors. In *The Golfer's Handbook* they have chosen to immortalize the following: "At Texas [the editors are often vague as to exact place names] Mr. Moody Weaver in a practice swing used such force that he broke his leg in two places." Or this: "At Darwin, Australian, in 1951, a lady, so excited by a successful shot, threw up her hands, stepped back and stumbled over her golf bag. She fell and broke her arms above the wrists."

By chance, I actually received further news from the Moody Weaver people. His daughter wrote, in fact, that *The Golfer's Handbook* information was not completely accurate. The father had fallen and broken *both* legs rather than one leg in two places. The event, which she wished cleared up, took place in Wichita Falls.

The *Handbook* editors are quick to chronicle the hazards of nature on the golf course: "At Rose Bay, New South Wales, D.J. Bayly MacArthur, on stepping into a bunker, began to sink. He shrieked for help and was rescued when up to the armpits." Or: "A magnificent beech tree with a trunk five feet in diameter, at Killermont Golf Club, Glasgow, collapsed when hit by a ball driven by a member."

Since the editors are often scanty with details about items that beg for amplification, one of the particular pleasures of browsing through the *Handbook* is the flow it can give one's imagination, as in the case of those rebound records. For example, the first item under the heading "Freak Matches" reads: "In 1912, the late Harry Dearth, an eminent vocalist, attired in a complete suit of heavy armor, played a match at Bushey Hall. He was beaten by two and one." One can only lean back and speculate. "Two and one" means that in match play—competing for each hole rather than for overall score, which is medal play—the armor-suited golfer was beaten when he was down two holes with only one to play. What sort of a golfer must his opponent have been to allow the armor-clad gent to stay in contention until the seventeenth hole? Was he somehow equivalently handicapped—playing out of a potato sack, for example? Perhaps his game suffered from the embarrassment of playing with someone who creaked and swayed in armor down the fairways. Did Dearth do any sudden singing? That could explain it. Just at the backswing to have that singer's voice boom out, muffled by the visor but still concussive, with an added timbre by dint of coming from the great voice box of iron.

Sometimes there is an item that is pleasant to visualize, like a cartoon: "At Dungannon Golf Links, County Tyrone, October 1936, a ram attacked two players on the seventh green. They tried to beat it off with their clubs but were unsuccessful . . ."

Typically, the *Handbook* does not specify what it means by "unsuccessful," whether, indeed, the players survived the assaults by the rams, and got back to the clubhouse to have a shaky whiskey, or whether the rams prevailed completely, and did them in, so that their lifeless forms had to be removed when discovered the next morning by the greenskeepers:

". . . Charlie, put in a call for a wheelbarrow. Have a couple of them sent down from the toolshed so we can get these two members carted away before the first foursome comes through."

"Right."

"Nasty business cluttering up the course like this. A matter for the Greens Committee . . ." etc.

I could always count on the *Handbook*. It was a fine relief from the realities of my travails out on the golf course.

The trouble with *The Golfer's Handbook* was that it was not a practical solution to my golfing woes. That evening, after supper, I came back to my room and looked at the notes I had kept of my day's play at Monterey. I found that one bad shot was almost invariably followed by another,

and then another, until there was a whole stretch of them to assault one's poise.

Fifth: Fair drive. Long iron to right of green, ball lodging under tire of Cushman pickup truck. Truck carefully moved. Poked ball on green with six-iron. Three-putted, missing two-footer.

Sixth: Feeling low about two-footer. Apologized to Bruno. Hit drive out of bounds. Hit another drive out of bounds. Apologized again. Picked up and left Bruno responsible for the hole.

Seventh: Hit drive fifteen feet into gully. In appalling mental condition. Apologized . . .

It is one of the precepts of golf that a bad shot is best dismissed from mind immediately. It is not easy to do. Perhaps the one who could do it best was Walter Hagen, who was famous for his bad shots, particularly off his woods, the weakest department of his game. He accepted the fact that a wild shot would come from time to time, and rather than fretting and being nervous and wondering when it would come, he allowed it to, and then did not let it disturb him when it did. I could not emulate him. My fingers twitched nervously as I thought back on those long strings of flubs.

I spent some time that evening going over my notebooks to see if there wasn't a phrase I had copied which would be helpful. I had written down a number of aphorisms—the golf books were absolutely chock-full of them—and my notion was that if studied they might have the same effect that slogans and such commands as THINK pinned on the office walls are supposed to have on company employees.

I turned the pages and stared at a Harry Vardon suggestion: "Perfect confidence and a calm mind are necessary for the success of every stroke."

I began shifting uneasily in the armchair as I reflected on the cluttered state of my own mind. Perhaps, it occurred to me, I could try the next day to let my mind go *absolutely blank* as I stood over the ball—that I could produce a vacuum rid of Japanese admirals, the paraphernalia of that battleship control room, voices and commands stilled—*that* might be the "calm mind" to which Vardon referred. There was a school of golf instruction, I knew, whose precepts were simply to forget everything and get up and sock the ball. But I had my doubts. Is there not the famous children's wager: "Hey, I'll bet you a dollar you can't stop thinking of the word 'rhinoceros' for two minutes, that's all, two minutes, starting *now*"? Well, it's impossible, of course, because no matter how hard you think of tulips or maiden aunts who died tragically in auto crashes, the rhinoceros nibbles at the edges of your mind, stomping around out there, and then suddenly he is *inside,* and if you are honest you pay up and admit that not only is he in your mind but he's crowding its borders with his bulk.

I had sensed that the same thing would happen with my Japanese—I might get them out of the control room for a while—the area suddenly vacant and vast like an empty silo—but soon enough a steel door would creak, and there they would be, smiling and bowing, reaching for the voice trumpets . . .

I skimmed the pages and came across another suggestion by Harry Vardon, this one a recommendation that the golfer wear suspenders and a coat. His notion was that it helped "hold the shoulders together."

I hurried to the next; culled from Henry Cotten's book, it read: "Imagine the ball has little legs, and chop them off."

Then I came to a sheaf of notes under a paper clip which seemed more worthy of study. I had put them together some months before. They dealt with the "waggle"—namely, the movement of the clubhead before beginning the swing. Could my trouble lie here? It seemed farfetched, but then I had collected the waggle material because many golf authorities believe that a very specific type of waggle is not only helpful but essential to the execution of a great golf swing. Bernard Darwin, in an essay engagingly entitled "Some Reflections on Waggling," felt that a change in waggle, if things were going badly, was a definite help.

The purpose of the waggle, of course, is to see that everything is perfectly adjusted for the stroke. It is simply impossible to hit a golf shot without some sort of preliminary physical action. In his chapter Darwin speaks of two schools of wagglers. In the first, there are those who indulge in the quickest action possible (three examples of his time were Taylor, Duncan and Ray). Doug Sanders would be a contemporary example of this school. There is a slight jiggle that moves the material of his golfing trousers as he sets himself, but his club stays right behind the ball until the actual process of his shot begins. In the second school are those who rely very heavily on the waggle to get started, who simply cannot begin without it—". . . like the toy animals," Darwin writes, "who have to have a key inserted in their stomachs before they will walk around the floor." Baird and Herd and Hilton were representatives of this latter school. Darwin wrote of Herd's waggle as being a cumulative preliminary, and that, gradually, with his waggles, he lashed himself into a "sort of divine fury before hitting the ball."

In more recent times Tommy Armour was noted for his waggle—maneuvering as many as fifty times before getting his shot off. He also thought of it as an exercise which "accumulated" power.

Perhaps the oddest waggle notion was that suggested by Eddie Loos. He was the author of the famous theory "let the club swing you," in which he urged golfers to forget about balance and arms and forward press and where the elbows are, and so forth—just forget all that doctrinaire advice and concentrate instead on getting the "feel of the club." To do this he suggested waggling one's name in the air, writing it out as if the club were a gigantic pen, the longer the name the better, and doing it as often as one could, not only as a waggle but while walking down the fairway or waiting for one's partner to hit. "Feel the clubhead and let it swing you." That was what Loos kept telling people. He evolved his theory from watching the golf game of a one-legged player who shot consistent rounds in the low seventies—Ernest Jones (a relatively short name to waggle in the air), a flier who had lost a leg in the war, and who could sit in a chair and hit the ball 200 yards. There were many golfers who subscribed to the theory. Leo

Diegel, just as an experiment, shot a round in the seventies standing on one foot. The father of Manuel de la Torre of our foursome—Angel, his name was—was employed as a professional at the Lakes Shore Country Club in Glencoe, Illinois, where the experiment started. I had asked Manuel if he was a proponent of the system. He said that he had been started off in the system, willy-nilly, because he was only eighteen months old when he was given his first club, cut down to a foot and a half, and since he couldn't talk or understand very much, certainly not the arcane instructive phrases of golf, at the beginning he was surely a natural student of the "Let the club swing you" school.

I set my notes aside and left the room for the lodge and a nightcap. I sat down at a small iron garden table in the bar and ordered a drink. The place was crowded.

"Mind if I sit down?"

I looked up. A long-faced man was standing by the table. He had a drink in his hand.

"Not at all," I said. "Have a chair."

He sat down and put his legs straight out.

"Had a good round today?" he asked. "I take it you're in the tournament."

"Yes," I said. "But I had a rotten round."

"Too bad." He had a very sunburned face, too pink for the almost leathery copper color of the pros. So I took him for an amateur. Probably a very good one. He had said "Too bad" with a certain superior sense of pity.

"I've just been sitting in my room reading about the waggle," I told him.

"The waggle?"

"Some people think it's important. You can see I'm reaching for straws. You're supposed to write your name in the air with your club."

"I'll say," he said. "The waggle? Hell, a waggle's a waggle."

"Darwin says . . ."

"Darwin? That old guy." He held up a hand. "Hold on," he said. He turned and gulped down his drink and ordered another. "I'll tell you what my philosophy is. What you need is confidence. Pure and simple. That's what the game is. Confidence. Concentration. Control. The three C's. That's all that the game is about."

"I see," I said.

"That's all you need to quote to yourself—those three C's."

"I know a Vardon quote," I said. "Just been reading it. Let's see: 'A golfer must never be morbid. Perfect confidence and a calm mind are necessary for the success of every stroke.'"

"Yes, yes," he said impatiently. "Boy, you certainly know some old fogies."

"Well, he agrees with you, it turns out," I said.

"Confidence *is* the thing," the golfer went on. "You got to have that. That's the first C. Very important. Byron Nelson used to say that at the height of his career when things were going good for him he could actually *tell* during a practice round whether he was going to win a tournament. He'd let his wife in on the secret. He'd say, 'Hey, stick that chicken in the oven 'cause we're going to celebrate!' Or take Ken Venturi. Before he got the shakes and that circulatory trouble in his hands, he could do it. His wife once admired a Ford Thunderbird they were giving away as a bonus to the tournament winner, and he said, 'Don't worry, honey, I'll get it for you.' Well, he did, and he said, 'I told you so.'"

"Well, I understand all that," I said. "I *want* to have confidence. But it isn't the sort of thing . . ."

"The most confident player I ever heard of was Max Faulkner. What confidence he had. In the Open Championship at Portrush, Northern Ireland, in 1951, he autographed a fan's book 'Open Champion'—and there were still two rounds to go. He made it too."

"I've read quite a bit about him," I said. "He used to have those old caddies. He had one called Turner, who had a great red flowing beard . . ."

The golfer looked at me and said: "You certainly pick up strange pieces of information. A reader, eh? Let me give you something that might be more helpful to your game."

"Yes," I said, "a redheaded caddie is not—"

"Take concentration—the second of those three C's. Let me tell you a story about Claude Harmon and concentration. Claude Harmon once told me that Hogan comes to him the year the Open was played at Winged Foot, which is Harmon's home course in New York and thus duck soup for him—every curl and swoop of it known—and Hogan says, 'You can win this. You should. But you won't. Because you play "jolly golf." '

"That riles the hell out of Harmon.

" 'I'm telling you absolutely honest,' Hogan says. 'You can't play your own course half-decent. You haven't got a game plan. I could give you one, but you won't accept it, because you're stuck on "jolly golf." '

"Harmon stomps around and that phrase 'jolly golf' upsets him so much that he says he'll put himself entirely at Hogan's disposal—y'know, he would accept whatever directions Hogan gives him.

" 'All right,' Hogan says. He lays down a number of directives. They were: 'Don't answer any phones, not for a day or so before the tournament; you being a home pro, people are going to be telephoning for tickets, parking stickers, God knows what all, and Winged Foot's got a good staff to handle all that; so no phones. Then, get to the tournament exactly one half-hour before tee-off time; practice, but don't talk to anyone. On the way to the first tee, don't lift your eyes off the ground; don't lift your eyes off the ground for the *entire round*—it'll save you having to talk or listen to anyone; no one's likely to start a conversation unless you're looking him in the eye; just plod around staring at the ground, and keep your mind on the game. Don't say anything to anyone—don't say "good shot"; don't say a damn word. On the eighteenth, after you hole out, clear off of the course; don't stay around; go home.'

"That's tough on Harmon," the golfer continued. "He says, 'Can't I say anything to anyone then?' Very petulant. He's a very gregarious sort, big jowls, a howling loud voice, full of stories and he loves to talk.

" 'No,' says Hogan. 'You go home, and you think about the next day.'

"Harmon tells me that was the hardest thing," the golfer explained. "You see, you walk by the front terrace at Winged Foot with all the members sitting there, and they call out your name and they know how you've done and you know they got a big grin working, waiting for you to look up, and if you don't, if you don't recognize them, you don't last long as a club pro."

"What happened?" I asked.

"Well, Claude told me he resisted it. But he sneaks out the back way."

"Did it work?" I asked. "Claude Harmon's game plan?"

"Damn right," he said. "He didn't cop it all—but he got a 284 to Billy Casper's 282, just two strokes off the pudding."

"I wonder if Hogan lives up to his own directives?" I asked. "Does he ever talk during a round?"

"Harmon tells me never," said the golfer. "Never says a damn word. He told me that the last day of the Masters at Augusta in 1947, he was paired with Ben. Harmon made a hole-in-one on the twelfth hole. Hogan never said a thing. The people were screaming, of course, when they went down the fairway, and they got to the green, and there was the ball wedged in the hole against the flag. The first words Harmon hears Hogan say are to his caddie. He says, 'Get that flag out of there.' Hogan had a long putt for a two and he made it for his par. On the way to the next tee he said something about Claude's hole-in-one shot but he waited until then—until he'd got his own ball down."

"That's quite a story," I said when he had done. "Did you try the Hogan plan yourself today?"

"Damn right," the golfer said. "Didn't say anything to anyone. Just plodded around looking at the ground. Maybe that's why I'm talking so much now. Got a whole eighteen holes of gab to get off my chest."

"Well, how did it work?"

"Didn't work at all!" he said. He gave a short burst of laughter and he took a swallow of his drink. "I shot a ninety-five on my own ball—didn't help the team a damn. I think we're lying ninety-second in the field. I tell you, trudging along looking at the ground through those last holes, I felt like a mourner following a coffin. I found a dime just off the twelfth green. Only positive thing I can say about the whole day."

"That's too bad," I said.

"Ah well. Now the third of those C's is Control," he said, moving on blithely. "What I mean by that is control of both the physical and mental. How are your nerves out there? Not so good, eh? Well, that's natural. And proper. Bobby Jones said that the worst symptom he could find in himself in a tournament was the absence of nervousness. But nerves must be kept under control. Sam Snead had a great word for it: 'cool-mad'—controlled tension, that's what he was talking about . . . You ever hear that phrase? Good one, isn't it? I think about it all the time. So there you have the three C's. Confidence. Concentration. Control. That's all the game is about."

"I know an interesting thing about Jones," I said.

The golfer looked at me across the brim of his drink.

"Well, he used to relax those nerves of his by lying in a tub of hot water after a round of golf and drinking a stiff highball. He said that was the finest relaxing combination he knew. Then he would get into bed and read. At Flossmoor, the year he was competing in the National Amateur Championship, he was reading Papini's *Life of Christ.*"

"No kidding?"

He put his glass on the table.

"Where do you get all this information?"

"I have this book bag," I said. "I browse through it. You get a lot of interesting stuff. I don't know how *valuable* it is. It's confusing sometimes. You read about Jones and his relaxing and reading, and *then* you find out that Hagen had three hours of sleep and a hangover when he won the National Open in 1919. Sometimes the stuff is pretty esoteric. I mean last night I read a long paragraph by Henry Cotton on how to tee up the ball—you'd think *that* would be easy enough, but no, he has a special way of using the back of the hand so you get the tee the same height each time."

"What else?" asked the golfer.

"Well, a little while ago I read that Vardon thought a golfer's game would be improved if he wore suspenders and a coat. He felt it kept the swing more compact."

"Oh, yes," said the golfer. "Well, he may have a point. I mean the game's crazy enough anyway. Maybe a guy *should* get himself dolled up in a suit—hell, an *overcoat.* Why not? And he should get himself a red-bearded caddie, like that guy you were talking about, and what's that book . . . ?"

"Papini's *Life of Christ?*"

". . . Papini's *Life of Christ,* and walk around the course with it under his arm. He might have a helluva round."

I couldn't tell if he was being cynical or not. He was turning his drink rapidly in his hand.

He shook his head. "Jesus, after today I tell you I'm willing to try anything."

"How about those three C's?" I said. "That seems an awfully solid base right there."

"Jesus, I don't know," he said.

Up the Tower

by **HENRY LONGHURST**

In an industry where there is often too much talk, Henry Longhurst invented "brilliant flashes of silence" and became maybe the best television golf commentator ever to call a shot. Longhurst's honesty, humor and vast golf knowledge won him admiration throughout the golf world. Here he describes his early adventures in medialand.

LIFE is a mixed bag—chances offered and taken, more often chances missed or not even noticed. Successes are sometimes to be scored by honest toil and solid worth, more often by happening to be standing somewhere, thinking of nothing, at exactly the right time. In the latter category may be placed my entry into broadcasting, which for about thirty-five years has been one of the most pleasurable activities of my life.

Television is, by comparison with radio, a pushover. In television—I am talking, of course, of golf—in times of local difficulty, which means quite often, you can always intersperse what Sydney Smith, referring to the loquacious Macaulay's conversation at dinner, called "brilliant flashes of silence," and, indeed, as I hope to show in due course, this may gain you much merit. In other words, you can always sit back

and let them look at the picture. In radio, if your mind goes blank for three seconds, they think the set has gone wrong. It is essential, therefore, in an emergency to possess the ability to "waffle on," and with this from the first I never had any great difficulty—on the radio or anywhere else, come to that!

I believe I can claim to have done the first "live" outside radio broadcast on golf when the BBC (British Broadcasting Corporation) set up a glass box on stilts at some vantage point far out on the Little Aston course outside Birmingham, overlooking two greens and three tees. In a way we were not unsuccessful. We saw plenty of play, chopping and changing from one hole to another, and had an added piece of good fortune when a past British Open champion, Arthur Havers, completely fluffed a short approach shot in front of our window. Perhaps he was unnerved by the thought of being on "live" for the first time in history.

Then the BBC brought in a portable apparatus with which it was to be possible actually to follow the golf, and here the initiator, at the English Amateur Championship at Birkdale the year before the war, was the doyen of our profession, Bernard Darwin. He set off onto the course accompanied by two engineers, one carrying a portmanteau-shaped apparatus strapped to his back with a long aerial sticking up vertically behind his head, and the other lugging around the batteries. I naturally listened with professional interest, having been invited to carry out a similar venture at the Amateur Championship at the Royal Liverpool Golf Club at Hoylake later on.

It was soon pretty clear that the venerable Darwin was finding it heavy going and it was no surprise when he declared, on returning to the clubhouse, that golf, so far as he was concerned, did not lend itself to this type of broadcasting.

At Hoylake on the morning of the Amateur Championship quarterfinals, we tried to follow the play but soon came up against the elementary stumbling block that in order to describe the play you had to see it, and in order to see it you had to be within range of the players, and they could therefore hear what you were saying, which was not only extremely embarrassing but led to persistent cries of "sshhhh" from the silent spectators. For the afternoon semifinals, we set ourselves up on a knoll beside the fifth fairway, well out of the way but with a reasonable view of the distant play. It seems incredible today but the signal for us to start was to be the lowering of a white handkerchief by an engineer perched on the roof of the Royal Liverpool clubhouse.

The exact hour of the broadcast in those days had to be printed in advance, so there was no flexibility in time. The first semifinal came to us and passed, then came the second. At this point the engineer raised the white handkerchief and we were under starter's orders. He lowered it briskly, and we were "off"—whereupon the second match vanished from sight, leaving our little trio silent upon a knoll in Hoylake, unable to move since our range was only a mile. I state with confidence that I gave an absolutely splendid and dramatic eyewitness account of the play, understandably interspersed with a good deal of the "Wish you were here . . . lovely view across the bay" sort of stuff, and I could not help feeling that not everyone could have waffled continuously or to such effect for ten whole minutes about nonexistent play. I thus returned to the

clubhouse feeling that a congratulatory hand or two might well be extended. Instead, we met the engineer. He was most apologetic. "We had to fade you out after a minute or two," he said, "on account of a technical hitch."

Much as I respect the club, Hoylake has never been my happy hunting ground for either radio or television. In 1936, when golf on the radio was comparatively new, the engineer and I were stuck in a tiny, glass-fronted box situated among the guy-ropes at the back of the refreshment tent, with barely room for ourselves and a suspended microphone. Firstly, one day's play in the Open was cancelled on account of a snowstorm—in July—and I had to do three ten-minute pieces on a program going out across the British Empire, filling in for a whole day's play that had never taken place. Then a couple of friends espied me from afar and with schoolboy delight advanced upon our humble box.

I was in full spate when they came and made rude two-fingered gestures outside the box, pressing their noses against the glass and generally carrying on as though provoking a monkey in a cage. Finally, when once again we were in full flow, a waitress came out behind the refreshment tent carrying an enormous pile of plates. The strange spectacle in our little box so distracted her attention that she tripped over a guy-rope and sank with a crash that reverberated throughout the Empire. I explained what it was and gather that it gave innocent pleasure as far away as New Zealand.

The first serious attempts in Britain to televise live golf were directed by Antony Craxton, who used to do the queen's Christmas broadcasts. Many were from Wentworth, which, in summer, with the trees in full glory and a shirt-sleeved crowd moving from hole to hole enjoying themselves in the sunshine, can present a magnificent picture. I remember Craxton saying how golf even then attracted quite a large "rating" by comparison with what had been expected, and how many housewives on housing estates said that they knew nothing about it but liked to watch because "it seemed such a lovely place." Nowadays, of course, this holds good to a much greater extent and some of the scenes in color—on British television so much superior to the American color, for once, due to different "line" standards—can be really heavenly.

For myself I always thought the "beauty shots" and the little irrelevancies—though we seem to have time for few of them these days—added to the appeal of golfing programs: the 360° panorama of, say, Turnberry, with the Clyde and the Isle of Arran and the long encircling arm of the Mull of Kintyre and Ailsa Craig; or Muirfield, with the distant tracery of the two great Forth Bridges and the Kingdom of Fife on the other side of the Firth; or St. Andrews and the bay and the snow-capped Cairngorms; or, again, the small boy at the eighth at Wentworth who, immediately after the last match had passed by, emerged from the undergrowth and started fishing in the pond; or the lark's nest focused upon by an alert cameraman at Muirfield during the Open. The producer had to sacrifice this camera for quite a while before the mother lark returned to the nest to feed the young, and there were many who afterwards said that this was the best bit in the program, never mind Jack Nicklaus. The same cameraman's roving eye and telephoto lens discerned a couple on the sand hills just outside the course and it was nip and tuck whether their subsequent union would appear, live and in color, for the first time on this or any other screen. If only the producer had been under notice from the BBC at the time, he might have risked his arm and given the world a most entertaining exposure—and I sometimes wonder what I should have made of the commentary.

What we put up with in the early days of TV golf never ceases to surprise me. For a Walker Cup match at St. Andrews I was stuck up on a tall tower out by the "Loop," where the holes crisscross over each other at the far end of the course, making it almost impossible on a small monitor to detect who is playing which hole and who is crossing over playing a different hole. Once again the wind howled in, direct from the North Sea and twice as strongly at forty feet up as on the ground, and soon it was so cold that one became numbed. Nor were the senses quickened

by the fact that the British team lost every match on both days. For the second sitting I borrowed a fine, fur-collared flying coat from the barman at the Scores Hotel, but once again I gradually froze, to such an extent that I eventually found myself huddled over the blurred picture, thinking how poor it was and that there wasn't even a commentary. It was quite a time before the penny dropped. I suppose I can claim the doubtful distinction of being the only BBC commentator who has actually forgotten to do the commentary.

Another time, at St. Andrews, it was the picture that failed and I heard frantic voices from London saying, "Tell him to do a sound commentary till we get the picture back." This was really like old times and the "lovely view across the bay" stuff came back as naturally as though it were yesterday. In fact, at St. Andrews, there *is* a lovely view across the bay. I kept this up for about twenty-five minutes till eventually we got going again, and at the end of it all strolled back from my perch at the seventeenth to the Royal and Ancient for refreshment, which I felt had been well earned. As I got inside the door, the porter handed me a telegram. It was from the Nore Golfing Society. FIRST RULE OF ELECTRONICS, it read; IF IT DOESN'T WORK, KICK IT.

What can be the mentality of the man who actually rings up the BBC during the course of a transmission, as did a doctor during the playoff for the British Open between Peter Thomson and Dave Thomas at Lytham? We were in full voice when the producer came in with: "There's a doctor who has just rung the BBC in London with a message saying, 'Tell Longhurst there is no "p" in Thomson.' " This is a moment for instant decision. The answer comes immediately to mind, but do you give it? Do you say, "I understand a doctor has just rung the BBC to say there is no 'p' in Thomson, and if it is of any interest to him this is by no means the only thing in which the p is silent"—or don't you? I didn't, but I still have a sneaking wish that I had.

Gradually it came to be appreciated that, if you wanted to "show the winner winning," the thing to do was to concentrate, as the Americans were already doing, on the last five holes, together with any "bonus" holes that the same cameras might be able to cover elsewhere—as, for instance, at St. Andrews, where the first five and the last five all share a common strip of ground.

It was also realized, as was really known all along, that the commentator need not be able to see what he was talking about, since his first task is to watch the monitor, the cardinal sin being to talk about something the viewer cannot see, thus driving the latter into absolute frenzies of frustration. Thus at last we began to be pitched nearer the clubhouse rather than miles out on the course, and up only one ladder, and the hand of civilization was extended towards us in the shape of little glass boxes to sit in.

It was to producer Ray Lakeland, and to the fact of happening once again to be in the right place at the right moment with my mouth open —literally, and with the right elbow lifted, at that —that I owe another experience in television which has given me more delight than I can say and has turned out to be a compliment not only, if I may say so, to me but also to "us." Lakeland was for some reason at the 1965 Carling tournament at Pleasant Valley outside Boston. I was also there but, having no work to do until the Friday, was idly sitting around having a drink, when he informed me that CBS, who were televising the event, wondered if it would interest me to go up one of their towers, it being their rehearsal day, and "see how they did it." I was naturally intrigued, and did so, joining John Derr, one of their announcers, as they call the commentators in the U.S.

So far as I remember I only said a few words into their microphone, but to my astonishment I got a note from the producer, Frank Chirkinian, inviting me to do the sixteenth hole next day. This turned out to be a long short hole of some 210-odd yards, where the players drove from an elevated tee down between two bunkers and onto a huge green, behind which we sat under a big parasol on a tower no more than twenty feet high.

"After all I've been through," as my mother is fond of saying, I soon discovered the luxury that is the lot of the American television an-

nouncer by comparison with home. Firstly, we ascended our little tower by a broad set of steps instead of a death-trap ladder. The next luxury was the thought of having only one hole to pay attention to, and a short one at that, so one did not even have to watch drives as well as second shots.

At any rate, at Pleasant Valley I did all I was called upon to do, which heaven knows did not seem very much, naming the players and their scores correctly as they came up to the tee, which one could hardly fail to do in view of the fact that a very efficient young fellow had already put a piece of paper in front of one's nose containing the information, and occasionally adding some commonplace comment before being told to "throw it to fifteen."

It transpired, however, that completely unwittingly, I had managed to cause two minor sensations in our limited little world. One was when, towards the end, a young golfer called Homero Blancas came to the sixteenth hole with the prospect looming before him of picking up, if everything went right, the equivalent of some £12,000 ($33,000). It proved to be a little much for him and, taking a two-iron, he hit the shot that a good many of us would have done in the circumstances; in other words, he hit it right off the sole, half topped, and it must have stung like the devil. "Oh, that's a terrible one," I said instinctively. "Right off the bottom of the club." In fact, it scuttled down the hill and finished on the green, but that wasn't the point. I had said it was a bad shot—which of course, it was—but no one, it transpired, had ever said such a thing before, at least in such downright terms.

This, though it took some time for the penny to drop, and I can sometimes scarcely believe it still, was the first "sensation."

The second took even longer to dawn on me. Golf being, like billiards, a "silent" game— that is to say that silence is expected while a man is making his stroke—it had never occurred to me from the very beginning that one should do other than remain silent while the golfer was actually playing his shot, so that "talking on the stroke" had always seemed to be one of the cardinal sins of golf commentating, even though, heaven knows, I have found myself often enough guilty of committing it. This had not been, up to that time, the accepted principle in America it has since become, and the "brilliant flashes of silence" turned out to be the second "sensation."

Also, of course, the most commonplace little expressions in one man's country may seem strange and catch the attention in another's. Towards the end of this (for me) momentous day, for instance, I announced that the eventual winner, Tony Lema, later so tragically killed in a private plane accident, had a very "missable" putt. This, I was told, was greeted with much applause by the crowd watching in the locker room: "You hear what the old guy said? He said, 'He's got a missable putt.'" For some extraordinary reason this commonplace and self-explanatory expression seemed never to have become part of golfing language in America.

Anyway, it was all good for trade, and not only was I invited again by CBS, this time to the Masters at Augusta, which must have a separate mention of its own, but also by ABC who handle such "prestigious" events as the U.S. Open and the PGA championships. This has meant not only a minimum of four visits to various parts of the States each year but also a whole host of new friendships among the general camaraderie of television, which, though I hope it does not sound pompous, is the team game to end all team games, since there are so many links in the chain between the original product and the viewer's screen that a single incompetent or bloody-minded link can ruin the whole enterprise.

In a modest way, too, my name has gone into the language of television, for by the time we all met in America I had already grown portly enough to wonder what I was doing, climbing these ladders at my weight and age, and made so bold as to wonder whether it would not be possible to somewhat civilize this mode of ascent. From that time onwards a form of staircase, complete with handrail, has been the order of the day, for which I and all my successors may be truly thankful. What I am really proud about, though, is the fact that, in the directions to the

scaffolders who erect the towers, these staircases are ordered by ABC under the name of "Longhurst Ladders."

Such is immortality!

As a result of the pleasant episode at Pleasant Valley, CBS, as I have said, invited me the following April to cover a hole at the Masters at Augusta, Georgia, and for years I have had the honor, to say nothing of the aesthetic pleasure, of sitting on a little tower at the back of the sixteenth there, too. It is once again a short hole and clearly, I should have thought, among the first half-dozen in American golf.

Who christened this tournament "the Masters" no one seems quite to know, nor is it certain that the pious founders would ever have started it at all if they had known what eventually they would be letting themselves in for. However that may be, the tournament they created remains unique. No advertisements are allowed to disfigure the scene either inside or outside the grounds—except when some supporter of Arnold Palmer (not, we may be sure, the great man himself) hired an airplane to fly noisily over the scene all day trailing a banner with the words GO ARNIE GO. Nor is any mention of filthy lucre permitted, and this really is something when you consider that the "leading money winner" seems to be the chief focus of interest in American golf. All the television directors and commentators have to submit to a solemn lecture forbidding mention of any tournaments other than the U.S. and British Open and Amateur championships and the American PGA (other tournaments on the professional tour simply do not exist) and especially forbidding them to mention money in any form. No prize money is announced beforehand and none presented at the time, it being held sufficient for the winner to have won the Masters and to have been invested with the traditional green blazer, which, thenceforward, even though he be a millionaire, he wears with justifiable pride. Only later is it revealed that the first prize came to $40,000, or whatever it may be.

Perhaps I may add one final comment on my own modest operations in television, namely that, whatever you may say, it is nice to be recognized, even if only by one's voice. This is not vanity. It adds much to the pleasure of a taxi ride (as well as to the tip!), for instance, if the driver says, "I'd know your voice anywhere," and starts talking about golf. Only the other day, hailing a cab opposite the American Embassy in Grosvenor Square, I said, "I wonder if you could take me to Cricklewood Broadway?" to which the man at once replied, "I'd take *you* anywhere."

Like so many London taxi drivers he was an avid golfer—they have a golfing society of their own—and actually had a golf magazine beside him in the cab, open at a picture of Arnold Palmer, who once, he said, the biggest day of his golfing life, he had driven in this very cab. All this is not, however, the irrelevance to the subject of the Masters that it may seem, for my peak was reached, and you can hardly blame me for relating it, when, on handing in my baggage at Cape Town airport in South Africa, I had had time to say only, "I wonder if you could check in this shooting stick as well as the suitcase?" when a transatlantic voice behind me said, "Hey! Aren't you the guy that does the sixteenth at the Masters?"

Scenes from a Marriage: A Golfers Lament

by PETER ANDREWS

The domestic consequences which face the avid golfer— male or female—must give us pause. Next to money and sex, golf leads as the prime source of ruined relationships. A couple embarking on a hopefully long accord must establish an understanding about how golf figures in their life together—or apart. As Peter Andrews discovered, golf can turn marriage topsy-turvy.

THE most climactic moments in my marital life have all taken place on the golf course. I am not referring, of course, to those evanescent matters so briefly engaged in and so swiftly forgotten. But rather to those deeply felt watershed events that indelibly color the relationship between a man and a woman. Joy and despair, elation and longueur. They have been the stuff of my marriage and all of them played out on the par fours of life.

I met Marjorie some twenty years ago and was immediately taken with her. She comes from an extremely good family. Her father, who once saw Walter Travis play, still has a serviceable eighteen handicap and uses the two-iron as if he really understands the purpose of that puzzling instrument. Her mother has a lovely compact backswing and plays a rock-steady game. She once hit into the rough in the spring of 1947, found it a bad place to be and has never been back. She is the kind of sweet, gray-haired old lady who lets you spot her seven shots a side and then putts your heart out.

Marjorie and I had courted during the winter and although we had not actually discussed playing golf together, I had, in view of her family, made certain assumptions. In my boyish enthusiasm, I had pictured the two of us teeing off down the fairway of our lives together, so to speak.

I was naturally delighted when Marjorie agreed to be mine, and immediately booked honeymoon lodgings at the Greenbrier in West Virginia. It was on those velvety confines that Sam Snead had once shot a fifty-nine, and I was certain that Marjorie, with her keen sense of the historical, would appreciate starting out our marriage on such a tradition-laden course. The morning after we were married, I got up to practice a few chip shots in the hallway and later, as I was shaving, I called out brightly, "got to get up, darling. We have an eight o'clock tee time and we ought to hit a few to warm up first."

Marjorie, however, snaked out a piece of French toast from the room service tray, looked at me coolly and said, "There are a lot of dumb things in this world, Peter, but lashing away at a golf ball has got to be the dumbest of them all. You can go out and play if you want to. I'm going to stay here in bed."

256

Less than twenty-four hours after we had exchanged sacred vows, I learned that the woman I was to live with for the rest of my life didn't play golf. And didn't want to. When she was absolutely forced to go outside she much preferred—she told me as if it were a matter of no importance whatsoever—tennis. Tennis? My bride was engaged in a sport that people play in their underwear. I was appalled and left our first marital chamber with hot cheeks and stumbled to an erratic ninety-four in spite of unusually easy pin placements.

Our life had gotten off to an indifferent start but one of the best things about the marriage business is that you get to be an old hand at it very quickly. I soon discovered the joys of living with a nongolfing woman far exceeded those of living with one who does play. For several years, I had the best of both possible worlds; unbounded felicity in the home and blessed separateness away from it. When we journeyed to Washington, D.C., for our annual spring visit, Marjorie would spend the day at the National Gallery looking at its exquisite collection of Vermeers while I went about the Lord's work attacking the crown greens of the Chevy Chase Country Club. Chevy is a lovely course, especially in May when the ornamental trees are in bloom. But there were few sights more enchanting than the vision of my wife gaily waving to me as I came off the eighteenth green. We would have a cocktail on the patio and tell each other exciting stories of what we had done that day. Oh, I tell you, it was a perfect marriage. I wonder what ever happened to it.

I know what happened. Marjorie decided to take up golf and the captain's paradise I had lived in for a decade fell apart like Johnny Miller's long iron game. At first it was a cloud on my horizon no larger than a wedge hurled angrily in the sky. Marjorie said she wanted to give up tennis for a while and learn to play golf so we could be together more. It seemed a reasonable enough desire at the time, but if I had known what was in store for me I would have gladly ponied up the dough to send her off for a weekend with Jimmy Connors so she could learn to talk dirty.

For a while it wasn't too bad. Marjorie

thrashed around at golf raising her anger levels higher than her golfing expectations. We played the Big G course at Grossinger's in upstate New York a couple of times armed with a dozen extra balls and a thermos jug of bloody marys in my bag for emergencies. "This is a damned stupid game," Marjorie muttered after dropping three straight fairway woods into the water by the par-five fourth hole. "I don't see why people subject themselves to it."

"I never said golf was fun, darling."

Playing with a truly horrific lady golfer did offer some moments of high drama. For a season or so, Marjorie was an almost perversely consistent golfer. She could have played an entire round along a cart path, provided the path had been cut approximately fifteen yards into the rough on the right. No matter what kind of shot she hit, slice, top, hook, fat or thin, she almost always wound up in the right rough. Every once in a while she would send a heroic pull into the left rough but then would slice back to where she was apparently more comfortable. After working her way up the right rough a few yards at a time, Marjorie would at last emerge in the area of short grass near the green. Working as stealthily as an underwater demolition team, Marjorie snuck up on to the green and then after two or three extremely tentative putts she got to within three or four feet of hole, which she referred to as her "range." Then Marjorie would suddenly turn into Wonder Woman in golf slacks and become the boldest, most ferocious short putter the game has ever known. Once she had a slightly uphill putt of not more than twenty inches. Marjorie took careful aim and rammed the ball—I am not making this up, I marked off the distance in front of witnesses—thirty-eight feet past the hole. I sent the documentation of this to the Guinness Book of World Records for inclusion as the longest leave from the shortest putt, but they wrote back saying if I was having marital difficulties I should try to solve them myself and not drag them into the situation.

Marjorie seemed to be fated to be the eternal lady duffer but she kept at it with a good will and we started to play together more on our vacations. It meant my having to give up a day or two to squire Marjorie through the woodlands, but it seemed a small enough sacrifice for a fine woman who had presented me with a beautiful daughter. Eventually, we settled into a pattern where we played together about nine or ten times a year. This seemed just about the right number of times to play with one's spouse on the golf course; enough to be a good sport but not so often your friends make fun of you when you beg off from your regular foursome to "play with the wife."

Marriage counselors will tell you that the disintegration of a marriage is an intricate matter involving years of minor dislocations and small disappointments that eventually lead to a parting of the ways. It was not so with mine. I can pinpoint the collapse of our relationship with considerable exactitude. It came about at exactly 3:17 on the afternoon of August 12, 1976, on the seventeenth hole at Black Hall, a difficult course in Connecticut whose mountainous fairways were hacked out of a forest that would have scared off Hansel and Gretel.

Marjorie had been playing her usual game; a fozzled wood here, a shanked iron there, and was finally laying a nervy seven about 165 yards from the green. Marjorie took her regular stance with a four-wood and then came back with a little loop at the top of the swing so reminiscent of a young Bobby Jones. Then she let fly. It was one of those glorious moments when every element of the golf swing falls into place; hips, shoulders and hands all in perfect synchronization. The ball leapt off the club like a cannon shot and arced into the sky. It seemed to hang in the air for a moment as if it were lost—no golf ball struck by Marjorie had ever before flown so far or so high—then it turned over with just a slight draw from right to left and dashed for the folds of the flag.

Now you must remember that Marjorie is an extremely gentle woman who has traveled through most of the civilized world, speaks three languages and always reads a few pages of Hazlitt before retiring. She stood transfixed as the ball bit into the green and then clawed its way toward the hole, finally coming to rest about four inches away.

"Jeeeezuz." she exclaimed. "Did you see that?"

I did. But it cannot be said that I have seen my wife in any significant sense of the word since then. With a single sweep of a fairway wood Marjorie became a total golf nut. Before, she was a regular earth mother who carefully tended the enormous amounts of greenery in our house, prepared gourmet meals and made her own linen from raw flax. Now, unless we hear her spikes clattering over the floor as she runs another of her innumerable golf outfits through the washer-drier, my daughter and I have no idea whether she is in the house or not. Except when it's raining, of course, and then she is in the living room putting.

Doing housework is something Marjorie will not even discuss anymore because it is well known that moving furniture to dust contributes to upper body tension. Cooking is out because it is not good to eat too much before a round. When last Christmas I suggested that a smallish cooked bird to commemorate the day would not be considered excessive, Marjorie said no because earlier that morning she had seen a small patch of sun and the weather could break any minute. Nor will she help wash up after dinner because the heat from dishwater desensitizes the fingers and makes for a poor putting touch. And everyone knows, for heaven's sake, that putting is the most important part of the game.

The other day I came home to find a note wedged under the door knocker which said, "Have gone to have a mid-iron lesson with Vince. There's a TV dinner in the icebox. Keep the left side strong."

Marjorie maintains a drumfire correspondence with every golfing mail order house in America and the British Isles that has not been shuttered by the authorities for making fraudulent use of the postal service. There is not a nostrum, piece of special equipment, correctional device or instruction kit she has not purchased. As a result, our house, which was once a showplace, now resembled the pro shop of a particularly seedy public course in Guatemala. When we go away, which can't be too often to suit me, instead of the two of us pursuing our separate pleasures we now have, God save the mark, total togetherness. Marjorie never lets me out of her sight in case I might try to slip off and get in a round of men's golf without her. We played Spring Lake in New Jersey early this year. I have always liked Spring Lake with its broad, forgiving fairways, but this time the only peace I knew the whole day was when I had a rum collins with the naked men in the locker room and now she is starting to make ugly Friedanesque noises about that simple pleasure. Retreating to the male preserves of Pine Valley is something I can just forget about. Marjorie says she will be on the phone to her attorney while my car is still getting out of the driveway.

When she is not playing with me, Marjorie is usually off playing with those whom she describes as "the girls." A coarse, loutish group of women, they are in the main given to extravagant patterns of speech of a particularly startling nature. To a woman, they seem to have ingested the entire rule book of golf and call penalties on each other that have not been invoked since the death of Harry Vardon. Worst of all, Marjorie has begun to adopt the ghastly patois of the seasoned golfer. To hear a woman with whom you have lived for a score of years suddenly start saying things like, "Boy, I really hit that little sweetheart on the screws," is not a pleasant turn of events, I can assure you. All this from a lady with whom I was always able to exchange a pithy remark or two on the affairs of the day. Now, if it isn't advertised at the Food Fair or written up in Bob Toski's *The Touch System for Better Golf*, Marjorie hasn't got a clue.

Where it will all end, I have no idea. We are already planning a summer trip and Marjorie can't make up her mind between Pinehurst or the seaside links of the Irish coast. For myself, I suggested we go to the Hermitage. I have a sudden desire to spend an entire vacation indoors viewing the art treasures of ancient Russia. But Marjorie won't consider it. She says she's heard it is a terrible course.

How Bobby Jones and I Blew the British Open:

by **CHARLES PRICE**

Charles Price speaks in such detail about the game's great figures that he gives the impression he may have caddied for old Tom Morris. If there is an expert on Bobby Jones, it is Price, and in this true story he reveals something of the Jones humor and his own ability to make himself the center of comic misadventures.

IN 1964 Bob Jones and I did a book together. I say "did" because actually Bob had done all the writing years before in a series of newspaper columns distributed internationally by the McNaught Syndicate between 1927 and 1932 and in a series of pearl-like essays for *The American Golfer,* the old Condé-Nast monthly magazine published until the Depression killed it off in 1935. Together, they added up to some 600,000 words, or about the length of six average novels. It was my job to cut them down to a publishable 90,000.

That job was not only the most pleasant I have ever had but the easiest. For one thing, Bob could write better than I ever could. For another, I could have thrown the entire collection down a flight of stairs and still have had enough pages left at the bottom to make as good a book on golf as I have ever read. Altogether, it was the most perceptive, most artful, most eloquent collection of thoughts on this maddeningly mysterious game I have ever assimilated, and I guess I have

studied or at least perused almost everything in the whole, considerable library of golf. It was powerful prose, some of it pure poetry. Edited down, it was published in 1965 by Doubleday & Company under a title that was simplicity itself: *Bobby Jones on Golf.* If it is not in *your* library, let me tell you something. You don't have a library.

I worked on the book all winter in my Manhattan apartment, sifting and cutting and dovetailing until my mind boggled and my soul ached, at which time I would hop a plane to Atlanta for a conference with Bob at his law office. After all, this was Bob Jones, the likes of which golf had never seen before and never would again. This book had to be right. He had not wanted to do it in the first place because of his flagging energies. But Doubleday and I had talked him into it, if for no other reason than to get it into libraries, where it would be read long after all other golf books—most of which had been unwittingly plagiarized or downright pirated from Bob's writings anyway—had been given to the Salvation Army. So far as my puny efforts were concerned, I was chiseling Bob's words on marble.

One morning in his office after a long discussion over the manuscript, we broke for our favorite lunch: two martinis and a hamburger, which were phoned out for by his secretary, Jean Marshall, from a local bar and deli. Bob hated to eat in public. He was then so crippled from that hellish disease, which doesn't strike down one person in ten million—syringomyelia—that he could barely handle a knife and fork. Just turning over the pages of the manuscript was a chore for him. He had always been a chain-smoker, but now merely stuffing a cigarette into the holder, which he used to keep from burning his fingers, had become a task that sometimes made him swear. "Damn!" he would mutter and then keep on trying. One thing he didn't want was help. But I would use these frustrating moments to light up a cigarette of my own whether I wanted it or not, and then use the lighter on his desk so I could also light his cigarette in a gesture of common courtesy he couldn't refuse, all the while trying to act lackadaisical and hoping he wouldn't see my eyes water. It was a simple enough lighter, encased in leather, which he could trigger by pressing a button. But sometimes he lacked even the strength to do that, this by a man who could once hit a golf ball effortlessly an eighth of a mile. That lighter today sits on my desk, and the Chinese Army couldn't take it away from me.

We puffed on our cigarettes and sipped our martinis. "You know?" he said, admiring his drink. "I shouldn't drink these. They interfere with my medicine."

"I know," I replied. "I shouldn't drink them, either. They make me drunk."

Bob chuckled. Nobody I have ever met chuckled as warmly as Bob Jones. It came clear up from his shoelaces.

We were now into our second martini. I used the aura of alcohol to spring on him an almost irreverent thought I had been harboring for years. I wanted his reaction. "You know something, Bob?" I said. "As golfers, you and I have something in common."

"What's that?" he said suspiciously.

"We both retired from competition at twenty-eight. You because you had beaten everybody and I because I had never beaten anybody."

It hurt his sides, but Bob decided to laugh anyhow. The line turned out to be a private joke between us that we shared for the rest of his days.

"What's your handicap?" he asked.

"It's still one," I said. "But I can't play to it anymore. Never could, as a matter of fact."

"Neither could I," said the amateur who had finished either first or second in ten of the last eleven American and British Open championships he had played in. He paused for a moment, obviously gathering some thoughts. "Why don't you go to the British Open this year? It's at St. Andrews."

"What the hell am I going to do there? Sell balloons?"

"No, play," he said. "I'm serious. You told me once you had never been to St. Andrews. This would be a good time to go. It would help you to better understand some of the things I've been talking about."

The whole idea was so absurd, so farfetched, so ridiculous, so fantastic, so preposterous that I almost laughed out loud. Here was the greatest championship player in the history of a 600-year-old game asking *me* to travel clear across the Atlantic to compete in the oldest athletic contest in the world over the most sacrosanct ground in golf. I felt like a pimp being asked by the Pope to visit the Vatican.

So I went.

But I did not go unarmed. I hit 7,000 practice balls and played ten rounds of golf in one week. I showed up at JFK Airport with a cracking leather golf bag the size of a steamer trunk, both black and brown brogues, six tweed sweaters, an array of argyles, four mouse-colored slacks, a leather cap, two rainsuits and a hip flask. If I couldn't play like a Scotsman, at least I was going to look like one.

I also carried with me a copy of a letter of introduction Bob had sent to the secretary of the Royal and Ancient Golf Club, of which he was a member and, at his own insistence, a dues-paying one, this despite the fact he had not long before been made, during a tear-jerking ceremony at the local town hall, what amounts to an honorary citizen of St. Andrews, the first American to have been so honored since Benjamin Franklin. For added insurance, I also had a letter from Joe Dey, who was then Executive Director of the USGA. If I couldn't get into the R&A clubhouse, I wasn't going. I was damned if I was going to have to eat in a refectory tent with the likes of Arnold Palmer, Jack Nicklaus, Gary Player and Tony Lema. Gawd! I was an amateur! A *gentleman* golfer! Besides, the bar was in the clubhouse.

One of the first things you learn at St. Andrews during the British Open is that almost anybody can get into the R&A's clubhouse. All you need is one of four different badges. One is marked "Member," of which the R&A has almost as many as the YMCA. Another is marked "Guest," which includes all the members' relatives, all their relatives' friends, and all their friends' relatives. A third is marked "Contestant," which means you are one of more than 300 hopeless optimists who have entered the championship but haven't yet qualified. The fourth is marked simply "Player," which means you are exempt from qualifying by virtue of having won something somewhere, such as the U.S. Open. Now I know what the pros mean when they point to a guy and say, "He's a player." You better damned sight be one when you play in the British Open at St. Andrews. The Old Course has a way of making you wish you had stuck to horseshoes.

The first thing you ask your caddie about the Old Course when you step to the first tee is, "Where is it?" In front of you is nothing even remotely resembling a golf course, just a sea of rolling gray mounds leading nowhere, a metaphysical morass of emptiness devoid of challenge or even direction. I've seen empty parking lots that were more beautiful.

But you learn. Lord, how you learn! I mean the hard way, even with a caddie like mine, Carnegie, who kept pointing me in the right direction and choosing all my clubs. Once when I wanted to hit a five-iron, Carnegie shook his head and tapped my three-wood. "You nay wan' no mashie here," he said. "Use you' spoon." Another time when I wanted to use my three-wood, Carnegie tapped my five-iron. "I know," I said, "I nay wan' no spoon here. Use my mashie." He was right, too. Every time. Carnegie, I was to discover, was something else again, a goddamn genius in my estimation. He was 102 years old and hadn't had a haircut since he had been ninety. Although it was July, he wore a gray, herringbone Chesterfield that came clear to his ankles and that had been given to him by Lloyd George just after the Versailles Conference. The coat, I was to learn, also served as his pajamas. With the natural stoop from age, he looked to me at first like Albert Einstein. After he had caddied for me all week, I thought he *was* Albert Einstein. And could he drink! He consumed more Scotch on a golf course than Hagen spilled off one. One morning he showed up with a particularly vicious hangover. The veins in his nose looked as though they had turned varicose and he was hobbling. What happened, I asked, staring at his game leg? It seems he had come home so drunk the night before that his own dog had bitten him.

There are two ways to play in the British Open at St. Andrews if your game is rusty, your nerves are shot and you have no talent to begin with. One is to try and win it, in which case you won't have to go home. You will be *taken* there. In a straightjacket. The saner way is to try not to win it, in which case you are offered three alternatives. One is to score a ten on the final hole if you are leading—which can be a bit embarrassing. The second is to purposely fail to make the cut, which is not as easy as it may sound. If the wind comes up, you can score two nineties and still find yourself obliged to play the last two rounds. The third and surest alternative is not to qualify in the first place. This is the tack I decided to take. I wasn't going to travel clear across the Atlantic to make an ass of myself. I'd post a couple of seventy-sixes or such, and go home bloodied but unbowed.

The two qualifying rounds were to be played over two other courses while the Old was left to the "players" for practice rounds. We "contestants" were assigned either to the New Course, which dates back to Queen Victoria, or to the Eden Course, which for all I know dates back to King Canute. I was assigned to the Eden. But it made no difference. I hadn't played either one and didn't intend to. I was too busy getting in my licks over the Old while I still had the chance.

I was paired with a local amateur who I shall call Angus because I can't remember his name and because I am sure he has tried very hard to forget mine. Carnegie and I dutifully reported to the first tee ten minutes ahead of my starting time. Had it not been that Carnegie knew Angus, we might never have met each other. I saw Angus

Courtesy of Wide World Photos, Inc.

The bane of contemporary golf is the parade of mechanical men who excel but do not emote. One of those fine players who did was the late "Champagne" Tony Lema, shown here after winning the 1964 British Open.

in the crowd, but I thought he was a hustler from Miami Shores. He had on white plastic shoes, canary yellow pants, a loosely knit purple cardigan and a tennis visor. Everything had either an alligator or a penguin on it. By contrast, everything I was wearing had a belt in the back: my black brogues, my gray tweed slacks, my leather cap, even—in what I thought would be smashing fashion—my Norfolk jacket. If I had had a beard, you would have thought I was old Tom Morris. "Tell me," said Angus after we had shaken hands, "do all Americans dress like you for golf?"

"Only when we want to keep warm," I replied, bowing my head and scraping my shoe against the ground.

"I see," said Angus, doubtfully. It was high noon. There wasn't a cloud in the sky or a breath of air. And the sun was hot as a boil.

I won't go into all the birdies I had in the first round because there weren't any. I scored a seventy-six, just as I had predicted, which left me a very comfortable twelve-stroke margin for failure over Cobie Legrange, a professional from South Africa, who had had a nifty sixty-four, thank God. Angus and I shook hands as we walked off the eighteenth green. "'Joyed it," said Angus crisply. "Crashing," I replied.

The next day—which, if everything went well, would be my last—I decided to do my Sherlock Holmes bit. You know. Deerstalker cap, meerschaum pipe and a greatcoat, which I tossed cavalierly over my shoulders without bothering to put my arms through the sleeves, continental fashion. It was 82° in the shade. Eyeing me for a full minute on the first tee, Angus finally pulled some words together. "You must know Bing Crosby," he said.

"No," I said. "Why do you ask?"

"No particular reason," he replied. "I just presumed everybody in show business knew Bing Crosby."

The round started off with a near catastrophe. I birdied the first hole. On the advice of Carnegie, I used my niblick for my second shot and hit it three inches from the hole. Well, what's done is done, I reminded myself, and went on to the second, where I made a nondescript par four by holing a wedge. To get to the third hole at the Eden Course you cross a bridge over the railroad tracks which lead from Edinburgh to nearby Leukers. Had I known what was ahead of me, I would have thrown myself across them and waited for a high-speed express. The third hole is a medium length par three with an immense green shaped like a caved-in fedora. I hit what I thought was a perfect shot, a cold top that rolled more than 100 meters onto the putting surface. The putt I had left would have to dip into a valley, roll up a hill, and then break sixteen feet to the right to get anywhere near the hole. I could four-putt and still not lose face. As luck would have it, the first putt stopped on the lip of the cup.

The fourth hole was built to fit my game: a wide-open dogleg to the right, which I couldn't have bogeyed if I tried. So I didn't and ended up making a birdie. I can't remember the very short fifth—a par four—but I do recall parring it after two woods. Then came the horrendous sixth—a 186-yard par three to a highly elevated green, the wind at my back from off the Estuary at about thirty-five knots. I cannot remember what club I used—it was something Carnegie tapped with his forefinger—but I distinctly remember taking a backswing. I'm positive of that. I must have, for the ball went into the hole! Carnegie told me it was the first hole-in-one made at St. Andrews during a British Open since the war; the last war, that is. Strictly speaking, though, it was not the British Open but only the qualifying rounds. And it was not the Old Course but the Eden. But it was still a hole-in-one. Carnegie would have told me anything to get that bottle of Scotch he knew he was going to get.

So there I stood—four under par after six holes while quietly trying not to qualify 3,000 miles from home for a championship I did not want to play in in the first place. Suddenly, newspaper reporters and photographers came from everywhere. Arnold Palmer had failed to file an entry and Tony Lema, who would eventually win the championship, had not yet shown up. So the story for the day was that an unknown Yank, and an amateur at that, was burning up the Eden Course. Class, someone once said, is the ability to undergo pressure with grace. So what did I do? I just did what comes naturally. I vomited.

The press bombarded me with questions. "Where do you live?" they asked.

"New York City," I answered.

"What is your occupation?"

"I'm a steamfitter."

"What's your home course?"

"Central Park."

"We didn't know there was a course there."

"Neither do the police."

"Did you ever win anything?"

"Yeah. The sixth at Aqueduct."

By the time I had made the turn, the gentlemen of the press acted true to their nature. They left me. Alone once again, things started going my way. I had an unplayable lie, lost two balls and hit three more out-of-bounds. To guarantee that no more miracles might happen on the eighteenth, I picked up. Now, at last, I was back where I belonged—in the gallery.

The day after the British Open I was back in New York, and three days after that I was back in Atlanta to see Bob Jones for our final conference on the book. "What happened at St. Andrews?" said Bob as I settled into a chair.

"I lost." I said.

"Well-l-l-l," said the greatest golfer in the world to the worst, "we can't win them all, can we?"

"There are no pictures of what you've done on the scorecards, only the figures," said Bruce Crampton after winning the Western Open with a scrambling, dramatic final round that appeared simply as a seventy-one in the record book. Following are statistics on golf's major events and pro tours. Behind many of the names, courses, tournaments and records lie myriad dramas. They are the history of golf in brief to help settle debates about who won what when.

80th. U.S. OPEN CHAMPIONSHIP

HOLE	1	2	3	4	5	6	7	8	9	10	11	12	13	14	15	16	17	18
LEADERS PAR	4	4	4	3	4	4	4	4	3	4	4	3	4	4	4	3	5	5
NICKLAUS	6	6	7	6	6	6	5	5	5	6	6	6	6	6	6	6	7	8
AOKI	6	5	5	4	4	4	3	4	3	4	4	4	4	4	4	4	5	6
HINKLE	5	5	5	4	4	3	3	3	3	3								4
WATSON	3	4	4	4	4	4	4	4	3	2								4
FERGUS	4	4		4	4	4	5	5	5	4								4
HAYES			2	2	2	1	1											0
TREVINO																		3
REID																		
SNEED ED																		

ALL-TIME LEADERS IN MAJOR CHAMPIONSHIPS

	U.S. Open	British Open	PGA	Masters	Amateur U.S.	British	Total Titles
Jack Nicklaus	4	3	5	5	2	0	17
Bobby Jones	4	3	0	0	5	1	13
Walter Hagen	2	4	5	0	0	0	11
John Ball	0	1	0	0	0	8	9
Ben Hogan	4	1	2	2	0	0	9
Gary Player	1	3	2	3	0	0	9
Arnold Palmer	1	2	0	4	1	0	8
Harold Hilton	0	2	0	0	1	4	7
Gene Sarazen	2	1	3	1	0	0	7
Sam Snead	0	1	3	3	0	0	7
Harry Vardon	1	6	0	0	0	0	7

USGA MEN'S OPEN

Year	Venue	Winner	Score
1895	Newport (R.I.) G.C.	Horace Rawlins	173
1896	Shinnecock Hills	James Foulis	152
1897	Chicago G.C.	Joe Lloyd	162
1898	Myopia Hunt C.	Fred Herd	328
1899	Baltimore C.C.	Willie Smith	315
1900	Chicago G.C.	Harry Vardon	313
1901	Myopia Hunt C.	Willie Anderson	331-85
1902	Garden City C.C.	L. Auchterlonie	307
1903	Baltusrol G.C.	Willie Anderson	307-82
1904	Glen View (Ill.) C.	Willie Anderson	303
1905	Myopia Hunt C.	Willie Anderson	314
1906	Onwentsia C.	Alex Smith	295
1907	Philadelphia C.C.	Alex Ross	302
1908	Myopia Hunt C.	Fred McLeod	322-77
1909	Englewood	George Sargent	290
1910	Philadelphia C.C.	Alex Smith	298-71
1911	Chicago G.C.	John McDermott	307-80
1912	C.C. of Buffalo	John McDermott	294
1913	The Country Club	a-Francis Ouimet	304-72
1914	Midlothian	Walter Hagen	290
1915	Baltusrol G.C.	a-J. D. Travers	297
1916	Minikahda C.	a-Charles Evans, Jr.	286
1917–18	No championship		
1919	Brae Burn C.C.	Walter Hagen	301-77
1920	Inverness C.	Edward Ray	295
1921	Columbia C.C.	James M. Barnes	289
1922	Skokie (Ill.) C.C.	Gene Sarazen	288
1923	Inwood (N.Y.) C.C.	a-R. T. Jones, Jr.	296-76
1924	Oakland Hills	Cyril Walker	297
1925	Worcester (Mass.)	Wm. MacFarlane	291-75-72
		a-R. T. Jones, Jr.	291-75-73
1926	Scioto C.C.	a-R. T. Jones, Jr.	293
1927	Oakmont (Pa.)	Tommy Armour	301-76
		Harry Cooper	301-79
1928	Olympia Fields	Johnny Farrell	294-143
		a-R. T. Jones, Jr.	294-144
1929	Winged Foot G.C.	a-R. T. Jones, Jr.	294-141
		Al Espinosa	294-164
1930	Interlachen C.C.	a-R. T. Jones, Jr.	287
1931	Inverness C.	Billy Burke	292-149-148
		Geo. Von Elm	292-149-149
1932	Fresh Meadow	Gene Sarazen	286
1933	North Shore G.C.	a-Johnny Goodman	287
1934	Merion Cricket C.	Olin Dutra	293
1935	Oakmont (Pa.)	Sam Parks, Jr.	299
1936	Baltusrol G.C.	Tony Manero	282
1937	Oakland Hills C.C.	Ralph Guldahl	281
1938	Cherry Hills C.C.	Ralph Guldahl	284
1939	Phila. C.C.	Byron Nelson	284-68-70
		Craig Wood	284-68-73
		Denny Shute	284-76
1940	Canterbury G.C.	Lawson Little	287-70
		Gene Sarazen	287-73
1941	Colonial C.C.	Craig Wood	284
1942–45	No championship		
1946	Canterbury G.C. Cleveland	Lloyd Mangrum	284-72-72
		Byron Nelson	284-72-73
		Vic Ghezzi	284-72-73
1947	St. Louis C.C. Clayton, Mo.	Lew Worsham	282-69
		Sam Snead	282-70
1948	Riviera C.C.	Ben Hogan	276
1949	Medinah C.C.	Cary Middlecoff	286
1950	Merion G.C.	Ben Hogan	287-69
		Lloyd Mangrum	287-73
		George Fazio	287-75
1951	Oakland Hills C.C.	Ben Hogan	287
1952	Northwood C.C.	Julius Boros	281
1953	Oakmont C.C.	Ben Hogan	283
1954	Baltusrol G.C.	Ed Furgol	284
1955	Olympic C.	Jack Fleck	287-69
		Ben Hogan	287-72
1956	Oak Hill C.C.	Cary Middlecoff	281
1957	Inverness C.	Dick Mayer	282-72
		Cary Middlecoff	282-79
1958	Southern Hills C.C.	Tommy Bolt	283
1959	Winged Foot G.C.	Bill Casper	282
1960	Cherry Hills C.C.	Arnold Palmer	280
1961	Oakland Hills	Gene Littler	281
1962	Oakmont (Pa.)	Jack Nicklaus	283-71
		Arnold Palmer	283-74
1963	The Country Club	Julius Boros	293-70
		Jacky Cupit	293-73
		Arnold Palmer	293-76
1964	Congressional C.C.	Ken Venturi	278
1965	Bellerive C.C.	Gary Player	282-71
		Kel Nagle	282-74
1966	Olympic C.	Billy Casper	278-69
		Arnold Palmer	278-73
1967	Baltusrol G.C.	Jack Nicklaus	275**
1968	Oak Hill C.C.	Lee Trevino	275**

1969 Champions G.C.	Orville Moody	281
1970 Hazeltine Ntl.	Tony Jacklin	281
1971 Merion G.C.	Lee Trevino	280-68
	Jack Nicklaus	280-71
1972 Pebble Beach	Jack Nicklaus	290
1973 Oakmont (Pa.) C.C.	Johnny Miller	279
1974 Winged Foot G.C.	Hale Irwin	287
1975 Medinah C.C.	Lou Graham	287-71
	John Mahaffey	287-73
1976 Atlanta A.C.	Jerry Pate	277
1977 Southern Hills C.C.	Hubert Green	278
1978 Cherry Hills C.C.	Andy North	285
1979 Inverness C.	Hale Irwin	284
1980 Baltusrol G.C.	Jack Nicklaus	272

a-Denotes amateur.

PGA CHAMPIONSHIP

1916 Siwanoy C.C.,	James Barnes	
Bronxville, N.Y.	d. J. Hutchison	1 up
1917–18 No championship		
1919 Engineers C.C.,	James Barnes	
Roslyn, L.I., N.Y.	d. Fred McLeod	6 and 5
1920 Flossmoor	Jock Hutchison	
(Ill.) C.C.	d. J. D. Edgar	1 up
1921 Inwood C.C., Far	Walter Hagen	
Rockaway, N.Y.	d. J. Barnes	3 and 2
1922 Oakmont	Gene Sarazen	
(Pa.) C.C.	d. E. French	4 and 3
1923 Pelham (N.Y.)	Gene Sarazen	
C.C.	d. W. Hagen	1 up (38)
1924 French Lick	Walter Hagen	
(Ind.) C.C.	d. J. Barnes	2 up
1925 Olympia Fields	Walter Hagen	
(Ill.) C.C.	d. B. Mehlhorn	6 and 5
1926 Salisbury G.C.,	Walter Hagen	
Westbury, N.Y.	d. L. Diegel	5 and 3
1927 Cedar Crest C.C.,	Walter Hagen	
Dallas, Tex.	d. J. Turnesa	1 up
1928 Five Farms C.C.	Leo Diegel	
Baltimore, Md.	d. Al Espinosa	6 and 5
1929 Hillcrest C.C.,	Leo Diegel	
Los Angeles, Calif.	d. J. Farrell	6 and 4
1930 Fresh Meadow	Tommy Armour	
C.C., Flushing, N.Y.	d. C. Sarazen	1 up
1931 Wannamoisett	Tom Creavy	
C.C., Rumford, R.I.	d. D. Shute	2 and 1
1932 Keller G.C.,	Olin Dutra	
St. Paul, Minn.	d. F. Walsh	4 and 3
1933 Blue Mound C.C.,	Gene Sarazen	
Milwaukee, Wis.	d. W. Goggin	5 and 4
1934 Park C.C.,	Paul Runyan	
W'msville, N.Y.	d. C. Wood	1 up (38)
1935 Twin Hills C.C.,	Johnny Revolta	
Oklahoma City	d. T. Armour	5 and 4
1936 Pinehurst	Denny Shute	
(N.C.) C.C.	d. J. Thomson	3 and 2
1937 Pittsburgh F.C.	Denny Shute	
	d. H. McSpaden	1 up (37)
1938 Shawnee (Pa.) C.C.	Paul Runyan	
	d. S. Snead	8 and 7
1939 Pomonok C.C.,	Henry Picard	
Flushing, N.Y.	d. B. Nelson	1 up (37)
1940 Hershey (Pa.)	Byron Nelson	
C.C.	d. S. Snead	1 up
1941 Cherry Hills C.C.,	Vic Ghezzi	
Denver, Colo.	d. B. Nelson	1 up (38)
1942 Seaview C.C.,	Sam Snead	
Atlantic City, N.J.	d. J. Turnesa	2 and 1
1943 No championship		
1944 Manito G. & C.C.,	Bob Hamilton	
Spokane, Wash.	d. B. Nelson	1 up
1945 Morraine C.C.,	Byron Nelson	
Dayton, O.	d. S. Byrd	4 and 3
1946 Portland	Ben Hogan	
(Ore.) C.C.	d. E. Oliver	6 and 4
1947 Plum Hollow	Jim Ferrier	
C.C., Detroit	d. C. Harbert	2 and 1
1948 Norwood Hills	Ben Hogan	
C.C., St. Louis	d. M. Turnesa	7 and 6
1949 Hermitage C.C.,	Sam Snead	
Richmond, Va.	d. J. Palmer	3 and 2
1950 Scioto C.C.,	Chandler Harper	
Columbus, O.	d. H. Williams, Jr.	4 and 3
1951 Oakmont	Sam Snead	
(Pa.) C.C.	d. W. Burkemo	7 and 6
1952 Big Spring C.C.,	Jim Turnesa	
Louisville, Ky.	d. C. Harbert	1 up
1953 Birmingham	Walter Burkemo	
(Mich.) C.C.	d. F. Torza	2 and 1
1954 Keller G.C.,	Chick Harbert	
St. Paul, Minn.	d. W. Burkemo	4 and 3
1955 Meadowbrook,	Doug Ford	
Detroit, Mich.	d. C. Middlecoff	4 and 3
1956 Blue Hill C.C.,	Jack Burke	
Canton, Mass.	d. T. Kroll	3 and 2
1957 Dayton Valley,	Lionel Hebert	
Dayton, O.	d. D. Finsterwald	2 and 1
1958 Llanerch C.C.	Dow Finsterwald	276
1959 Minneapolis	Bob Rosburg	277
1960 Firestone C.C.	Jay Hebert	281
1961 Olympia Fields	Jerry Barber	277-67
(Ill.) C.C.	Don January	277-68
1962 Aronimink G.C.	Gary Player	278
1963 Dallas (Tex) A.C.	Jack Nicklaus	279
1964 Columbus C.C.	Bobby Nichols	271**
1965 Laurel Valley G.C.	Dave Marr	280
1966 Firestone C.C.	Al Geiberger	280
1967 Columbine C.C.,	Don January	281-69

Denver, Colo.	Don Massengale	281-71
1968 Pecan Valley C.C.	Julius Boros	281
1969 NCR, Dayton	Ray Floyd	276
1970 Southern Hills	Dave Stockton	279
1971 PGA National G.C.	Jack Nicklaus	281
1972 Oakland Hills C.C.	Gary Player	281
1973 Canterbury G.C.	Jack Nicklaus	277
1974 Tanglewood G.C.	Lee Trevino	276
1975 Firestone C.C.	Jack Nicklaus	276
1976 Congressional C.C.	Dave Stockton	281
1977 Pebble Beach G.L.	Lanny Wadkins*	282
	Gene Littler	282
1978 Oakmont C.C.	John Mahaffey*	276
	Jerry Pate	276
	Tom Watson	276
1979 Oakland Hills C.C.	David Graham*	272
	Ben Crenshaw	272
1980 Oakland Hills C.C.	Jack Nicklaus	274

1970	Billy Casper	279-69
1971	Charles Coody	279
1972	Jack Nicklaus	286
1973	Tommy Aaron	283
1974	Gary Player	278
1975	Jack Nicklaus	276
1976	Ray Floyd	271**
1977	Tom Watson	276
1978	Gary Player	277
1979	Fuzzy Zoeller*	280
	Tom Watson	280
	Ed Sneed	280
1980	Seve Ballesteros	275

*Won sudden-death playoff. **Record.

MASTERS

1934	Horton Smith	284
1935	Gene Sarazen	282-144
1936	Horton Smith	285
1937	Byron Nelson	283
1938	Henry Picard	285
1939	Ralph Guldahl	279
1940	Jimmy Demaret	280
1941	Craig Wood	280
1942	Byron Nelson	280-69
1943–45 No championship		
1946	Herman Keiser	282
1947	Jimmy Demaret	281
1948	Claude Harmon	279
1949	Sam Snead	282
1950	Jimmy Demaret	283
1951	Ben Hogan	280
1952	Sam Snead	286
1953	Ben Hogan	274
1954	Sam Snead	289-70
1955	Cary Middlecoff	279
1956	Jack Burke	289
1957	Doug Ford	283
1958	Arnold Palmer	284
1959	Art Wall	284
1960	Arnold Palmer	282
1961	Gary Player	280
1962	Arnold Palmer	280-68
1963	Jack Nicklaus	286
1964	Arnold Palmer	276
1965	Jack Nicklaus	271**
1966	Jack Nicklaus	288-70
1967	Gay Brewer	280
1968	Bob Goalby	277
1969	George Archer	281

BRITISH OPEN

Year Site	Winner	Score
1860 Prestwick	Willie Park, Sr.	174
1861 Prestwick	Tom Morris, Sr.	163
1862 Prestwick	Tom Morris, Sr.	163
1863 Prestwick	Willie Park, Sr.	168
1864 Prestwick	Tom Morris, Sr.	167
1865 Prestwick	Andrew Strath	162
1866 Prestwick	Willie Park, Sr.	169
1867 Prestwick	Tom Morris, Sr.	170
1868 Prestwick	Tom Morris, Jr.	157
1869 Prestwick	Tom Morris, Jr.	154
1870 Prestwick	Tom Morris, Jr.	149
1871 Not played		
1872 Prestwick	Tom Morris, Jr.	166
1873 St. Andrews	Tom Kidd	179
1874 Musselburgh	Mungo Park	159
1875 Prestwick	Willie Park, Sr.	166
1876 St. Andrews	Robert Martin	176
1877 Musselburgh	Jamie Anderson	160
1878 Prestwick	Jamie Anderson	157
1879 St. Andrews	Jamie Anderson	170
1880 Musselburgh	Robert Ferguson	162
1881 Prestwick	Robert Ferguson	170
1882 St. Andrews	Robert Ferguson	171
1883 Musselburgh	Willie Fernie	159
1884 Prestwick	Jack Simpson	160
1885 St. Andrews	Robert Martin	171
1886 Musselburgh	David Brown	157
1887 Prestwick	Willie Park Jr.	161
1888 St. Andrews	Jack Burns	171
1889 Musselburgh	Willie Park Jr.	155
1890 Prestwick	*John Ball	164
1891 St. Andrews	Hugh Kirkaldy	166
1892 Muirfield	*Harold H. Hilton	305
1893 Prestwick	William Auchterlonie	322
1894 Sandwich	John H. Taylor	326
1895 St. Andrews	John H. Taylor	322
1896 Muirfield	*Harry Vardon	316

1897 Hoylake	*Harold H. Hilton	314
1898 Prestwick	Harry Vardon	307
1899 Sandwich	Harry Vardon	310
1900 St. Andrews	John H. Taylor	309
1901 Muirfield	James Braid	309
1902 Hoylake	Alexander Herd	307
1903 Prestwick	Harry Vardon	300
1904 Sandwich	Jack White	296
1905 St. Andrews	James Braid	318
1906 Muirfield	James Braid	300
1907 Hoylake	Arnaud Massy	312
1908 Prestwick	James Braid	291
1909 Deal	John H. Taylor	295
1910 St. Andrews	James Braid	299
1911 Sandwich	Harry Vardon	303
1912 Muirfield	Edward Ray	295
1913 Hoylake	John H. Taylor	304
1914 Prestwick	Harry Vardon	306
1915–1919 Not played		
1920 Deal	George Duncan	303
1921 St. Andrews	Jock Hutchison	296
1922 Sandwich	Walter Hagen	300
1923 Troon	Arthur Havers	295
1924 Hoylake	Walter Hagen	301
1925 Prestwick	James Barnes	300
1926 Royal Lytham and St. Annes	*Robert T. Jones Jr.	291
1927 St. Andrews	*Robert T. Jones Jr.	285
1928 Sandwich	Walter Hagen	292
1929 Muirfield	Walter Hagen	292
1930 Hoylake	*Robert T. Jones Jr.	291
1931 Carnoustie	Tommy Armour	296
1932 Princes	Gene Sarazen	283
1933 St. Andrews	Denny Shute	292
1934 Sandwich	T. Henry Cotton	283
1935 Muirfield	Alfred Perry	283
1936 Hoylake	Alfred Padgham	287
1937 Carnoustie	T. Henry Cotton	290
1938 Sandwich	R. A. Whitcombe	295
1939 St. Andrews	Richard Burton	290
1940–45 Not played		
1946 St. Andrews	Sam Snead	290
1947 Hoylake	Fred Daly	293
1948 Muirfield	Henry Cotton	284
1949 Sandwich	Bobby Locke	283
1950 Troon	Bobby Locke	279
1951 Portrush	Max Faulkner	285
1952 Royal Lytham and St. Annes	Bobby Locke	287
1953 Carnoustie	Ben Hogan	282
1954 Royal Birkdale	Peter Thomson	283
1955 St. Andrews	Peter Thomson	281
1956 Hoylake	Peter Thomson	286
1957 St. Andrews	Bobby Locke	279
1958 Royal Lytham and St. Annes	Peter Thomson / David Thomas	278-139 / 278-143

1959 Muirfield	Gary Player	284
1960 St. Andrews	Kel Nagle	278
1961 Royal Birkdale	Arnold Palmer	284
1962 Troon	Arnold Palmer	276
1963 Royal Lytham and St. Annes	Bob Charles / Phil Rodgers	277-140 / 277-148
1964 St. Andrews	Tony Lema	279
1965 Royal Birkdale	Peter Thomson	285
1966 Muirfield	Jack Nicklaus	282
1967 Hoylake	Roberto de Vicenzo	278
1968 Carnoustie	Gary Player	289
1969 Royal Lytham and St. Annes	Tony Jacklin	280
1970 St. Andrews	Jack Nicklaus / Doug Sanders	283-72 / 283-73
1971 Royal Birkdale	Lee Trevino	278
1972 Muirfield	Lee Trevino	278
1973 Troon	Tom Weiskopf	276
1974 Royal Lytham and St. Annes	Gary Player	282
1975 Carnoustie	Tom Watson	279
1976 Royal Birkdale	Johnny Miller	279
1977 Turnberry	Tom Watson	268
1978 St. Andrews	Jack Nicklaus	281
1979 Royal Lytham and St. Annes	Seve Ballesteros	283
1980 Muirfield	Tom Watson	271

*Amateur.

USGA MEN'S AMATEUR

1895 Newport G.C. Newport, R.I.	Charles B. Macdonald d. C. E. Sands	12 and 11
1896 Shinnecock Southampton, N.Y.	H. J. Whigham d. J. G. Thorp	8 and 7
1897 Chicago C.C. Wheaton, Ill.	H. J. Whigham d. W. R. Betts	8 and 6
1898 Morris County G.C. Morristown, N.J.	Findlay S. Douglas d. W. B. Smith	5 and 3
1899 Onwentsia Club Lake Forest, Ill.	H. M. Harriman d. F. S. Douglas	3 and 2
1900 Garden City (N.Y.) G.C.	Walter J. Travis d. F. S. Douglas	2 up
1901 C.C. of Atlantic City, N.J.	Walter J. Travis d. W. E. Egan	5 and 4
1902 Glen View Golf, Ill.	Louis N. James d. E. M. Byers	4 and 2
1903 Nassau C.C. Glen Cove, N.Y.	Walter J. Travis d. E. M. Byers	5 and 4
1904 Baltusrol G.C. Springfield, N.J.	H. Chandler Egan d. F. Herreshoff	8 and 6
1905 Chicago G.C. Wheaton, Ill.	H. Chandler Egan d. D. E. Sawyer	6 and 5
1906 Englewood (N.J.) G.C.	Eben M. Byers d. G. S. Lyon	2 up
1907 Euclid Club	Jerome D. Travers	

Cleveland, O.	d. A. Graham	6 and 5
1908 Garden City	Jerome D. Travers	
(N.Y.) G.C.	d. Max H. Behr	8 and 7
1909 Chicago G.C.	Robert A. Gardner	
Wheaton, Ill.	d. H. C. Egan	4 and 3
1910 The Country Club	William C. Fownes, Jr.	
Brookline, Mass.	d. W. K. Wood	4 and 3
1911 The Apawamis	Harold H. Hilton	
C., Rye, N.Y.	d. F. Herreshoff	1 up, 37
1912 Chicago G.C.	Jerome D. Travers	
Wheaton, Ill.	d. C. Evans, Jr.	7 and 6
1913 Garden City	Jerome D. Travers	
(N.Y.) G.C.	d. J. G. Anderson	5 and 4
1914 Ekwanok C.C.	Francis Ouimet	
Manchester, Vt.	d. J. D. Travers	6 and 5
1915 C.C. of Detroit	Robert A. Gardner	
Grosse Pointe	d. J. G. Anderson	5 and 4
Farms, Mich.		
1916 Merion Cricket C.	Charles Evans, Jr.	
Ardmore, Pa.	d. R. A. Gardner	4 and 3
1917–1918 No championships		
1919 Oakmont	Davidson Herron	
(Pa.) C.C.	d. R. I. Jones, Jr.	5 and 4
1920 Engineers' C.C.	Charles Evans, Jr.	
Roslyn, N.Y.	d. F. Ouimet	7 and 6
1921 St. Louis C.C.	Jesse P. Guilford	
Clayton, Mo.	d. R. A. Gardner	7 and 6
1922 The Country Club	Jess W. Sweetser	
Brookline, Mass.	d. C. Evans, Jr.	3 and 2
1923 Flossmoor	Max R. Marston	
(Ill.) C.C.	d. J. W. Sweetser	1 up, 38
1924 Merion Cricket C.	Robert T. Jones, Jr.	
Ardmore, Pa.	d. G. Von Elm	9 and 8
1925 Oakmont	Robert T. Jones, Jr.	
(Pa.) C.C.	d. Watts Gunn	8 and 7
1926 Baltusrol G.C.	George Von Elm	
Springfield, N.J.	d. R. T. Jones, Jr.	2 and 1
1927 Minikahda C.C.	Robert T. Jones, Jr.	
Minneapolis, Minn.	d. C. Evans, Jr.	8 and 7
1928 Brae Burn C.C.	Robert T. Jones, Jr.	
West Newton,	d. T. P. Perkins	10 and 9
Mass.		
1929 Del Monte G. &	Harrison R. Johnston	
C.C., Pebble Beach	d. Dr. O. F. Willing	4 and 3
1930 Merion Cricket C.	Robert T. Jones, Jr.	
Ardmore, Pa.	d. E. V. Homans	8 and 7
1931 Beverly C.C.	Francis Ouimet	
Chicago, Ill.	d. J. Westland	6 and 5
1932 Baltimore	C. Ross Somerville	
(Md.) C.C.	d. J. Goodman	2 and 1
1933 Kenwood C.C.	George T. Dunlap, Jr.	
Cincinnati, O.	d. M. Marston	6 and 5
1934 The Country Club	W. Lawson Little, Jr.	
Brookline, Mass.	d. D. Goldman	8 and 7
1935 The Country Club	W. Lawson Little, Jr.	
Cleveland, O.	d. W. Emery	4 and 2
1936 Garden City	John W. Fischer	
(N.Y.) G.C.	d. J. McLean	37 holes
1937 Alderwood C.C.	John G. Goodman	
Portland, Ore.	d. R. E. Billows	2 u
1938 Oakmont	William P. Turnesa	
(Pa.) C.C.	d. B. P. Abbott	8 and
1939 North Shore C.C.	Marvin H. Ward	
Glenview, Ill.	d. R. E. Billows	7 and 5
1940 Winged Foot G.C.	Richard D. Chapman	
Mamaroneck, N.Y.	d. W. B. McCullough, Jr.	11 and 9
1941 Omaha Field C.	Marvin H. Ward	
Omaha, Neb.	d. B. P. Abbott	4 and 3
1942–45 No championships		
1946 Baltusrol G.C.	Stanley E. Bishop	
Springfield, N.J.	d. S. L. Quick	37 holes
1947 Del Monte G. &	Robert H. Riegel	
C.C., Pebble Beach	d. J. W. Dawson	2 and 1
1948 Memphis C.C.	William P. Turnesa	
Memphis, Tenn.	d. R. E. Billows	2 and 1
1949 Oak Hill C.C.	Charles R. Coe	
Rochester, N.Y.	d. R. King	11 and 10
1950 Minneapolis G.C.	Sam Urzetta	
Minneapolis, Minn.	d. F. Stranahan	1 up, 39
1951 Saucon Valley C.C.	Billy Maxwell	
Bethlehem, Pa.	d. J. F. Gagliardi	4 and 3
1952 Seattle G.C.	Jack Westland	
Seattle, Wash.	d. Al Mengert	3 and 2
1953 Oklahoma City	Gene A. Littler	
G. & C.C.	d. Dale Morey	1 up
1954 C.C. of Detroit	Arnold D. Palmer	
Grosse Pointe	d. R. Sweeny	1 up
1955 C.C. of Virginia	E. Harvie Ward	
Richmond, Va.	d. W. Hyndman, III	9 and 8
1956 Knollwood C.C.	E. Harvie Ward	
Lake Forest, Ill.	d. C. Kocsis	5 and 4
1957 The Country Club	Hillman Robbins	
Brookline, Mass.	d. Dr. F. Taylor	5 and 4
1958 Olympic C.,	Charles Coe	
San Francisco	d. T. Aaron	5 and 4
1959 Broadmoor G.C.,	Jack Nicklaus	
Colorado Springs	d. Charles Coe	1 up
1960 St. Louis C.C.	Deane Beman	
Clayton, Mo.	d. B. Gardner	6 and 4
1961 Pebble Beach	Jack Nicklaus	
(Calif.) G.L.	d. D. Wysong, Jr.	8 and 6
1962 Pinehurst	Labron Harris, Jr.	
(N.C.) C.C.	d. Downing Gray	1 up
1963 Wakonda C.C.	Deane Beman	
Des Moines, Ia.	d. R. H. Sikes	2 and 1
1964 Canterbury G.C.	Bill Campbell	
Cleveland, O.	d. Ed Tutwiler	1 up
1965 Southern Hills	Bob Murphy	291
C.C., Tulsa, Okla.	Bob Dickson	292
1966 Merion G.C.,	Gary Cowan	285-75
Ardmore, Penn.	Deane Beman	285-76
1967 Broadmoor C.C.,	Bob Dickson	285
Colorado Springs	Vinny Giles	286
1968 Scioto C.C.,	Bruce Fleisher	284
Columbus, O.	Vinny Giles	285
1969 Oakmont C.C.,	Steve Melnyk	286
Oakmont, Pa.	Vinny Giles	291
1970 Waverley C.C.,	Lanny Wadkins	279
Portland, Ore.	Tom Kite	280
1971 Wilmington, C.C.,	Gary Cowan	280
Wilmington, Del.	Eddie Pearce	283
1972 Charlotte C.C.	Vinny Giles	285
Charlotte, N.C.	Ben Crenshaw	288
1973 Inverness C.,	Craig Stadler	

Toledo, O.	d. David Strawn	6 and 5
1974 Ridgewood (N.J.) C.C.	Jerry Pate d. John Grace	2 and 1
1975 C.C. of Virginia, Richmond	Fred Ridley d. Keith Fergus	2 up
1976 Bel Air C.C. Los Angeles	Bill Sander d. Parker Moore	8 and 6
1977 Aronimink G.C., Newton Square, Pa.	John Fought d. Doug Fischesser	9 and 8
1978 Plainfield (N.J.) C.C.	John Cook d. Scott Hoch	5 and 4
1979 Canterbury G.C., Cleveland	Mark O'Meara d. John Cook	8 and 7
	Hal Sutton	
Carolina, Pinehurst	d. Bob Lewis	9 and 8

BRITISH AMATEUR CHAMPIONSHIP

1950 St. Andrews	Frank Stranahan d. Dick Chapman	8 and 6
1951 Porthcawl	Dick Chapman d. Charlie Coe	5 and 4
1952 Prestwick	Bud Ward d. Frank Stranahan	6 and 5
1953 Hoylake	Joe Carr d. Bud Ward	2 up
1954 Muirfield	D. Bachil d. Bill Campbell	2 and 1
1955 Royal Lytham and St. Annes	Joe Conrad d. Alan Slater	3 and 2
1956 Troon	John Beharrell d. Leslie Taylor	5 and 4
1957 Formby	Reid Jack d. Harold Ridgley	2 and 1
1958 St. Andrews	Joe Carr d. Alan Thirlwell	3 and 2
1959 Royal St. George's	Deane Beman d. Bill Hyndman	3 and 2
1960 Royal Portrush	Joe Carr d. Bob Cochran	7 and 6
1961 Turnberry	Mike Bonallack d. Jimmy Walker	6 and 4
1962 Hoylake	Richard Davies d. John Povall	1 up
1963 St. Andrews	Michael Lunt d. John Blackwell	2 and 1
1964 Ganton	Gordon Clarke d. Michael Lunt	1 up, 39
1965 Royal Porthcawl	Mike Bonallack d. Clive Clark	2 and 1
1966 Carnoustie	Bobby Cole d. Ron Shade	3 and 2
1967 Formby	Bob Dickson d. Ron Cerrudo	2 and 1
1968 Troon	Mike Bonallack	

	d. Joe Carr	7 and 6
1969 Hoylake	Mike Bonallack d. Bill Hyndman	3 and 2
1970 Royal County Down	Mike Bonallack d. Bill Hyndman	8 and 7
1971 Carnoustie	Steve Melnyk d. Jim Simons	3 and 2
1972 Royal St. George's	Trevor Homer d. Alan Thirlwell	4 and 3
1973 Royal Porthcawl	Dick Siderowf d. Peter Moody	5 and 3
1974 Muirfield	Trevor Homer d. Jim Gabrielsen	2 up
1975 Hoylake	Vinny Giles d. Mark James	8 and 7
1976 St. Andrews	Dick Siderowf d. John Davies	1 up, 37
1977 Ganton	Peter McEvoy d. Hugh Campbell	5 and 4
1978 Troon	Peter McEvoy d. Paul McKellar	4 and 3
1979 Hillside	Jay Sigel d. Scott Hoch	3 and 2
1980 Royal Porthcawl	David Evans d. David Suddards	4 and 3

Event inaugurated in 1885.

USGA WOMEN'S OPEN

1946 Spokane C.C., Spokane, Wash.	Patty Berg d. Betty Jameson	5 and 4
1947 Star, Forest C.C., Greensboro, N.C.	Betty Jameson *Sally Sessions	295 301
1948 Atlantic City C.C., Northfield, N.J.	Babe Zaharias Betty Hicks	300 308
1949 Prince George's, Landover, Md.	Louise Suggs Babe Zaharias	291 305
1950 Rolling Hills C.C., Wichita, Kan.	Babe Zaharias *Betsy Rawls	291 300
1951 Druid Hills G.C., Atlanta, Ga.	Betsy Rawls Louise Suggs	293 298
1952 Bala G.C., Philadelphia, Pa.	Louise Suggs M. Bauer, B. Jameson	284 291
1953 C.C. of Rochester, Rochester, N.Y.	Betsy Rawls Jackie Pung	302-71 302-77
1954 Salem C.C., Peabody, Mass.	Babe Zaharias Betty Hicks	291 303
1955 Wichita C.C., Wichita, Kan.	Fay Crocker Faulk, Suggs	299 303
1956 Northland C.C. Duluth, Minn.	Kathy Cornelius *B. McIntire	302-75 302-82
1957 Winged Foot C.C., Mamaroneck, N.Y.	Betsy Rawls Patty Berg	299 305
1958 Forest Lake C.C.,	Mickey Wright	290

Detroit, Mich.	Louise Suggs	295	C.C., Pittsburgh	Wiffi Smith	288
1959 Churchill Valley	Mickey Wright	287	1958 Churchill Valley	Mickey Wright	288
C.C., Pittsburgh	Louise Suggs	289	C.C., Pittsburgh	Fay Crocker	294
1960 Worcester C.C.,	Betsy Rawls	292	1959 Sheraton Hotel C.C.,	Betsy Rawls	288
Worcester, Mass.	Joyce Ziske	293	French Lick, Ind.	Patty Berg	289
1961 Baltusrol G.C.,	Mickey Wright	293	1960 Sheraton Hotel C.C.,	Mickey Wright	292
Springfield, N.J.	Betsy Rawls	299	French Lick, Ind.	Louise Suggs	295
1962 Dunes G.&B.C.	Murle Lindstrom	301	1961 Stardust C.C.,	Mickey Wright	287
Myrtle Beach, S.C.	Prentice, Jessen	303	Las Vegas, Nev.	Louise Suggs	296
1963 Kenwood C.C.,	Mary Mills	289	1962 Stardust C.C.,	Judy Kimball	282
Cincinnati, O.	Suggs, Haynie	292	Las Vegas, Nev.	Shirley Spork	286
1964 San Diego C.C.,	Mickey Wright	290-70	1963 Stardust C.C.,	Mickey Wright	294
Chula Vista, Calif.	Ruth Jessen	290-72	Las Vegas, Nev.	Mills, Faulk, Suggs	296
1965 Atlantic City C.C.,	Carol Mann	290	1964 Stardust C.C.,	Mary Mills	278
Northfield, N.J.	Kathy Cornelius	292	Las Vegas, Nev.	Mickey Wright	280
1966 Hazeltine Ntl. G.C.,	Sandra Spuzich	297	1965 Stardust C.C.,	Sandra Haynie	279
Chaska, Minn.	Carol Mann	298	Las Vegas, Nev.	Clifford A. Creed	280
1967 Cascades G.C.	*Catherine Lacoste	294	1966 Stardust C.C.,	Gloria Ehret	282
Hot Springs, Va.	Stone, Maxwell	296	Las Vegas, Nev.	Mickey Wright	285
1968 Moselem Springs	Susie Berning	289	1967 Pleasant Valley C.C.,	Kathy Whitworth	284
(Pa.) C.C.	Mickey Wright	292	Sutton, Mass.	Shirley Englehorn	285
1969 Scenic Hills C.C.,	Donna Caponi	294	1968 Pleasant Valley C.C.,	Sandra Post	294-68
Pensacola, Fla.	Peggy Wilson	295	Sutton, Mass.	Kathy Whitworth	294-75
1970 Muskogee C.C.,	Donna Caponi	287	1969 Concord G.C.,	Betsy Rawls	293
Muskogee, Okla.	Haynie, Spuzich	288	Kiamesha Lake, N.Y.	Mann, Berning	297
1971 Kahkwa C.C.,	JoAnne Carner	288	1970 Pleasant Valley C.C.,	Shirley Englehorn	285-74
Erie, Pa.	Kathy Whitworth	295	Sutton, Mass.	Kathy Whitworth	285-78
1972 Winged Foot G.C.,	Susie Berning	299	1971 Pleasant Valley C.C.,	Kathy Whitworth	288
Mamaroneck, N.Y.	Rankin, Barnett,		Sutton, Mass.	Kathy Ahern	292
	Ahern	300	1972 Pleasant Valley C.C.,	Kathy Ahern	293
1973 C.C. of Rochester,	Susie Berning	290	Sutton, Mass.	Jane Blalock	299
Rochester, N.Y.	Ehret, Hamlin	295	1973 Pleasant Valley C.C.,	Mary Mills	288
1974 LaGrange C.C.,	Sandra Haynie	295	Sutton, Mass.	Betty Burfeindt	289
LaGrange, Ill.	Stone, Mann	296	1974 Pleasant Valley C.C.,	Sandra Haynie	288
1975 Atlantic City C.C.,	Sandra Palmer	295	Sutton, Mass.	JoAnne Carner	290
Northfield, N.J.	*Lopez, Carner, Post	299	1975 Pine Ridge G.C.,	Kathy Whitworth	288
1976 Rolling Green G.C.,	JoAnne Carner	292-76	Baltimore	Sandra Haynie	289
Springfield, Pa.	Sandra Palmer	292-78	1976 Pine Ridge G.C.,	Betty Burfeindt	287
1977 Hazeltine Ntl. G.C.,	Hollis Stacy	292	Baltimore	Judy Rankin	288
Chaska, Minn.	Nancy Lopez	294	1977 Bay Tree G. Plant.,	Chako Higuchi	279
1978 C.C. of Indianapolis	Hollis Stacy	289	Myrtle Beach, S.C.	Bradley, Rankin, Post	282
	Carner, Little	290	1978 Jack Nicklaus G.	Nancy Lopez	275
1979 Brooklawn C.C.,	Jerilyn Britz	284	Ctr., Mason, Ohio	Amy Alcott	281
Fairfield, Conn.	Massey, Palmer	286	1979 Jack Nicklaus G.	Donna C. Young	279
1980 Richland C.C.	Amy Alcott	280	Ctr., Mason, Ohio	Jerilyn Britz	282
Nashville, Tenn.			1980 Jack Nicklaus G.	Sally Little	285
			Ctr., Mason, Ohio		

*Amateur

†Won sudden-death playoff.

LPGA CHAMPIONSHIP

1955 Orchard Ridge	Beverly Hanson	
C.C., Ft. Wayne	d. L. Suggs	4 and 3
1956 Forest Lake C.C.,	†Marlene Hagge	291
Detroit, Mich.	Patty Berg	291
1957 Churchill Valley	Louise Suggs	285

ALL-TIME MONEY LEADERS
(In tour events, through 1979)

Player	Since	Total
1. Jack Nicklaus	1962	$3,408,827
2. Lee Trevino	1966	2,088,178
3. Arnold Palmer	1955	1,798,431

4. Tom Weiskopf	1964	1,741,155	1947	31	352,500	11,371
5. Billy Casper	1955	1,683,618	1948	34	427,000	12,559
6. Tom Watson	1972	1,671,433	1949	25	338,200	13,528
7. Gary Player	1957	1,581,124	1950	33	459,950	13,938
8. Hale Irwin	1968	1,580,064	1951	30	460,200	15,340
9. Gene Littler	1954	1,509,870	1952	32	498,016	15,563
10. Miller Barber	1959	1,418,892	1953	32	562,704	17,585
11. Bruce Crampton	1957	1,374,294	1954	26	600,819	23,108
12. Hubert Green	1970	1,326,213	1955	36	782,010	21,723
13. Ray Floyd	1963	1,239,635	1956	36	847,070	23,530
14. Johnny Miller	1969	1,210,771	1957	32	820,360	25,636
15. Al Geiberger	1960	1,169,074	1958	39	1,005,800	25,789
16. Lou Graham	1964	1,149,972	1959	43	1,102,474	25,639
17. Dave Stockton	1964	1,068,402	1960	41	1,187,340	28,959
18. Dave Hill	1959	1,065,458	1961	45	1,461,830	32,485
19. Don January	1956	1,024,951	1962	49	1,790,320	36,537
20. J. C. Snead	1968	1,017,917	1963	43	2,044,900	47,497
21. Frank Beard	1962	1,008,426	1964	41	2,301,063	56,123
22. Julius Boros	1950	1,004,861	1965	36	2,848,515	79,403
23. George Archer	1964	983,590	1966	36	3,074,445	85,401
24. Charles Coody	1963	957,464	1967	37	3,979,162	108,356
25. Bob Murphy	1968	949,407	1968	45	5,077,600	112,835
26. Bobby Nichols	1960	944,651	1969	47	5,465,875	116,295
27. Ben Crenshaw	1973	933,402	1970	47	6,259,501	133,181
28. Lanny Wadkins	1971	932,864	1971	52	6,587,976	126,689
29. Tommy Aaron	1961	871,151	1972	47	6,954,649	151,188
30. Chi Chi Rodriguez	1960	834,649	1973	47	8,657,225	184,196
31. Jerry McGee	1967	828,241	1974	43	7,764,449	180,568
32. Dan Sikes	1961	819,601	1975	41	7,402,750	180,555
33. Lee Elder	1968	798,784	1976	44	8,648,852	196,564
34. Tom Kite	1972	791,558	1977	44	9,015,000	204,886
35. Bruce Devlin	1962	779,414	1978	44	9,216,832	219,448
36. Gay Brewer	1956	775,593	1979	42	11,679,802	278,090
37. Doug Sanders	1957	771,284				
38. John Mahaffey	1971	746,357				
39. Jerry Heard	1969	743,536				
40. Grier Jones	1968	742,566				
41. David Graham	1971	702,777				
42. Bert Yancey	1964	688,125				
43. Jim Colbert	1966	674,715				
44. Kermit Zarley	1963	668,538				
45. Homero Blancas	1965	658,851				
46. Mark Hayes	1973	641,632				
47. Bob Goalby	1957	641,417				
48. Art Wall	1950	637,316				
49. Rod Funseth	1961	630,562				
50. Jerry Pate	1975	621,211				

TOURNAMENT PRIZE MONEY
(In tour events only)

Year	Events	Total Purses	Average Purse
1945	36	$435,380	$12,094
1946	37	411,533	11,123

PAST LEADING MONEY WINNERS

Year Player	Money
1941 Ben Hogan	$18,358
1942 Ben Hogan	13,143
1943 War bond prizes.	
1944 Byron Nelson	37,967
1945 Byron Nelson	63,335
1946 Ben Hogan	42,556
1947 Jimmy Demaret	27,936
1948 Ben Hogan	32,112
1949 Sam Snead	31,593
1950 Sam Snead	35,758
1951 Lloyd Mangrum	26,088
1952 Julius Boros	37,032
1953 Lew Worsham	34,002
1954 Bob Toski	65,819
1955 Julius Boros	63,121
1956 Ted Kroll	72,835
1957 Dick Mayer	65,835

1958 Arnold Palmer	42,607
1959 Art Wall	53,167
1960 Arnold Palmer	75,262
1961 Gary Player	64,450
1962 Arnold Palmer	81,448
1963 Arnold Palmer	128,230
1964 Jack Nicklaus	113,284
1965 Jack Nicklaus	140,752
1966 Billy Casper	121,944
1967 Jack Nicklaus	188,988
1968 Bill Casper	205,168
1969 Frank Beard	175,223
1970 Lee Trevino	157,037
1971 Jack Nicklaus	244,490
1972 Jack Nicklaus	320,542
1973 Jack Nicklaus	308,362
1974 Johnny Miller	353,021
1975 Jack Nicklaus	298,149
1976 Jack Nicklaus	266,438
1977 Tom Watson	310,653
1978 Tom Watson	362,429
1979 Tom Watson	462,636
1980 Tom Watson	530,808

ALL-TIME PGA TOURNAMENT WINNERS
(In tour events, 1930–1979)

Player	Since	Total
1. Sam Snead	1937	84
2. Jack Nicklaus	1962	68
3. Ben Hogan	1938	62
4. Arnold Palmer	1955	61
5. Byron Nelson	1935	54
6. Billy Casper	1955	51
7. Lloyd Mangrum	1939	34
8. Cary Middlecoff	1947	33
9. Jimmy Demaret	1935	31
10. Gene Littler	1954	29
11. Lee Trevino	1965	25
12. Jim Ferrier	1944	21
Gary Player	1957	21
Tom Watson	1972	21
14. Doug Sanders	1957	20
15. Doug Ford	1950	19
16. Julius Boros	1950	18
17. Harold McSpaden	1932	17
Johnny Miller	1969	18
19. Mike Souchak	1953	16
Hubert Green	1970	16
22. Dutch Harrison	1930	15
Paul Runyan	1929	15
Tommy Bolt	1946	15
Jack Burke Jr.	1947	15
Bruce Crampton	1957	15

| 27. Art Wall | 1950 | 14 |
| Ken Venturi | 1957 | 14 |

VARDON TROPHY WINNERS

Year	Player	Average
1947	Jimmy Demaret	69.90
1948	Ben Hogan	69.30
1949	Sam Snead	69.37
1950	Sam Snead	69.23
1951	Lloyd Mangrum	70.05
1952	Jack Burke	70.54
1953	Lloyd Mangrum	70.22
1954	E. J. Harrison	70.41
1955	Sam Snead	69.86
1956	Cary Middlecoff	70.35
1957	Dow Finsterwald	70.29
1958	Bob Rosburg	70.11
1959	Art Wall	70.35
1960	Bill Casper	69.95
1961	Arnold Palmer	69.82
1962	Arnold Palmer	70.27
1963	Bill Casper	70.58
1964	Arnold Palmer	70.01
1965	Bill Casper	70.59
1966	Bill Casper	70.16
1967	Arnold Palmer	70.18
1968	Bill Casper	69.98
1969	Dave Hill	70.34
1970	Lee Trevino	70.64
1971	Lee Trevino	70.41
1972	Lee Trevino	70.91
1973	Bruce Crampton	70.69
1974	Lee Trevino	70.53
1975	Bruce Crampton	70.50
1976	Don January	70.56
1977	Tom Watson	70.32
1978	Tom Watson	70.16
1979	Tom Watson	70.27
1980	Lee Trevino	69.73

ALL-TIME MONEY LEADERS

Player	Since	Money
1. Kathy Whitworth	1959	$858,460
2. Judy Rankin	1962	761,129
3. Jane Blalock	1969	708,935
4. JoAnne Carner	1970	649,979
5. Donna Young	1965	602,808
6. Sandra Palmer	1964	596,020
7. Sandra Post	1968	525,590
8. Carol Mann	1961	498,532
9. Sandra Haynie	1961	498,387
10. Pat Bradley	1974	452,616
11. Nancy Lopez	1977	410,440

12. Marlene Hagge	1950	372,251
13. Mickey Wright	1955	368,215
14. Amy Alcott	1975	366,434
15. Jo Ann Prentice	1956	358,299

ALL-TIME TOURNAMENT WINNERS

Player	Since	Total
1. Mickey Wright	1956	82
2. Kathy Whitworth	1959	80
3. Betsy Rawls	1951	55
4. Louise Suggs	1949	50
5. Patty Berg	1948	41
6. Sandra Haynie	1961	39
7. Carol Mann	1961	38
8. Babe Zaharias	1948	31
9. Judy Rankin	1962	28
Jane Blalock	1969	26

VARE TROPHY WINNERS

Year	Player	Ave.	Year	Player	Ave.
1953	P. Berg	75.00	1967	K. Whitworth	72.74
1954	B. Zaharias	75.48	1968	Carol Mann	72.04
1955	P. Berg	74.47	1969	K. Whitworth	72.38
1956	P. Berg	74.57	1970	K. Whitworth	72.26
1957	L. Suggs	74.64	1971	K. Whitworth	72.88
1958	B. Hanson	74.92	1972	K. Whitworth	72.38
1959	B. Rawls	74.03	1973	Judy Rankin	73.08
1960	M. Wright	73.25	1974	J. Carner	72.87
1961	M. Wright	73.55	1975	J. Carner	72.40
1962	M. Wright	73.67	1976	Judy Rankin	72.25
1963	M. Wright	72.81	1977	Judy Rankin	72.16
1964	M. Wright	72.46	1978	Nancy Lopez	71.76
1965	K. Whitworth	72.61	1979	Nancy Lopez	71.20
1966	K. Whitworth	72.60			

AMATEUR PUBLIC LINKS CHAMPIONSHIPS

Year	Team Champ.	Ind. Champ.
1955	Miami, Fla.	Sam Kocsis
1956	Memphis, Tenn.	James Buxbaum
1957	Honolulu, Hawaii	Don Essig, III
1958	St. Paul, Minn.	Dan Sikes, Jr.
1959	Dallas, Tex.	Bill Wright
1960	Pasadena, Calif.	Verne Callison
1961	Honolulu, Hawaii	R. H. Sikes
1962	Seattle, Wash.	R. H. Sikes
1963	Toledo, Ohio	Bobby Lunn
1964	Los Angeles, Calif.	Bill McDonald
1965	Phoenix, Ariz.	Arne Dokka
1966	Pittsburgh, Pa.	Monty Kaser

1967	Dayton, Ohio	Verne Callison
1968	Dallas, Tex.	Gene Towry
1969	Pasadena, Calif.	John Jackson
1970	Chicago, Ill.	Robert Risch
1971	Portland, Ore.	Fred Haney
1972	Portland, Ore.	Bob Allard
1973	Seattle	Stan Stopa
1974	San Francisco	C. Barenaba Jr.
1975	Honolulu	Randy Barenaba
1976	Detroit, Mich.	Eddie Mudd
1977	Tacoma, Wash	Jerry Vidovic
1978	Louisville, Ky.	Dean Prince
1979	Phoenix	Dennis Walsh
1980	Los Angeles	Jodie Mudd

Event inaugurated in 1922.

WESTERN AMATEUR

1955 Rockford (Ill.) C.C.	Edward Merrins d. H. Robbins	1 up (37)	
1956 Belle Meade C.C., Nashville, Tenn.	Mason Rudolph d. J. Parnell	6 and 4	
1957 Old Warson C.C., St. Louis, Mo.	Dr. Ed. Updegraff d. J. Campbell	9 and 8	
1958 The C.C. of Florida, Delray Beach, Fla.	James Key d. M. Rudolph	3 and 2	
1959 Waverley C.C., Portland, Ore.	Dr. Ed. Updegraff d. C. Hunter	7 and 6	
1960 Northland C.C., Duluth, Mich.	Tommy Aaron d. Bob Cochran	Default	
1961 New Orleans (La.) C.C.	Jack Nicklaus d. James Key	4 and 3	
1962 Orchard Lake C.C., Detroit, Mich.	Art Hudnutt d. Bud Stevens	1 up	
1963 Point O'Woods G. & C.C.	Tom Weiskopf d. Labron Harris, Jr.	5 and 4	
1964 Tucson C.C., Tucson, Ariz.	Steve Oppermann d. Dr. Ed Updegraff	3 and 2	
1965 Point O'Woods G. & C.C.	Bob Smith d. George Boutell	37 holes	
1966 Pinehurst C.C., Pinehurst, N.C.	Jim Wiechers d. Ron Cerrudo	1 up	
1967 Milburn C.C., Kansas City, Mo.	Bob Smith d. Marty Fleckman	3 and 1	
1968 Grosse Ile (Mich.) G. & C.C.	Rik Massengale d. Kemp Richardson	3 and 1	
1969 Rockford C.C., Rockford, Ill.	Steve Melnyk d. Howard Twitty	3 and 1	
1970 Wichita C.C., Wichita, Kan.	Lanny Wadkins d. Charlie Borner	4 and 2	
1971 Point O'Woods G. & C.C.	Andy North d. Barney Thompson	1 up	
1972 Point O'Woods G. & C.C.	Gary Sanders d. Gil Morgan	19 holes	

1973 Point O'Woods	Ben Crenshaw	
G. & C.C.	d. Jimmy Ellis	4 and 3
1974 Point O'Woods	Curtis Strange	
G. & C.C.	d. Jay Haas	20 holes
1975 Point O'Woods	Andy Bean	
G. & C.C.	d. Randy Simmons	1 up
1976 Point O'Woods	John Stark	
G. & C.C.	d. Mick Soli	3 and 1
1977 Point O'Woods	Jim Nelford	
G. & C.C.	d. Rafael Alarcon	2 and 1
1978 Point O'Woods	Bob Clampett d.	
G. & C.C.	Mark Wiebe	2 up
1979 Point O'Woods	Hal Sutton	
G. & C.C.	d. Mike Gove	1 up
1980 Point O'Woods	Hal Sutton	
G. & C.C.	d. Dave Ogrin	5 and 4

Event inaugurated in 1899.

NORTH AND SOUTH CHAMPIONSHIP

1960	Charlie Smith d. Peter Green, 5 and 3
1961	Bill Hyndman d. Dick Chapman, 4 and 3
1962	Billy Joe Patton d. Hobart Manley, 7 and 6
1963	Billy Joe Patton d. Bob Allen, 7 and 6
1964	Dale Morey d. Billy Joe Patton, 3 and 2
1965	Tom Draper d. Don Allen, 4 and 3
1966	Ward Wettlaufer d. Marion Heck, 4 and 2
1967	Bill Campbell d. Bill Hyndman, 10 and 9
1968	Jack Lewis d. Bill Hyndman, 7 and 6
1969	Joe Inman Jr. d. Lanny Wadkins, 2 and 1
1970	Gary Cowan d. Dale Morey, 5 and 4
1971	Eddie Pearce d. Vinny Giles, 5 and 4
1972	Danny Edwards d. Eddie Pearce, 3 and 1
1973	Mike Ford d. Bill Harvey, 1 up
1974	George Burns III d. Danny Yates, 4 and 2
1975	Curtis Strange d. George Burns III, 2 up
1976	Curtis Strange d. Fred Ridley, 6 and 5
1977	Gary Hallberg d. Michael Donald, 5 and 3
1978	Gary Hallberg d. Hal Sutton, 5 and 4
1979	John McGough d. Scott Hoch, 1 up
1980	Hal Sutton d. Kevin Walsh, 12 and 10

Event inaugurated in 1902.

NCAA CHAMPIONSHIP

Year	Team Champ.	Ind. Champ.
1945	Ohio State	John Lorms
1946	Stanford	George Hamer
1947	Louisiana State	Dave Barclay
1948	San Jose State	Bob Harris
1949	North Texas	Harvie Ward
1950	North Texas	Fred Wampler
1951	North Texas	Tom Nieporte
1952	North Texas	Jim Vickers
1953	Stanford	Earl Moeller
1954	S. Methodist	Hillman Robbins
1955	Louisiana State	Joe Campbell
1956	Houston	Rick Jones
1957	Houston	Rex Baxter Jr.
1958	Houston	Phil Rodgers
1959	Houston	Dick Crawford
1960	Houston	Dick Crawford
1961	Purdue	Jack Nicklaus
1962	Houston	Kermit Zarley
1963	Oklahoma State	R. H. Sikes
1964	Houston	Terry Small
1965	Houston	Marty Fleckman
1966	Houston	Bob Murphy
1967	Houston	Hale Irwin
1968	Florida	Grier Jones
1969	Houston	Bob Clark
1970	Houston	John Mahaffey
1971	Texas	Ben Crenshaw
1972	Texas	Tom Kite
		Ben Crenshaw
1973	Florida	Ben Crenshaw
1974	Wake Forest	Curtis Strange
1975	Wake Forest	Jay Haas
1976	Oklahoma State	Scott Simpson
1977	Houston	Scott Simpson
1978	Oklahoma State	David Edwards
1979	Ohio State	Gary Hallberg
1980	Oklahoma State	Don Blake

Tournament inaugurated in 1897.

USGA SENIOR CHAMPIONSHIP

1955 J. Wood Platt, Philadelphia	
d. Geo. Studinger, S.F.	5 and 4
1956 Fred Wright, Watertown, Mass.	
d. J. C. Espie, Indianapolis	4 and 3
1957 J. C. Espie, Indianapolis	
d. Fred Wright, Watertown, Mass.	2 and 1
1958 Thomas G. Robbins, Pinehurst, N.C.	
d. J. Dawson, Palm Springs, Cal.	2 and 1
1959 J. C. Espie, Indianapolis, Ind.	
d. J. W. Brown, Sea Girt, N.J.	3 and 1
1960 Michael Cestone, Jamesburg, N.J.	
d. David Rose, Cleveland	20 holes
1961 Dexter Daniels, Winter Haven, Fla.	
d. Col. Wm. K. Lanman, Golf, Ill.	2 and 1
1962 Merrill Carlsmith, Hilo, Hawaii	
d. Willis Blakely, Portland, Ore.	4 and 2
1963 Merrill Carlsmith, Hilo, Hawaii	
d. Bill Higgins, San Francisco	3 and 2
1964 Bill Higgins, San Francisco	
d. Eddie Murphy, Portland, Ore.	2 and 1
1965 Robert Kiersky, Oakmont, Pa.	

d. Geo. Beechler, Prineville, Ore. — 19 holes
1966 Dexter Daniels, Winter Haven, Fla.
d. George Beechler, Prineville, Ore. — 1 up
1967 Ray Palmer, Lincoln Park, Mich.,
d. Walter Bronson, Oak Brook, Ill. — 3 and 2
1968 Curtis Person, Memphis, Tenn.,
d. Ben Goodes, Reidsville, N.C. — 2 and 1
1969 Curtis Person, Memphis, Tenn.,
d. David Goldman, Dallas, Tex. — 1 up
1970 Gene Andrews, Whittier, Calif.
d. Jim Ferrie, Indian Wells, Calif. — 1 up
1971 Tom Draper, Troy, Mich., d. Ernie
Pieper, San Juan Bautista, Calif. — 3 and 1
1972 Lew Oehmig, Lookout Mtn., Tenn.
d. Ernie Pieper, San Jose, Calif. — 20 holes
1973 Bill Hyndman, Huntingdon Valley, Pa.
d. Harry Welch, Salisbury, N.C. — 3 and 2
1974 Dale Morey, High Point, N.C.
d. Lew Oehmig, Lookout Mtn., Tenn. — 3 and 2
1975 Bill Colm, Pebble Beach, Calif.
d. Steve Stimac, Walnut Creek, Calif. — 4 and 3
1976 Lew Oehmig, Lookout Mountain, Tenn.
d. John Richardson, Laguna Niguel, Calif. — 4 and 3
1977 Dale Morey, High Point, N.C. d. Lew Oehmig, Lookout Mtn., Tenn. — 4 and 3
1978 K. K. Compton, Marble Falls, Tex.,
d. John Kline, Houston — 1 up
1979 Bill Campbell, Huntington, W.Va. d. Lew Oehmig, Lookout Mtn., Tenn. — 2 and 1
1980 Bill Campbell, Huntington, W.Va. d. Gen. K.K. Compton — 3 and 2

USGA JUNIOR BOYS

1950 Denver C.C. — Mason Rudolph
1951 U. of Illinois G.C. — Tommy Jacobs
1952 Yale G.C. — Don Bisplinghoff
1953 Southern Hills C.C. — Rex Baxter
1954 Los Angeles C.C. — Foster Bradley
1955 Purdue G.C. — William Dunn
1956 Taconic C.C. — Harlan Stevenson
1957 Manor C.C. — Larry Beck
1958 U. of Minn. — Buddy Baker
1959 Stanford U. — Larry Lee
1960 Milburn G. & C.C. — Bill Tindall
1961 Cornell U. — Charles McDowell
1962 Lochmoor C. — Jim Wiechers
1963 Florence C.C. — Gregg McHatton
1964 Eugene C.C. — John Miller
1965 Wilmington C.C. — James Masserio
1966 California C.C. — Gary Sanders
1967 Twin Hills G. & C.C. — John Crooks
1968 The Country Club — Eddie Pearce

1969 Spokane C.C. — Aly Trompas
1970 Athens C.C. — Gary Koch
1971 Manor C.C. — Mike Brannan
1972 Brookhaven C.C. — Bob Byman
1973 Singing Hills C.C. — Jack Renner
1974 Brooklawn C.C. — David Nevatt
1975 Richland C.C. — Brett Mullin
1976 Hiwan G.C. — Madden Hatcher III
1977 Ohio State U. — Willie Wood Jr.
1978 Wilmington C.C. — Don Hurter
1979 Moss Creek G.C. — Jack Larkin
1980 Pine Lake C.C. — Eric Johnson

USGA WOMEN'S AMATEUR CHAMPIONSHIP

1950 Atlanta A.C. Atlanta, Ga. — Beverly Hanson d. Mae Murray — 6 and 4
1951 Town & C.C. St. Paul, Minn. — Dorothy Kirby d. C. Doran — 2 and 1
1952 Waverley C.C., Portland, Ore. — Mrs. Jackie Pung d. S. McFedters — 2 and 1
1953 Rhode Island C.C. — Mary Lena Faulk d. Polly Riley — 3 and 2
1954 Allegheny C.C., Sewickley, Pa. — Barbara Romack d. M. Wright — 4 and 2
1955 Myers Park C.C., Charlotte, N.C. — Pat Lesser d. J. Nelson — 7 and 6
1956 Meridian Hills, Indianapolis — Marlene Stewart d. J. Gunderson — 2 and 1
1957 Del Paso C.C., Sacramento — JoAnne Gunderson d. A. Johnstone — 8 and 6
1958 Wee Burn C.C., Darien, Conn. — Anne Quast d. B. Romack — 3 and 2
1959 Congressional, Washington, D.C. — Barbara McIntire d. J. Goodwin — 4 and 3
1960 Tulsa (Okla.) C.C. — JoAnne Gunderson d. Jean Ashley — 6 and 5
1961 Tacoma (Wash.) C.C. — Anne Quast Decker d. Phyllis Preuss — 14 and 13
1962 C.C. of Rochester, N.Y. — JoAnne Gunderson d. Ann Baker — 9 and 8
1963 Taconic G.C., Williamstown, Mass. — Anne Quast Welts d. Peggy Conley — 2 and 1
1964 Prairie Dunes, Hutchinson, Kan. — Barbara McIntire d. J. Gunderson — 3 and 2
1965 Lakewood C.C., Denver, Colo. — Jean Ashley d. Anne Q. Welts — 5 and 4
1966 Sewickley Hts. G.C. (Pa.) — JoAnne Gunderson Carner d. Marlene Streit — 41 holes
1967 Annandale G.C., Pasadena, Calif. — Lou Dill d. Jean Ashley — 5 and 4
1968 Birmingham (Mich) C.C. — JoAnne Gunderson Carner d. Anne Q. Welts — 5 and 4

1969 Las Colinas C.C., Irving, Tex.	Catherine Lacoste d. Shelley Hamlin	3 and 2
1970 Wee Burn C.C., Darien, Conn.	Martha Wilkinson d. Cynthia Hill	3 and 2
1971 Atlanta C.C.	Laura Baugh d. Beth Barry	1 up
1972 St. Louis C.C.	Mary Budke d. Cynthia Hill	5 and 4
1973 Montclair G.C., N.J.	Carol Semple d. Mrs. Anne Sander	1 up
1974 Broadmoor G.C., Seattle	Cynthia Hill d. Carol Semple	5 and 4
1975 Brae Burn C.C., W. Newton, Mass.	Beth Daniel d. Donna Horton	3 and 2
1976 Del Paso C.C., Sacramento, Calif.	Donna Horton d. Marianne Bretton	2 and 1
1977 Cincinnati C.C.	Beth Daniel d. Cathy Sherk	3 and 1
1978 Sunnybrook G.C., Plymouth Meeting, Pa.	Cathy Sherk d. Judith Oliver	4 and 3
1979 Memphis C.C.	Carolyn Hill d. Patty Sheehan	7 and 6
1980 Prairie Dunes C.C	Juli Inkster d. Patti Rizzo	2 up

Tournament inaugurated 1895

USGA NATIONAL WOMEN'S SENIOR

1962 Manufacturer's C.C.	Maureen Orcutt
1963 C.C. of Florida	Mrs. Allison Choate
1964 Del Paso C.C.	Mrs. Hulet P. Smith
1965 Exmoor C.C.	Mrs. Hulet P. Smith
1966 Lakewood C.C.	Maureen Orcutt
1967 Atlantic City C.C.	Mrs. Marge Mason
1968 Monterey C.C.	Mrs. Philip Cudone
1969 Ridglea C.C.	Mrs. Philip Cudone
1970 Coral Ridge C.C.	Mrs. Philip Cudone
1971 Sea Island G.C.	Mrs. Philip Cudone
1972 Manufacturer's C.C.	Mrs. Philip Cudone
1973 San Marcos C.C.	Mrs. David Hibbs
1974 Lakewood C.C.	Mrs. Justine Cushing
1975 Rhode Island G.C.	Mrs. Albert Bower
1976 Monterey Penin. C.C.	Cecile Maclaurin
1977 Dunes G. & B.C.	Dorothy Porter
1978 Rancho Bernardo C.C.	Alice Dye
1979 Hardscrabble C.C.	Alice Dye
1980 Sea Island G.C.	Dorothy Porter

WOMEN'S WESTERN AMATEUR

1955 Olympia Fields C.C.	Pat Lesser
1956 Guyan C.C.	Anne Quast
1957 Omaha C.C.	Meriam Bailey
1958 Oak Park C.C.	Barbara McIntire
1959 Exmoor C.C.	JoAnne Gunderson
1960 Mission Hills C.C.	Ann C. Johnstone
1961 Annandale C.C.	Anne Q. Decker
1962 South Bend C.C.	Carol Sorenson
1963 Broadmoor G.C.	Barbara McIntire
1964 Oak Park C.C.	Barbara Fay White
1965 Wayzata G.C.	Barbara Fay White
1966 Barrington Hills C.C.	Peggy Conley
1967 Bellefonte C.C.	Mrs. Mark Porter
1968 Broadmoor G.C.	Catherine Lacoste
1969 Oak Park C.C.	Jane Bastanchury
1970 Rockford C.C.	Jane Bastanchury
1971 Flossmoor C.C.	Beth Barry
1972 Blue Hills C.C.	Debbie Massey
1973 Maple Bluff C.C.	Kathy Falk
1974 C.C. of Indianapolis	Lancy Smith
1975 Tanglewood G.C.	Debbie Massey
1976 C.C. of Colorado	Nancy Lopez
1977 Flossmoor C.C.	Lauren Howe
1978 Fox Chapel G.C.	Beth Daniel
1979 Maple Bluff C.C.	Mary Hafeman
1980 Shaker Heights C.C.	Kathy Baker

WOMEN'S NATIONAL COLLEGIATE

1960 Stanford	JoAnne Gunderson
1961 Michigan	Judy Hoetmer
1962 New Mexico	Carol Sorenson
1963 Penn State	Claudia Lindor
1964 Michigan State	Patti Shook
1965 Florida	Roberta Albers
1966 Ohio State	Joyce Kazmierski
1967 Sand Point C.C.	Martha Wilkinson
1968 Duke	Gail Sykes
1969 Penn State	Jane Bastanchury
1970 San Diego State	Cathy Gaughan
1971 Georgia	Shelley Hamlin
1972 New Mexico	Ann Laughlin
1973 Mount Holyoke	Bonnie Lauer
1974 Singing Hills C.C.	Mary Budke
1975 U. of Arizona	Barbara Barrow
1976 Michigan State	Nancy Lopez
1977 Hawaii	Cathy Morse

1978 Grenelefe G. & R.C.	Deborah Petrizzi
1979 Stillwater, Okla.	Kyle O'Brien
1980 U. of New Mexico	Patty Sheehan

USGA JUNIOR GIRLS

1949 Philadelphia C.C.	Marlene Bauer
1950 Wanakah C.C.	Patricia Lesser
1951 Onwentsia C.C.	Arlene Brooks
1952 Monterey Pen. C.C.	Mickey Wright
1953 The C.C., Brookline	Millie Meyerson
1954 Gulph Mills C.C.	Margaret Smith
1955 Florence C.C.	Carole Jo Kabler
1956 Heather Downs C.C.	JoAnne Gunderson
1957 Lakewood C.C.	Judy Eller
1958 Greenwich C.C.	Judy Eller
1959 Manor C.C.	Judy Rand
1960 Oaks C.C.	Carol Sorenson
1961 Broadmoor C.C.	Mary Lowell
1962 C.C. of Buffalo	Mary Lou Daniel
1963 Woolfert's Roost C.C.	Janis Ferraris
1964 Leavenworth C.C.	Peggy Conley
1965 Hiwan G.C.	Gail Sykes
1966 Longue Vue C.	Claudia Mayhew
1967 Hacienda G.C.	Elizabeth Story
1968 Flint G.C.	Peggy Harmon
1969 Brookhaven C.C.	Hollis Stacy
1970 Apawamis C.	Hollis Stacy
1971 Augusta C.C.	Hollis Stacy
1972 Jefferson City C.C.	Nancy Lopez
1973 Somerset Hills C.C.	Amy Alcott
1974 Columbia Edgewater	Nancy Lopez
1975 Dedham C.	Dayna Benson
1976 Del Rio G. & C.C.	Pilar Dorado
1977 Guyan G. & C.C.	Althea Tome
1978 Wilmington (Del.) C.C.	Lori Castillo
1979 Little Rock C.C.	Penny Hammel
1980 Crestview C.C.	Laurie Rinker

WOMEN'S PUBLIC LINKS

1977 Yahara Hills G.C.	Kelly Fuiks
1978 Myrtlewood G.C.	Kelly Fuiks
1979 Braemar G. Cse.	Lori Castillo
1980 Center Square G.C.	Lori Castillo

RYDER CUP

1955 Thunderbird R.&G.C.	United States	8
Palm Springs, Calif.	Great Britain	4
1957 Lindrick C.,	Great Britain	7
Worksop, Eng.	United States	4
1959 Eldorado C.C.,	United States	8½
Palm Desert, Calif.	Great Britain	3½
1961 Lytham-St. Annes	United States	14½

G.C., Lancashire, Eng.	Great Britain	9½
1963 East Lake C.C.,	United States	23
Atlanta, Ga.	Great Britain	9
1965 Royal Birkdale C.,	United States	19½
Southport, England	Great Britain	12½
1967 Champions G.C.,	United States	23½
Houston, Tex.	Great Britain	8½
1969 Royal Birkdale G.C.,	United States	16
Southport, England	Great Britain	16
1971 Old Warson C.C.,	United States	18½
St. Louis, Mo.	Great Britain	13½
1973 Muirfield G.L.,	United States	19
Gullane, Scotland	Great Britain	13
1975 Laurel Valley G.C.,	United States	21
Ligonier, Pa.	Great Britain	11
1977 Lytham-St. Annes	United States	12½
G.C., Lancashire, Eng.	Great Britain	7½
1979 Greenbrier, White	United States	17
Sulphur Springs,	Great Britain-Europe	11
W.Va.		

Event inaugurated in 1927.

WORLD CUP

1953 Beaconsfield G.C.,	Argentina	287
Montreal, Can.	Canada	297
1954 Laval-sur-lac,	Australia	556
Montreal, Can.	Argentina	560
1955 Columbia C.C.,	United States	560
Washington, D.C.	Australia	569
1956 Wentworth C.,	United States	567
England	South Africa	581
1957 Kasumigaseki C.C.,	Japan	557
Tokyo, Japan	United States	566
1958 Club de Golf,	Ireland	579
Mexico City, Mex.	Spain	582
1959 Royal Melbourne C.,	Australia	563
Melbourne, Aust.	United States	573
1960 Portmarnock G.C.,	United States	565
Ireland	England	573
1961 Dorado Beach G.C.,	United States	560
Dorado, Puerto Rico	Australia	572

Winning team: Snead, Demaret.
Individual champion: Snead, 272.

| 1962 Jockey C., Buenos | United States | 557 |
| Aires, Argentina | Argentina | 559 |

Winning team: Arnold Palmer, Sam Snead.
Individual: Roberto de Vicenzo, Argentina, 276.

| 1963 Saint Nom la Breteche | United States | 482 |
| C., Versailles, France | Spain | 485 |

Winning team: Nicklaus, Palmer.
Individual champion: Nicklaus 237 (63 holes).

| 1964 Royal Kaanapali G. | United States | 554 |
| Cse., Maui, Hawaii | Argentina | 564 |

Winning team: Nicklaus, Palmer.

Individual champion: Nicklaus, 276.

| 1965 C. de Campo, | South Africa | 571 |
| Madrid Spain | Spain | 579 |

Winning team: Gary Player, Harold Henning.
Individual champion: Player, 281.

| 1966 Yomiuri C.C., | United States | 548 |
| Tokyo, Japan | South Africa | 553 |

Winning team: Palmer, Nicklaus.
Individual champion: George Knudson, Canada, 272
(won playoff from Hideyo Sugimoto, Japan)

| 1967 C. de Golf Mexico, | United States | 557 |
| Mexico City, Mex. | New Zealand | 570 |

Winning team: Arnold Palmer, Jack Nicklaus.
Individual champion: Palmer, 276.

| 1968 Olgiata G.C., | Canada | 569 |
| Rome, Italy | United States | 571 |

Winning team: Knudson, Balding.
Individual champion: Al Balding, 274.

| 1969 Singapore Island C.C., | United States | 552 |
| Singapore | Japan | 560 |

Winning team: Lee Trevino, Orville Moody,
Individual champion: Trevino, 275

| 1970 Jockey Club, | Australia | 545 |
| Buenos Aires, Arg. | Argentina | 555 |

Winning team: David Graham, Bruce Devlin.
Individual: Roberto de Vicenzo, Argentina, 269.

| 1971 PGA Ntl. G.C., | United States | 555 |
| Palm Beach, Fla. | South Africa | 567 |

Winning team: Jack Nicklaus, Lee Trevino.
Individual champion: Nicklaus, 271.

| 1972 Royal Melbourne C.C., | Taiwan | 438 |
| Melbourne, Australia | Japan | 440 |

Winning team: Hsieh Min-Nan, Lu Liang-Huan.
Individual champion: Hsieh Min-Nan, 217.

| 1973 Nueva Andalucia Cse., | United States | 558 |
| Marbella, Spain | South Africa | 564 |

Winning team: Johnny Miller, Jack Nicklaus.
Individual champion: Miller, 277.

| 1974 Lagunita C.C., | South Africa | 554 |
| Caracas, Venezuela | Japan | 559 |

Winning team: Bobby Cole, Dale Hayes.
Individual champion: Cole, 271.

| 1975 Navatanee G.Cse., | United States | 554 |
| Bangkok, Thailand | Taiwan | 564 |

Winning team: Johnny Miller, Lou Graham.
Individual champion: Miller, 275.

| 1976 Mission Hills C.C., | Spain | 574 |
| Palm Springs, Calif. | United States | 576 |

Winning team: S. Ballesteros, Manuel Pinero.
Individual champion: E. Acosta, Mexico, 282.

| 1977 Wack Wack G.C., | Spain | 591 |
| Manila | Philippines | 594 |

Winning team: S. Ballesteros, Tony Garrido.
Individual: Gary Player, South Africa, 289.

| 1978 Princeville G. Cse., | United States | 564 |
| Kauai, Hawaii | Australia | 574 |

Winning team: Andy North, John Mahaffey.
Individual: Mahaffey, 281.

| 1979 Glyfada G.C., | United States | 575 |
| Athens, Greece | Scotland | 580 |

Winning team: John Mahaffey, Hale Irwin.
Individual: Irwin, 285.

WALKER CUP MATCHES

1957 Minikahda C.,	United States	8½
Minneapolis	Great Britain	3½
1959 Muirfield,	United States	9
Scotland.	Great Britain	3
1961 Seattle C.C.,	United States	11
Seattle, Wash.	Great Britain	1
1963 Turnberry G.C.,	United States	12
Ailsa, Scotland	Great Britain	8
1965 Baltimore (Md.)	United States	11
C.C.	Great Britain	11
1967 R. St. George's,	United States	13
Sandwich, England	Great Britain	7
1969 Milwaukee C.C.,	United States	10
Milwaukee, Wis	Great Britain	8
1971 St. Andrews,	Great Britain	13
Scotland	United States	11
1973 The Country Club,	United States	14
Brookline, Mass.	Great Britain	10
1975 St. Andrews,	United States	15½
Scotland	Great Britain	8½
1977 Shinnecock Hills G.C.,	United States	16
Southampton, N.Y.	Great Britain	8
1979 Muirfield G. Cse.,	United States	15½
Scotland	Great Britain	8½

Event inaugurated in 1922.

WORLD AMATEUR TEAM

MEN

| 1966 C. de Golf Mexico, | Australia | 877 |
| Mexico City, Mex. | United States | 879 |

Winning team: Kevin Donahue, Kevin Hartley,
Harry Berwick, Phil Billings.

| 1968 Royal Melbourne | United States | 868 |
| G.C., Australia | Great Britain | 869 |

Winning team: Bruce Fleisher, Jack Lewis, Jr.,
Marvin Giles III, Dick Siderowf.

| 1970 Real C., | United States | 857 |
| Madrid, Spain | New Zealand | 869 |

Winning team: Lanny Wadkins, Vinny Giles,
Allen Miller, Tom Kite.

| 1972 Olivos C., | United States | 865 |
| Buenos Aires, Argentina | Australia | 870 |

Winning team: Ben Crenshaw, Vinny Giles,
Mark Hayes, Marty West.

1974 Cajuiles Cse., La Romana United States 888
Dominican Republic Japan 898
Winning team: Jerry Pate, Gary Koch,
George Burns, Curtis Strange.
1976 Penina G.C. Gr. Br. & Ireland 892
Portimao, Portugal Japan 894
Winning team: Ian Hutcheon, Michael Kelly,
John Davies, Steve Martin.
1978 Pacific Harbour G. Cse., United States 873
Fiji Canada 886
Winning team: Bob Clampett, John Cook,
Scott Hoch, Jay Sigel.

WOMEN

1966 Mexico City C.C., United States 580
Mexico City, Mex. Canada 589
Winning team: Mrs. Teddy Boddie,
Shelley Hamlin, Mrs. David Welts.
1968 Royal Melbourne United States 616
G.C., Australia Australia 621
Winning team: Jane Bastanchury,
Shelley Hamlin, Mrs. David Welts.
1970 C. de Campo, United States 598
Madrid, Spain France 599
Winning team: Martha Wilkinson,
Jane Bastanchury, Cynthia Hill.
1972 Hindu Club, United States 583
Buenos Aires, Argentina France 587
Winning team: Laura Baugh,
Jane Booth, Mary Budke.
1974 Cajuiles Cse., La Romana United States 620
Dominican Republic Gr. Brit.-Ireland 636
Winning team: Cynthia Hill,
Debbie Massey, Carole Semple.
1976 Vilamoura G.C. United States 605
Vilamoura, Portugal France 622
Winning team: Nancy Lopez,
Debbie Massey, Donna Horton.
1978 Pacific Harbour G. Cse., Australia 596
Fiji Canada 597
Winning team: Edwina Kennedy,
Lindy Goggin, Jane Lock.

Event inaugurated in 1964.

CURTIS CUP MATCHES

1956 Prince's Course, Great Britain 5
Sandwich, Eng. United States 4
1958 Brae Burn, C.C. Great Britain 4½
W. Newton, Mass. United States 4½
1960 Lindrick C., United States 6½
Workshop, Eng. Great Britain 2½
1962 Broadmoor G.C., United States 8
Colorado Spgs., Colo. Great Britain 1
1964 Royal Porthcawl G.C., United States 10½
Wales, G. Britain Great Britain 7½

1966 Cascades Cse., United States 13
Hot Springs, Va. Great Britain 5
1968 Royal County Down United States 10½
G.C., N. Ireland Great Britain 7½
1970 Brae Burn, C.C., United States 11½
W. Newton, Mass. Great Britain 6½
1972 Western Gailes G.C., United States 10
Scotland Great Britain 8
1974 San Francisco G.C. United States 10
 Great Britain 4
1976 Royal Lytham United States 11½
and St. Annes Great Britain 8½
1978 Apawamis C., United States 12
Rye, N.Y. Great Britain 6
1980 St. Pierre G. United States 13
& C.C. Great Britain 5

Event inaugurated in 1932.

PGA TOUR RECORDS

72 holes —257 (60-68-64-65), by Mike Souchak at Brackenridge Park Golf Course, San Antonio, Tex., in 1955 Texas Open.

54 holes —189 (63-63-63), by Chandler Harper at Brackenridge Park Golf Course, San Antonio, Tex., in last 54 holes of 1954 Texas Open; 192 (60-68-64), by Mike Souchak in 1955 Texas Open for first 54 holes.

36 holes —125 (63-62), by Ron Streck in third and fourth round of 1978 San Antonio-Texas, lowest consecutive rounds; 126 (64-62), by Tommy Bolt, Virginia Beach, 1954, lowest first two rounds.

18 holes —59, by Al Geiberger in second round of 1977 Danny Thomas Memphis Classic.

9 holes —27, by Mike Souchak during his round of 60 (33-27) in the 1955 Texas Open; also by Andy North on second nine of first round at 1975 B.C. Open.

Consecutive birdies —8, by Bob Goalby in the fourth round of the 1961 St. Petersburg Open; also by Fuzzy Zoeller in the first round of the 1976 Ed McMahon Quad Cities Open.

Fewest putts —18, by Sam Trahan in the second round of the 1979 IVB-Philadelphia Classic.

Fewest putts (72 holes) —99, by Bob Menne at the Sawgrass G.C., Jacksonville, Fla., in the 1977 Tournament Players Championship.

Consecutive wins —11, by Byron Nelson in 1945.

Consecutive times in money —113, by Byron Nelson in the 1940s. Jack Nicklaus had a streak broken at 105 (1970–1976) at the 1976 World Open.

Most wins in a single season —18, by Byron Nelson, 1945.

Consecutive major championships —Walter Hagen's 4 PGA Championships (1924–1927).

Youngest tournament winner —Gene Sarazen, 20, when he won the 1922 U.S. Open, is the youngest pro winner of an official tournament since the PGA was formed in 1916.

Oldest tournament winner —Sam Snead was 52 years, 10 months and 7 days old when he won the 1965 Greensboro (N.C.) Open.

Most money for a single season —$530,808, by Tom Watson, 1980.

Longest sudden-death playoff —Lloyd Mangrum and Cary Middlecoff played 11 extra holes after they had tied for the 72-hole lead in the 1949 Motor City Open in Detroit without deciding the title. Darkness intervened and the players were declared co-champions. There have been longer playoffs, but all started with an 18-hole stroke round which was tied, then went on more holes.

LPGA TOUR RECORDS

72 holes —271 (68-65-69-69), by Hollis Stacy, 1977 Rail Muscular Dystrophy Classic.

54 holes (in 54-hole tournament) —200, by Carol Mann in 1968 Lady Carling Open, Palmetto, Ga. Ruth Jessen also shot 200, in the 1964 Omaha Jaycee Open, but record invalidated by "preferred lie" local rule in effect at time.

36 holes (in 54-hole tournament) —131 (66-65), by Kathy Martin, 1976 Birmingham Classic; also by Silvia Bertolaccini (66-65), 1977 Lady Keystone Open.

18 holes —62, by Mickey Wright in 1964 Tall City Open, Midland, Tex. Other 62s, by Miss Wright in 1967 Bluegrass Inv., Louisville, Ky., and by Kathy Whitworth in 1968 Holiday Inn Classic, St. Louis, Mo., invalidated by "preferred lie" local rule in effect at time.

9 holes —29, by Marlene Hagge, on first nine in first round of 1971 Immke Open, Columbus, Ohio. Also by Carol Mann, on first nine in first round of 1975 Borden Classic, Dublin, Ohio; Pat Bradley (twice), on second nine, first round of 1978 California Golden Lights and first nine, first round of 1979 New York Golden Lights; Silvia Bertolaccini, first nine, second round of 1979 Orange Blossom.

Most wins in single season —13, by Mickey Wright in 1963.

Most consecutive victories —5, by Nancy Lopez, 1978 (skipped one scheduled event after three wins); 4, by Mickey Wright, twice, in 1962 and 1963, and Kathy Whitworth, 1969 (4 consecutive scheduled events), and by Shirley Englehorn, 1970 (skipped one scheduled event after first win).

Most official money in a single season —$197,488, by Nancy Lopez, 1979.

Most birdies in one round —10, by Nancy Lopez in second round of 1979 Mary Kay Classic.

Consecutive birdies —7, by Carol Mann in the 1975 Borden Classic, Columbus, Ohio.

Fewest putts —19, by Beverly Klass, 1978 Women's International, second round.

Youngest winner —Marlene Hagge, 18 when she won 1952 Sarasota Open.

Oldest winner —Patty Berg, 44 when she won 1962 Muskogee Open; Betsy Rawls, 44 when she won 1972 GAC Classic.

MISCELLANEOUS
LOWEST ROUNDS

Lowest known score on a course of at least 6,000 yards is a 57 (32-25) recorded by Bill Burke, 29, St. Louis, at the 6,389-yard, par-71 Normandie C.C., St. Louis, May 20, 1970. Burke's 25 ties for the lowest score ever made on nine holes of at least 3,000 yards. Douglas Beecher, 13, Williamstown, N.J., shares the nine-hole record with a 33-25—58 at the 6,180-yard, par-71 Pitman (N.J.) C.C., made July 6, 1976. Beecher's 58 is the lowest ever recorded by a teenager.

In 1962, Homero Blancas, a University of Houston golfer, shot a 55 at the Premier Golf Course in Longview, Tex. However, the course measured only 5,002 yards.

MOST UNDER-PAR HOLES IN SUCCESSION

Professional Roberto de Vicenzo scored six birdies, an eagle, then three more birdies on holes one through 10, on April 6, 1974, at the Villa Allende Golf Club, Province of Cordoba, Argentina. He eventually scored 61 for the round.

FEWEST PUTTS

Richard Stanwood, a professional, in 1976 played a round at the 6,220-yard, par-71 Riverside G.C., Pocatello, Idaho, in which he putted only 15 times. He had eight putts on the front nine, seven on the back and chipped in five times in scoring 34-31—65. The amateur women's putting record is 19, by Beverly Whitaker, Pasadena, Calif., in 1974 and by Dorothy Hurd, Pittsburgh, in 1924.